THE SOUL'S GUIDE TO BIRTHING

BIRTHING A NEW PARADIGM

Katherine Zorensky
Padma Aon Prakasha

ISBN 978-0-578-31538-6

Published by Katherine Zorensky Hawaii, November 2021

Copyright © 2021 by Katherine Zorensky & Padma Aon Prakasha

All rights reserved. No part of this book may be reproduced or utilized in any form or by any means, electronic or mechanical, including photo-copying, recording, or by any information storage and retrieval system, without permission in writing from the authors.

THE SOULS GUIDE TO BIRTHING

The Souls Guide to Birthing is the soul's handbook for parents to have a soulful pregnancy, blissful birth and raise their children consciously. The Soul's Guide to Birthing is the soul's perspective on healing and preparing women AND men on how to birth their child naturally in a caring, loving and emotionally intelligent birth process.

Conscious Birthing is transformative, a Rite of Passage for the whole family helping man, woman and child birth and embody hidden parts of their own soul. Women embody more of their feminine soul, yet birthing is equally a man's opportunity to embody his deeper masculinity.

This pathway is being Remembered again with the Renaissance of feminine consciousness. Sexuality and conscious relationship are the basis for conscious birth, using the full range of our emotions, hearts and bodies. In the hormonal rollercoaster of pregnancy and birth lie great opportunities to heal our family and ancestral traumas with our inner child. Shedding these patterns means we pass these benefits onto our children: they do not need to suffer the same pains we have.

The Souls Guide to Birthing brings together science and indigenous wisdom from around the world to give you and your family the head start you deserve in life. In this book you will learn to:

- Prepare and deepen into the four trimesters of conscious birth
- Navigate the emotions and hormonal ride of pregnancy
- Open the doors to a Blissful Birth
- Amplify your connection to Earth as a direct portal for conscious birthing.
- Discover the 7 Gates of the Womb and true feminine power
- Understand the role of the father in pregnancy, labour and beyond
- Understand the role of mother and birthing as a spiritual pathway
- Discover ways to consciously raise your new child
- Open and heal what arises in pregnancy and birth
- Use exercises to open into all aspects of the pregnancy and birth journey

The Souls Guide to Birthing is a modern, comprehensive and wide-reaching journey into the many dimensions of soulful pregnancy, blissful birth and becoming a conscious parent. It is practical and soulful, sharing the deeper dimensions of the entire birth journey to empower parents and their child into their highest potentials. This empowerment comes from consciously taking the Initiation into one of the most powerful experiences you will have in life: Conscious Birthing.

CONTENTS

- TABLE OF CONTENT 4
- DEDICATION 7
- FOREWORD 9
- INTRODUCTION 13
- **PART I: THE FOUNDATION** 25
  - CONSCIOUS RELATIONSHIP 27
    - THE CONTAINER 29
    - COMMITMENT 33
    - TRUST AND RESPECT 40
    - SOUL and SOURCE 43
    - SEX, SOUL and SOURCE 45
  - THE FATHER 51
    - THE PILLAR of THE FATHER 56
    - THE ANCIENT LINEAGE of FATHERS 60
    - THE SACRED LINGAM PILLAR 62
  - THE MOTHER: THE MAGNET 65
    - THE SEVEN CYCLES OF THE MOTHER 70
    - 1. BLACK LIGHT: WOMB SPACE 70
    - 2. WEB OF LIFE 74
    - 3. VESSEL: THE DANCE BETWEEN HUMAN AND DIVINE 78
    - 4. NURTURING AND THE BREASTS 83
    - 5. MOTHER AS LOVE/LOVER 89
    - 6. MIDWIFE 94
    - 7. THE BODY OF MOTHER: EMBODYING THE FEMININE SOUL 96
- **PART 2: THE EVOLUTIONARY IMPULSE** 101
  - THE EVOLUTION .... Error! Bookmark not defined.
    - YOUR GENETIC PROGRAMMING 105
    - THE INNER CHILD 107
    - HEALING WITH YOUR PARENTS 115
    - THE BENEFITS OF GENETIC ALCHEMY 122
  - EARTH RESONANCE 133
    - THE EARTH HUM FREQUENCY 136
    - BIRTHING A NEW PARADIGM 140
    - THE UNITY GRID of EARTH 146
    - SACRED SITES 150
    - EARTH AND BIRTHING 154
  - WOMB CONSCIOUSNESS 159
    - BECOMING WOMB CONSCIOUS: THE THRONE of YOUR WOMB 163
    - WOMB BREATHING 167

OPENING THE WOMB 170
THE OVARIES 173
YOUR MAGNETIC FOUNDATION 179
THE SEVEN GATES of THE WOMB: 187

PART 3: BIRTHING 229
CONSCIOUS CONCEPTION 231
   CONSCIOUS CONCEPTION 233
   THE CONTAINER 241
THE THREE TRIMESTERS of SOULFUL PREGNANCY 261
   THE FIRST TRIMESTER: ESTABLISHING THE CONTAINER 266
   THE SECOND TRIMESTER: COMMUNICATION AND CONNECTION 272
   THIRD TRIMESTER: COMMUNING with CREATION 282
BLISSFUL BIRTH 313
   PLEASURE IN BIRTH 315
   THE MASCULINE PILLAR IN BIRTH 326
   THE GOLDEN SPIRAL IN BIRTH 334
BIRTH and THE SEVEN GATES 338
   BIRTH IN IT'S MOVEMENTS 343
   THE GOLDEN HOURS 349
   THE PLACENTA and UMBILICAL CORD 351

PART 4: THE FOURTH TRIMESTER 364
40 DAYS OF BEING 366
PRACTICES: .... Error! Bookmark not defined.
   REINHABITING THE WOMB 366
   WEAVING THE NEW MOTHER INTO UNITY THROUGH THE ELEMENTS 369
   YONI REJUVENATION EXERCISES 379

PART 5: RAISING YOUR NEW CHILD 382
BONDING 385
THE SOULS DESIGN FOR PARENTING 389
FATHERS ROLE IN RAISING A CHILD 391
SOUL EMBODIMENT FOR CHILDREN 394
WHY BABIES CRY 400

PART 6: THE NEW CHILDREN 416
THE NEW CHILDREN 419
WHAT DOES A NEW CHILD NEED TO THRIVE? 430

RESOURCES 434

THE AUTHOR 435

ACKNOWLEDGEMENTS 437

DEDICATION

This book is dedicated to my son Sunyam. You are the light illuminating a future beyond what I can see. You answered my deepest heartfelt prayer to know unconditional love through my womb, my heart. You forge me into my love, wisdom and power as your mother. Your fierce independence and innocent tenderness keep me dynamic in my dance of letting go and embrace. Thank you for your patience as I grow to see you clearly beyond my own veils. May you feel the love of your parents, the love of the earth, the cosmos and all life as a foundational support in your life and mission to 'Be you.'

This book is dedicated to my daughter Annabella. For giving me the gift of your birth, which birthed me into this path. For showing me that our children come through us, but don't belong to us. You are your own. May you have the blessing of knowing your mother loves you always.

Finally, this book is dedicated to all the New Children and the parents choosing to consciously create a new paradigm. May you have all the support, guidance, joy, love, and grace you deserve on this most courageous journey.

FOREWORD

The Soul's Guide to Birthing presents information both new and ancient. New for these times we live in and the New Children who are coming to earth, and ancient in the sense that this book brings together a resurfacing of wisdom about the womb and birthing that has been largely forgotten.

An emotionally integrated and soulfully bonded family emerges from the full and conscious engagement of father and mother in the entire birth process, from pre-conception to pregnancy, labour, birth, and raising their child. In so doing, they embody and embrace more of their essential femininity and masculinity. Their joint and mutual effort becomes a foundation for their own integration of the Rite of Passage of Birth and Parenthood, the foundation for a healthy, loving child, and an enlightened human civilization.

Both roles of mother and father are unique, different and crucial to the whole process. Both have to be fully engaged with the process. By becoming a pillar of strength, care and wisdom the father-to-be creates a sound container to safely and soulfully guide his partner and child. In this space, the mother-to-be can soften and surrender to the deeper currents of magnetic presence, wisdom, nurturance and love that brings wholeness to her family, through her feminine essence.

We are dependent on our children to become parents. Our children are dependent on us as parents, to be children. In this relationship, we discover aspects of love that we will not authentically encounter in any other relationship or spiritual practice. When the relationship between mother and father is based on unconditioned love and truth, there is a sound foundation for child, family and humanity to blossom into an enlightened civilization.

The Soul's Design for Birthing was borne from my direct experience of healing my womb through the two transformative births of my children. The guidance and direct practices I received throughout my pregnancy, birth, and from the deeply intimate experiences I had as a birth doula guiding other women, helped birth this book.

The first time I gave birth was primal, potent and powerful. My daughter was born in Kealakekua Bay, known as 'The Place of the Gods,' on the western side of the Big Island, Hawaii under the watch of a full moon. It was where the dolphins, whales, sea turtles and sharks all come to birth.

In the final months of my pregnancy I swam with the dolphins every morning until my daughter's arrival. They greeted me belly to belly, and swam spirals around us in joy and delight. The ocean nurtured and nourished me, guided me into surrender and supported me in remembering the way of water birth as it has been done for thousands of years.

My daughter's birth was my first initiation into a remembrance of the feminine spiritual path of embodiment. My previous life of meditation and healing work as a massage teacher, cranio-sacral therapist and in-depth study of Chinese Medicine, allied with years of meditating and living in a Zen monastery practicing and teaching yoga, led me into guiding wilderness expeditions for ten years, taking addicts and their pain out into extreme wilderness zones for healing and nurture from the Earth.

Yet all of this neglected some of the most profound feminine secrets of my soul. And I knew it. The more masculine path I was on was missing a key that held the way to my deepest healing, happiness and soul fulfillment; my womb. The birth of my daughter in a small tide pool on the edge of the most remote island chain in the world gave me a glimpse into the power and vastness of my womb.

A few years later, I was on pilgrimage in Italy visiting sacred sites. I had a done a good deal of deep soul work and womb clearing. The more I inhabited my womb, the more I felt a burning desire to devote every part of myself to the embodiment and service of the Divine Feminine on earth. In a spontaneous moment of prayer, I asked to receive my soul-purpose deep in my womb. What I received was the gift of pregnancy, birth and parenting in the Soul's Design.

A few weeks later when I found I was pregnant with my son, a journey began: birth Co-Created with the Divine, Earth, mother, father and child. The experiences and communions that happened over his nine-month gestation evolved my birth experience from my first birth of an intuitive primal dance with the natural world, into deeper octaves of refined consciousness and Divine communion.

Through a healed womb, a sound family container, home-birth and a deepening connection with the Divine, I birthed my son into the world whilst birthing part of my soul and souls purpose into embodiment here on earth.

As a parent of a New Child, my life is a multi-dimensional dance with many roles. I stand with one foot in an old paradigm, not of it, but in it. I do my work to support and guide others who are willing to extract themselves from this limiting matrix.

I stand with my other foot in the emerging New Paradigm of a 5th Dimensional earth. Here I plant the seeds that have been entrusted to me to grow a new and ancient way, namely through birth. In my arms is my son, whom I care for, nurture and carry. He gives me insights, guidance and a larger perspective to keep me moving toward something much greater than I can conceive, and I show him the ways of life on earth, in gravity, in a body and with other humans.

His father is our pillar, creating a container for growth, stability and protection. He catalyzes the wave that actualizes the world we are moving toward, in our lives and beyond. We are three individual souls, sharing and coming together in many ways to embody, evolve and expand ourselves and a purpose much larger than any of us.

Birth in this way is how we can usher in the New Children, and set a true foundation for them to carry out their purpose: to evolve humanity into a new species, the expression of the full human potential in the Divine Image.

I present to you *The Souls Guide to Birthing* as a support for you to birth from the soul's perspective, to guide you into a life, and birth, lived through the soul.

INTRODUCTION

Our natural birth process is designed to be loving and inclusive, with both parents fully engaged and involved in all aspects of the journey. Both parents have unique roles, vital for the child and for their own soul's growth.

Our natural birth process is designed to be blissful, safe, harmonious and loving. It is designed to bring each of you into your next octave of evolution and your next level of consciousness.

The Soul's Guide for Birthing is a handrail to lead you beyond the influences of external conditioning, traumas, ancestral and personal wounds, into an inclusive, life-affirming pathway that brings you an initiation into your soul and a reclamation of parts of your deep masculine and feminine essence.

Conceiving, gestating, birthing and raising your child in a conscious way, connected to the earth, your sexuality, womb consciousness, all three souls and the safe cocoon of your conscious relationship and home, is part of this journey. When this journey is embarked upon with consciousness, it gives us a new experience and expression of our souls, as well as ushering in our own next evolutionary leap.

As women, we have the gift of deep connection with the flow of Life through our wombs. In sexual union we can open into the joy, ecstasy and intimacy that is part of our soul blueprint. In pregnancy we are offered a sacred, precious opportunity to carry another life within the most intimate folds of our body. In birth are revealed the very secrets of creation, happening through our own bodies in love, feminine power and pleasure; in motherhood we expand into a deeper aspect of our own femininity, through love-in-action.

The man who walks beside his woman is entrusted with the noble role of protecting, upholding and guiding aspects of that journey. Through foresight and action, he carves out a pathway for mother and child to birth and bloom. In accepting and enacting his role, man claims part of his deep masculinity, becoming more embodied, more loving, more whole in himself.

In conscious conception, soulful pregnancy and blissful birth, we have an opportunity to embody our own self-love and soul's wisdom, aligning with the exciting new paradigm consciousness of these times. When we gestate and birth our children in bliss, in intimacy, in harmony with our souls and with our partners, in sacred sexuality and Womb Consciousness, in resonance with the earth and Source, we can take the initiation and Rite of Passage that conscious birthing is designed to be.

Birth is a universal experience, like love. Everyone has experienced it! The initiation of birth is designed to be an evolutionary expression of the love, soul purpose and learning opportunities of all three souls involved, benefiting all of them in many ways. When we step into the souls pattern of birthing consciousness we step into a timeless spiritual pathway that is now being remembered again through the renaissance of the feminine consciousness and feminine power in harmony with the masculine.

The Soul's Guide to Birthing is a map of the essential elements that clarify and exalt one of the most powerful and life-changing experiences we will ever have. This book is a living thread of connection back into the primordial rhythm, harmony, and understanding of how consciousness is birthed. This book, this wisdom, is not only relative to birthing children, as it can be applied to birthing anything, from people and projects to paradigms.

REMEMBERING WOMB CONSCIOUSNESS

The Creator gathered all of Creation and said,
"I want to hide something from the humans until they are ready for it."
The eagle said, "Give it to me. I will take it to the moon."
The Creator said, "No. One day they will go there and find it."
The salmon said, "I will bury it on the bottom of the ocean."
The Creator said, "No. They will go there, too."
The buffalo said, "I will bury it on the Great Plains."
The Creator said, "They will cut into the skin of the earth and find it even there."
Grandmother Mole, who lives in the breast of Mother Earth, and who has no physical eyes but sees with spiritual eyes, said,
"Put it inside of them."
And the Creator said, "It is done."

Hopi Creation Story

For many women, a womb is an organ just like the rest of the organs in our bodies. Like the heart, liver, kidneys, we all know the womb is there, but do we give any thought to it other than when we think of menstruation or pregnancy? What else is it there for? What if we asked the questions: What else does my womb do other than give birth? What is the wisdom and power within my womb?

The deepest most ancient secrets of life lie within the womb of every woman. The womb is the holiest temple in our body, our inner sanctum and guru, the place where our inner voice, clarity, stillness, creative expression and primordial power as Woman arises from. It is our primordial voice and our interface into the Web of Life, the interdependent matrix that weaves all living beings together in the dance of life.

We are all birthed from the womb, yet it is one of the least known parts of ourselves. It holds the greatest power that a woman possesses: the power to nurture, grow and create life *on many levels of consciousness.* This power of creation is what each woman carries, yet rarely accesses, even in the process of giving physical birth.

The womb is not just a place of physical birth. It is a consciousness that can birth *us,* that can birth new realities and evoke deep transformation. The womb is a woman's feminine core, the generator of tremendous creative potential, vitality, boundless well-being, power *and manifestation.*

The womb births our children and it births the fullness of our feminine spiritual potential, our soul's purpose and our healing. It brings forth a felt foundation for the depths of intimate relating for which we all yearn. It helps unify the masculine and feminine, bringing balance and loving wisdom to our deepest relationships.

The womb does this in alliance with the heart. The womb is the heart's fertile, warm, ever present, safe foundation, the fecund soil which enables the heart to drop down, to truly feel, to feel safe and held within, and to crack open to more love.

In the past and in present-day sacred traditions women have known *The Way of the Womb*, the wisdom, practices and power of womb-consciousness, and how to use it to create and evolve on a profound level. Some of these great women from both East and West include Mary Magdalene, the female Bodhisattva Yeshe Tsogyal, the Priestesses of Isis, the Daoist and African Sisterhoods, and the druid Shamanesses of Europe and the UK.

In many cultures worldwide, the womb was revered and worked with by both men and women. The womb is a cave of pure creativity where woman becomes creator. The womb is your inner council where you discover your doctor, adviser, confidant, sage, decision-maker, and artist. It is the root, the foundation of the feminine self, and the safe, rich, fertile ground upon which the feminine heart can bloom and flower.

It is important to know we can create from this center within us. Once the womb is discovered and its spaciousness inhabited, women can enter a space that takes us from playing victim to playing creator, our true authentic self. This womb woman is empowered in her body, through her emotions, sexuality and soul into the authentic feminine power.

This woman manifests her soul mission, and has intimate, fulfilling relationships, engaged in the spontaneous joy of life. Without reservation, without compromise, this woman uses her loving emotional and sexual energy to dynamically fuel her evolution, health, relationships and lifestyle.

Discovering the womb's power and voice is essential for the healing journey for every woman and man who is thinking of having a child. The healed womb becomes a sound container for your child to enter this world.

Yet women have now become divorced from the womb, our primal center of gravity, joy, creativity and soul connection. The flowering of the feminine rose has become dwarfed by the pillar of the masculine, instead of each exalting the other, side by side in harmony. As women, we have forgotten our true reference of feminine power, wisdom, and love. In this forgetting, men too have forgotten how to relate fully to the feminine and to their own emotions, forgetting how to be truly human, building walls of denial, rationalization, intellectual abstraction and anger around the wounds that have been created by this separation.

Many ways of 'normally' accepted human behavior have been influenced by this separation, creating a grossly distorted view of the feminine, masculine, God, spirituality and social behavior that has formed our current cultural narratives. The effects on human culture of this imbalance are many and manifold, impacting every area of human life, from birth trauma, the degradation of the environment, to needless war, the loss of heart centered life affirming values, the loss of family values, and the failure of intimate relationships between man and woman.

In short, the loss of Womb Wisdom has created a huge imbalance on planet Earth that impacts all of us, creating an unstable foundation for our cultures and our lives.

When a woman is authentically living in her feminine power, she lives and inhabits the space of her womb-heart connection. A woman's center is in her womb-heart, not her head. She lives on Earth, connected through relationship, not in an abstract concept of what life is. As a woman's center of gravity shifts to the womb, her primal center of embodiment, she becomes centered, empowered, present and grounded. This then allows the heart to deeply and organically bloom open.

The strength and fertile depth of the womb provides a secure foundation deep within you to be able to feel and express your heart freely. The head and heart work within grounded foundations sunk deep within the womb. The head by itself cannot come into the heart. The womb brings the mind down into a woman's true center of gravity, and then the mind can act as the servant of the heart.

The womb has its own unique voice that is wise, knowing, deeply intuitive and primordial. It is sunk down deep in roots that allow the tree of the soul to feel steady, to grow and expand. The womb holds the space, the container and the crucible. The womb is a safe and steady place, an unwavering center of creation, still and reliable. With this foundation, the heart feels safe and secure, feeling an organic and natural ground to rest and rely upon, a place to arise from in wisdom and strength.

Through the womb you become more able to trust yourself and what is uniquely individual to you. This process of transformation depends upon your ability to feel and fully experience essential feminine values safely, within yourself, with men, and with other women. Having an authentic inner relationship to our feminine and making it our own empowers us into our deep-felt belly wisdom and gut knowing. All life benefits when we have the courage to live and love from this place of truth.

When women hold this deep-felt belly wisdom and gut knowing, when women come to love their wombs and live from this truth, *all life benefits*, for the womb is the generator and keeper of Life. This activating of the womb is a powerful process that can heal many deep-seated, age-old wounds in both the feminine and masculine consciousness.

When the womb is cleared and restored in connection to the heart, women come into their full feminine power. By doing so, their men too become balanced, whole, and healed in a way they could never before have imagined or felt. With the resurrection of our wombs comes the resurrection of man. Man will remember a new identity, a timeless and primordial presence that is activated in the presence of the activated and clear womb-heart.

So men: stand up and support the women in your life! Do not be scared that you will lose your power, for you will in fact gain the greatest power of all: love born through humility, that which makes you a real man, a King. Listen to the womb; it will serve you to enter truth, the greatest bliss, the greatest softness, the deepest power, the wisdom of which will support you into becoming a King.

Women: delve deep into your primal power, beyond the appearances, customs, societies and religions of the day. Delve into the Knowing you have always had, and always will. It is here right now. Delve deep into your belly brain: your original voice, the voice that will always lead you to the truth of love in action, the consciousness of joy and peace: The Voice of Life itself.

THE SOUL'S DESIGN FOR BIRTHING

Have you ever wondered why our children are born totally defenseless and dependent on their parents for their very survival and existence? No other species on earth needs so much care and attention to be able to survive in the first years of life like we do.

Human children cannot really do anything without their parents. They need their parents to guide them in every aspect of human existence. Success with eating, walking, talking, expression, social interaction and love is dependent on their parents' presence. This total dependence is unique to the human species alone.

Yet we are interdependent as parents and children. We need them for our soul's growth as much as they need us. We cannot be parents without our children! This interdependency encourages us to more deeply experience our vulnerability and to dig deeper into the strength and consistency of our love. Our children grow us as much as we raise them.

Conscious pregnancy and birth enable both mother and father to become truly human. This happens not through transcending our humanity, but by embracing all of it. The process of raising our children anchors humility and consistent unconditioned love into our humanity. Supporting and guiding our children on every level physically, emotionally, mentally and spiritually breathes us more into the fullness of our own soul's blueprint.

The delight, play and joy we feel with our children is one of the most endearing characteristics of being a human being. The care and love we feel for them helps define and bring out our own souls. This love will evoke amazing qualities within us we have never experienced before. It will also trigger and bring up wounds within us that have resisted love, that have not experienced love, *for true love will always bring up that which It is not within us.* This may include some growth edges, some unfelt pains and other learning challenges to assist us to become more of who we truly are. And yes, our children help us with all of this, in their way.

The love and devotion we feel for our children penetrates to the core of our hearts. It touches the same place within us from which our communion with the Divine happens. The love we feel for our children touches this profound place of creation, of sincerity, of love extending itself naturally from our core.

The devotion we have for our children expresses in wanting them to have everything that we could not have, or did not have, when we were children. There is a deep seeded genetic impulse and soulful desire seated in our core that wants our children to be better than us. We want our children to be better than we are, go beyond where we have gone, do greater things than we have done, and be more evolved, loving and wise than we are.

When we allow this desire to express, we give our child the love we never received from our parents. We provide for them the opportunities, spiritual and material, that were not available to us. We share with them our valuable earthly lessons and soulful learnings that took us years of pain and mistakes to learn, not to take this learning away from them, but to enable them to build their souls foundation on deeper roots than we ever did.

In following this innate desire, we love selflessly and unconditionally, extending our souls in ways we never did before. We develop a greater patient kindness AND the greater detachment of true love that allows and embraces all things. The deeper the love we have for our children, based on our own solid foundation of sovereign Self-love, the freer we allow our children to Be their own unique selves and to follow their own unique purpose, passion and blueprint. This is a different form of bonding than the wounded need for love or grasping for love that many believe is love, and which they may then pass onto their children in some way.

We want to give our children the best of everything. *All our children ever really want is our attention and love*, and for us to help *them keep the channels of giving and receiving love open*, which they already innately have. It is in the closing down of these channels of the soul[1] that many of the wounds of incarnation happen, which then create conflict, suffering and pain.

In keeping these channels open, we come to know our true selves, and come to a deeply felt experience and understanding of *what love is, and what love is not*. By our Knowing this, our child will come to know this. Both parent and child can help each other Remember the fullness of what love is. This is our Soul's Design.

The New Paradigm is built on Love. The old paradigm was built on fear. Conscious Birthing and birthing a new paradigm means healing from the wounding and traumas woven through our genetics, our birth traumas, our sexuality, our hearts and our bodies. This enables our children to emerge into a world of empowered clarity and consciousness, free to express and create from the purity and magnificence of their own unique blueprints without the baggage we have had. We are the bridge between old and new, allowing our

---

[1] which includes the need to please their parents which many children have and which many parents mistakenly encourage

children to emerge onto solid ground and take their first steps in a fertile soil of possibility. From here they will employ their gifts to enable a new humanity.

THE STRUCTURE OF THIS BOOK

In this book, chapter-by-chapter, are shared the foundations of a caring, emotionally intelligent and conscious birth journey that initiates man, woman and child into their soul, into their deeper masculine and feminine essence, and a whole new octave of wholeness.

PART 1: THE FOUNDATION

Sacred Relationships are the basis for conscious conception, soulful pregnancy and blissful birthing. In developing a strong container between both partners, and embracing the intimacy and healing that arises in sacred sexual relationship, we create foundations of trust, commitment and honour between partners and for our child as well.

The Father is one half of the birthing process. His Pillar of support, safety, protection, strength, guidance and masculine heart allows mother and baby to bloom in all ways. In the process he reclaims part of his own deep masculine self. The Mother's physical and spiritual vessel, nurturance, love and magnetism draws the field of family together and births them all into being.

PART 2: THE EVOLUTIONARY IMPULSE

The Evolutionary Impulse is driving forwards the accelerated shifts happening in the world today. When we bring this impulse into healing our parental patterns and releasing the burden of our ancestral lineages, we accelerate our evolution and pave the way for our children's futures to be bright and free of the suffering we have inherited. By taking this deeper into our inner child healing, we release ourselves from our childhood conditioning and enable ourselves to engage with our children more soulfully, enabling them to not take on our conditionings.

Earth grounds our biology and our electromagnetic fields into wholeness. Earth is the fertile ground for the birthing of anything as our indigenous traditions teach us. In Earth we find an aspect of ourselves, and by practically immersing into her frequency we embody a grounded yet expanded sense of living fully.

Womb Consciousness is the space where all birthing occurs, from our children to galaxies. This is a living, feminine consciousness that has seven magnetic portals in a woman's sacred sexual self and womb that open a woman and a couple into womb consciousness. This wisdom has been taught by Priestesses worldwide for thousands of years and is a practical art and science of feminine consciousness, feminine power and embodied sexuality.

PART 3: THE BIRTH

In the four trimesters of the souls birthing, many dimensions, skills, gifts, healings, insights and wisdom become available to us. There is a science of consciousness underlying each trimester, encompassing our biological shifts, our sexual shifts, our emotional movements and the consciousness of woman, child and man.

Soulful Pregnancy is the gestating of a child in a healing opening womb that becomes a fertile soil for woman, child and man, emotionally, physically and spiritually. Blissful Birth occurs when we have opened up to our feminine power and can emotionally flow with the ecstatic, orgasmic rushes of labour. The actual physical and energetic movements of baby in the birthing process are found in how the womb consciousness operates.

PART 4: THE FOURTH TRIMESTER

We are at our most tender, open and sensitive after birth. We have been opened biologically, sexually, emotionally and spiritually beyond our believed capacities, and it warrants gentleness, nurturing, connection and slowness to call all the parts of our being back into our new reconfiguration. Just as we hold and care for the new born baby in our arms, so we must care for the parts of our own selves that are newly born.

The Fourth Trimester is the crucial time after birth for the Rites of Passage mother, father and child have just experienced to become integrated in a caring, loving way. The shamanic initiation of birth needs a safe Return, bringing us into wholeness rather than fragmentation and depression.

PART 5: RAISING YOUR NEW CHILD

In the journey of preconception to birth and beyond, you will have grown in many ways. All the experiences and initiations you have taken have naturally and intuitively equipped you physically, emotionally, mentally and soulfully to feel and know what your child needs, and what you need, to stay balanced and in harmony.

Raising your new child allows you to further grow and live into a new paradigm. There are many practical ways we can support the innocence and high vibration of our new child.

PART 6: THE NEW CHILDREN

The New Children are humanity's future leaders and teachers, and collectively they will revolutionize the planet, establishing a tangible basis for an awakened civilization in all facets of life, from the economic, artistic and scientific, to the technological, spiritual and environmental.

These New Children are in connection with their soul essence, and are being born to conscious parents who have prepared themselves to receive them. These Children are conduits for new creations, and see the world with different eyes. They hold a key to the Template for the Fifth Dimensional Earth and the next evolution of the human species.

PART I:
THE FOUNDATION

CONSCIOUS RELATIONSHIP

THE CONTAINER

'The highest form of spiritual practice, for those of us who aspire to create Heaven on Earth, are our relationships with one another.' [2]

Conscious, sacred relationship is the foundation for blissful birthing. A high vibrational, emotionally intelligent and self-responsible couple produces a high vibrational, emotionally intelligent child. You and your partner are the emotional and spiritual bedrock for your child's well-being and growth on all levels, which leads to the truth that sacred relationship is the basis for an awakened civilization.

You and your partners emotional condition and emotional intelligence, your togetherness as a team, your felt respect, trust and honor for self and each other all impact your child from the moment of conception. He/she will feel this in their deep subconscious, and this will provide a pattern for their life and their birth. The ways you treat each other, the ways you love each other, the ways you speak to each other, the ways you are there for the other, or not, will all impact your child's soul and life journey.

The container for the Rite of Passage of loving birth is created by the bond between father and mother, and the quality of this relating. Sacred Relationship gives a man a basis to become a King and sets a foundation for a woman to become a Queen.

The whole Birthing process, from beginning to end, brings you into the deep masculine essence and deep feminine essence. In this process, much of what you have learned from the masculine and feminine role models you have had will come up to be questioned, improved upon, discarded, healed and integrated. You will find new ways of being feminine, new depths of the masculine, and new ways to love and hold each other in deeply touching and vulnerable ways.

Sacred Relationship and the pregnancy journey brings up many emotions and deep seated beliefs that have previously been unseen, unfelt and untouched within you, into your awareness. In the swirl of hormones and emotions as life grows within you, untouched and unknown parts of your own mother and father arise to be seen and embraced. Your ancestral patterns, your emotional losses, your abandonment, your fears, your sexual healings, your shame and grief can all be triggered by pregnancy.

The chaos that often ensues in pregnancy is simply because these emotions and forgotten places within you start to arise full force because they want to be seen, felt and embraced. They want your love: they want your partners love. They need to be loved. They are reaching out for your love, and now is the time for a Great Healing to occur so that a new cycle can begin.

The process of creation you embark upon in pregnancy is anchored in a deep biological and emotional commitment to two other people as well as yourself. It is a process of ever

---

[2] *Andrew Cohen*

increasing care, honor and soulful responsibility. It is said that love brings up everything it is not, and in pregnancy we tangibly get to feel the places within us where love is absent, where love has not yet touched us, where love has been forgotten within us. Some of these growth edges are difficult and painful, but in the end they always serve to open our hearts.

Birthing in sacred relationship is a key to our evolutionary destiny, where we reactivate our primordial voice and our pure sexual and emotional expression in harmony with the Divine. To facilitate this, we must take some essential healing steps.

Sexuality requires a conscious transfiguration, as well as all that is held within our hearts, DNA and psychology. Our emotions and feelings make us who we are, and define the flows of our soul. Experiencing all our feelings by fully allowing them and moving through them allows us to become truly alive. Our feelings, in their vitality, bring us deeper into our embodiment, and our connection to all life. They are also our bridge to the Divine.

Sacred Relationships are the initiatory temples of today. They are where we learn to truly feel, give and receive. They bring us to the heights of bliss and plummet us into the depths of our pain. They are our boon and bane.

THE CONTAINER OF CONSCIOUS RELATING

"All the great attainments in the area of spiritual practice and realization, wonderful as they are, have hardly begun to transform the overall quality of human relationships on this planet, which are still driven by the most primitive of motivations and emotions." [3]

Sacred Relationship is the unifying of two souls sexual energy and emotions through our bodies as an offering to the Divine. In this sacred trinity the relationship becomes an alchemical container of transformation. In the container and furnace of this relationship, divine men and divine women are forged. Kings and Queens are not born through isolation, they forge and reveal each other through the dance of sacred relating.

A container is a crucible and sound structure that allows the energies of intimacy, surrender, trust and union to form, dance and alchemize. A container is a shared field, womb or matrix that allows both souls to bring different parts of them into full manifestation. A container is created when two or more "choose" to come together to share their combined energies for a common soul purpose, and to fulfill and manifest the soul contracts between them both. When this choice is conscious, they claim responsibility for all that arises in the alchemic fire of this crucible.

This container or consciousness is made of feelings and commonly held soul purposes, principles and values that form a loving, rhythmically intelligent, responsive and interactive third being in your relationship. A true container consciousness is greater than the sum of its human parts. It continuously interacts with its creators, influencing them and

---

[3] *The Sacred Mirror*, Welwood

being influenced by them. It works progressively by stimulating and assisting its creators, as long as they behave and act in line with its original aims.

The more time and energy you spend together, the richer and more developed your container will become. The balance, meeting point and mutuality between you is found in this third point or consciousness of the container. Where both meet in the warmth of love is this third, a consciousness of union that knows only love, that only responds to love. It is an actual alive being, a blueprint of union always there, waiting for both of you to slip into it, because *it is you* in sacred union.

The container can become so strong that even if its creators died it would continue to exist, and could even be contacted centuries later by people. The container and template of Sacred Relating created by Christ and Magdalene is one example.

A solid container needs trust, confidentiality, a sense of togetherness in privacy, and a holding in integrity of the other person. Keeping each other's deeper secrets and more vulnerable aspects in trust allows more vulnerability and intimacy. Rumi reminds us, "Love blooms away from prying eyes."

A solid container needs space. Giving freedom, free will and space to each other, and choosing to connect in meaningful ways allows more room for your emotions to breathe, and for the rekindling of your spark of attraction and love for the other. Only through taking space alone for ourselves can we integrate what is happening within us, and the growth that is happening in our relationship. Taking space may be as simple as a walk or a daily meditation time.

In this space, sometimes we meet residual emotions and beliefs, yet taking space usually results in more closeness and sharing as each soul deepens into themselves. In space we find our individuality, our polarities in relation to each other and this fuels the eros or attraction that each individual brings to the relational container.

The dance of the relationship is renewed and kept lively through this, and you remember why you love the other. You meet the other anew, refreshed and more able to see the other person. We want intimacy, but often we are afraid of it because of the pain it has brought in times past. When two people agree they desire closeness, when they state they are willing to clear their barriers to it, intimacy begins.

Men who have integrated and healed with their father sustain a safe, strong and sound physical, emotional and spiritual container. When a woman feels this, she can rise into her femininity and drop into her magnetic foundation of safety and trust: her womb. She needs to feel held, nurtured and safe in a secure environment. She needs to trust, respect and admire you.

Women who have integrated and healed with their mother sustain a safe, strong and sound physical, emotional and spiritual container. When a man feels this, he can soften what is rigid within him and let go into the depths of his masculinity and his gentle, patient heart.

He needs to feel received, not judged, and able to freely and fully express all parts of himself. He needs to trust, respect and admire you.

This mutual presence, love and support creates a loving container for the combined energies of your shared intent, purpose and soul agreements to flow into, and take form. This field is vital to maintain the integrity and manifestation of what is being created, *for all processes in creation need a container to bring the formless into form, to bring an idea into manifestation.*

The containers purpose is to "hold" the two together. One quality is magnetic and embracing, gathering all the open and intimate shared moments in lovemaking, commitment and communication. Another quality is when all the issues you face and have overcome together are Remembered and integrated, which contributes to the growing strength of the container. In return, it will influence and bring forth the courage and resources for you both to continue together.

We come more into the container of our relationship when we are both in a state of self responsible teamwork rhythm. We also experience it's manifestation at vital crossroad times, at the gates of a breakthrough, breakdown or big soul opening.

The flowering of a container also depends on honest monogamy. When you seal the back doors and convenient exit strategies you have created to escape the heat of emotional conflict, when you throw away the key in your back pocket you use to run away from trying times and things you project onto your partner and do not like, then you choose to fully surrender to the alchemy of all that arises within the crucible of the relationship. We get to confront what is happening, and who we really are. This is the threshold into living the love we have always longed for.

When the container between two people is sound, they can allow Divine Love to enter and anchor through deep emotional intimacy, and a shared desire and surrender to that which is eternal. Sacred relationship is a container to inhabit the Divine on earth.

ESTABLISHING A CONTAINER FOR CONCEPTION, PREGNANCY and BIRTHING

In sacred relating and birth, there are key qualities mother and father need to have established within themselves and between them. The necessary qualities are commitment, truth, friendship, trust and respect.

COMMITMENT

A Committed Relationship is one in which two souls support each other in being whole, complete individuals. Themitment is to going *all the way*—letting the relationship be a catalyst for you to live and express your full potential, wisdom, love and creativity. Commitment is to Truth, Love, Your Sovereign Self and your Beloved other. All qualities support each other in a True Relating.

A Co-Creative Relationship is one in which two souls become more creative as a result of their loving interaction. An enhanced energy springs forth, enabling both to make a greater contribution than either one could have made alone. This is the fertile ground for the physical manifestation and/or conception of a child, a project, or a paradigm.

There are three things to do to bring your commitments into manifestation.

Feel All Your Feelings and be totally self-responsible for them- it is not about the other person. This is where the triggers exercise above is helpful.
Tell The Truth with all its details and half truths, be willing to be naked on every level physical, emotional, and spiritual.
Keep Your Agreements and Vows with the other to keep the container strong.

It takes two to play this game. If one person wants to have commitment and the other does not, commitment is not possible. It is only when both people agree to play that real intimacy becomes possible. If you are willing to make the following commitments but your partner is not, it is likely you are in a martyr/ co-dependent relationship. If this is the case, you need to examine why you have set up your life this way, and feel the deeper emotions that are keeping you in this hope.

For the following commitments to work, each person must make them a priority.

Commitment One: I Commit myself to full intimate, emotional and sexual closeness. I Commit to clearing up anything within me that stands in the way of this. I Commit myself to acting from the awareness I am one hundred percent the source of my reality. I Commit myself to my own complete development as an individual.

A Prayer: 'It is our *heart's desire to live in a committed relationship. May we have courage of heart to feel all our emotions, to tell the truth and to keep all agreements that we make with ourselves and with one another.'*

You cannot have ultimate closeness without being able to be separate. In other words, the more developed and whole you are as an individual, the more you are able to fully give and receive love in a relationship. This stems from owning everything in your life and not making your life about anyone, or anything, else.

As children, many of us saw relationships in which people had to compromise their individual development in order to maintain the relationship. Each individual had to get smaller to squeeze into an ill-fitting box. It is time for you both to agree that individual development as well as closeness to the other person are the same; both feed the other.

In a Committed Relationship, each takes 100% responsibility for his/ her life choices, emotions, actions and for the results this creates. There are no victims in committed relationships, there are no victims in the New Paradigm. In fact, victimhood is impossible when both people are willing to acknowledge they are a cause of what happens to them. There is little conflict, because neither person plays the accusatory or victim role. With the energy saved through lessened conflict, both people are free to investigate themselves and therefore to feel deeper love for self and the other, and to express this more.

If either person is being less than one hundred percent, the ground is ripe for power struggles. Each person may look for the places where the other person is at fault, and may diminish the other person to match your wound or extract something from them that you still need.

Commitment Two: I commit to revealing myself fully in the relationship, not to concealing myself

A major opening to love occurs when we shift from concealing to revealing. Most of us learned to hide our wounded selves AND true selves in order to survive the process of growing up. We then take this into our later relationships. It costs, because a close relationship thrives on transparency and mutual communication, feeling that you are seen, accepted and loved without judgment.

Fully communicating and being transparent heals the shadow and releases life force and stuck emotions. It brings forth more vulnerability, love and closeness. If your energy is tied up in concealing who you are and how you feel, there is little energy left for intimacy. It takes more energy to conceal something than to live free of it.

Be open, vulnerable, honest and totally transparent about everything that is going on within you, even if you do not feel it affects the other – it may very well do! Be humble and self-responsible, in speech, silent feeling, sensitivity and discovery of self and other. Patient yet not stagnant, loving but not sentimental, clear yet soft, open, fluid and ready to shift, without fixation or blame.

Whenever we cannot treat ourselves or our partner with sincerity and love, there is an invitation to embrace a part of ourselves that is in separation.

Commitment Three: I commit myself to having a good time in my close relationships.

As a child, how many people did you see around you who were in a state of joy in their relationships? What about right now? As Gay Hendricks[4] says, " a formal commitment to having a good time is necessary to move into a state of co-commitment. We do not know the meaning of life, but we are sure it is not to have a bad time.'

Why not take a conscious stand for joy in your close relationships?

Commitment Four: From this moment on, a commitment needs to be made.

I commit to only partake in authentic love-making. I commit to never allow myself to have sex unless both of us are in honor, giving, appreciation and love.
I commit to make love and to not have 'sex.'
I commit to not follow lust, and to not chase an orgasm.
I commit to not having sex to please or control my partner.
I commit to not compromising my heart and soul in any way through sex.
I commit to being an authentic, elegant, and empowered man/woman.

Place the whole of you behind these vows, and stand for what you know to be true. In surrendering to these vows, all the very human aspects of you will arise to be seen and embraced. It is not about living in perfection, but embracing all the aspects of imperfection as they reveal themselves in our desire to be in truth. These vows are not about being perfect. Aligning with them brings the opportunity for you to be more honest and loving with yourself and choose to grow.

TRUTH

"Only the truth shall set you free."

All Commitment is based on Truth. Truth is both your own personal truths gleaned of the lessons you have come to learn in your life, and the One Truth of universal laws. Truth goes hand in hand with love. Truth leads to love and love brings us deeper into truth. The more love we have realized, the more truth we live and access. The more truth we live, the more love we have in our lives.

The more aligned with truth we become, the more painful and obvious any misalignment with truth becomes. We align with truth by recognizing, speaking, and taking action around all that is not in truth. Truth brings a feeling of relaxation (even when it is hard to face). It has a powerful impact on those around us, and the more we feel, speak, and take action in pursuit of it, the more we embody our essential nature.

Sometimes, we do not want to hear the truth about ourselves or another, and will resist it with all our might. Then, the Universe will eventually seed the truth within us through our

---

[4] From Conscious Loving: The Journey to Co-Commitment by Gay and Kathlyn Hendricks

interactions with others and perhaps painful or confronting situations that will make us recognize that truth.

When we allow the pain that comes with truth, we become more humble. This movement into humility opens us to receive more love. When we justify, excuse, deny and rationalize, we are defending and closing ourselves off from life force and love. When we surrender into the pain we can release the blockage of what is unresolved. This will directly change the external circumstances that brought about this painful reflection. In this way we realize how deeply empowered we are simply by living by the laws of truth.

Truth breaks us open into our naked selves. Honesty is a high form of intimacy. It strips away our facades and reveals our wounded self, and then leads us by the hand into our shining, pure, glorious Self.

Truth is clarity. The simpler we can express something complex the more we have embodied and mastered it. The simpler we are in our prayers, sharings, and creative endeavors, the more successful they become and the more they are heard.

Only a master can say no to anything. He/she is clear in what the universal truth is, what their own personal truth is, and where they meet and merge, therefore he/she is empowered to say no to anyone or anything because they know the truth about themselves and Divine Truths. You are free to say no to anything.

The more we fearlessly investigate all parts of ourself in all situations with different types of people, the more we get to know ourselves and the truth. Traveling around the world is good for this, as are sacred relationships, a form of inner travel.

The more authentic our connection is to life and our own soul, the more we come to know Universal Truths. Both personal truth and Universal Truth integrate in our journey when we are humble and place truth as our priority. In truth we are supported, abundant, and loved. The more we let go of our manipulations to get things, to see ourselves truthfully in our grasping, the more we open to receive what was beyond what we could imagine for ourselves.

Truth is individual until it becomes selfless. Truth has no self to it, therefore it is everywhere and nowhere, always flowing and available. The truth is that there is nothing to hold onto, no concept, teaching or relationship. All of this *as an attachment* has to dissolve in order for you to live the truth. In this the universe meets us in the truth of who we are in every moment.

Prayer
'I wish to feel the naked truth about myself. I want to know where I am out of truth in my life. I wish to feel all the fears I have. I wish to feel all the ways I control myself and others. I wish to feel my pride and unworthiness that cuts me off from Truth.'

Action
Where are you out of alignment with truth right now? Where are you not following your personal truth? Where are you not following Divine Truths in your life? How many times this week have you neglected to speak a truth to another and yourself? How many times this week have you thought or felt a truth about yourself or another and failed to put it into action? *Why did you not do this?*

WORKING WITH TRIGGERS

An emotional reaction is a message from the soul that tells us we are in duality. Life is neutral and when we don't feel and release the pain of our wounds we will continue reacting to life and others from a place of our historical pain. In order to respond to life instead of reacting to it, we have to face our unfelt pain.

Being triggered is a great opportunity to go into the deeper layers of feeling. Owning our reaction is a great act of self-love, taking us deeper into ourselves and the reclaiming of aspects of our psyche and emotions that have fragmented. Having the tools to be able to work with the intensity of emotion that is stirred in our most intimate relationships is essential to building a long lasting foundation of trust and growth within the container of a couple and a family unit.

The following exercise is an inquiry using the entry point of an event that stirred an emotional reaction. When the reaction is felt and explored down to the soul level of the original wound, the charge can be released from our bodies, from our projection onto our partner, and from our experience. In this way we become empowered by the moments of friction that inevitably happen in relationships, empowering us to use them as a means to do deeper healing and to align with the present moment.

Choose a recent event in your life that triggered you, where you had an emotional reaction.

1. *How did you feel?*
Not seen, not heard, not understood, rejected, abused, used, not loved, helpless, overwhelmed, invaded, trapped, blamed, disrespected, insignificant, pre-occupied, humiliated, exposed, abandoned, attacked ignored, etc. Really feel in your body where this experience is held. Breathe into it.

2. *What did you feel?*
Guilt, frustration, anger, fear, anxiety, anguish, hate, sadness, panic, etc

3. *How do you defend?*
There are 3 ways of defending: submission, aggression and withdraw, or fight, flee and freeze. Submission is when we silence ourselves, forgive too easily, or say yes to the other too soon. In submission we put ourselves in a place of being a victim. Aggression is our expression of wanting to be right, blaming, judging, attacking, exposing or destroying the other. Withdraw is feeling numb, when we disengage our of pride or fear, when we simply cannot be bothered, or we freeze.

4. ***What are the beliefs?***
The structure of a belief is : If this happens, then ....
I am not seen, I will not exist, If I am used I will lose everything.

5. ***What are the memories that are stirred by this experience from your childhood? Who were they with:* mother, father, siblings, school or an overall emotional climate?**
When the past comes into the present, we can release history's grasp on our experience. Breathe deep into your heart and womb/hara, allow this experience to be fully felt. Hold yourself as a child at the age this event occurred, and really give this child what it needed in the moment. Place one hand on heart, on hand on hara/womb and feel your pulses synchronize. This will recalibrate your nervous system. [5]

FRIENDSHIP

In Sacred Relationships we need to have a personal friendship with our partner AND a larger friendship based on your soul's desires and purpose and the others soul's desires and purpose. Being Friends is an important part of partnership and involves loyalty to Truth and a higher Love.

Human friendship is brought into its highest potential by each one of you desiring each other's highest potential and being united in this common goal. In this deepening and ever-revealing, humbling process, feelings of fraternal love arise from walking the path in vulnerability with these friends.

This bond is Free for it is moving towards the infinite, and is designed to support our soul's growth. Friends have a selfless love for each other, regardless of our own agenda and needs. They will always point out the truth to each other, (and never collude) for this is an unconditional love and honoring of the purpose of the soul, and indeed the very creation of the soul itself.

You support each other's free will, regardless of how it may affect you, for you desire for the other what you desire for yourself. You love them as the Divine loves you, and treat them as you treat yourself.
Every true love and authentic soul friendship is a story of unexpected transformation. If we are the same person before and after we loved, that means we have not loved enough. [17]

As we deepen in our embodying, our relationship to the Divine becomes clearer as we realize how perfectly we are loved and the more perfectly we love ourselves. Born through this love comes a soulful affection for others as Friends of The Heart. The more you love yourself, the more you love others.

---

[5] Thanks to Fabiana Sacca

This also extends to those you are less familiar with, as well as those who may perceive themselves to be your enemies. Sharing affection with your 'enemies,' being kind to them in their anger or fear towards you, is a sign of this love being perfected. *Wherever there is pain, there is the opportunity for love to bloom once the pain is felt, because all pain shows us where we have not been loving or been loved.*

Being Friends gives a partnership a foundation beyond the body and sexuality. It allows us to be totally who we are. The presence of true support for the deepest part of the soul is priceless, and allows the deepest honesty, vulnerability and true expression of the soul to reveal. This helps open the soul into its true nature.

Prayer
'I desire to know my companions of destiny, Friends of the Heart, guides and allies, now. I receive you, my guardians, guides, soul pod and companions of destiny! I walk in life with trust, love and acceptance for all beings.'

Who are your Friends of the Heart? Who are the people who are always honest, speak truth to you, are open and there for you? Are you connecting with them regularly? Who are those people you trust with the deepest parts of your soul?

TRUST AND RESPECT

Respect each other's freewill and what the other feels to do, even if you do not agree to it; *share, not demand*, for love is a gift to be shared, not demanded. Respect the boundaries of yourself and the other in self-love. Respect and follow your desires and passions; allow others the same.

One way we can respect another is to see and affirm their goodness and worth through appreciation and gratitude. We can only sustain respect and love for our partner if we truly sense and acknowledge, regardless of their words and actions, that 'the other' never loses their innate goodness, only their awareness of it.

And the same goes for our own self too. If we do not love, respect and trust our own self, we send a message that we believe the other also is not worthy of respect. We cannot fully respect, accept or value the other if we do not respect, love and value our own self. This can be quite a journey for many souls.

On another level, respect, like trust, needs to be earned over time. We need to see the integrity and honor of the other person through their actions, not just their words.

Choose to not give much validation to either yours or the other's personality, but rather a continual seeing and speaking to the soul. In this, gossip and mental chatter are not encouraged. Instead, the deeper nature of the soul's expression and feelings are consistently shared and upheld by both souls, as best they can with each other. This honors the soul and strengthens it. *This is sexually arousing for a soul inspired man or woman,* and will lead to more soulful and great lovemaking!

This means that you both share with each other when you stray from truth and love, and support yourself and the other to stay in truth without demanding perfection or expecting it. Honoring the soul means you both do not stand for anything less than this, both in yourself and the other. Pay attention to each other, not multitasking, ignoring or 'shouted from the other end of the house' communication.

Trust is the cornerstone foundation of intimate relationship. It is the Key to a great container. True trust comes over time. It is through our actions and by keeping our words and commitments that trust can bloom. In its heights and depths, trust is a precious aspect of Love, a pure, safe and empowering feeling felt by both souls when they open to each other, daring to reveal all their weakness, shame or pain as well as the glory of Love, in its awe and wonder.

Love requires Trust. The two go hand in hand. We need to trust ourselves. We need to trust our partners, and we need to trust Life. We need to differentiate between the voice of our soul and the voice of our wounded self.

Trust is based on a willingness to explore, to be vulnerable and to take the time to listen to yourself and the other. We simply cannot trust a person we don't respect, don't accept and are not vulnerable with. Without trust, love is infantile and selfish.

In any challenge, this being does not fall apart or get hysterical, but instead turns inward and moves in the direction of the container. This internal process has to be the backbone of your spiritual practice. When couples lack inner confidence, have no real faith in a greater source of wisdom than their human minds, and are ambivalent towards one another, how on earth can this internal shift ever take place?

Without a palpable connection to the container and to the Divine, and each one's inner Wholeness, this great journey together will not come to fruition. It takes not only intention and desire, but practice. We have to stay as humble as possible. We have to commit to a daily infusion of prayer/meditation, space, humility, openness and truth on every level. Without consistent replenishment, our spiritual backbone may break.

In relationships trust is the first thing to go, and the last thing to return! It's hard to trust someone you do not respect. Until you are honest with yourself, you will not be able see the real cause of your withdrawal of trust in others. Sure, you can discern not to trust another, but always look at yourself as well.

Until we *feel* beneath our own fears to their *cause first*, we will mistrust others for some reason and justification, constantly sabotaging our relationships and our ability to give and receive love. *These include:* constantly denying our true feelings, minimizing the impact that our experiences have had on our sensitive emotions and souls; justifying our own and others actions, forgiving them too soon without having truly felt first; and blaming others for our own emotional reactions, experiences and lessons.

The fear of being hurt leads to mistrust. This is usually based on past experiences where we felt hurt/let down by someone, or betrayed. We think we can avoid a recurrence of this hurt if we close down a part of ourselves to cope with this ancient pain. All this does is avoid our own lessons. The trigger exercise at the beginning of this chapter helps to follow feelings of mistrust to the causal experience in your history, so you can release this on a deep level, opening you more capacity to trust NOW.

Try and meet others, even those you know, innocently. Do this today with someone you have known for a while. Do this today with someone you may have previously judged by their appearance or past actions. How would you approach them? What would you say? Pretend you do not even know them, and this is your first day of meeting. You may be surprised!

One rule to remember is that people CAN AND DO change, including yourself, and our opinions of others are often clouded by our own filters, past experiences and wounds. Do not spend time analyzing, judging and thinking about others like a gossip column; look at yourself.

AN INTIMATE PRACTICE TO TRUST

Place your fingers, or your partner's fingers, gently and lovingly, with conscious attention, at the lips of the yoni or lips of the lingam. Simply feel it; the texture, the warmth, the contours, the feeling of the skin.

Ask if the lips of the yoni or the lingam *emotionally feel* any of these six ways of distrust. If they do, then simply rest into and feel each emotion and sensation.

Now, ask these questions out aloud, and feel into the answers:
Has she/he ever felt respected, appreciated, honored, nurtured or admired by another?
Can you remember the feelings of what it felt like? If so, what was it?
Have you ever respected, appreciated, trusted, honored, nurtured or admired her/him yourself?

Check each one slowly, allowing whatever feeling to arise for each one.
Do this next check in for the lips of the yoni and the lingam lips for the man.
Does she/he feel safe and secure within you?
Does she/he feel like she can trust?
Does she/he feel that she/he can open up, and is trustworthy?
What is blocking her/him?

When you are ready, gently send appreciation and praise, from your heart, down through your arms, to him/her. Intuitively feel what you wish to share with him/her.

When your sexuality starts to open, it can feel sweet, humbling, tearful, affirming, joyous and powerful. In this opening, we can feel the pain of missing that part of us, the sweet joy of finding that again, and gratitude.

SOUL and SOURCE

"We cannot solve our problems with the same thinking we used when we created them."
Einstein

There is something larger than ourselves that is the fundamental resource for all that is manifesting through us. When we open to the possibility of the energies and consciousness of a Divine Mother and Divine Father, we can feel the feminine and masculine in their most exalted forms, and our experience of being an expression of this. To know anything fully, one has to go to the next octave beyond that which has been created.

To know our own soul fully, one has to get to know That which created us. When we spend time everyday deepening into this connection, communing with this Divine Love, we anchor ourselves into a divine life. When we invite divine connection into our healing, our lovemaking, our birthing, it brings infinite support, infinite wisdom and infinite love into us. When devotion is part of our soul's journey, a deep sovereignty and unconditional love emerges from us in loving others and ourselves.

The soul is covered by our emotions. These emotions include all the wounds and learning challenges of your life, such as sadness, anger, fear, unworthiness and emotional pain we avoid. In this avoidance, we build walls of beliefs and create our own programs about what reality is.

Feelings, which our pure soul flows through and is fueled by Shakti or life force, are based on love's qualities such as appreciation, gratitude, compassion, joy, humility, and holy desire. As one becomes established in the pure soul, one acts from this intelligence.

To co-conceive a Child with the Divine requires we have intelligence based on feelings, which happens when we release emotions that stop us from being loving and Present. We can only be fully present with others and ourselves if we have done this deep work. The more we release these emotions, the more we become situated in our feeling or magnetic soul.

Our soul stirs and awakens in our heartfelt desires, passions, what moves, touches, and inspires our very core. Within the soul is our innate ability to give and receive love in all forms, freely and unconditionally, with all beings, with all life, in the interconnected web of life.

Your soul is the part of you that has the possibility of living forever, the only part of you that can merge into the eternal. It is the real you, the eternal you, and it is accompanied by its vehicles of the spirit body, which is how it moves throughout multi dimensional creation, and the physical body, which is how it moves on Earth and the third dimension. Your soul has a physical body to help in its individualization process. The human soul is created with an innate desire to express and receive love from others, but this desire is distorted through conditioning and imprinting you have received.

The soul feels, not thinks, and it is through deep feeling that it grows more and truly connects with other souls. Your soul has free will and choice. This enables your soul to grow in truth and love, or decrease in love. Your soul holds your true purpose, mission and deepest fulfillment. It is the most natural part of you, and is always wanting to communicate with you, through it's longing and desires.

Sacred Action: Have you been feeling disconnected from the source of love and the lineage of your soul? Are you feeling lost and on your own?

Take a moment to come into feeling communion with your essence, no matter how desperate you are feeling. Open yourself with a deep breath to the innate blessing and love that you are, and that the universe is extending to you.

Allow your defenses, layers of protection and resistance to drop in this moment for as you humble yourself so you can receive. This is your birthright, to know and receive this love intimately and totally.

The soul grows through:

- Giving and receiving love freely.
- Humility and self-responsibility: your desire to fully own and fully feel all your emotions, both the deepest love and pleasures, and the deepest pains. This also involves owning when you punish, blame, judge or harm yourself or others, and take responsibility for feeling your own pain that caused you to react in this way.
- Free will choice: The more curious we are about our limitations, the more we open to what is possible as we dissolve the false constructs of safety.
- Being sovereign: having your own real, felt connection to Self and Source, dependent on no one else.
- Heartfelt desire, sincerity, longing and passion in your life.
- Loving and serving others.
- Discernment and wisdom regarding what is love and what love is not: what is truth and what is untrue; investigating this with everyone in all aspects of your life.
- Following the souls intelligence, not the mind alone.
- Making 'radical' actions in the world based on your souls knowing.

SEX, SOUL and SOURCE

Soul and sexuality evolve together. When we separate our essence from our life force we limit our capacity for growth, realization, and joy. To heal sexually, the soul and its wounds have to be felt and included on the journey. To heal our souls, which are partly fueled and embodied by sexual energy, sexuality has to be included along the journey.

The intimacy, emotions and soulfulness that come from truly loving someone and opening your soul to them allows true nakedness to occur. This is known as the path of Beloved Tantra. Beloved tantra is about union with the Divine with and through the support of another. When we harness our soul's desire for union with the most powerful force available to humans, our sexual energy, we employ a radical and transformative capacity for realization.

Sacred Union is where both partners are focused on the union of human and Divine. In this journey of uniting sexuality with Divine Love, much gets healed and a soul becomes embodied. All the places where love is absent within you will arise fast. Once triggered in the sexual act, with a little humility, your wounds can be felt and seen within you. This allows a flowering of loving sexuality through the open womb-heart and lingam-heart.

The gift of sexuality allows us to experience another form of emotional intimacy, growth and union. This is one of the many ways we can experience every aspect of love. Our design is to be soulfully orgasmic, to enjoy the feeling in our bodies and souls, to feel it here on Earth, in the third dimension, in every way.

Sexuality in loving feeling is a deeply blissful, magnetically ecstatic state and is one of the highest frequencies in creation. One of the primary purposes of our physical and spiritual design is sexual expression in love. This deepens connection within ourselves, with our partner, and is the means for conceiving a child. When we harness our sexual energy we can connect with all life in a way that is honoring. Sexuality in it's highest form can bring us into full union and dissolution. When a couple has done the preparation work, sharing this in a sacred container with another is one of the fastest ways to full becoming fully realized as an embodied human being.

We access union through pleasure. When part of your sexuality is not open to fully feel, we are cut off from pleasure. The denial of sexual desire often blocks deeper holy desire. To feel deeper desire for union with the eternal involves you freeing up your sexual energy. We all have to make steps along the way, exploring, investigating, healing and refining our sexual identities, finding out more of who we are in this respect.

You can spend periods of time away from sexually engaging to refine and develop your soul, and this is wise and true, but our souls are also sexual in nature. It is part of the substance of your soul, so you cannot really embody or reach full union without engaging with it, alchemizing it, refining and sublimating it in some way.

The opening and activation of the womb is a precursor to engaging in true lovemaking or sacred union.[6] This union has been described in many cultures as *sacred marriage*, *yab-yum* and *hieros gamos*. As the womb heals through the opening of the 5 portals [7] lovemaking enters a whole new sphere where the touching of souls occurs in a profound way. One starts to make love in a different way and with a different purpose: for a woman it is to be penetrated by consciousness and for a man it is to enter the womb. Both partners enter a vaster bliss, an infinite space.

Pure feelings, yearnings, deep desire are the language of the soul reaching into Source. This sincerity is the doorway that opens us into receiving the love from the cosmos. Prayers are most deeply felt when they are no longer words or thoughts, but soul emanations, communicated through desire and love from your soul. *The true prayers of a longing soul are more powerful, and will bring response than all the powers of angels, spirits and devils combined.*

This form of prayer shapes the soul, crafting and refining her into Essence. In these sublime depths, ecstasies and heartbreaking moments, the soul prays wordlessly; the mind knows not, speaks not. Prayers are answered more fully when they are no longer intentions, but rather become a giving of all of yourself without reservation.

Precise prayer is when you direct your desire to feel specific emotions, specific parts of your soul, and specific prayers to strengthen your soul. Prayers are answered if they come from humility and soul recognition. Prayers are answered more when you make the effort in all areas of your life to uncover where you are unloving and untruthful. *If we ask* sincerely, and if we are humble enough to accept the truths shown to us, we will receive what is innately ours. Only you yourself can prevent this, so if you ask, be sure you are ready to receive.

We are given what we need rather than what we erroneously believe we need born out of the false wisdom of our wounds, needs and earthly appetites; choices that are out of harmony with love. Changing the very nature of the primordial power of desire into pure holy desire for the Beloved is how prayer can really activate us.

---

[6] Similarly, the healing of both parents' sexual wounds and birth traumas were seen as part of the pre-birth process, and would be done as part of a preparation before one even conceived a child.
[7] For more, read *The Technology of Love*

A SOUL SEXUAL person is:

One who is turned on by the purity, humility and sacredness of another's soul
One who is aroused by the lights and elegance of another's soul
One who is inspired to move to their higher potentials by the others connection to Love
One who trusts and stands by the soul
One who knows their own Self and desires the other to know their Self
One who brings a selfless higher Love into themselves and the relating
One who can give and receive love freely
One who stands by truth and can share this with you
One who opens their heart and soul fully to you in the bedroom, living room and meditation room
One who can meet you in the silence
One who can meet you in the noise
One you can learn with, and from
One who gets aroused by the other souls devotion
One who makes love like prayer
One who makes love with all their heart and shakti
One who opens your heart up to the fullness of your sexuality
One who connects to the higher Love and invites you there
One who can bow to you, receive your bows, and can bow to God in front of you
A man who can open your womb and a woman who can open his heart so you both come into union
A man who stands in Presence when you lose yours
A woman who reminds you of Love when her man is in his head
A man who reminds you of the truth, human and eternal
A woman who reminds you of kindness and love for all in the eternal
A man who can be vulnerable and share with you
A woman who can receive this in a space of magnetic presence
A woman who opens up into the Beyond in surrender with you
A man who can take her there
A man who kisses with his soul in depth, passion and stillness
A woman who can surrender and be overwhelmed in this
A man who refuses to have sex without love
A woman who thanks him for this
A man who can evoke the presence of the divine masculine
A woman who can evoke the presence of the divine feminine
One who knows and listens to the inner voice
One that prefers feeling more than other ways of moving

SACRED RELATIONSHIPS: BIRTHING A NEW PARADIGM

Sacred Relationship is a Dance between two individuals and their teamwork and togetherness as a couple. One part of your Sacred Relationship is Knowing what fulfills you and the other, what both of your deepest desires are, what both of your lessons are in life, and how to heal them.

This is a Dance of inclusion with the other: how do they fit with your own souls purpose, passions and desires? Does the other meet you in the areas you want to be met? Is there mutuality? Is there an active and conscious working towards this between you, or is it largely unconscious? Do you fit together?

Nothing lasts forever. This is when the divine comes into complete the Trinity of your Sacred Relationship. She is Eternal, and this is your journey, with a supporting cast of characters to help you Realize this. If you can support another in this, and if they can support you in this journey, you have a wonderful basis for your Relating to fulfill its highest purpose and ultimate Goal.

This divine Third Party in your Relating will only ever bring more love and more truth to you both, complementing your humanity with an Infinite Love and bringing an ever deepening humility to you both. In this Trinity, man and woman find their right places and roles with each other. Woman surrenders, man holds; woman receives, man guides; woman moves the Shakti, man is the pillar. And they swap at different times, to complete their own inner male and female.
This happens when we no longer need our partner as a crutch, to fill a hole within us, and we can be happy with them *and* without them. We desire them simply because we enjoy them, we enjoy our love, our meeting, our lovemaking, our sharings, our fun, our friendship and the spontaneous adventure of life taking us into the vast unknown.

In the old Paradigm we wanted someone to live with, grow old with, to share the bills with, to have kids with, to make life here easier, to make life more manageable: the other became a crutch of sorts. Look at your parents.

In the New Paradigm, we do not need the other. We have our own money, our own emotional security formed from our own deep inner Work, our own soul purpose and soul sovereignty, our own wholeness and aloneness we enjoy. We can live and die alone, and we choose to relate to others out of an informed freedom of choice and willingness to share, not out of desperation, loneliness or sadness, but out of exuberance, fulfillment and peace.

This sacred relationship brings you *freedom to express all parts of you*, known and unknown. One way we viscerally, palpably taste the Goodness of this is through lovemaking. When all of a woman's body, soul and womb becomes one, throbbing, pulsating, ripe, juicy, surrendered and oh so attractive and magnetically alluring, a man embodying the Lingam Pillar of Light enters. In entering his woman from yoni through womb to heart, crown and beyond, she becomes imbued, infused by Presence. Both enter ecstasy. This Union is with your own soul *as well as* with the other to lead you into the greatest Union ever possible. This Sacred union is the ground for conscious conception, to birth a New Child, a New Paradigm, and a New World.

THE FATHER: THE PILLAR

'Dad Deprivation' is eroding modern society. [8] One of the world's most respected campaigners on men's issues believes dad deprivation is directly causing "a boy crisis," and unless society urgently intervenes, we will be in danger of writing off a whole generation of men.

Warren Farrell, pioneering men's activist and author of *The Myth Of Male Power,* states that Dad-deprived boys are less likely to display empathy, are less assertive, more likely to become depressed, have nightmares, talk back and be disobedient. He points out that *in every one* of the largest 70 developed nations, boys have fallen behind girls.

"These boys will be more likely to have low self-esteem, fewer friends, and are likely to do worse in every single academic area, especially reading, writing, maths and science. These boys hurt: and boys who hurt, hurt us – and themselves.

These boys have no positive male role models. That makes them vulnerable to strong, destructive alpha males like gang leaders or drug dealers. These boys are most likely to be brought up by mums, and then move from a mother-centered home to a woman-centered school.

Boys need to see males caring at every stage of their lives. We need to encourage men into the caring sectors, to challenge the cliché that caring work is women's work. To an eight-year-old boy, their dad is God. Backing off or abandoning them leaves the child feeling not important. Dads must fight to be a part of their children's lives, for Fatherhood is about passing on character, which is an empowering and gratifying feeling. We should celebrate gentle, caring, loving values in men; not just power, but responsibility".

There is not much support for prospective fathers-to-be in the birthing world. The lack of information about a father's role in pregnancy and birth leaves many men feeling marginalized, confused and helpless. Many fathers instinctively KNOW they are here to help with birth, and would like to do something, but they just do not know what to do emotionally or soulfully. Their parents, their first port of call for advice on birth and parenting, usually do not know either.

This is why there is such a large section in this book dedicated to the father. Mothers usually get a lot more attention and support in pregnancy, whereas fathers are left to fend for themselves and "be a man" about it.

As a father in my first pregnancy, I was flailing around, going to birth centres and birth classes, speaking to my parents, family, asking friends who had babies what to do, how I should prepare myself, what everything should look like.... and a hundred other questions and thoughts. None of the people or resources I consulted spoke to my heart or my questions on what I dimly perceived to be my upcoming initiation into fatherhood. I knew this was an important time for my partner and me, yet nobody could share with me what I was "supposed" to do.

---

[8] In an article in the UK's Telegraph Newspaper by Martin Daubney 22 June 2016

How many men have done this, and are still doing this today? How many men want to take this initiation, this rite of passage into the deeper masculine, but have no idea how to? Perhaps you are one of these men, who wants to take this initiation and honour your soul, your partners soul, and the soul of your precious child who has specifically *come to you* to be their papa.

You don't know what you don't know until you come across it! There is a flame in the deep, masculine heart that KNOWS how important a man's full presence is during pregnancy and birth. You may know it innately, but may not have been able to articulate it until now.

By giving, you will receive. By giving your full male presence and by fully engaging in the pregnancy and birth process with your partner and child, with every part of your being, you will become a fuller man. In giving fully of yourself, you will receive more of yourself. This is the promise of fatherhood, which starts at conception.

This promise is a seed, a seed borne in you from the moment you were born on this earth, a seed which wants to grow into a solid tree of masculine presence, giving you the depth, the solidity, the earthly presence, softness and unconditional you always wanted to experience deep down. In true fatherhood, you gain a valuable part of your humanity; something all the spiritual practices in the world cannot give you.

Every man, deep down, wants to be the pillar, the anchor and the rock. This is part of the male genetic makeup. Living this genetic imperative propels us into the spiritual growth we always wanted, but never could put our finger on. Yet, what can be more spiritual than creating life? This is what God does, and in birthing, we are given a taste of this life-affirming gift for ourselves. God created us with the power to create, and if we follow this Design, we get to Know more about the whole process of creation and of life itself.

DNA evolves through mutation. The New Children are accelerating this mutation, and with each one born through their Souls Design, the entire collective consciousness of humanity steps into more of its potential. This potential is innate within us.

Each one of these New Children born on earth is heralding in a new chapter in Earth's history. Maybe the next quantum leap in evolution will come from one of these Children waking up and creating something entirely new, something completely different, to all that has come before. Something previously inconceivable to the parameters of evolution thus far on Earth is dawning in humanity.

THE WOUNDED WARRIOR

Many men are wounded warriors who yearn to return to the womb for the primordial comfort, nourishment and healing they have forgotten and lost in life's journey. They seek to reconnect to the source of life, and can do so by becoming emotionally present, sexually aware and emotionally intelligent to their partner and child in the rite of passage of pregnancy, labour, birth and raising a child.

A woman's depth of womb presence in the whole process of pregnancy and birthing can help a man to grow emotionally and spiritually into becoming a true pillar of a man, a rounded, grounded human being. Becoming a true man is a part of every man's soul purpose whilst on earth, just as being a true woman is a part of every woman's soul purpose whilst on earth.

Birthing is an important factor in this process. The womb in the nine months of birthing 'pulls' out certain energies from the father that can rarely be accessed in other circumstances; this drawing out or catalyzing draws him further into the womb space, where his own deepest wounds can be seen, felt and healed. This healing can be a deep process for an emotionally aware man who is engaged in the pregnancy and birth process, as it involves primal, preverbal energies that connect soul to soul, and that the personality mind or ego cannot understand.

Birthing time is a great way for a man to become more fluid, more intuitive and more feminine, and therefore own and embody his true masculinity. To be a true man requires he be fully feminine as well; to be a true woman, a woman has to have embodied her masculine too.

The birthing process dredges up deep untended needs, desires and longings that need to be shared openly, vulnerably and honestly in order to be resolved. This can result in the birthing of a new man, the birthing of the true masculine within a man. This more soulful perspective towards life and birthing is often ignored in modern day society, making it difficult for men and women to find soulful reference points during their birthing process. This process can be a struggle, as a man may not understand what is happening to him.

Even if he does understand it, he may not know how to deal with it, so tempestuous can be the emotional whirlwinds and subconscious promptings spinning inside him and his partner. His work is to feel and release the effects or surface layers of these emotions, working through them to release the cause.

In order to be fully empowered in the depth of his masculine essence, he must feel embraced by the feminine womb. This will bring up deep issues for him, for love brings up everything that it is not. In this process he will feel many places within him where love has been absent, denied, repressed or unfelt, and in so doing, he can heal himself.

A man must first find himself before he finds his woman. Otherwise he will continuously damage every woman he comes into contact with along the way.
Vernon Smith

In healing yourselves dear fathers, you help the whole collective masculine consciousness of our planet, and in turn, with your willingness and desire, this can ripple out to the feminine consciousness and ease the burden of age-old wounds and inequalities.

THE PILLAR of THE FATHER

All of us have deep needs for safety, security and a need for love from others. This is a natural and innate emotional need and calling card for our emotional body. Our needs partially stem from what our fathers did, *or did not*, give us as children. As children, we were dependent on our parents for our source of love.

We are dependent on our fathers to provide us with a solid inner foundation in order to flourish and become who we truly are as individuals, NOT to become someone else or to ape wounds and dysfunctional patterns from the family or ancestral line. We are dependent on our fathers being there for us in order to empower us into becoming sovereign individuals and to acquire the resources to achieve this later in life.

To do this, we as fathers or fathers to be, must embody the pillar. When a father provides a consistent pillar of safety, trust, depth, listening to his child, always being there for his child, receiving his child, providing discipline, masculine strength and care with presence, then these qualities are passed on and imprinted onto the child. This is a father's role, and benefits him too, as it empowers the father into a deeper aspect of his own masculine.

This benefits the child as ancestral gifts from the masculine lineage, positive qualities of father, grandfather and so on, are passed on that the child will need. As the child grows up, he/ she will feel safe, secure, and able to make choices from their sovereign centre unfiltered by anyone else. The child will not have a deep subconscious insecurity borne out of a hunger for love that clouds their decision making, making them create unhealthy relationships.

The child will not be unable to direct its power. The child will not need approval and admiration from a needy insecure place within them, which often means we try and fit into society and please others, always looking outside for security, comfort or dregs of love. The child will be able to be present. The child will feel held within and more able to overcome fear swiftly, able to organically unfold into who they uniquely are. The child will be able to feel their emotions without filters or dampening/repressing them, thus intuitively knowing what is best for themselves and having less hesitation in putting this into action.

The child will trust him/herself, and be able to adventure freely and intuitively. The child will have their own inner pillar, and be centred. Paradoxically, the child will be able to flow much more with life's situations, its ebbs and flows, from his/her centre, and manifest its purpose, gifts and lessons more directly and gracefully.

For a father to directly imprint his child (and mother) with this inner pillar begins at conception until the child is 27 months old. Some fathers will take longer to do this, sometimes until the child is 21. *Usually, most fathers will never do this, and never take this initiation of fatherhood.*

The true masculine is a pillar for others to lean on and confide in, a source of strength and depth that is ever present, ever reliable. He is there no matter what, living in integrity, and would do *anything* for his loved ones. He is the pillar of strength his woman and child can rely on and always come back to.

This pillar is much more powerful for his partner than a woman confiding in her girlfriends behind her partners back, and not sharing with him. Why? Because a deeper bond is created through vulnerability that allows both man and woman to embody their true femininity and true masculinity.

For example, in labour just before birth, a woman will often say, "I can't!" This is when her man moves in close, holds her hands, looks in her eyes and lends her his strength. This allows the expectant mother to share in his strength, his solidity, his pillar, and therefore re-access her own strength, encouraging her to travel deeper into herself.

The male pillar anchors and firmly grounds the container for alchemy to happen. The male anchor keeps everything in its right place, both physically and in the realms of consciousness. He keeps things stable, linking heaven to earth, securing and connecting one to the other.

Husband 'means one who keeps the house and everything in its right place. Another meaning of *husband* is to look after, cultivate, *to till the soil*, to wisely manage.[9] A husband or pillar wisely manages his household, cultivating the relating, bringing life into the fields of the relating, turning it over and keeping it fresh so new life and new opportunities can happen.

This man, solid, steady and true, brings simplicity to the dance of relating, bringing he and his woman back to their own respective centre points. He brings everything into perspective, helping each individual understand the larger context.

He helps his woman and inner feminine return to her souls truth, passion and purpose when she is caught up in the emotional swirls of her own process. He brings her back to the solid container of trust. He sees and holds the 'big picture, 'allowing both souls to find their own flows and unique expressions. He is the reminder, the balance point in the middle of it all.

The responsibility to be a strong pillar for everyone can stop a man from being vulnerable and human. He can become frozen, no longer flowing with his own emotions, becoming isolated and trapped in a role. If a man cries and expresses his vulnerability, he may fear his woman will feel unsteady and scared around him, and perceive that he is no longer the rock she can lean on. He may feel he has neglected his duty and responsibility, by dropping his façade of invulnerability.

In this taking of false responsibility for others, a man can deny himself and others their lessons for growth and empowerment. When a man ceases to flow with and embrace the movements of his emotions in order to be a static pillar that everyone, and everything, depends on, he loses a part of himself.

Crying, being gentle with ourselves, sharing this with others, having our own space alone, allows us to drop deep into the vulnerable heart that then becomes a stronger foundation for the pillar to rest on. It brings people closer to you and deepens the bond of intimacy with them. A man needs to integrate and experience this part of his femininity before he can become the true masculine pillar, just as a woman needs to integrate and experience her masculinity in order to become the true feminine.

THE PILLAR EMBODIED

The Pillar is a soft yet strong Presence. He holds a vast, impersonal unconditional love that deeply affects and holds the feminine in an intimate, personal way. From this basis of the pillar, the man is free to fully and unreservedly express his unconditional and personal love from a place of safety, strength and openness.

A child feels the pillar of his father as a safe, strong, electric Field of light around him/her. In this field, the child can fully be him/herself. He/she feels held and guided, safe to play, explore and discover more of who they are and the world around them. As one grandmother shares, ''I felt so happy to see him really happy with his family, he is completely nourished by his Papa's love, he knows his Papa is there for him and he is secure and complete. '

As a man integrates his pillar more, he settles into Holding unconditionally all those around him because he is rooted and settled into his own ground of consciousness in an organic, feeling, body centred and natural way. The mind becomes a servant of this consciousness. He feels like an invincible pillar of consciousness built from love, soft as he is strong.

The Pillar loves purely with or without sexual energy being emanated; rather, it can be contained and sublimated into a holding love of Self and others. This is deeply felt by those around him, and can be deeply healing for mother, child and friends. It is this love that many women need and want, a love they never got from their father or lovers.

This love can also help unearth and heal many forms of sexual wounding and shame in women, as an emotionally intimate, touching love can be shared without any need or sexual charge. Feeling intimate love without sexual charge, need or grasping from a man can be deeply healing and opening for a woman.

In Being the Pillar, a man's physical body is still, relaxed and alive, encased in a soft inner peace. This exudes strength, trust and safety to the feminine magnetic form, allowing her to drop out of her mind and surrender into her heart and body more. This masculine magnetism is soft and holding, yet electrically powerful and rooted at the same time.

His auric field or spirit body envelops whomever he is holding, allowing them to let go and feel loved and safe. His clarity of feeling from a quiet mind, quietened because he is emotionally clear, leads to clear action. This organic masculine, where everything is held, viewed and loved in the same clear Consciousness becomes integrated within him as a feeling way of being, rather than a mental or meditational abstraction or fleeting state of consciousness.

From the Pillar, a man's inner child or soul feels safe to express itself totally and to play in all ways. Play is a great form of learning. From the Pillar, any shadow within a man can be easily felt as a distortion, something strange and not of That.

From the Pillar, a man's heart blooms. His soul embodies more from being situated in this organic, emotionally integrated, embodied Pillar than any other form of spiritual practice, body work or spiritual work. This is his basis as a man, and this needs to be in place for him to embody. Otherwise he cannot, no matter what he does.

From the Pillar, God becomes part of man. It is in this Pillar that God awakens within the man. Otherwise, God Cannot awaken within man fully and transform him (if you are on this pathway of sacred fatherhood). The doorway to this Divine Human comes through our humanity. All parts of our heart need to be embraced, our humanity received and nurtured, our humanity given its expression and fully allowed; then the Pillar can anchor in immoveable roots, sunk deep into the soil of our humanity.

When a man stands in his Pillar fully, he automatically comes into flow with the Harmony of Life, the goodness, order, balance, coherency, justice, truth, morality and righteousness of love, known as *Ma'at* in Egypt, *Pono* in Hawaii, *Rtam* in India. The Pillar enables a man to be able to flow with the web of life, for the *Pillar is his own Anchoring Point and Interface with the Web of Life,* Shakti and the love that flows throughout all existence. It connects through his Hara, heart and his sexuality, (just like the Womb does for a woman) blooming out and enveloping his whole being and electromagnetic-auric field.

THE ANCIENT LINEAGE of FATHERS

The Pillar anchors when a man's ancestral healing and parental healing is completed in unconditional love. Some men can have aspects of the Pillar for their partners and families before this, but may not have it for themselves or have God awaken within them as a result of this process of embodying the pillar.

All fathers are linked on an intimate chain of love with the Ancient Lineage of Fathers, fathers throughout history who are organically interconnected because they have taken the Rite of Passage into Sacred Fatherhood. Beings such as Abraham, Ram, Osiris and many others from cultures worldwide are role models for Sacred Fatherhood.

This Sacred Brotherhood is always available for guidance, support and help for any man on the path of Sacred Fathering, and by you taking your own full initiation into fatherhood, you will join this noble and honorable lineage of men.

The father quality is innate in all men, and is activated through conscious birthing and healing the wounds of your childhood and sacred male sexual self associated with your own father and ancestors. The father quality is important for both man and woman as it allows both to rest, accept and feel safe in their foundation, with their sexuality rooted into heart and hara, allowing one to feel and express their depths.

This integrated father quality provides the pillar that allows relationships to deepen because there is a still, unshakeable core that cares for and looks after both people. In India, the feminine Shakti is seen dancing around the still, calm masculine, sitting in perfect balance and equipoise. When the man is this, Shakti can play, weave and create to her hearts content. She is free to express and Be who She is.

The Dance of Relating involves many roles. At certain times, we all need to be a father or mother type figure to our inner child and our partner, to allow deeper emotional openings and expression to happen. This does not mean you become their literal father, merely the archetypal energy for a moment or two.

If you are becoming too much of a father to your partner, there is emotional healing needed for you both to come into balance. This balance is where the integrated father, a caring, patient, deep and unconditional field, becomes a natural part of your flow.

MEDITATION TO CONNECT WITH ANCIENT LINEAGE of FATHERS

This Meditation and Invocation is simple and direct. It depends on your sincerity of heart, the power of your invocation, and centering in yourself before you start. Beforehand, prepare 5 questions you want answered. Be as precise and clear as you can be in your questions.

Now: Sit on the Earth and take some deep breaths into your Hara to centre, calm and still yourself. Visualize a three dimensional cube around you. Focus on this with concentration.

From your pineal, ask this cube to spin clockwise at 7/10ths the speed of light. Ask the Cube to clear your field of any negative energies, distractions, and negative residues.

Once you feel this motion, focus on your crown and from your crown and heart *as one stream*, say: 'Beloved Divine Father, Beloved Ancient Lineage of Fathers, I call you forth.'x3.

Breathe into your crown and heart. Say: "I call forth the clear light of God. I ask to be woven into the Web of Life. I Ask for MY children to be woven into the Web of Life. I ask that the Divine Spark of Light I AM now fully ignites and returns back to its Creator through me, in light and perpetuity. Amen."

Now: Sit in Testes Mudra. Put your thumbs and first fingers on each hand together in a circle. Place your hands in this mudra over your testes.

Inhale glowing, iridescent, deep wine-red energy down into the seed of your testes for 6 seconds, so your balls rise up. As you deeply exhale, your balls fall back down. Do this 12 times. Exhaling releases wastes, and if done with specific desire, (for example to feel and release shame etc) can release emotions.
Pray: "Beloved Divine Father, send me 18,000% Red Ray of Spiritual Warrior to charge my testes circuit now."

Inhale radiant, glowing, iridescent, fluid white energy, deeply into the core of your testes for 6 seconds so they rise up, then slowly exhale out, 12 times.
Pray: 'Beloved Divine Father, send me 18,000% White Ray to cleanse my testes circuit now.'

Inhale shining, glowing, iridescent fluid black energy deeply into the seed of your testes for 6 seconds so your balls rise up, and slowly exhale out, 12 times.
Pray: 'Beloved Divine Mother, send me 16,000% Black Ray to anchor my testes circuit now."

You will feel a cool tingling between the two testes. Now, "sip" ALL this energy through your pursed lips into your Hara x12. Move your sacrum down and then pull it up. Rock your pelvis back and forth, gently, deeply, sensually. ENJOY!

Now breathe all this energy into your heart, back and forth x12.
Now breathe all this energy from your heart into your crown, back and forth x12.

Now, rest in your crown and call forth:
'Beloved Divine Father, Beloved Ancient Lineage of Fathers, I call you forth." x3.

Now: ask your 5 questions for guidance. Be open and listen. The guidance and answers can come through immediate responses, feelings, pictures and sensations. Some answers may come later in the day or week from other people, situations and triggers. Be aware and allow. Everything will unfold.

THE SACRED LINGAM PILLAR

The healed, sacred lingam is a tool for love, a pillar of light connected to the heart of man, whose heart is connected to the Soul. Lingam means "Wand of Light," and describes the field of activated light *around* the physical lingam, a Field that enters the Womb and ignites it.

The sacred lingam is a nourishing healing energy for a woman when used well. It is the extension of the Pillar in form and action. It is open, supple, flexible, not disposed to lust, violent entry or usage; he is a servant of love. He is not rigid, overly hard and stiff, and can bend and fit into all parts of the yoni and womb, opening and filling it completely with his body of light, no matter his physical size. This wand of light penetrates into the womb, becoming a pillar, filling the woman completely from yoni through to crown and beyond, taking her into bliss and into the cosmos.

The lingam becomes sanctified after it has been crowned and anointed by the womb, after he has been allowed into the wombs embrace and opened into her depths. This is where a man becomes a King.

The sacred lingam is turned on and inspired by a woman's radiance, love, devotion and loving field. He is turned on from the heart. He awakens through beauty, and the gift of innocent loving devotion from a woman. Purity brings the sacred lingam into sexual reverence; the sacred inspires his erection.

In making love with a sacred lingam, much healing can happen. The yoni and womb open to depths never experienced before, and she desires to create even more space within her to give her all to this man, and to something far bigger than this man: to God.

Seeing, feeling and experiencing a sacred lingam opens a woman into a place of trust and reverence. Many of her past fears or issues with men can dissolve, as she returns to her original innocence, reawakening her longing to give herself in open vulnerability and surrender.

A sacred lingam is comfortable and assured in his heart's power, his pure masculine essence-feelings wed to his sexual virility and knowing that He Is. This allows a woman to safely feel her deepest emotions around her own body, sexual and emotional nature in ways that therapy and neo tantric sexual healing can never reach.

For a man with a healed and sanctified lingam, the power he wields is immense, as is the responsibility, care and humility in using it. He uses it to open and serve his woman, and takes care of her vulnerability and openness to help her become more of herself. He is still and clear within himself as he feels deeply into his woman's yoni and womb. Both woman and man experience the lingam as sacred and beautiful.

Just seeing a sacred lingam touches a woman's heart and womb. In making love the woman feels to give all of herself to this act of love, to expand, welcome and embrace her man.

Prayer: *'I Am ready to heal my lingam of all negative emotions recorded in it. Help me bring my heart's presence into the act of love! I desire to be a King, shepherding in the New Age of Divinity within myself and all beings. Please help me and my lingam become a pillar of strength and solidity for myself, and for my woman. Amen.*

THE MOTHER:
THE MAGNET

In the past, becoming a parent was seen as an obstacle to becoming awakened. Parents simply did not have the time and energy needed to meditate for many hours every day, as is the norm in many traditions. This reflected a separation between human life and the Divine. However, parenthood offers the opportunity to merge both human and divine, as this capacity is built into our physiology and soul as a means for our soul embodiment here on Earth.

Innate within motherhood is the sustaining nurturance and stillness that we need to live into our multidimensional self. There becomes less separation between meditation/prayer and human daily life, as both become authentic opportunities for 'being' love. 'Being love' is the ultimate catalyst for soul growth. In every experience that arrives at a mother's doorstep, she is offered an opportunity to choose love, whether that be self love or giving and receiving love with another.

Many cultures believe a woman is not a full woman until she has biologically and soulfully bloomed through the portal of birth into motherhood. The permanent changes in a woman's body, womb and brain in this process stimulate the magnetic circuitry of her feminine self, bringing her into an innate receptivity and giving direct from her body and soul to those she loves.

The foundation of love with family is fertile ground to unlock some deeper recesses of the feminine soul. From this loving heart-womb space we have the capacity to make whole, to nurture, tend to and love others. To live in 'mother essence' asks that we align and navigate from our womb/heart. When we aren't, it is a sign an emotion is arising to be felt and embraced in order to bring us back home to ourselves, back into being love.

"MA" is the most commonly used word in all languages. When we step into Motherhood, the energy of "MA," we step into a deep, vast river woven by the ancient lineage of Mothers that moves through all mothers who have taken the rite of passage of conscious pregnancy and birth to become part of this fractal web of life.

Motherhood opens us deeply to the tenderness of all life, the precious vulnerability in ourselves and others. Motherhood embraces everything that life brings in one moment, and in the next moment lets it all go. Motherhood is the continual process of birthing something from our most intimate place within, and releasing it into the world in love.

Motherhood is an initiation into a deeper aspect of the feminine soul. Becoming a mother is a Call to birth into the next octave of our being. Motherhood asks that we listen with our purest intuition to the flow unfolding through us, and around us. This flow is continually birthing the next step of our evolutionary expression, of our souls, our relationships, our projects, our prayers. Motherhood fortifies our trust. It is here that we receive guidance for everyone's best interests, and it is from here that we receive our soul's next unfolding.

Motherhood is an invitation to deepen into one of the purest and wisest expressions of the feminine. Motherhood is the marriage of intuition, wisdom, experience and love in action, here and now. The journey of being a mother is not about leaving all things human behind in our search for God. The journey is about surrendering to the experience of being human, and this being a doorway into finding God.

This awakens a true human felt compassion. This compassion is fuel to enact our earthly purpose, what moves us to bring heaven to earth: this is Shekinah, the feminine principle of God-in-action working through us on earth. This is how a mother becomes a Divine Human and helps birth The New Paradigm.

Innate within the design of motherhood is the sustaining nurturance and stillness that we need to maintain multidimensional flows. Pregnancy is the time for us to strengthen and deepen our internal channels of connection to ourselves, our guides, to God so that they can be touched in an instant once the busy-ness of mothering is here.

Nursing, transitioning our children to sleep and cuddling are all times of sweetness where we can touch back into the Source that feeds us all. It is here we let go of our efforts of containing ourselves and our children and melt into that embrace of Divine Mother that is always holding us. Many of the same things that our children need, we need, such as routine, time on the Earth, connection and rest.

Within this there is the balance of deepening in your own soul and expression beyond the role of mother. Mother is an important aspect for actualizing femininity, but not the only aspect. When a woman becomes consumed with tracking her child, she can lose sense of herself, her own needs, desires and expression. She can lose connection with her soul, leading to depression.

Life becomes only three dimensional and dull and she slips into a mode of surviving rather than thriving. It is easy to then look to the child for connection, light and inspiration as a crutch and to fulfill the need for love, instead of finding it within herself, and with her own passions, desires and soulful purpose.

It takes responsibility and humility not to fall into the etched out roles of victim and martyr. When we are vulnerable with those who support and love us and ask for what we need, we open the channels for more love to flow, and for ourselves to have our own space and time to be with, and express, our soulful passions and desires. This only makes us better mothers.

Behind every good mother is a good father. Mother Mary had the pillar and love of Joseph that helped enable her to be the loving presence of softness and strength she is known for. By surrendering to the sound container father provides, mother can move deeply into her womb, the gestating home of her child, the foundation for her own heart and the source of her innate knowing in how to raise her child. Her womb is a source for her to access and express the gifts of her soul, beyond her role as a mother.

The mother needs time to herself to connect with her soul, and feel her own emotions. In the immediacy of caring for a child, it is easy to lose perspective on the larger picture. The father's more detached position maintains a better vantage point that can bring the mother back into her soul beyond keeping herself fed, changing nappies and nursing.

Just as the father can have the overview or big picture view, the mother can have a more intimate understanding and experience of the child through pregnancy, birth and early on. The more she communicates with father and shares the emotional and physical nuances of her time with baby, the more father is brought into the world that she and baby share.

It is through embracing her family in the circle of her womb that she experiences a greater wholeness, a deeper embodiment of her feminine essence. From this loving womb space she has the capacity to make whole, to nurture, tend to, and love others. Through her womb she can creatively navigate the practical tasks in the 3D world with the soulful covenants to herself and her family.

In embracing this, inevitably all the fragmented aspects of her soul will arise to be healed. I remember waking up one day when my son was a few months old, and feeling I was terribly out of sync. For the previous few weeks I had felt scattered, emotional, unable to complete anything. I was attempting to do so many things, and couldn't do any of them well. My son was going through a phase of no naps, nursing for much of the night, and wanting to be held almost continually.

On the surface I felt frustrated that no one understood the challenges of being a mother, and it took his father's perspective to help me own and recognize the reflection of my inner world that was playing out in my outer life. A deeper layer of fragmentation in my own soul had surfaced to be healed, stimulated by the deep love and support I felt with my family.

As I moved into feeling the layers of pain that were surfacing, I became aware of all the ways I justified not healing because I felt I had to be a 'mother.' In truth, when I let go of my to-do list, and sunk into the feelings, I became much more present. I started taking 20 minutes in the morning and evening just to deep belly breathe into my womb. The feeling, the chaos, the distraction all dissipated, and I felt connected, whole and loving again.

Being a mother and being whole asks, demands, ,that we align and navigate from our womb/heart. There is no set recipe, no set 'way' to be a mother. Mother is a continual creative navigation of all the factors presented to us in each moment, and how we forge our way through and stay true to the laws of love.

THE SEVEN CYCLES OF THE MOTHER

The Seven Cycles of Mother are deeply interwoven. They create a full spectrum of the mother expression, from human to Divine.

1. BLACK LIGHT: WOMB SPACE

The Mother holds the space for you to expand into the Black Light if you soften yourself enough and allow your boundaries to become fluid, to expand out into the embrace of space. Here, Mother embraces all life.

The highest octave of Mother, which spans and extends throughout all creation, is held in the Black Light. Mothering is an aspect of perpetual birthing, happening all the time, birthing, creating, expanding in every single second.

Nothing can be added or taken away from the whole. In this wholeness, of constant embrace and creating in every moment by the Mother, everything can exist. Mothering is allowing everything to exist as it is, and in that there is *Ma'at*, the cosmic harmony of creation. "Mother" is the universal holding, being, existing as that harmony.

Black Light is the matrix that holds all existence together in Love. It is palpable when we pause, drop into feeling and soften, opening to the breath of undulating silence waiting for us between inhale and exhale. She is constant, steady, the breath of Divine Mother, nourishing, healing, dissolving all that is rigid. She is the resting place of our soul's origin, the gravity of essence that birthed us into being. From her our soul was born, and to her we shall return.

You will start to feel blessed constantly as you sink deeper into the Black Light, the origin of all things, the origin of all states of consciousness, the foundation of life. It is the fundamental, loving presence that existence IS, that supports us unconditionally, the trust in the unfolding of life. A woman in the Black light creates space, which the man then activates and ignites, bringing forth what is held in the formless into dynamic manifestation.

The Black Light is the presence of the universal womb, before light visible, before color, before matter. The universe is pervaded by this tender, loving, presence, holding, unfolding all that we are, containing all that we are in her womb. Before there was light, and an idea of darkness, lies Black Light, the sweet emptiness, the heart surrendered.

In Black Light, it feels like your heart is gently but perpetually breaking wide open, with no object for its breaking. It is crystal clarity, pure, deeply touching, and feminine in vastness. There is no object for its love and compassion, for there is nothing there, no reference point, no concept or form, nothing to hold onto, no memory, no past, no future.

It is the deepest intimacy one can ever know. It embraces you, not you it. It touches you in places nothing else can, and nobody else ever will. It makes you cry for it is the deepest remembrance of Love a human can ever have. It is the Beloved that has no face, no form and no substance. It contains itself completely within itself, pure before it becomes form.

It is only by means of our passage through matter we evolve. This is the ultimate purpose of our incarnation. While we are in the stage of our evolution subject to the push and pull of the body, mind, or matter the Black Light is our Dark Night of reason. It dissolves reason.

Scientists say that 94% of the universe is 'dark matter', reachable only beyond the measurements of the senses. Within this 94% lies what you call subspace. This subspace is actually a liquid space accessible through the light body, and is felt as a fluid motion, similar to the Cerebral Spinal Fluid felt in the spine that bathes the brain. All obstructions in this pathway must be dissolved to allow the flow of light all the way from the base to the brain.

Within the womb lies the power of the sun RA, and within the centers of all suns themselves lies the Seed of the Black Light. Suns are grown from the Black Light, and when they explode into supernovas they return into Black Light. The Black Light is the beginning, and end, of creation. When you are born, you come from Black Light in your mother's womb. When you die, you go through the Black Light as the soul makes its journey back to the creator.

The Black Light holds the power to create from the space where all things are held in potential before they manifest. Black Light is the greatest alchemy, and the most powerful magic of love, the potential that all women hold within the womb. It transforms by holding and bringing everything you are back into its pure, undifferentiated unformed state; original innocence. In this state, all wounds can dissolve, and all things are made possible. All things are made new.

When you create anything of great impact, or huge significance that truly taps into universal forces and power, then you to have to enter the Black Light to birth this. If you do not enter the Black Light, then the creation you are birthing does not have full impact; it may be useful for some people, it may generate awareness amongst the masses, but it will not change anything fundamental in consciousness.

The Black Light, as epitomized in the form of the Black Madonna, is the state from where all realities arise from. Christ, Buddha and other Great Ones have all entered this Black Light to ground their transformative actions onto the earth plane. Every birth, the first and most momentous journey, begins in darkness.

In the heart of the subconscious lies a charge deeply rooted in the primal brain. This charge is a denial of love that was required to bring spirit into matter, a separation that defined one into form. To truly bring spirit into matter requires that we go into the depth of this subconscious, this charge, and unfold it from within itself. In this way we go so deep into illusion that we see the truth at the heart of it, and so come through it out the other side.

We walk into our total individuation or aloneness to realize our All One Ness. This is allowing the full flowering of the sub-consciousness into consciousness.

EXPANSE

Expanse is the embrace of the Black Light. Mother essence holds the space for us to expand into the embrace of the Black Light, where we feel deep relaxation on a soul level. We feel held by a field that allows all constituent parts of us to simply Be. In this 'beingness 'we can soften, open and become more responsive and receptive to love. We feel this undulating velvety vibration moving through us, dissolving, melting, expanding. In this expanse of spaciousness we find our deepest rest.

Mother enables a magnetic expansive field of deep rest: the original womb space. This is the fertile ground through which all true creations emerge. It is in this place of expanse that Spirit is brought into matter. This gentle but all powerful light penetrates into and transforms matter, even under the most impossible of situations. All creativity emerges from a place of space. All true solutions are derived from an expanse beyond the consciousness of the current problem.

Black Light is embodied through womb resonance with three aspects of the Earth: her electromagnetic fields, her soil and elements, and her inner core. Her electromagnetic fields align with a woman's Shakti and electromagnetic fields, connecting her more deeply to the Unity grids of Love. Earth's elements become her own internal building blocks for manifestation, of children, purpose, projects, and the substance to ground these things into. Earth's core bridges directly to Galactic Center, the void.

Through her connection to these three aspects of Earth she can bring herself, her children, her partner more into the Black Light. This deep rest and peace of being held in womb space is a sense of being held in an intimate love. From womb embodiment Mother can co-create with the forces of Earth in an organic fluid way.

A PRACTICE: TOUCHING THE VOID

1. Sit with spine straight and hips slightly higher than the knees. Place one hand on heart, one on womb and feel these 2 pulses synchronize, relaxing you deeper into your body. If you can access a sense of gratitude in your heart, or your body, this opens you deeper to receiving. Feel the earth beneath you, and the sun above you, and yourself in the center.

2. Begin with full lower belly breathing by inhaling expanding the belly in all directions. As you exhale, draw the navel toward the spine and draw up the muscles of your pelvic floor and anus up. Do this powerfully 13 times to clear out any stale air and life force.

3. Find the point halfway between the navel and the pubic bone against the front side of the spine (or back side of the womb). There is a small hole here...sniff it out with your breath, and see if you can enter here. This can be an access to the void, entered through the body, but is beyond the body. Spend 11 minutes or more returning and exploring here.

4. Place one hand on womb, one on heart, and seal the practice deep in your body. From here you can offer any blessing or gratitude outward to someone specific or to all life.

2. WEB OF LIFE

The second aspect of Mother is in connection to the Web of Life. The Web of Life is our innate energetic connection to all sentient life. Communication happens through the web via frequency or sound carried by the threads or superstrings which compose the web of life, which then informs the spaces in-between the threads. Our depth of connection to the Web of Life determines our capacity to resonate things into harmony. From this resonating space, mother's instinctual, intuitive, and elemental intelligence of Shakti flows in its own rhythmic intelligence. This energy gets emanated into the various parts of herself that need it, or emanate through her into other people who need it.

This is not a mental construct or organization. This is a way of being, a way of life, a happening, a spontaneous rhythm and organization that spreads out like the branch of a tree, touching, moving and going where it is naturally drawn to, where there is lack, need, nurturing or empowerment needed.

This innately comes through our deep connection to the Earth, her womb, her elements, and her fields. When we fully breathe and bring her into our body, she too becomes part of our body. We become the three aspects of Earth, merged with her, fluid with her, at one with her, completely transparent in this Web of Life. Once we are flowing in the Web of Life, we have been initiated into this level of mothering.

We connect to the web of life by offering and giving ourselves to it. Gratitude is the attitude of the web of life. Everything in the web can be seen as a glowing silver-white web, threading, weaving and sustaining harmony in all things. Your body, your flesh, your nerves, your cells, your very being is permeated by this web, the same light that is giving birth to every plant, every tree and every star spread throughout the cosmos.

Offering ourselves sincerely to the web allows us access. Through our entire body and womb becoming our focal point of resonance *and* the conduit, giving to the earth, rather than just taking, allows us access. In the offering we receive, and become the conduit that is in constant flow, receiving and giving through the open heart.

A PRACTICE: CONNECTING TO THE WEB OF LIFE

Initially, the best way to do this is whilst visiting a sacred site in nature, where you feel resonance, where you feel at home. Sit down at twilight or at night, or on a night where the moon is visible, where you are near some trees, and away from city lights, city noise and interference, if possible.

Take your shoes off and sit barefoot on the Earth. Focus on your heart. Breathe. Focus on your womb and ovaries; for men the penis and testes. Breathe. Now focus on your feet, and the field of energy that extends down from the feet into the Earth. Visualize it.
Breathe down through the soles of your feet into this field. Push down the breath, and visualize the field extending.

Now extend this field of energy from your feet into Gaia downwards; deep down. Allow yourself to plunge down, through the soil, through the many layers of rock, earth, and fire, into the womb of the earth. This is a vast, black, all enveloping space. Sit here for a moment. Now ask, and pray to Mother Gaia, in your own words, from your own heart, to feel and extend your connection to her. Offer her yourself, offer her your service, and thank her for being your foundation, your anchor, your home. Breathe into this connection, connecting heart, womb, feet, to Gaia. Feel this space within you; for it is part of you, and you are part of it, as part of your origins, your roots, and your foundation.

Now open your eyes, and focus on a tree, or a group of trees. Soften your gaze until it becomes slightly blurry. Relax and breathe gently from the belly. Start to see the aura of the tree, the energy field surrounding it. Be patient. Follow the field of the tree in its expansion outwards. See or visualize a silver white thread / web extending outwards, and upwards, to the Moon. Look up to the moon, and feel your feet. Welcome to the web of life. Giving your soul, giving the menstrual blood, giving the sexual juices – all this gives Gaia a signal that you wish to reconnect. In this reconnection, one gets taken into the web, and it starts to guide and pull you into itself – into Life. This reconnection starts to create an energetic renewal, where we become quickened. We begin to recognize the need to set aside reactive thoughts, personal agendas and fear, allowing all feelings to be there.

THE ANCIENT LINEAGE of MOTHERS

When we step into Motherhood we step into a deep, vast river woven by an ancient lineage of Mothers. All mothers throughout the ages who have taken the Initiation and Rite of Passage into Sacred Motherhood are interlinked on an intimate chain of love in the Ancient Lineage of Mothers. Beings such as Mother Mary, Isis, Sita and many others from cultures worldwide are good examples of Sacred Motherhood.

This Sisterhood is always available for guidance, support and help for any woman on the path of Sacred Mothering, and by taking your initiation into motherhood, you will join this noble and honorable lineage of women. This flow of life force is a flow of love. Moving through us, we become part of this fractal web of creation.

This Sisterhood is intimately connected with Beloved Divine Mother and Her Love. In this inter-connected stream of love, Mother operates in action. Simply drop into your heart, and ask to feel your connection to the Ancient Lineage of Mothers.

The mother quality is important for woman and men as it allows both to rest, accept and feel safe in their magnetic foundation, with their sexuality rooted into heart and womb/hara. This allows us to feel and express our depths. The integrated mother quality is innate in all women, and is activated through conscious birthing and healing the wounds of your childhood and sacred sexual self associated with your own parents and ancestors.

This integrated mother quality provides the magnetic womb space and seat that allows relationships to deepen because there is a still, unshakeable core that cares for and looks after both people. In India, the feminine Shakti is seen dancing around the still, calm masculine, sitting in perfect balance and equipoise. When a man can sit in this field held by her, her Shakti can play, weave and create to her hearts content. She is free to express and Be who She is.

The Dance of Relating involves many roles. At certain times, we all need to be a mother type figure to our inner child and our partner, to allow deeper emotional openings and expression to happen. This does not mean you become their literal mother, merely the archetypal energy for a moment of healing and release.

The integrated mother, a caring, patient, magnetically soft unconditional field, becomes a natural part of your flow. A mother in her fullness will be resonating with the Web of Life, and this is a great way to give her child whatever they need and desire to be, grow and evolve.

MEDITATION TO CONNECT WITH ANCIENT LINEAGE of MOTHERS

The following meditation is simple and direct. The power of it depends on your sincerity of heart, power of your invocation, and your centering in yourself before you start. Prepare a list of five questions, desires, intentions you wish to bring focus and guidance into. Ask them at the end of the Meditation.

Begin by doing some deep womb breathing so you are still, centered and your field is clear.

Sit down and visualize a multidimensional, three-dimensional pyramid around you.
From your pineal, ask the pyramid to begin spinning clockwise at 7/10ths the speed of light.

Ask the pyramid to clear your field of any negative energies, distractions, any residue.
Focus on your crown and from your crown and heart as one stream say, "Beloved Divine Mother, Beloved Ancient Lineage of Mothers, the Soul Doulas of the Earth, the soul doulas who midwife spirit into womb, and spirit into the world. We call you forth, we call you forth, we call you forth." x3

Now say, from crown and heart united, "We call forth the clear light of Source. We ask to be woven into the Web of Life. We ask for our children to be woven into the Web of Life. We ask that the fallen Divine Spark of Light I AM fully ignites and returns back to its Creator through me, in light and perpetuity."

Begin breathing deeply into your ovaries then connecting and uniting them with crown and heart.
Call forth the feeling and image of the Ancient Lineage of Mothers and Divine Mother again. Breathe deeply into this connection.

Now ask your prepared 5 questions, guidance, desires, requests.

3. VESSEL: THE DANCE BETWEEN HUMAN AND DIVINE

Being transparent as well as being a container, being a vessel, is how embodiment truly occurs. Mothering is an intersection where human and Divine play and dance with each other. Our vessel is our meeting point of this infinity loop. This expresses in a dynamic interplay of communion and connection, lived experience and manifestation.

Human mother brings Shakti, tenderness, and form, Divine Mother brings unconditionality, wisdom and refuge. Human mother has her needs and desires. Divine Mother has no need. A human mother will be attempting to fulfill her needs and deep desires, and will be reconciling herself continually with the deeper urges and callings she is feeling to expand into her embodiment of Divine Mother.

Motherhood opens us to the tenderness of life, the precious vulnerability in ourselves, in our children. Motherhood is a balance of unconditional embrace and the voice of truth that melts the illusions of separation. Motherhood stretches our concepts of space and time. It teases us into our multi dimensional, multitasking, intuitive and expressive selves. It demands that we listen with our purest intuition to the flow unfolding through us, and around us.

This is how we transcend the bounds of space and time and complete the washing, nurture our family, sanctify our souls, and pour ourselves deeper into the expressions of our soul's purpose. It encourages us to bend the hours in a day to allow for all the layers of our being to be expressed, nourished and addressed.

Motherhood strengthens our courage, our voice, our boundaries. There is not the luxury to bleed energy, effort and time into that which does not serve us, our purpose or our loved ones. It means strengthening our container and filling it with that which is truly in alignment with our souls, not just for our own sanity and foundation, but for our children, who feel all that we engage with.

Motherhood fortifies our trust in Divine nature that supports and sustains us beyond our own self-sufficiency. It solidifies our trust in ourselves to bring Love, Power and Wisdom into all our relationships and projects. It deepens our humility, in demanding that we ask for help, for care, for love, when our own human resources run dry and depleted.

It tunes our inner and outer listening, and deciphers the layers of knowing within us. It challenges us to turn down the volume on our thoughts and turn up the vibration of our feelings. It is here we receive the telepathic communication from our children. It is here that we receive the guidance for their best interests, and it is here that we receive inclinations of our own soul's next unfolding.

Motherhood is an initiation into a deeper aspect of the feminine soul. It is the call to be birthed into the next octave of our being, and the responsibility to nurture and sustain the soul purpose and children that emanate from that. Mothering is a continual dance, a continual negotiation of the spectrum from human to Divine. A harmonious balance through the infinity loop intersection where human and Divine play and dance with each other is required. With the right support and communication with her family and friends this can happen. With clarity, direction and purpose everything can be brought into a harmony.

SURRENDER

Surrender is one of the most deeply defining qualities of mother. It is the meeting point in the infinity loop between human and Divine. It is how we become a vessel for that which is greater than our individual selves. It is necessary from the moment of conception when we surrender our bodies, our hearts, our souls, our egg to the penetration of our partner's love and his seeding consciousness.

It is present as we soften our physical container in the blooming of our bodies into pregnancy. It is asked of us in the throes of birth as we open and meet the intensity of rushes with our pure presence and allow our yonis and wombs to melt and expand. It is invited as we surrender our human limitations to our Divine capacities.

It is our willingness to surrender that opens us to birth that which is greater than us. It is our commitment to surrender that brings us into our next paradigm of possibility, releasing the confines of what we have known, and bringing our pure presence to witness the next impulse asking to be born through us.

Surrender is a process, a continual experience, which happens every day. It is never done or completed; it never stops, it is never a statement; one is always surrendering, continually giving over the mind to what lies here and now, in the present moment, in each thought, each choice.

Surrender softens what is rigid within. It gentles us, taking us more internal, deeper into the silence of the open heart that is awake and sensitive. This awakening guides us back from that which is not love, by embracing all thoughts and feelings that arise that are not love. Having the felt awareness of what is not love moves awareness to love, so more love can flow.

Surrender leads to true vulnerability, vulnerability that cleanses the heart and releases fear, leading to expansion into more love, which in turn leads to more vulnerability, and more fears arising … until all that is left is a pure heart as a conduit for love to flow through. You move when the living force of love moves you, because you have become so available, so present, that only what comes in this moment is what you know to be true, because it is happening right now.

The commitment to the journey of birthing from the Soul's Design requires surrender. The impulse of creation is a wave that can carry us into a deepening evolution and expression of our soul. When we completely surrender to this wave, and the depth of wisdom and manifestation asking to be expressed through it, we surrender old identities and configurations of who we thought we were. This seats us in a more anchored place of service, of unconditionality, and steadfast commitment to truth.

The Souls Design for Birth weds us into this impulse of creation, into the threads of evolving consciousness moving through our bodies and our expressions. In surrender, we surrender our vessels to be used for that which is part of the Cosmic unfolding…and in this we actually become more of who we truly are. Surrender carries us into the deepest individuality of our soul, and then beyond.

In surrender, all things are given through you. You do what you need to do, with care, with full attention, and then move onto the next thing to do, that unfolds organically. This step by step approach allows the full death of the previous moment in order to create space for the next new moment, where we know nothing about the future, and have forgotten about the past.

This involves deep trust, trust in that whatever is needed will come. This is the only way we can mother and truly stay present amidst such demands on all levels. This is the only way we receive all the resources, support, and direction we need to fully parent our children, while nurturing ourselves. This is the only way we can stay truly connected to the flow of giving and sustaining life, love.

From the moment our child emerges through our yoni, we begin the process of letting go. Nothing will ever physically touch us as deeply as our gestating children in our wombs. And when we let go of this profound history into the moment that is happening with that soul now, we allow space for love to rush in.

Letting go is one of the hardest things to do, be it letting go of the search for the Divine, letting go of habits, or letting go of ideas, people, and beliefs that have served you until this point, but can no longer take you where you need to go in order to evolve. In letting go, there is no need, just resting, and from resting, joy arising, and from joy, peace as the gateway to the golden silence within your core: the present. This letting go is a literal emptying of the self, an active, willing, letting go in order to give yourself space to Be.

You die a little every day living this. Through surrender to being here, to including and embracing all aspects of life, we become one with the creation. Everything is included in surrender, and nothing is left out. All that you have believed, thought, felt and experienced has to be offered, and given away. Everything has to go, and you have to leave no back door, no escape route, no way for the resistant self to come back.

This surrender creates opening, a space where you can be pulled, where love can pull you, that can then take you to your destination, wherever that may be. Surrender opens the door to love, so that love may take you wherever it wishes.

Surrender is the last quality to master you, before one lives the surrendered life. When you live a surrendered life there is little, if no thought, arising within you. You may not know the words that come out of your mouth in any moment, and have no need to remember what they are, or what the actions are that flow through your body-mind and speech. You learn by what comes through you. There is great delight and joy in this, for in this allowing of ourselves to be nobody, we become able to relate with anybody, in any moment.

OPENNESS and TRANSPARENCY

Openness and transparency are the keys to allowing the magnetic flow of Mother. The more fluid we are and the more we allow ourselves to be a conduit for the flow of life and love through us, the more we rise into a knowing beyond what we 'thought 'was possible. In this way we are deeply connected to the Web of Life to offer our children, families and work all that is warranted. In this way we become a 'vessel.'

In being a vessel there is holding, transparency and flow. We hold that which is entrusted to us, while continually expressing and releasing aspects of ourselves. This is a dynamic balance that situates us in an amazing seat of rapid evolution. As we adjust our bodies, our minds to this flow, we release all that is not serving us anymore and open to that which is necessary in the next moment. This is a challenge and a blessing. This openness and transparency allows the flow of the web of life to move through you, to exit you, and to help create the safe container.

Vulnerability is part of humility. Vulnerability invites all of the secret places in our heart to come out into the light: all we are scared of, all we are ashamed of, and all that we hide in dark places within. Vulnerability is a great attractor to other people and to other benevolent energies, and inspires support. Vulnerability brings us all closer together, and opens the way for someone to be at your side. When we are not vulnerable, we push others away, and stop ourselves from receiving what we truly need and want. Vulnerability brings us the loving balm that our souls need to grow, and when we have integrated this into our daily lives with transparency and honesty, we become open.

Openness means we are open to whatever life brings us, knowing that it is for our good. Openness is the end of attachment to any outcome. We may still have preferences, but we are not attached to them. Openness is true flow, where we become like water, able to flow into any situation and environment. We can be truly present whether paying for food at the market, singing our child to sleep, or making love with our partner. We can be speaking to a beggar one moment and a king the next, and we are equally open with them both, meeting them where they are, sharing what is needed to be shared in the moment.

Having this foundation of openness means we are open to the greatest transformations. We can flow with whatever comes, secure and safe in our emotional center. We are open to the greatest alchemy of all: enlightenment, and we can accept it as it comes. Openness brings us all we ever wanted, as we can now receive it without barrier or block. God always wants to bring us everything. Can you be open enough to receive it?

In this transparency we are whole. Nothing can get to "you", as there is no "you" to be got to; it has been surrendered, so the "you" is no longer an obstacle, and everything flows through. This then becomes a beacon to others, lightening their load and giving them a different perception, a new possibility. This presence in you grows through sharing and giving, as it can never lessen when more of it is being ignited around itself.

In surrender, there is the living experience that Life is Living through you and this extends to all relationships you engage in. As you engage with others you stay in your own connection to this life flow, and engage from this space.

4. NURTURING AND THE BREASTS

The fourth level of Motherhood is nurturing. A mother nurtures her child and her man through her body and soul. As she nurtures, she is nurtured. Nurturing from a woman's magnetic womb and heart through her breasts is connected deeply to primordial biology. This enables a mother's magnetic ground to expand in her body and with her hormonal changes. When this nurturing capacity is honored, tended to, accentuated and celebrated, her biology itself can hold a greater depth of light and love. Her magnetics, her feeling body, blooms.

As a woman, when love flows unhindered through us, our Shakti innately nurtures all that we come into contact with. Nurturance is a deep magnetic quality that solicits a deep offering of love, from our hearts, our breasts, our bodies and our souls. Nurturing is triggered from us when those that we love come close. It ushers forth an offering of substance that fuels and sustains those we are connected to.

The breasts and breast milk offer our children some of their first physical and emotional nurturing and sustenance outside the womb. From a nutritional standpoint, breast milk is the best food we can give our children, for it has all the necessary nourishment to sustain their bodies for the first six months. When combined with whole, living foods after six months it is a continued source of living enzymes, immune support, good proteins and fats.

From the soul's perspective, breastfeeding is a time of deep bonding, love and communication. It is an opportunity to commune and connect, a time for sharing sounds, touch, smiles and cuddles. It is also an opportunity for a woman to embody more deeply into her feminine soul and to consciously give love at this time to her child through her breasts. This is the beauty of our Divine Design; through nurturing our children, we grow in love.

When I nursed my son, he received sweet, living, nutritious milk while feeling the warmth of my skin, the love in my heart and the profound connection in our eye contact. We would play together, and he felt a real depth of touch, holding and nurturance. This is priceless, for an emotionally balanced child who feels loved and nurtured biologically and emotionally, will grow up to be a balanced, valuable, contributing member of society and a loving, secure person.

Breastfeeding is also a time for play. Sometimes I would tickle his skin and he smiled, or we would play games with our fingers. Sometimes I massaged his feet, or sometimes he tickled my chest. These simple interactions bring us into a shared present moment with each other for whatever deeper nurturance and love wants to happen.

Nursing was also a time when we gazed deep into each other's eyes. I spoke to him about the light of his soul. I shared with him how deeply I love him. He smiled, gazed deeply, or winked. It was intimate and close, soul nourishing and deep, for both of us. It built a steady and firm foundation between us, of love, communication and trust.

As a woman, breastfeeding brings us into an aspect of our feminine soul through nurturing. It stimulates the magnetic circuitry of our feminine self, bringing us into our innate receptivity and giving direct from our bodies to those we love. This energy is soft, pearlescent, undulating, pulsing, sensual, soulful, and pure.

Before we can experience these qualities within us, we must release the imprints and emotions carried within our breasts. Many losses and unresolved emotional and relational impacts in our lives are recorded here. In the breast circuit we lock away the emotionally painful moments and scenarios in our life that exceed our capacity to understand and digest. Our breasts become a store-house for what is out of balance, what is out of love, and what is out of feminine harmony within us.

In allowing the magnetic circuitry of the breasts to fully flow, these wounds are revealed for us to reconcile in love and embrace. When we authentically presence this, we realize a deeper layer of our own humanity and vulnerability. Through this we encounter the pure intimacy of our feminine soul, in its vulnerability, humility, and willingness to grow in love.

This softening enables us to be happier, more peaceful, more feminine, and more compassionate. This compassion becomes a fuel for pure action, an impulse that enacts our earthly purpose through love. This is what moves us to bring heaven to earth, to uplift the status quo into the status we know is possible. This is the Shekinah, the feminine principle of God in action working through us on earth.

As this circuit is opened, we become more soulfully and magnetically present. More present to ourselves, our family, our lives. Our biology becomes the three dimensional doorway into our multidimensional souls, and these acts become opportunities to usher forth more tenderness, softness, and presence.

In our bosom's magnetic circuitry lies the innate capacity to nurture and sustain life. Here is where we hold an organic sense of wholeness. Within this sense of wholeness lies the recognition of what is not whole. This awareness can then draw from within our bosom, and the rich full veins of magnetic love and nurturing, that which is needed to make whole. This capacity to recognize and offer pieces for emotional wholeness is an innate aspect of our 'mother essence.'

This emotional capacity is also demonstrated physiologically through our breast milk. Our biological make-up enables us to custom fortify our milk to meet our children's changing needs. Each time our child latches onto our breast to feed, their saliva imprint sends a chemical signal to our hormone system indicating its nutritional needs. Our system intelligently responds by adjusting and adapting our milk to fit the current nutritional necessities for our child.

Just as our physiology naturally receives and responds to a child's call for nourishment, so too does our feminine soul. Our breasts carry our impulse to come forth in love to embrace, nurture, and protect. When we are not clear in our breast circuitry, we can feel overwhelmed, burdened, and martyred.

Breastfeeding is an example of love in action. When I feel how much I love my son, my milk immediately starts to gush forth to feed him. The same gushing happens when I feel my son calling me or needing me, whether I am in the room or twenty miles away. I am moved by love to feed and nourish him, biologically and emotionally. This is innate in being a mother.

Perhaps one reason breastfeeding women get depressed or stressed after birth is because this deeply emotional circuit is being so stimulated, probably more so than in their entire lives. All of the blocked emotions arise to be felt *and released if* the woman knows what is happening, and has the tools to do so.

THE MAGNETIC CIRCUIT of the BREASTS

Between both nipples in the breasts lies a magnetic energy circuit that enables a free flow of feminine nurturance and compassion. All physical and emotional problems associated with breastfeeding can be traced back to unresolved emotions held in this circuit. Aversion or resistance to nursing your child signifies an emotion to be cleared from this area. As a woman and a mother, this is one of the most sacred and important interfaces between yourself and your child and partner.

When clear, this flow creates a safe, protective, and loving field for our children. The sound of our heartbeat, the smell of our milk and skin, the warmth and love from our hearts, enables a familiar and sound anchor for them to begin to experience the earthly world around them. This is one reason why it is so beneficial to carry or wear our children for much of their first year.

When the energy is blocked in the breast circuit, it impacts a mother's capacity to give and receive love. Sometimes this will show up in the child as him/her needing to nurse more, as he/she is not receiving the physical and emotional nurturing they need. If this remains unaddressed, a cycle will continue of more nursing and more depletion.

PRACTICE: OPENING THE MAGNETIC CIRCUIT of THE BREASTS

The following meditation will help clear and connect you deeply to the magnetic circuitry between your breasts and nipples. As we move through and release the layers of our personal grief and sorrow, we open ourselves to feel a deeper connection to our child, partner, and a compassion for all beings.

1. Begin in a comfortable seated position with your belly soft and your back straight. Take a few deep breaths into your belly to bring your focus out of your mind and into your body.

2. Cross your arms and place your palms over each breast with your palms pressed gently against your nipples. Take a few gentle yet deep breaths and allow your breasts to feel supported and warmed by your hands.

3. Now become aware of your nipples. Feel the pulse in each nipple and wait for them to organically synchronize. As they synchronize, you may feel a pearlescent white three dimensional infinity circuit connect between them.

4. As you feel this circuit, become aware of any blocks or stagnations. Use your breath or hand movements to help move or open these blocks. They will most likely correspond to a deeper emotion that may arise in the moment, a few hours or a day later. As you breathe into these energetic areas, bring love from your heart.

5. Sound the following syllables 12 times slowly while you continue to feel the pulse in your nipples: *OOM MAOM MA*

1. As these emotions arise, allow yourself to feel them completely. They are clearing to open up the channels for your love, your milk, and part of your feminine essence to flow more freely.

PRACTICE: HEART ARC LINE MAGNETIC ACTIVATION

In this 15 minute practice (one can go longer if you wish), you are stimulating the magnetic circuitry of your heart arc line. This practice will increase your magnetic flow and activate your ovaries. It will bring you down from your head into your heart. Use your intuition, with specific intention and strong desire and much can unfold.

You can do this practice with specific desires and intentions before and during it. You can do it to clear out past lovers, help you to feel and release deep blocks in your heart, prepare yourself before breast feeding. You can also do it before making love, and your partner can then nurture himself from this, and you can both really enjoy the enhanced magnetic flow and take that deeper into your making love.

Begin by stimulating the right nipple until it gets perky.
Counter clockwise move around the most sensitive part of the nipple 17 times.
Repeat 17 times, sensually sounding the syllable OON, until you feel the nipple really stimulated in a sensual, soft way.
Trace this into the center of your chest and allow the magnetic frequency to express through the sound of URR 9-12 times.
Move to Left nipple. Do clockwise circle 17 times, then counter clockwise 17 times.
Trace this energy to the center of your chest and give the frequency the shape and sound of LAH.

"When I first began clearing my magnetic circuit between my nipples, my right and left side felt completely out of balance. As the energy began to flow, I felt some of my deepest grief arise, about situations in my life that I had not fully accepted. Upon feeling this grief, I was aware of the disconnection I felt between parts of myself, and physically between my right and left sides.

I did the circuit everyday for about 2 weeks. As the grief cleared I felt a soft, deep, velvety love for myself begin to radiate. I had touched a level of self-love I hadn't known yet. The circuit became very warm, soft, light and expansive. My son would crawl into my lap to nurse each time he felt this energy begin to flow. As the energy began to flow through these places, I felt a heaviness begin to leave me.

Feeling the emotions in my breasts infinity circuit was a very different experience than feeling emotions in my heart. It was as if I was feeling a feminine part of me that had been dormant and unused. As I expanded my awareness into this area, I felt an innate gentleness and expansive love. I wanted to hug and embrace all humanity as my children.

I used to wake up every morning to a slight depression. What I realized in doing this meditation repeatedly, was that it came from a subconscious feeling of helplessness, stemming from feeling a dissonance in and around me, and feeling helpless to do anything about it. When I moved through my feelings of grief held in this circuit, the helplessness left, and I was opened to a profound love and empowerment for myself, and a deep compassion for humanity. This love moved me to take action in further actualizing my own soul purpose, and the ways I could truly serve.

My self love increased tremendously as a result of opening this circuit. I felt more joy, more love, more connection, and more ability to authentically and lovingly engage with others."
The essential qualities of the breasts are nurturing, sustaining, erotic and sensual. Mothering and nurturing births us more into these essential human qualities. The purity and radiance of a new mother is the magnetic freshness that comes when mother is well loved, rested and taken care of.

A mans healed and heart connected lingam can also give a woman a primordial experience of nurturing from the sacred sexual masculine self. Through the breasts a woman can nurture, through the lingam a man can nurture. In allowing and receiving this mutual nurturing, something deep in the primordial self gets touched, moved and activated. This can create a tender magnetic bond, where each trusts the other to nurture each other in this giving of ones magnetic self through lingam and breasts.

The nurturing, sustaining quality of the mother is intimately inter-linked to her feeling fresh and vital, i.e feeling and being rested, nurtured and supported. She being supported is good for partner, child and herself. Many mothers don't have this, but in the soul's design for mothering it is vital. It is for mother, father, caregivers and family to set this up in some way.

5. MOTHER AS LOVE/LOVER

The breasts bring us a union of mother and lover. The ripeness and sensuality in a mother's body, in a lover's body, are connected. These two emanations of the feminine soul express through sensuality, embrace, devotion and unconditionality.

Embrace is at the heart of the mother. Physically and emotionally it is the holding of fetus in our wombs, babes in arms, with toddlers who have skinned their knee. It is the organic expression of 'mother 'in our bodies and the all encompassing expression of mother in our souls.

The impulse of embrace carves us out into a much deeper love, not only for our children, but ourselves, our partners and all humanity. Embrace enfolds what is presented to us, brings it in, and extends this enfolding outward toward its specific subject. It holds, it loves, it dissolves separation. It is wired into the chemistry and expression of the mother.

Embracing takes whatever we feel is unacceptable and makes it transparent. It asks that we bring the vibration of the unacceptable inside our hearts, and envelop, embrace and extend ourselves into that vibration. There is no judgment in embrace.

Embrace is not personal and yet it is deeply intimate. When we embrace, we embrace the quality that is asking for love, that is not love, and we bring it deep into the folds of our heart. We meet it, see it, allow it to be what it is without needing to change it. In this way of being seen, it softens, relaxes. As we do this with our outer world, we do it with our inner world. As we embrace our children in their most un-loveable moments, we embrace the un-loveable parts of ourselves.

The Mother embraces and accepts what IS happening in any moment. In embrace, we bring others into our own heart, feel the truth of who they are, and then give them what they need in that exact moment. In the deepest embrace, we bring the planet, and the suffering of all humans into our heart. There is nothing that is singled out as wrong, unacceptable, or unworthy of embrace.

As a mother we can be initiated into a capacity of embrace beyond our own children. We step into an unspoken responsibility and capacity to embrace others, humanity, the planet in a way that is beyond a certain pre-existing selfishness. As we are birthed into personal mother, we can open ourselves to this deeper initiation to universal mother.

The way we navigate through this role is both deeply personal and transpersonal. Our depth in one impacts the power in the other. As we embrace ourselves, we more deeply embrace our children. As we embrace our children, we more we can deeply embrace ourselves.

As we embrace our own personal mandala of souls who have been entrusted to our love, we embrace humanity as a whole. Embrace is a quality, an action, an emanation far beyond personal. In the Buddhist practice of *Tonglen* there is a similar experience, taking that which we feel is painful and harmful, that which we don't like or love in ourselves and others, and drawing it deep within, offering our breath, our love, our knowing of innate goodness to this.

This experience is available to anyone if you are open, genuine, vulnerable, and willing to go deeper. As you allow this to happen more by embracing all before, and within you, then you yourself will start to feel embraced by all of existence, provided for, supported and loved.

Our own inner aspect of lover essential in our mothering is in allowing the man to be a man. A woman rarely allows a man in his deeper aspects to be a man. On the surface aspects many women know this, practice this and find satisfaction and contentment on these levels.

On a deeper level of a woman truly allowing a man to be a man, she surrenders, she inspires. Even when she is pregnant, she can still inspire a man through her giving, radiance, her beauty, and her love. She can still inspire a man to go deeper. This is still important to do in pregnancy, as the man needs this and you need this.

You need to be in contact with this ever blooming, ever burgeoning, ever deepening feminine essence that is blooming through you. Allowing a man and inspiring a man will bring out a deeper depth in you and will also bring out deeper depths in him which he will feed back to you, to then increase your own depths in this beautiful feedback circle of love.

Keep on inspiring your partner, keep on fueling his devotion to you through your love for him. Of course there will be times when you are tired, hormonal, emotional and other times when you are full of energy, full of life. Share some of this to inspire or touch your man. Allow him to step into his own masculine, his newly blooming and newly burgeoning masculine self.

If you keep this dynamic going for the pregnancy, this will allow you as mother to more fully embody through your biology, and this will deeply affect the man too. He will be affected by your new biological emanations. The more he is affected, the more he will be primordially inspired to serve his woman and to be devoted to her, because he is genuinely moved by her giving from this state of radiant, sensual wonder.

DEVOTION

Devotion is a field of tender respect, serving, holding and honoring. It is a giving of all parts of ourselves, even the ones we don't know yet. In devotion we give and we allow. In devotion we offer ourselves to other, the man, the child. We give them all they need.

Devotion softens all that is rigid within us; it melts the harsher parts of ourselves and humbles us. In this humbling we are actually being exalted. In this humility we are being raised, our vibration is being raised, our love frequency is accelerating, our openness and transparency is being amplified, our willingness to love selflessly expands, our softness and depth increases. Any emotion or belief that stands in the way of this will arise in you. Simply embrace the history (as emotion) that is passing through and releasing.

Devotion is a part of bonding. Devotion allows bonding between human and God and human and human. It bonds mother and father, lover to lover. Devotion brings forth the quintessence of the heart seed. It activates and blooms the heart seed. It stretches and expands us, and can break all resistance.

An essential part of mothering is devotion. Devotion will give rise to many beliefs around what it means to be a woman in the world. Beliefs around codependence, wounding around father/mother can arise. Many feminist ideals will be challenged, to be brought into their rightful place in harmony with the masculine. Many ideas of freewill and choice will also be challenged.

Devotion is a choice-less choice and a way of being with love: a way of love. Devotion needs Shakti within it to manifest, to be expressed, to actualize, to be palpably and viscerally felt. Loving devotion has Shakti intertwined with it; it is not a separate phenomenon. Devotion is an aspect of Shakti, an aspect of love.

When a mother lives devotionally, she activates the magnetic thread of connection that enables her family to be held in soft tender reverence, and for the bowl of a woman's womb to be held in a soft magnetic light.

Tending to and nurturing your devotion, engaging, sharing and expressing this every day allows a great safety for child, self and partner. The safety and container that devotion affords means everyone can step into their right place, right role, right position, right expression and enter into an aspect of fullness within themselves.

Both woman and man feel loved, respected, honored, adored, and then both can give that back as well, and vice versa. The palpable quality of devotion allows both parents to cradle and hold their child in this magnetic loving field. This devotion that touches the seed of both parent's hearts in love and selfless giving to each other allows everyone to step more into their essence.

WISDOM

In becoming mother we find a union of wisdom and unconditional love. Wisdom without unconditional love is cold and abstract. Love without wisdom is disempowering, because there is a lack of true knowing and discernment. Unconditional love becomes stabilized through selfless service for the good of others, over time.

This change of working for others, rather than working to survive ourselves, helps purify our psyche and consciousness. We move from identity as body or mind, and stabilize our identity as a living soul. Through this embrace, love establishes the soul as the ruler, and mind as the servant. As this happens, a deep release of core tension occurs. When we drop all knowledge, all ways of being that are imposed on us, given to us by others, or that we have taken on, then we enter innocence. We become like our children, innocent and pure.

This love, this longing, this innocence, lies within each and every one of us, and resonates with everyone. We all share this vibration within the heart, and like a harp string plucked, we can feel its vibrations echoing throughout our beings.

The mark of a mother is to be able to feel and embrace all the emotions of the personal heart, and yet to stand unwaveringly in the knowing that love is unfolding in perfection under any condition. This is the union of embrace and allowance. This is the supreme strength in softness. This is what ultimately carries us beyond the trials and pains of the world into the infinite Feminine Heart.

This underlying commitment to love enables us to open our hearts fully, extending compassion to all that we see and experience. In this way everyone becomes our child, we become a universal mother. Expressing these qualities in a man's world also requires a great deal of power, a great discipline, a great commitment, and a total identification with the Black Light, that which holds this space indefinitely, and is ever present for all beings.

In this space we keep one foot in our human heart…that cries, feels sorrow, pain, hunger. Our other foot is anchored in our communion and knowing of the Divine, and that love emanating through us, as us. This koan, this living as the bridge between heaven and earth, is something that forges us in our individual creative reckoning and surrender.

How we do this determines the depth of our embodiment, the depth of our humility and desire, the depth of our love. Mother is that bridge from form into formless, from tenderness and intimacy to unconditionality. Mother's expression embodies us through our own negotiation of this role, this love for our children and partners…and in this we become manifest.

It is here that we may come to the crossroads of wisdom, having to discern and then unify the wisdom of the soul and the wisdom of the heart. The wisdom of the heart is what enables us to love, to relate in our horizontal experience of giving and receiving love. It is the wisdom of our soul that will take us all the way vertically into God.

In these defining moments of choice, when we move on behalf of the soul, we anchor ourselves on a more infinite course. One is steeped in a love that is beyond the finite constructs of this world and its creations. This is not without consequence, for in these defining moments there is a pain of letting go of a more personal love, into a deeper surrender of a Will and Love greater than our own.

As we deepen in the emanations of love and being a mother we inevitably integrate more deeply with our own inner child. The more we have brought her, which is in essence our pure soul, into a dialogue, communion, conversation with the other parts of ourselves, the more we are unified in love.

Mothering an external child happens to its fullest potential once you have mothered your inner child and brought that into a more integrated place within you, a place of communion, where that inner child is allowed to be, to express, to play, to communicate and freely do so in any moment. This is a crucial foundation to being a mother. One cannot embody without having done this first: this is the doorway.

ALLOWANCE

Allowance settles us in the deep remembrance that our children come through us, but they are not our own. From the moment they are born through our yoni lips into the world, we are in a process of letting go, of allowing them to be and become who they innately are.

When we allow others to be themselves, beyond what we believe they are at this moment, beyond what we need them to be for us, we open up to an even greater possibility for love. Allowance is a deepening in trust in our selves, in the Divine Plan and the truth that we are loved and supported on every level.

Allowance starts to settle into our lives when we realize we have no control over our life, and in fact we never did. All resistance and judgment arise in allowance to be seen and accepted. We see ourselves, and begin to surrender who we thought we were, into what actually is.

In allowance we come to see the truth about ourselves. Our pains, our patterns, and our veils to love living through us. In allowance, we allow the pain, the sadness, the anger, the grief and the unworthiness to bubble up and be in us, simply to be present. And this is a marvel. Marvel at this for a moment; enjoy your naked beauty.

In allowance we open the door of our heart to be touched by something far greater than us, and in a felt sense 'give way 'to this feeling the more we practice it. In the space of allowance each individual can be and express as they are, who they are, in the freedom of being more of themselves.

As mothers, when we allow our children and our partners to be and move through their phases, without judgment or control, we let them live and experience the full spectrum of their humanity and discover for themselves a healthy resting place of expression that is true for them.

This leads to Acceptance. Acceptance is the ultimate initiation. It melts and softens all hardness into the truth of what we, our children and our partners have been created to be. And it speaks only truth, for acceptance knows the nature of reality as open. Acceptance is the soft, inner peace that has no charge towards anything or anyone. It allows all expression to simply be what it is. Allowance leads to acceptance, and acceptance opens the heart to embrace whatever is presented to us, thus transforming everything in its wake.

6. MIDWIFE

A Midwife is a shaman: one who has a foot in all worlds. She is a bridge between the Earthly, guardian angel and Celestial Lights. Her role is to embrace and unify in love, power and wisdom these realms of instinctual, elemental, primordial forces within earth and within woman, and help connect that flow to the celestial.

In being a mother it is essential to be able to bridge worlds. It is necessary to have one foot in the invisible realms receiving guidance and direction for ourselves and our families, whilst being anchored on Earth and the tangible existence of a third dimensional life. When we are integrated we can effortlessly move from one realm to the other. We can also ask for any support we need whilst in any of these realms, and put this guidance into action.

A midwife guides the birthing process, holding the space for the descent of spirit into form. She opens the way, becoming a supplementary magnetic ground of strength and care that allows others to relax into the process of manifestation. The midwife harnesses and holds a multiple frequency vibrational field within her body, not her mind. The mind is tertiary.

She holds it in her body in its instinctual, primordial, rhythmic, feminine intelligence. It is from here she can respond and move through all the realms. Her mind is a servant to the actualization of this. Her body's capacity is what holds all three realms together on the highest levels of consciousness. Midwife as mother will learn how to do this throughout her pregnancy, labor and birth, and will then embody this as she moves into physical motherhood.

A true midwife works through her connection to the Web of Life. She understands on a felt level the deeper inner-connection of all parts of the whole. She works with the Law of Harmony that no gain happens at the expense of another. In this there is no hierarchy, just a perfect circle in which each player has their unique role in the wholeness. In this is total trust, total surrender, and total engagement in the role that is hers to play.

In our intimate lives as mother, lover, midwife, sister, daughter or friend, we create our own personal Web of Life, that in its connections creates a dynamic hologram of our soul's expression and manifestation. In conception and pregnancy it is important to create a container of family with this web.

We can build this container by connecting directly to our own personal Web through the Womb Mandala, our heart seeds, our child's heart seed, the Cosmos and the Earth, and the Ancient Lineage of Mothers/Fathers. This creates a pentagram of 5 emanations. As we keep this mandala nurtured and whole within us, it becomes a microcosm of the macrocosm.

These five aspects connect you to the greater web of life in the processes of pregnancy, birth and early childhood. Nurturing it everyday allows your own personal hologram of the Web of Life to be fulfilled and complete. When we nurture, maintain, and evolve each of these relationships in their right place, we are supported and embraced in our own deeper embodiment and expression.

When I feel a stickiness or resistance to any of those represented in my personal web of life, it usually is illuminating a place within me that is out of love, needing to be seen, embraced, tended to and brought back into harmony.

As our children are born, they too will also have their own web of life consisting of Mother, Father, Source, Earth, and grandparents/God parents or other significant figures in their lives. You will innately 'feel' who these people are for them. Let go of any mental constructs or attachments around this. Father and Mother are entrusted with the upkeep for our children in relation to their own Web. This is essential to their embodiment process, as love from the different aspects magnetizes their soul more deeply into the human experience.

7. THE BODY OF MOTHER: EMBODYING THE FEMININE SOUL

Divine Mother holds all together in her body and her womb. She is the holder of the blueprints of creation. When the soul and the physical body are in one flow, we are embodying. The feminine soul is mediated through the yoni and womb. Many women's heads and yonis are disconnected. This is then felt as having less sensation, less deep feeling, less pleasure, and less love in her sexual organs. A woman may 'think 'she wants sex, but her body does not respond. When soul and body are aligned there is an innate depth of pleasure expressed through her sensual loving.

Our experience of mothering is inextricably woven into the fabric of our sexuality and body. Our children are conceived in the deepest folds of our wombs. Here they are embraced and gestated until they travel through our biological portals into the world. Then they are nurtured and sustained by our breasts and held in our arms until they have emerged into their individuated capacity to walk. Our bodies are the first home, sustenance and experience of mother.

When a perspective mother has done her embodiment work, she can be her inner child, dance between human and Divine, enter void and enter the embrace of all life that Mother is. This is the connection of your Shakti and sexuality to your heart, your soul intelligence in the body, and to God. The greatest work begins at home, in her body where a true mother has to, and does, live.

THE KIDNEYS

The kidneys hold feminine gentleness, softness, clarity and flow. They offer a direct connection to the feminine soul. Working with our kidney energy helps us transform fear and anger, embracing our feminine side. If we are nervy, stressed, tired, reactive, mental, emotionally disconnected or scattered, it may well be the kidneys that need cleansing, rejuvenating, nurturing and restoring.

During pregnancy the kidneys are working harder to filter and cleanse almost a double volume of blood. It is especially important to nourish them during this time, and after birth. I have found that a few minutes a day of kidney breathing helps me stay connected to my innate sense of flow, and I can more easily navigate the consistent multitasking presented in mothering.

The kidneys help to neutralize excess masculine or mental energy from the head and re centre us back into the womb, our natural centre of gravity. They redistribute feminine energy to wherever it needs to be, to places that have been stuck, numb or stagnant. Their colour is sky-blue, like the sky on a perfect cloudless day. Kidneys, along with the ovaries, are the organ most responsible for your overall health, longevity, energy, growth and vigour. All the organs derive part of their operating chi from the kidneys. Kidney chi is an important part of sexual energy, and allied with the liver, the potency and strength of the kidneys helps to regulate our sexual activity, our sexual drive *and* menstruation in women.

PRACTICE: KIDNEY BREATHING

(Do this for 11 minutes each day)

Stand outside in nature, or with a view of nature or a water source.

1. Place your feet parallel to each other, pigeon toed, as in a Tai chi stance. Bend your knees as much as is comfortable, so you are the edge of discomfort. Keep your spine straight.

2. Create a Prayer or an intention, for instance, "To feel and release all fear from my kidneys."

3. Relax your perineum and bottom, and place your hands on your kidneys, which are situated either side of your lower back, with palms facing upward.

4. Breathe deeply, yet gently, into the kidneys for 10 minutes. Imagine blue and green energy flowing into the kidneys through your palms, energizing and revitalizing them.

   You may feel heat, tingling, sweating and shaking as energy starts to flow through you. Listening to emotional music will help. Now, sit down, with hands on kidneys.

5. Say: " *Beloved Divine Mother, please help me rejuvenate and strengthen my kidneys. Please help me feel and release all my fear, my anger, my resentment keeping me from my feminine flow. Please help me drop deeper into my feminine soul.*"

The deeper aspects of embodiment are interwoven into our magnetic ground. Magnetism is at the heart of all mother qualities. The more deeply integrated and connected our magnetic ground is to our Shakti, our soul, the Web of Life, the more we become the innate bowl and being to hold all our creation.

THE SHADOW SIDE OF MOTHER: MARTYR

The shadow side of mother is mothering without wisdom, allowing our children or loved ones to rule and dictate us without having the discipline and strength necessary to love ourselves, be strong, and set boundaries with others.

Here, we can stifle and smother the other, overlooking their blind spots and debilitating the soul growth of our self and the other. This may occur through our own need to look like we are loving, our own need to be seen as good, our own need to be a people pleaser. Underneath this all lies our own unfulfilled need to be loved.

The deepest love is for another's soul, not their mind or wounded self, and sometimes this takes tough decisions that the wounded self will not like.

For too long 'mother' has been mistaken for 'martyr.' This is not true mothering. We must be mothering ourselves in order to properly and soulfully care for our families. We must be connected intimately to our partners, our selves, the Earth and cosmos and have a continual flow of giving and receiving love to help sustain us. One of the deepest lessons in being a mother is that of self-love. Both the tenderness and the fierceness to presence and protect one's own soul, and keep the balance of giving to our children.

So many who identify with the archetype of mother really identify with the archetype of martyr. They orient around a deep wound that keeps them from being present with a child, a wound from their own childhood of abandonment, of not receiving the love they needed from their own mother. They give and give and give from a place of not feeling they deserve to receive love in return. In our souls design, mother is at the center of her own circuit of giving and receiving… receiving as much as she is giving.

Many wishing to embody mother want to be seen as loving, generous, kind, and 'there 'for others, always serving others. This usually happens at the expense of their own self, their own needs and desires and their own sovereignty and self love. They need to boost their own diminished self worth, to make them feel loved and wanted. They can rarely say no to another, as they want everyone to know how selfless, lovable, and wonderful they are, when in fact they have a deep sense of unworthiness, shame and guilt about truly receiving love.

Love extends, shares, embraces, welcomes and creates more of itself. Love embraces every experience in relationship. Relationship is the testing ground for love. This selflessness requires inner power otherwise one leaks energy, and becomes drained. An image to remember here is the picture of Mother Mary with a Child in one arm and a sword in another. To be the Mother requires great strength, the sense of fearless protection that a lioness has for her cubs, great independence, and great Self-love.

Playing spontaneously rather than being stuck in routines allows this quality to unfold. Doing something different, being childlike, playing with friends, and allowing yourself just to BE can open up arenas that you never thought possible.

You can also practice staying in you while others are present. Work with these statements: "Allowing me, allowing you, allowing us." Say this from your heart.

The role of mother is an interface between heaven and earth, formless and form. Mother is the connector, translator, adapter, stepping down frequencies into digestible tones and elevating/raising her creations into the fullness of their design.

PART 2:
THE EVOLUTIONARY IMPULSE

GENETIC ALCHEMY

Our DNA is a quantum system that stores massive amounts of information in a very small physical space. Ancient cultures have used quantum principles based on the Laws of Vibration to encode knowledge in our DNA, our most hidden yet most obvious storage system. Our DNA is a holographic system that contains the codings of life, not just for humans but for all life.

DNA stores information on multiple different modes of vibration simultaneously, not just on one frequency waveband. The more modes of vibration we resonate at, the more complex and intricate the information can be released. What we see, hear, feel, speak and think are waves of vibration, composed of light, sound and electromagnetism. In this vibratory Universe, every thought, emotion and idea we have has a unique vibration. Every time we think or feel, a vibration arises.

All these vibrations are continually moving, perpetually undulating and creating new forms and patterns. Human beings vibrate at 570 trillion HZ per second. This means that we are moving incredibly fast every single second of our lives - we are just not aware of it. We are vibration, and in this constantly vibrating, ever shifting universe, everything that exists lives in a web of wave energy. This dance is happening all the time, right now, inside you. DNA receives and transmits vibrations from our inner and outer environments, linking the external world and our own inner reality.

The Human Genome Project has decoded about 3% of our total DNA. The remaining 97% is called "junk", implying it has no meaning or purpose. Mainstream science simply does not understand the function or the coding of this 97% of our DNA. The human body is efficient, and anything of no use evolves out of existence eventually. If 97% of our DNA is junk, why do we still have it?

Junk DNA are self replicating loops that do not connect to anything else. The 'ON ''switch is off. Think of it as a spaghetti junction that does not lead anywhere, rather it just goes round and round itself in a closed off circuit. From this closed loop, all manner of emotional dysfunction, physical disease and mental constructs/ beliefs occur, *and these are occurring all the time*. Yet within this 'junk 'DNA lies a virtually limitless well of potential waiting to be connected and activated.

Both our connected strands of DNA and "junk" or disconnected DNA constantly emanate vibratory signals, pulses, messages and transmissions throughout your whole body-mind-soul all the time. Right now, this is happening, and this informs your perception of reality on a deeply subconscious level.

Both our connected strands of DNA and "junk" or disconnected DNA create a genetic hologram or mirror that manifests in the 3D world around you: a model of reality that is emotionally based. The hologram fueled by 'junk' DNA creates a matrix of fear, amnesia, ignorance, conflict and repressed emotion that the collective mind of humanity has come to believe itself to be. This hologram feeds and lives from negative emotions and inherited family/ancestral trauma and behavior patterns.

This hologram farms energy from DNA on personal, ancestral and collective levels to support this matrix, feeding it with our life force so it can sustain itself and grow. These distortions become entrenched, creating a feedback loop and another junk DNA pattern: a vicious cycle.

When we become aware of, feel, and transmute these distortions we can leave this ancient ancestral mind behind, and our own energetic connections to it within ourselves. This is vital in order for us to evolve, and for our children to not continue living these patterns out. We can change this, for them and for ourselves by removing the ancestral emotions and behaviours that lie within our DNA.

When the DNA field is cleared and transmuted, it aligns with our unique Soul Blueprint, and we can then connect through the 'Thread of the One'. As the Mayans so eloquently stated, it is here we become "the road to the sky leading to the umbilical cord of the universe", connecting us to the womb of Galactic Center. These strands are cosmic lifelines of vibration and communication from us, to Source or universal intelligence.

When the DNA is cleared of ancestral patterns and emotional traumas, we can resonate with this "Thread of the One". In India this is known as the "Sutra Atman" – the Thread of Souls. All souls are strung upon this Thread, like pearls threaded on a silver string, connecting all life forms, humans, animals, and other civilizations in all distant parts of the Galaxy, to the Creator, and to each other.

We are all beads on this "superstring" that weaves its way throughout all time, all space in the web of life. We are all connected on this Thread, that weaves the web of life throughout time and space, which has infinite perspectives contained within it, derived from a Single Awareness, connecting in an unbroken chain all the living beings of our world and our universe.

The Code of Life is in your DNA. The code of all Life in this Universe is held in YOUR DNA. Imagine: everything you see, all life forms on earth, all other beings on all other planets, stars and galaxies: their codes are within your DNA. Everything alive is held within you. Look around you. Anything alive is literally within you, vibrating within you at this very moment! You contain all life in seed form within you. These strands of DNA are not just in your physical body; they extend and span out like super strings into the whole Web of Life, on every level of consciousness.

YOUR GENETIC PROGRAMMING

"If you think you are enlightened, go spend a week with your family."
Ram Dass

At conception you inherit and receive matched and paired recessive genes from your two bloodlines, from your mother and father. These genes hold memories, emotions, beliefs and gifts that offer us great opportunities for healing forgotten, fragmented and wounded aspects of our body, mind and soul.

Our ancestors have both positive gifts to share with us, and negative traits. Many of their positive traits have not been passed fully onto us because of our own parent's and ancestors inabilities to do so. The negative traits are ours to transmute and dissolve. We chose our parents and their bloodlines in order to facilitate these experiences as a mirror of our own learning.

In Ancestral Healing, you feel and release these genetic imprints within yourself, your ancestors, the collective consciousness thought forms you are connected to, and your star seed origins that stand between you and your natural Self. In so doing, you gain the gifts of all your ancestors and heal the fragmented parts of your families and ancestors that you, and your children, still carry. You can prevent your children from carrying these patterns and having to suffer like you have done from them, by doing the healing on yourself now.

There are 7 layers to our genetic programming.

Your mother and father and inner child
The First Seven Generations of your ancestors
Your Solar Ancestors
Your Star Seed Origins
The Head of your Bloodline
The First Parents of Humanity
Creator of Humanity

Between 15%-25% OF OUR ENTIRE HEALING IS GENETIC BASED.

Underneath the streams of our lives lie rivers of all the experiences of our ancestors, imprinting into our DNA. We are a 'web' of experiences within the larger web of life, and until we release our own personal web or cage of experiences, we cannot access the web of life fully.

In the process of clearing and bringing into harmony your first 7 Generations of ancestral healing, which deeply involves your father and mother, you extend your soul awareness into your soul family or Monad. This flows deeper into your DNA and the threads on the Web of Life you are connected to and impacts your children.

The next step then extends into your solar ancestors and then your stellar ancestors, your Star Seed origins-the star you feel most connected to and may even call 'home.' In stepping into your larger bodies, or True Self, you meet the Head of your Bloodline. This then enables you to clear genetic, karmic and cellular memories recorded in you, the magnetic fields of the earth, our solar system, our galaxy and eventually the Universal body. You become a Light of the World.

In doing this, you become a Genetic Way Shower, a soul who clears and releases old genetic, karmic and cellular patterns held in your DNA and the collective consciousness grids, which are intimately intertwined with the planetary grids. By clearing these pathways, the entire collective human consciousness benefits greatly, as does the earths fields and of course your own genetic lines.

The New Human Design, which many children are now embodying, need these pathways to be clear for them in order to initiate the next leap of genetic evolution into a new species of human being: *homo luminus*, or being of light.

As Nicolya Christi shares, *"We are the ones on the 'frontline' of the 'Family Story' who are redressing not only our own historical wounding and karma but also that of our ancestors. We are the ones who are carrying in our DNA the endurance and suffering of the generations who have gone, and those still to come. We are now healing and closing these timelines.*

It is our mission to ensure 'It Ends Here'. This is no easy feat and, for many of us, especially those unaware of the fact that we are healing not only ourselves but also the ancestral lines, the Path has been a long and arduous one. Yet, we find ourselves now, in these auspicious times, standing upon a threshold of unprecedented promise and transformation.

As we faithfully and diligently clear the residues of past, present, personal and genetic timelines, we embody an even greater purpose as high frequency, high vibrational, co-creators of Heaven on Earth."

THE INNER CHILD

In order to birth and raise a child lovingly, our inner child needs to be released from their wounds, traumas and hurts. In healing the wounds of your own childhood, so that you can be at ease and reclaim your original innocence, play and joy in life, means that your physical child will not have to experience the pain, fear and traumas of childhood like you did.

To heal your inner child, you need to go where that child lives—inward—to your *inner child*. The pain we experience in childhood and from birth makes deep emotional and somatic imprints that last throughout our lives, until we decide to feel these wounds and experience the unmet emotional needs at their core.

The unmet need is always for love. Children are dependent on their parents and family for their source of love. They need a consistent love, care and attention to allow them to be who they are.

The inner child part of ourselves is the one who permits a door to open into deep, caring embrace. Healing our Inner Child allows the possibility of true intimacy in our adult lives. The Inner Child needs our love and healing, as it is the key to our magical, joyful and full experiencing of life. It is our Inner Child who, in our early childhood, was deeply connected to the multi dimensional universe, to God, angels and guides; it is the child who trusts absolutely and innocently.

If our Inner Child has been wounded, this lives within us into adulthood and leads to sabotaging choices, unhealthy relationships, addictions and many forms of destructive behaviour. This wounding limits our ability to connect to others, and diminishes our capacity to give and receive love, the lifeblood of the soul. It is our ability to fully give and receive love in all ways that connects us to all parts of our Self, and therefore others. It makes us whole.

When the inner child is wounded, it influences our adult decisions. A part of us is constantly trying to protect the inner child by doing the same things we did as a child to protect ourselves–like leaving our bodies, fighting, escaping into a fantasy world, running away and hiding.

A part of most adults has never matured and healed their wounded inner child, and this piece that is unintegrated can lead to many forms of infantile behaviour as an adult. This makes it hard to raise and parent a child and connect to them on their level successfully and consistently.

It is almost impossible for the adult self to feel completely fulfilled or to be able to completely surrender when their wounded Inner Child is busy protecting itself. How then does this play out with your physical child? Can you see any similarities?

Enlightened beings have the joy, humour and playfulness of a child. Play is an important way that the soul and inner child expresses itself. They can feel instantly and are able to emote easily. They do not hold onto anything-rather they feel in the moment and release the emotion in the moment. They do not stuff the emotion down, try to rationalize it, deny it or protect themselves. They feel and release the emotion, and then continue playing.

If you notice how a small child is, they simply feel what is happening, whether it is painful or pleasurable, and express it. They do not need therapy or healing because they can do this. They do not compartmentalize their emotions or save it for another time: they feel it in the street, in the park, in a crowded place, and have no shame about feeling these emotions. It is the natural feeling of emotion that allows us to become who we really are, as we are not holding onto anything, and can allow life to freely move through us, and out. Better out than in!

The protective mechanisms and conditionings of our childhood become obstacles as adults. Many of us try to heal the inner child in adult ways, but in order to reach the child, we must enter the emotional realm and come into feeling communion with this fragmented part within us.

When we enter intimate relationships, it is only a matter of time before this deep inner work rises up for healing in *both* partners. This is natural. It does not mean that the relationship is "not working." Any depth of love and intimacy in relationship and the cauldron of pregnancy can bring up everything that Love is not.

In essence, we have to become both mother and father to *our* own inner child. Be aware that when two Inner Children are relating, complete dysfunction can result OR complete joy can happen!

In the dysfunction when wounded inner child issues arise, one partner can hold Presence in a loving way, allowing the other partner's Inner Child an opportunity to heal. These are the times when we are called, in moments, to adopt a mothering or fathering quality for our partners Inner Child - as they let go of being an adult and feel into their own inner child's needs for wholeness.

This is where our unconditional support comes in. As acceptance and non judgmental presence is felt,, the inner child comes forward in vulnerability and trust, with the willingness to share his or her needs, wounds and desire for wholeness.

Your Inner Child is also a son or daughter to your own mother and father. To accept this place in your heart, in honour and humility, through family and ancestral healing methods, completes *you*. Your Inner Child needs to feel part of this evolutionary chain, and to be heartfully included in this cycle. Honour sets you free.

Your Inner Child goes by your birth name. He or she has always had its parents, whether they were loving or not. To be loved by your parents, to love them, despite what may have happened, and without falsely forgiving them and thus having felt and integrated the hurts you have experienced with them, is important.

Those people who have integrated this dynamic in a harmonious order have a certain innocence and freshness to them, because they have accepted they are a son or daughter, and act with a morality and good heartedness. They are accountable, and being held accountable brings us into a moral code of right and wrong, loving or unloving choices and actions.

The inner child being aligned in harmony to mother, father and ancestors completes the circle of Harmony. The Inner Child heals more through this Ancestral Order of Love. Discovering and living into this integrity is a Rite of Passage, for almost all of us were raised with the lies of our culture and the additional woundings of our families. We were not shown what is real, loving and true.

To become a true father or mother and take this Initiatory Rite of Passage of healing the inner child within you enables you to raise your physical child with your inner child engaged in the process. This means you can enjoy it more, relate to your physical child more, and be able to have your adult self seamlessly flow with the whole process. Being a parent means having your inner child and adult self working together for your benefit and your physical child.

MEDITATION

Take the time today to meet and embrace your Inner Child.
Breathe deeply and center yourself. Remember: your Inner Child has your birth name, not a later assumed name you may now have.

"Beloved Mother Father God, Help me connect with my Inner Child. Guide me to the place within me where my little one is residing. Help me come into feeling communion and deep listening with him/her. Help me to touch the heart of my Inner Child so I may feel what she/he needs. Help me establish a dialogue with him/her. Please help my Inner Child to trust again, to play again. Beloved Mother Father God, as my divine parents – guide me as to how I may restore my child back into harmony with my parents, and into your loving arms."

Start a conversation and dialogue. Call your inner child forth by name, gently and with love. Ask him or her how they feel; ask what they need from you. Hold your Inner Child on your lap and give them love. Tell them you love him/her. Embrace him/her.

This may take time at first, but the more sincere effort you make to contact your Inner Child, the more he/she will come to you, learn to trust you, and eventually integrate within you as part of you.

Dedicate 15 minutes every day for one month to communing with your inner child, honoring his/her emotional needs for love. After this piece is done you may experience years of obstacles being lifted. Many patterns of your life, both inner and outer, can change.

THE ORIGINAL SELF

As we grow up, the wisdom and innocence of your inner child can get lost in the world, abducted through illusions, beliefs, struggle and strife. Once lost, our inner child yearns to re-experience and feel this union of security, safety and unconditional love here on earth. From this feeling of separation we experience emptiness and feel fear within our emotional body. This impetus can start your inner child on a journey to finding its way back home to unity.

Your Inner Child is part of your original self, part of who you really are, the pure soul I AM, a Spark of Love. This Spark of Love can commune with everything in Creation in innocence, can connect and play and relate with anyone. It is This aspect of you that can truly connect to all beings.

This I AM is the smiling golden child you are, perpetually innocent, absolutely timeless, yet fresh. I AM not learned anything, for there is nothing for this child to learn. I AM plays. I AM is innocent.

Just try this. Sit for 5 minutes: drop into your heart and state this: I AM Innocent.

Come into contact with your pure soul, for every time you do, you are aligning to this inner child I Am. Every time you give selflessly, play and engage innocently and joyfully, with self and other, you are living this.

The journey of life is the journey of the inner child pure soul. All authentic spiritual paths and teachings are trying to return to the original innocence of the pure soul. What is called the inner child today in most spiritual circles is actually the unloved, unheard, unmet, injured part of you from your childhood that did not receive the love it needed, or had parental wounds projected upon it. The inner child just wants to be magnetically received and listened to, paid attention to, heard, joined in with, met and cared for.

THE INNER CHILD WITHIN YOU, and YOUR PHYSICAL CHILD, NEEDS TO BE RECEIVED:

Physically –hugs, holdings, touches, bodily affection, massage, play
Emotionally –embraced, accepted, held, honoured, communicated with, heard, given space, respected, cherished, celebrated, joined in with affection, trust, and played with and thus met
Mentally –connected, understood, heard, engaged with, interested in, met
Soulfully –In filling body-heart-soul-womb

The inner child is what hides within everyone. This hiding is by no means any fault of our own. This is what the inner child has learned how to be, how to cope with a world, a culture, a society, an environment that does not recognize the child as being a whole, individual being having anything to contribute to their adult life.

The first thing to know is that the inner child is in hiding, submerged and set adrift amongst a worldly morass of apparently important things, a tidal drift of debris and distractions. One has to clear the debris, clear the waters, and clear the distractions first before one can really embody the inner child.

The inner child will often arise as your deepest pain and will often be triggered in these moments of deepest pain. The inner child lives in your heart, your amygdala, and your genitalia. The inner child is naturally and innocently sensual. It is connected to your deepest needs and desires. This is what the inner child thrives on; this is its fuel, its wonder fuel. Your inner child needs this fuel.

All children feel deeper. They feel more emotionally, and with their senses. They are innately tuned to their magnetic feeling currents, so they are more naturally open to life and connection, which is more sensual. This is also why some paedophilia happens. Wounded adults are looking to regain part of their childhood innocence, part of their sensitivity, and part of their natural sensual self: they see this in children and they want it. Much of this is coming from a wounded needy place, not necessarily always from a vindictive place, although this too happens.

In the child like sensual opening into sensations, into feelings, into the currents of the life force, is where the inner child thrives and dwells. One has to return to these places within one's self in order to live that inner child.

The inner child is a part of your magnetic foundation found in your pelvic bowl, just under the hara and womb, connecting the pelvic bowl to the hara and womb. This is part of the magnetic foundation for your soul to embody on earth. If your childhood and inner child was fragmented, disrupted, separated, or disconnected this has to be brought back into your body, your heart, your genitalia, your amygdala, to come to rest in your magnetic foundation.

Bringing the innocence, curiosity, play and inner sensuousness back into your sexuality, back into your sexual expression, doesn't mean you act like a baby when you make love, but this energy is present and enjoyed, not over-sexualized or *adultified,* but allowed to be in its natural, playful flow.

A PHYSICAL PRACTICE

The inner child brings an emotional, physical, sexual union within the adult self. Embodying it means that we rest in and express all these parts of us, and the more we do so, the more we feed that inner child. The more it is given attention, the more it knows it doesn't have to hide, because your body is welcoming, encouraging that and expressing him/her.

This practice can be used to relax you into your magnetic foundation of which the child is a part of.

There are two points to touch on the sides of your pubic bone in your groin area (on either side). Touch and breathe deeply into these points. Invite your inner child by name to enter, (your birth name.)

You can have another person holding these points whom you feel that play/love/ inner child connection with. You could also have the heels of your partner's feet pressing into each of these sockets. Breathe deeply, invite the inner child.

Breathe this connection into your hara/womb and anus, as one flow, and back again. You may start feeling a light field or wave.

This simple practice for 15 minutes starts to adjust your armoring into the natural free flow you had as a child. It brings more feeling-safety into your body, more solidity in gentleness.

INNER CHILD RECONNECTION
By Lakis Chrysanthou, Inner Child Therapist

The light of your soul is held within your inner child. This spark of your incarnation, an aspect of your divinity, is here to experience an earth bound existence. From the moment you incarnate into your body you start making meaning of the world, interpreting what happens in your life according to your experiences, making mental constructs and beliefs about yourself, other people and the world around you.

In adulthood these memories and subsequent resultant beliefs become the signposts to your reality and how you co-create in your life: the lens through which you see and interpret the world.

Positive and nurturing childhood memories propel us forward in life whilst negative and painful memories hold us back. The subsequent misperceptions and negative beliefs that you created as a child live within you into adulthood, mirroring the feelings you have for yourself, your inner child.

Looking at you today through the eyes of the past stops you from seeing what the present moment has to offer. Getting in touch with your inner child, that part of you which carries all these feelings from your childhood experiences, is the first step to bringing resolution to all the childhood memories you don't like, those memories that hold pain, hurts and wounds.

Once connection has been established, a process of re educating, re-parenting and re nurturing begins, giving love, support and wisdom to your inner child. This helps facilitate gentle and profound resolution to your memories, as they will not hurt anymore.

This change in perspective and new emotional flow re maps your consciousness, collapsing other alternate realities connected to your past, bringing resolution in the now as you become the love, support and wisdom your inner child never received.

Freeing yourself of the old emotional and mental constrains of the past, whilst integrating your subsequent learnings, brings forth feelings of spaciousness, joy, freedom and excitement to now flow through you.

You initiate movements into seeing yourself as a creative being in all areas of your life, becoming your full potential, flowing as part of the world around you, journeying to your core essence, fulfilling your destiny, remembering that you are a beautiful being of light held gently with love at all times within the the universe.

MEDITATION

Connect to and visualize your heart centre. Imagine a sacred candle here, burning brightly. These are the warmth forces of your soul. Now visualize golden energy above you descending towards you, connecting in the upper part of your body... flowing through you, within you and around you.

Now connect and visualize your inner child who lives within you.... by giving your child a coloured essence or vibration. Imagine your inner child's essence flowing through you, within you and around you, particularly in the lower half of your body.

Now imagine uniting and merging these two vibrations within your being, to bring forth inner child healing and nurturing. Breathe this new coloured essence vibration through your whole being, allowing it flow through every part of you.

HEALING WITH YOUR PARENTS

Christ said: "He that loves father or mother more than Me is not worthy of Me: and he that loves son or daughter more than me is not worthy of Me."

The 'Me' here that Christ is referring to is not Jesus the person. It is Christ or the God Self I AM, the God that is in all souls. We have been taught by religion to look outside for this God, yet is has always been, and always will be within us, and can only ever be Realized like this.

Yet there is another meaning to this as well if we are not yet in unity consciousness or fully awakened. Your human parents are not the Original Parents or Creators *of your soul*. Your soul is far beyond this earthly incarnation, sourced from the joy, play and love of Divine Mother and Divine Father. This Being created your essence that lives beyond this body, this earth, your parents, your partner, your children and all your ancestors.

Your human parents are temporary custodians and co-creators of your body-mind: not your soul. We have been attracted to them because our lessons mirror theirs in certain ways: they show us our own lessons and qualities we need to master. Our soul purpose with our human parents is to learn who we really are and heal that which is not who we really are, so we can reunite with our Divine Parents, i.e re-unite in our True Self, Becoming At-One with That.

Our human parent's purpose is to be caretakers of their children whilst they grow, to allow them to become who they are, to give and receive love with their children, and pass onto their children the qualities of the true masculine pillar and true feminine presence. As parents, we are Ambassadors and examples for our child of their Divine Parents. We are the First Reminder to our children of God. The child will view his human parents as 'a god' in the first years of his/her life, so it is our responsibility as parents to model this, AND point our child towards his/her Creator,(and true Self) who loves him/her more than we ever can.

The togetherness, respect, love and solidarity of mother and father creates a resonant field in which the child receives the stimulation, protection, safety, nurturance and love to awaken and activate their own being in a safe container. Through this family unit greater things can be anchored.

Both parents create a magnetic anchor and center of gravity for their child. They are responsible for setting a template for their child's own unique hologram, rather than imposing their own agenda and expectations which are informed by their own ancestral and emotional wounding. This requires us as parents to be conscious and aware of our flaws, and to have done some deep healing on ourselves.

Most parents subconsciously want their children to be like them, and most children want to be like their parents. We are all here to be ourselves in truth. Rather than children being themselves, their own free and wonderful beings, we may subconsciously need them to be part of our own patterning. This is neither sovereign or loving. We are merely guardians of their soul, not makers of it or formers of it.

As parents we are here to make sure our child becomes who they are, rather than what we need them to be. This is our soul responsibility: to honor their free will, their desires, their movements, their soul purpose and passions, rather than shut them down, dumb down their aspirations or expect them to conform to our own expectations or society's agendas.

"It is no measure of health to be well adjusted to a profoundly sick society."
J. Krishnamurti

As parents, it is our responsibility to provide the right people, resources, environments and stimulus to activate our children's unique soul. If we are in flow, this will be a synchronous and graceful happening. Parents do not have to be everything for their children, but they are responsible for drawing the Right things into their children's life through discernment and listening to their own intuition, listening to their child and seeing what they like and want, and being emotionally and physically available.

As parents, we need to follow our child's desires for expression and engagement, whatever that looks like, rather than forcing our own ideas (he should be a doctor/lawyer etc) onto them. Respect, listening, observing them brings us keys to this.

As parents, we introduce our children from an early age to what earth life is about on a fundamental level. Why are we here? If we model this to our children in joy, play and openness, they will follow this and carry it forwards into their adult lives. They will be able to listen to themselves and carry out their inner urges and passions, answering that most fundamental question for themselves. This is very empowering!

Unfortunately, most parents do not do this, as they themselves are disempowered and have not taken their own initiations into the deeper masculine and feminine through the Rites of Passage of Birth, Raising a Child, Puberty, Manhood, Spiritual Initiation and Sacred Relating.

So, the cycle continues: wounded parents creating wounded children. This cycle has to end somewhere, and the most auspicious time to end it is before even conceiving a child, and if not then, in pregnancy, if not then before the child is 7, and lastly before the child is 14. The buck stops with you, if you have the courage and the willingness to do so.

Much of humanity's wounding and healing comes from one simple cry: Why did my parents not love me as I needed to be loved? There is a simple answer to this: because they are human. They can share some human love with you, but there is a difference between human love and the unconditional love we all desire, and indeed physically need to grow our brains as children.

It requires conscious, emotionally intelligent, ancestrally healed parents to sustain unconditional love. When we receive this love as children, it helps us to self-actualize: it helps us to have full trust in who we are, to actualize our soul passions, joy and purposes in the world. It allows a deep inner security and self-knowing to bloom.

We have part of this foundation within us when we are conceived in love and bliss, communed with and held in love in pregnancy, and experience the initiation of blissful birth. This foundation continues to develop when we raise a child with loving consciousness based on our taking the initiation of birth. From this true foundation: then we are helping to create heaven on earth.

We can then live out our true design as souls, without spending many years of our life stuck in old patterns, spending a lot of time, energy and money trying to heal ourselves or learning tough lessons through the repetition of relationships.

Would you not want that for your children?

If your relationships and wounds from your mother and father remain unhealed, this will always interfere in your feelings and perceptions of the soul. Parental injuries are a major block in establishing any direct soul to soul relationships AND a direct soul to soul relationship with God. Combined with the religious mis-understandings and distortions about the nature of God and love, many people feel alienated from Source or angry, because of their own life lessons.

All wounds have a structure to them, and because it is limited it can be known. What is finite can be known. All your wounds have structures, and once you are out of the wound you can see the structure of the wound. Once you are out of the Matrix, you can see what the Matrix is built of. Once you are outside the building you can see the building, but when you are in the building you cannot.

In having healed your parental issues you are just this: you are out of the building. You love your parents the way the Divine loves you, and the way that the Divine loves them. If you are in unconditional love then it does not matter whether they are or not, as you are in that loving place within yourself, and by natural extension with them.

Your parents are people just like everyone else, and they have a special relating to you as well. See the truth of your parents too: their wounds and their gifts, and navigate with discernment accordingly. It is not as common as people may think that their blood families are their soul family. It happens, but is not the norm. We draw our blood parents to us as they mirror our own lessons and wounds in various ways. Only we can learn these lessons.

SEVEN WAYS TO HEAL PARENTAL WOUNDS

Family Constellation Healing
Genetic Alchemy Practices
Parental Dialoguing
Ancestor Rituals from indigenous traditions
Relationship and Sexual Healing Practices
Self Inquiry and Prayer to feel/release the wounds
Somatic/Depth Psychology

PARENTAL DIALOGUING AND HEALING

The first step in healing the genetic injuries your parents have passed down to you is *accepting and feeling that there are emotions within you generated by your interactions (or not) with them*, and recognizing how this affects your life, and most importantly the emotions this generates within you.

Be in honest dialogue within yourself about the patterns, behaviors, attitudes and emotions you feel with your parents, and if your parents are alive you can have a honest dialogues with them about it.

When you go into honest dialogue with your parents with the intent of expressing your hurt, your pain, your fears, it can be quite intense; there can be a lot of charge. So it is important to make sure you keep your expression about you, expressing your pain, hurt and disappointment and OWNING IT AS YOUR OWN. Do not make it about them and what they did or did not do.

Then they are more likely to receive it. Express what you are feeling, and try not to blame them. You may be surprised at how you may have the best and most loving conversation that you have ever had with them ...or not!

Be honest with your feelings to them. So you can start off by saying, "*I have something important to share with you about my feelings from my childhood with you, and I would like you to hear me while I speak and not interrupt,*" and then just say it. What they say back to you will trigger more emotions in you, which will assist your healing. But it is not about them.

Your parents cannot give you the attention and love NOW that you wanted from them as a child and did not receive, especially when you have reached beyond your teenage years. That time has passed. Many of us still hanker after that love, still need that love, and carry that need into our intimate relationships. This will sabotage any deeper connection to your partner, and you may end up being a mother or father to them and abandon other parts of you.

You cannot get your parents love that you so needed as a child NOW. It will not fill the hole within you. That is a missed opportunity. You can however receive that love from healing yourself, and this will also help heal the wounds your ancestors and parents have passed onto you.

In having an open, honest dialogue with your parents, understand that you are going to see them and speak to them *to really feel your own wounds*: you are walking in there to trigger your wounds, and then you are going to walk away to feel your wounds and be with them. They can never heal you, they can never give you what you want.

For example, if you experience your father's anger or fear, which is covering his wounds, what does that then trigger in you? And then you need to go deeper into that feeling *in you*.

Use these situations so you can feel the deeper layers of your wound: go and speak to them because you are here to heal yourself.

And this is actually the most loving thing for you and them, as you are owning everything in humility and self-responsibility. By healing yourself, you will also be helping their healing process as well, giving them the opportunity to soften into the unconditional love they have within them *for you*.

Your physical parents are an effect of a cause that you are gifted with in order to heal something that is now within you.

One thing to say to yourself could be, "Okay, what am I trying not to feel here?" because underneath the thought lies the true emotional cause. Simply remind yourself, *"What do I not wish to feel here?"* and then relax and allow yourself to feel.

In this honest dialoguing with your parents, often fear and anger arises. These are just the surface emotions, and underneath this may be deeper causal feelings of grief, hurt and abandonment. Both you and your parents can stay on the surface; they are in anger and you are in fear, or vice versa. The point is to understand, '*oh this is just a surface emotion*', and you are actually hiding from and protecting yourself from going into the deeper causal emotions where real healing lies.

Many souls are afraid to lose their parents love. On an unconscious level, like an unspoken rule, family members rarely push each other too far into the cause of their wounds, as then they fear the (false) bond they have would be broken, or taken into an unknown place, and possibly separation. Secrecy and shame are the bedfellows of this fear.

But families are here to help each other's souls, not continue their bondage.

Parental and ancestral wounds are here for you to learn, embrace and accept all sides of yourself in deep feeling. Their wounds reflect a part of you, whether you like it or not. In resistance to this truth, seeing your parents as nothing to do with you or the way your life has turned out, you deny your own gateways to Love *brought into human expression just for you*. Your parents are here to help you heal your soul, maybe not in the idealized way you envisioned it, but nonetheless this is the soul agreement between you both.

You cannot be in Union with Your Self, never mind God, without healing your human parental lessons and wounds first. Your human parents live on in you, even if they are physically dead, as their DNA is carried within you *until* it is transformed. So, ask to feel it all, rather than live underneath it.

If you are not mothering, loving and nurturing your own soul, then you may mother others in an attempt to not feel your own wounds. Often, we mother and father others because it is easier to do so than mother and father our own soul. We may try and muffle and cover our wounds with others who have a similar wound, colluding to create a ''wound-ship '' rather than a friendship.

Many times, we turn towards our human partner when we feel lack around our human mother/father; we look for succour, comfort, nurturing, strength, guidance and courage when we lack this. Truly love yourself by clearing the wounds with your human parents, for this will then enable you to meet and love your partner without need, wounds or filters. This can then eventually lead into you being the unconditional love that God Is.

These healings are important steps for you to take to get closer to your soul and God. Often, we become parents to our own parents in various ways because of their own needs and lack. They may subconsciously place you in the place of being their mother, father or even lover if they did not have their own mother-father or love relating. As their child, you may place yourself in a parental position towards them out of concern, false responsibility and a misplaced sense of 'love 'for them.

This is damaging to your soul and intimate relationships, as it will create a false belief around what love is and what love is not. Mother and father wounds govern our emotional openness, our ability to give and receive love fully and vulnerably, and our ability to manifest abundance in the world. These are huge keys to our happiness and peace.

Healing our parental wounds enables us to step into a more pure expression of mother and father, free from attempts to balance what we did or did not receive. Here we are free to rest in the organic expression of parenting that wants to emerge through us.

SACRED ACTIONS

Look now in your life and *all* your relationships to see where you are over mothering and fathering others.
Why are you doing this? What emotion is underneath it?
What new actions can you take to stop these situations and imbalanced relationships?

When you take these actions you will release energy and emotion, enabling you to feel and heal faster, and love yourself more.

THE BENEFITS OF GENETIC ALCHEMY

"We can regain our authentic power and clear the pain of our ancestors in our system. Imagine how the quality of humankind could change in one generation by changing our birthing practices and bringing our children into a world of love and safety."
Elena Tonetti-Vladimirova

1. SOVEREIGNTY

We can only truly be ourselves when we are not *being* anyone else, trying to be like someone else, or unconsciously aping inherited behaviours, wounds and traits of your parents and ancestors. To be yourself, to be natural and free, to express yourself fully, sets the best example for your children to be who they are: by you being truly who you are.

We cannot be ourselves with ancestral burdens and unresolved wounds running through our lives, our emotions, our minds and bodies. These genetic signals course through our subconscious, co-creating our external reality and informing our choices and relationships and impacting our children who will also continue these traits and burdens. With these ancestral and genetic burdens, we also "buy into" the collective fear based consciousness of humanity, as they resonate with each other.

We cannot be ourselves when we are still being our parents and our parent's parents, and neither can your children be themselves fully either. Ease those burdens, release those emotions, those beliefs borne from another time: changing your DNA is what Genetic Alchemy brings to us when we travel deep into it.

To be your natural self is one of the greatest gifts you can give to yourself and your children. When you flow with this passion and purpose coming from Your Center, this joy, this happiness, this empowerment, you arrive at the cutting edge of evolution and emanate that out to all others.

This creates change in your blood relatives, especially your children, who receive these vibratory signals from you. The most effective time to clear your genetics and do ancestral healing is before your children are conceived, during pregnancy, and when they are between the ages of 0-7.

Between 7-14 years old, your genetic healing will still have an impact, albeit lesser, on your children, and after they are 14 years old the impact of your own genetic healing will be lesser still. Your ancestral healing gives permission to, and carves out a path for your children to relax into and be their natural, unique selves without carrying old pains, hurts, griefs and dysfunctional patterns that you, your parents, and your ancestors hold.

Sovereignty is Independence, self-government and authority to rule all aspects of your Self. Centered in our *own* sovereignty, we can resist any fearful need to clip another's wings or suppress another's sovereignty. We must be mindful of that which still remains unfelt and unloved within us that might cause us to claim our 'sovereign' state by coercion, or out of anger and rebellion; true sovereignty arises out of harmony and balance with all parts of us and others in our web of life.

The more sovereign we are, the more we can accept this in another, and indeed revel in and enjoy it! True sovereignty is a reciprocal energy—we carry it within, and resist any temptation to curtail it in another. When we respect others sovereignty, it often requires us to let go of control, greed, or the wishes of our wounded self.

Recognizing our own and others sovereignty is an unselfish act of love. It works to release us from the spell of wounded, conditional, selfish 'love'. As we let go of the desire for our own pleasure at the expense of another, as we let go of needing our childrens love to fill up our own need for love that we did not get from our parents, this changes the old paradigm of control and fear into an unconditional respect and love. Parenthood is an initiation into unconditional love.

Sovereignty is part of the true use of choice or free will. To become fully able to use our free will is a rare thing on earth, as most of us are not aware of the full scope of possibilities and potentials available to us, never mind actively using them. To become sovereign, we enter the full power of new and previously unimaginable choices, putting them boldly into action. This is greatly helped by doing our family and ancestral healing.

Paradoxically, this freedom requires boundaries. Freedom blooms when you have healed the hurts of your incarnation and ancestral wounds. Be exactly who you are and express this without reservation, hesitation or delay in all ways, physically, emotionally, mentally, soulfully and sexually.

Freedom is *not* hedonism, doing whatever your wounded selfish self wants, doing whatever your hurt inner child screams for, and putting up with this with others. This just causes harm. Freedom is grounded in a soft, warm and yet vast heart.

2. THE EVOLUTION OF THE GENE POOL

The human gene pool holds the collective genetic information and total number of genes available in our species. The gene pool has a strong sexual energy within it for obvious reasons and is the total 'breeding stock' available to our species. The potential for this is still largely untapped due to our ancestral and family genetic patterns, all of which are part of the human gene pool and your own gene pool which you will pass onto your children and your childrens children.

Where does our own personal gene pool come from? Our ancestors and our parents having sex and passing on their genetic information to us. Multiply this for all humans and you can see a picture emerging. These are the links in the collective suffering of humanity, and it is this chain that we need to heal, embrace and therefore transcend in order to create a new species of human. This new type of human being is *genetically free* from the past pain.

There are numerous benefits to family/ancestral healing on all levels of consciousness, spiritual, emotional, mental and physical. Chronic and apparently 'incurable' illnesses can be healed. There can be immediate relief of physical pain and distraction, and the triggering of physical symptoms until the healing is completed.

Physically you can feel more centered, whole, spacious, stronger and grounded. You can have more life force by becoming more connected to the ancestral flow of love that is our souls design and the natural order of life. You have more energy to be in the flow, to be in the present moment in a heart centered space.

The deep need for belonging that is so essential to our well being starts to be fulfilled in a healthy, sovereign and empowered way. *What do we need to belong to?* Our family, a peer group, the collective consciousness of humanity? We have a deep need to belong to an origin, to belong with the people we come from, and spend time with.

We want to have our rightful place, our role in the whole, our harmony in the whole web of life. So do our ancestors. By accepting them and helping them, we help ourselves. We can then receive their gifts and their love, and come into harmony and a right position with them within our own selves. For the families we are born into are a reflection of aspects of our own selves and mirror our need for belonging, or the feeling that sometimes we do not belong to anything. Do you want your children to feel this too? Or to be secure, safe, and whole within themselves?

Receiving our ancestors positive gifts, talents, abilities and love for us enables us to live into our own Self. Our ancestors, our parents, have much goodness to share with us that perhaps they could not pass onto us before because of their own wounding, their own inability to give love, and our own resistances and inability to receive love. Doing our ancestral healing allows these gifts to be transmitted to us.

This can manifest in many ways. For example, your father was meant to give you a sense of an inner pillar, a core, a center to live from as a unique individual, and appropriate healthy and loving boundaries to empower you. Perhaps your father never had that within himself to give, so you looked for this in other ways. In ancestral healing this can be remedied, even if your father has passed away. You can assume your right position with each other as sovereign beings and accept the gifts of the father in your life, beyond the hurt of not receiving it before.

In ancestral healing, feelings of sadness, isolation, and loneliness stop being so existential and strong. Our capacity to expand our heart and embrace self and others without judgment increases. Our ability to forgive self and others, and ask humbly for forgiveness, deepens.

We can embrace our parents, ourselves and our ancestors, feeling and forgiving our actions and the actions they have done, which in turn expands our capacity to unconditionally love, and be present with our own children, and everyone else. We can experience peace, a deeper embodying of the heart.

Restlessness, nervousness, tension and busyness can all come into a deeper point of stillness. These symptoms are often the precursor of deeper illnesses in the body. Burn out, fatigue, laziness and exhaustion are often part of ancestral issues.

As we ancestrally heal from our families, physical and emotional fragmentation of the soul resolves, as pieces of us come back together. There are aspects in the fractal of the collective consciousness that harbor the same emotions our ancestors and we are connected to. Your authentic transformation of this within you also helps healing to happen for many other souls. The impact of this is deep and freeing, and is truly for the benefit of all beings.

3. THE SACRED COVENANT WITH YOUR BLOODLINE

Your parents and ancestors have deep pains that play out through your DNA and your children, marking your life. Every bloodline depends on one person to help redeem and liberate themselves. Many of the more conscious people on earth, like you, have chosen this role out of unconditional love for your parents, your ancestors, your (future and present) children and yourself.

In the release of family and ancestral imprints, our ancestors, past, present and future also receive a healing. This includes our present day families and children. This healing impacts our future too. Ancestral healing changes the possibilities available to us, shifting our potential timelines and future possibilities from one outcome into another.

What seemed improbable or even impossible suddenly becomes do-able, and more than that, tangibly manifests in your life and relationships. Your future time-lines change as you heal, and your DNA changes its vibratory rate the more it is released from its layers of burdens. This in turn creates a whole new set of possibilities and future outcomes aligned to your hearts desires.

Are you stuck doing a job you do not like? Cannot see a way out of a current situation or relationship? Do you keep attracting the same scenarios and patterns? Do you still maintain the same belittling and unsatisfying position in your life, career, relationships? Do you have issues with money and abundance? Are you a mother or father to others and not to yourself? Do you want this to be passed onto your children?

Genetic patterns are passed on from family to family, ancestor to ancestor, stretching all the way back to your very first ancestor - your first father or mother. At each step along the way of this long genetic chain, each generation adds positive qualities or defects to the DNA pattern, passing this information down to the next generation, and so on.

For example, the mother of a scientist friend of mine bent and broke her finger in her early 20's. When John was born, this manifested in a curled up finger, which then also manifested in his daughter ... and so on. Other examples would be a genius passing on his genius to his son or daughter, a spiritual master passing on his transformed DNA to his child, or an emotionally traumatized person passing on fear, abandonment and mistrust to their children.

Inheritances can be of all kinds, positive and negative. This cycle continues until one person resolves and heals the ancestral burdens within them on the soul-emotional-genetic-physical level, culminating in their literally becoming a redeemer or a "Christ" for their entire bloodline.

In this cycle, there are seven layers to Genetic Alchemy. As we progress through these layers, we step into our true sovereignty and individuated Self. Most ancestral healing methods on the planet only go into three or four layers of this healing. Once we step beyond the fourth layer we begin the process of becoming a Christ to ourselves and our bloodline.

True genetic healing on the deeper layers is a potently visceral physical, emotional and spiritual experience. It changes the DNA, brain and body mind, and you feel it deeply in your bones. The experience of feeling your ancestors around you, giving you support, is deeply moving. Feeling the loving humility of this place, the purity of the healing in process, and the deep connection to you is honoring and profound.

4. THE NEW HUMAN RACE

A new way of Birthing our children is vital for the genetic evolution of humanity. It is through a new evolution of our current species that suffering can lessen on earth. Many Masters have said that in order for humanity to evolve into its next phase of evolution a new species will have to be born on Earth, a species as different from humanity today as we are to the evolutions that have preceded us. This means becoming biologically different, genetically different, and discontinuous with the fear based structures and emotional veils of the present day mass consciousness constructs of humanity.

One of the basic laws of Alchemy requires that we separate in order to become whole. We differentiate from something else in order to become who we are. In India the yogic saying, *"neti neti," I am not this, I am not that*, allows us to then Know who we truly are. In this separation to become whole, part of the process of True Alchemy, we help redeem our bloodlines, liberating ourselves and our ancestry to the extent that they are able to let go. In practice this means that our mothers, fathers, daughters and sons become 'separate' from us because our own DNA has changed, which affects all our ancestors, stretching all the way back to our first ancestor.

This is a wonderful thing! True love is unattached. In this genetic release within me, I felt freer, open, more loving and more joyous with my parents. Both my biological father and mother, and everyone who meets us, notices how different our relationship is as compared to other parents and their children.

There is more love, spaciousness, and genuine meeting between us as individual souls, without agenda, expectation, genetic heaviness and role-playing. We are all free to be whom we are, and to enjoy and share that with the other. *Separation allows union is the paradox.*

The next step in the evolution of humanity is already here on Earth, awaiting further nurturing to bloom into fullness. These New Children of Light are a transitory species, a bridge between the old *homo sapiens* and the new *homo luminus*, or light being. They are building this bridge one body, one soul at a time, and they are flocking in droves to earth to achieve this.

Adults who have the desire, the freedom of choice, and have released their conditioning can access this transitioning species. These adults and New Children are paving the Way for the new species of *homo luminus* to incarnate, and to provide this new species with the best possible chance of growth here.

The purpose of *Homo luminus* is to create a new civilization through uncorrupted vessels that allow latent energies within the DNA to fully bloom so humanity can become 'like gods '(part of God) on earth.

To admit this is possible and do-able to your self is the beginning of anything great.

New Children do not have the same burdens we have had. They are not so much a part of the genetic and mass consciousness fields of present day humanity. The more of these New Children are born, the more this new field anchors, and the more possibilities open for our own evolution. By helping them, we are helping ourselves and all beings. This is a new expression of the Bodhisattva Vow: helping all beings move out of suffering on a grand scale, one birth at a time.

Evolution is a long journey that is reaching a crucial turning point and rapid acceleration with the birth on earth of the New Children. They do not have to struggle like we did, which means their light, their brilliance, their creativity, their sovereignty and infinite potential is already alive at an early age, without obstacle. Of course, they too have wounds/lessons, BUT with their conscious parents support, these wounds can be more easily released than with adults or normal children.

It is easy to notice the difference between a New Child and a normal child. You may see it when you walk down a street, or meet one of these New Children. They actually look, feel and emanate a different light to other children. This has been corroborated by modern science, who have proved that a human has been born with triple strand DNA, instead of the 'normal 'double helix. A young boy in the UK, Alfie Clamp, was born blind with severe disabilities, which led doctors to carry out various tests. They revealed his seventh chromosome has an extra strand of material which has never been publicly documented anywhere in the world.

Of course there are more of these children, yet they will not have 'disabilities 'or not be tested by modern science. Alfie Clamp's 'disabilities 'are part of the genetic mutation process, as millions of years of genetic evolution culminate. It is a mutation of our species into something which is not yet known.

These New Children carry within them seeds for a New Humanity. When watered with our love and protected in a safe container, they bear fruit, realigning humanity's path to the next higher expression of possibility. They carry a light that we can raise ourselves upto in its purity, instead of trying to dumb them down to our experience and culture. In this surrender to what they bring, we will arrive at our next evolutionary possibility.

These New Families create a tunnel through the old paradigm into a new birth for humankind. These new children have much to share with us if we are willing to listen and open beyond our normal means of communication. They take us on journeys beyond our edges to show us a greater plan.

I remember one morning I was resting in bed nursing my year old son. He began to speak to me, as he often does, in images, and he took me on a journey, beyond the earth to a distant star. From here I could see earth and the whole of humanity. Within the larger pattern of chaos, I could see subtle waves forming.

I understood there were a few souls who had incarnated on earth at this time to help bring harmony back to humanity, and these waves were the momentum of their actions manifesting. My son indicated these souls were laying the foundation for the New Children, paving the way for the next species of human being to emerge.

Sri Aurobindo, a sage, visionary and founder of Auroville Community in India, foresaw this new species. *"For the manifestation of a divine body here on earth there must be an initial transformation, the appearance of a new, greater and more developed type. Materiality can be turned into a material solidity of divine nature …by a radical transformation of the functioning, structure, mechanical, material impulses and driving forces of the body system…."*

What we can do is provide the conditions and environments, inner and outer, to facilitate this for these Children. This new species blooms and anchors on earth by a spiritual change in our being, as they bring fundamental and radical change in our evolution, akin to a revolution, in our very nature.

To live into the opportunity gifted by these New Children, the opportunity to create a new humanity, we have to enter the state of being and consciousness they are in. They help us, we help them, and the soul covenant is complete for all.

Evolution on earth has been a long and slow process, but this does not have to be so. It has only been long and slow because it has been an emergence from the subconscious. With these New Children, this is not the case, as they do not have the same burdens we have had.

Sri Aurobindo continues …*"Theirs can be an evolution in the light, not in the dark, in which the evolving being is a conscious co operator and participant. Their evolution is not from ignorance and wounding to knowledge and consciousness; it is from knowledge to greater knowledge, consciousness to greater consciousness, from Being to even greater Being.*

In this, there is no longer any necessity for the slow pace of ordinary evolution; there can be rapid conversion, quick transformation after transformation, which would seem to us now a succession of miracles. In this (new species) there are no contradictions: whatever would seem to be opposites for the mind, here carry in themselves their own right relation and reconciling agreement, if indeed any reconciliation were needed, for the harmony of these apparent opposites is complete.

This change might happen not only in the few, but extend and generalize itself in the race. This possibility, if fulfilled, would mean that the human dream of perfection ....of all its ways of action and living, would be no longer be a dream but a truth, that could be made real and humanity lifted out of ignorance."

The New Children and the New Earth need each other. Each mutually enhances, feeds and builds the other. When New Children interact with the earth's fields, they help earth herself to move through obstacles in her own evolution into the Fifth Dimension.

The New Children interact with the Template for The New Earth held in Earths's Fields, and trigger their own DNA. Both need each other in order to grow. The New Earth can only manifest when enough of us are embodying the healed DNA, and the majority of these souls will be the New Children and possibly their parents.

DNA is the code of all life. *All life everywhere is held within our DNA, and the soul is the key to activating it.* When more of our disconnected DNA is activated, 'god like' abilities and capacities will become the norm for much of humanity, and suffering will disappear. *As Christ said, "Ye are like Gods."* He saw this potential within all of us, and he activated it within himself.

The human being is a physical body (particle) AND a spiritual Being (wave). As a wave, the individual is part of the collective consciousness, in touch with it in its entirety. From 2013, there has been a New Particle introduced into the human collective and this particle, the Golden Children, who have not existed before in the collective, are the next step in the evolution of human consciousness.

This wave/particle will continue and propagate to eventually reach all parts of the collective, building a bridge for all beings to be able to access a new level of vibration that will affect the entire species. This wave is cascading out like a spider's web to resonate and permeate the entire collective via its wave form or resonant frequency, building a bridge by "catalytic proximity" to the Zero Point Field.

Evolution is triggered by a mutation of one member of a species, which is then passed onto other members of the species by DNA and vibrational resonance. When one member of a species moves to a higher vibrational frequency and crosses from being identified as just a physical being to being part of the Wave of the Creator, (in Aramaic: *Ha-Shem*) this information is then seeded into the collective consciousness and a pathway is opened that others can follow.

In the same way as a physical mutation is passed along to the rest of the species by DNA, it is passed into the collective consciousness via the Law of Resonance. This new frequency and resonance permeates the field, to be matched by those beings who approximate the source frequency. If the evolutionary trigger is one member of the species, say a Christ or a Golden Child, and the whole is the sum of its parts, it therefore follows that the parts influence the nature of the whole.

In this case, the New Children are having a catalytic effect on the whole of humanity. Their vibrational imprint is at work in the collective consciousness already, and we are probably too close to observe it properly, but its effects will become more visible as time goes on.

Where do these new children come from?

The birthing of a new human race *homo luminus* is based on conscious relationships, sacred sexuality and authentic emotional intimacy between couples. These are the active agents of unified love, wisdom and power, the basis of an awakened civilization. Between the two of the sacred couple lies the third, the *egregore,* the field between them, the intelligence of loves wisdom and/or a child.

In the old paradigm nuclear family structures, control, fear, and ancestral/birth wounding ran the family unit. Now, these family structures are transforming into something new with the healing that these couples do. *Nuclear family*, the base unit of the old collective foundations, is now morphing and changing into becoming an extended *soul family*, where the souls resonance with others is valued wherever it may find itself, and detaches from abusive and dysfunctional family members and values. In this, we transcend our genetic ties, so there is no repeating of wound patterns.

The waves carried into the collective Gene Pool by these sacred couples and new family units, (those who have released their genetic patterning) impact all humanity. Their new genetic information is resonating into the collective gene pool, carving a pathway open for others to follow this trail of genetic florescence and illumination.

Awakening brings you into transcending your genetic imprinting. Ancestral healing and genetic alchemy is our horizontal axis, the divine is our vertical. We come into balance as we release deeper layers of genetic patterns.

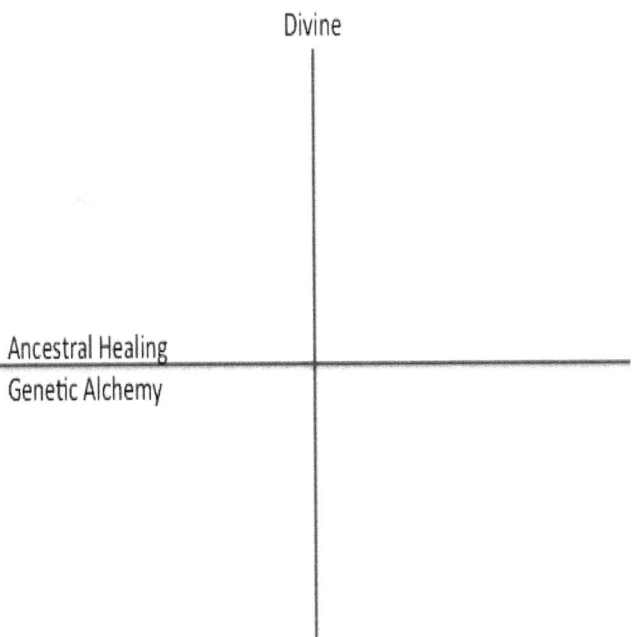

Awakening is our second birth. Our first birth was through the womb, the flesh, the genetic imprinting we took on in our birth. The second birth is of the pure soul manifesting itself, free of all conditioning. In India, they call this process ' dwija" or becoming twice born. It is a complete erasing of the genetic imprinting of your birth process and traumas, your time in the womb in pregnancy, your conception, your parental issues, and all your ancestors, stretching all the way back to the first parents of your bloodline, the first human parents of all humanity, and finally the Creator of our DNA itself.

All of these layers can all be simply called your karma made manifest.

EARTH RESONANCE

"An awakening must come in the earth nature and the earth consciousness, which will be, if not the actual beginning, at least the effective preparation and the first steps of its evolution toward a new and diviner world order."
Sri Aurobindo

Earth is our physical home, our support, the place where we live, our mother. She is part of us, as we are part of her. She provides the container for the preciousness of our lives and love to occur. She is the ground beneath our feet that enables us to walk our evolutionary lessons and offers us the opportunity for our lives to bloom into fullness. Her electromagnetic fields mirror our own electromagnetic fields, and we cohabitate symbiotically in a living web of relationship.

Earth is one of our greatest allies. Her body supports us in so many ways, our food, our home, our sustenance, physical support, warmth and protection. Earth brings together all the elements and coagulates them into form, giving us the opportunity to be embodied, to be here now, to bring together all parts of us into wholeness. The more we live in harmony and connection with her, the more she can nurture, sustain and support us in living a life of soulful, physical and worldly fulfillment.

Earth has a womb, just as we do. The crystalline core of her womb center is vast and loving and is always available to hold and receive us, in our deepest sorrows and our greatest celebrations of life.

Earth holds many keys for our evolution, embodiment and connection to the vastness of our own souls. We also hold many keys for her. Her magnetic fields connect with our own. We are part of her body, as she is part of ours. The more connected we are with her, the more we are connected to ourselves, and the more easily our incoming children can enjoy and adapt to life on earth as soul.

In birth, a woman's body becomes a bridge between heaven and earth. The spiraling currents of life-force that flow through her womb creates a vortex through which the spirit of her child enter Earth's magnetic fields. When mother is deeply aligned with herself, the Divine, and Earth, she surrenders her being and her body into the Golden Phi Spiral of life, allowing her child to emerge in harmony with the innate movements of creation.

When we align our rhythms with Earth's rhythms, we come into sync with the pulse of life. The organic unfolding of our needs and desires can be met. We move in synchronicity, crossing paths with other souls, places and events that are aligned with our current unfolding and purpose.

When we nurture our innate connection with the Earth, through time and communion with nature and her spirits, with her magnetic fields and her womb, with the elements, in play, gratitude and silence, we allow the web of life to flow through us. We connect more to ourselves, everyone else and all life when we are more connected to Earth in our body! The deeper we ground into Earth in all her aspects, the more you can expand in your consciousness, as earths womb is a portal to the Galactic Centre, as many ancient sacred traditions knew.

Earth's fields and consciousness is a fifth dimensional field that connects to all life everywhere. She is not just this planet earth in the third dimension. Being grounded does not mean being heavy, trapped, worldly or earthbound. Communing with Earth takes us into a vast expanded groundedness rooted in our bodies that is multi dimensional. In giving and receiving love with the Earth, we enter the Cycle of Love, the Sacred Hoop.

The three aspects of Earth we can align with are her womb core, her magnetic fields, and the element of earth itself, which is within our bodies as well as being the planet herself. Her womb crystal core connects to our own womb and the womb of the Galactic center. Her electromagnetic fields anchor the Unity Grids, the template for Love reflected in the magnetic flows of our own Shakti circuitry. As we open and heal our own magnetic circuitry, emotions, feelings and memories, the expression of our soul through our Shakti, through our bodies, opens more too. This all opens us upto the flow of the Web of Life.

THE EARTH HUM FREQUENCY

The Earth's natural heartbeat rhythm or frequency has hovered for many years around 7.8 Hz, until recently. This frequency, known as the 'Schumann Resonance' after the scientist who discovered it, is a wave and vibrating pulse that connects to and sustains all living organisms on earth.

Whenever your frequency is out of alignment with the Earth Hum, you are out of alignment with your natural rhythms, genetically, spiritually and physically. As Earths fields are now changing rapidly, so too is this frequency, and this is the cause for many disturbances in us, and on earth, today. Much human disease, pressure and stress comes about because of disconnection and disturbances between your electromagnetic field (your spirit/auric body) and the fields and resonant frequency of Earth.

The Earth Hum is a frequency oscillation that moves far more slowly than most modern human beings are used to. Many indigenous societies have maintained their connection to the Earth Hum, their living connection to the Earth, as part of their lifestyle and way of being and moving, which is why they move more slowly and are frequently more happy than their "advanced first world" counterparts.

The more deeply you move with the Earth Hum, the more magnetic or emotionally attuned you become, able to flow, let go into, and trust the natural feelings and cycles of life *and* of being a human being. As Rudd shares from The Gene Keys, "The agitation of the lower frequencies experiences these slower, yet higher, frequencies as dullness."

For example, you can be vibrating so fast, at such a high frequency, that you actually are still. Inner stillness, inner silence happens when your frequency has risen, when your frequency has gone up, not down. That's because you are spinning so fast that you become still. The faster and higher your vibration and frequency is, the stiller you become.

When the frequency of your DNA entrains with the Earth Hum, your experience of time changes. If we look at the Aboriginals in Australia, they measure time in millennia, not days or months as the more mental western world does. They are in no hurry at all, as they used to collectively know the Earth Hum, and move with her. As they live closely to the earth's natural rhythms, they live the wisdom that comes of moving more slowly in the world and at a higher frequency.

There is a higher magnetic power latent within your DNA which connects to the Earth Hum and Earth's electromagnetic fields. Such magnetic resonance is part of the foundation for the Law of Attraction – the universal law that draws towards you that which serves your purpose, souls desires and learning, be it relationships, teachings, events or resources. Until you resonate with the Earth Hum, the Grace of this law is not fully realized in your life. The Earth is part of the attractor.

Magnetism emanates through your auric field or spirit body. As Goethe said: *'Everything alive creates an atmosphere around itself.'* All life forms radiate bio-energetic energy fields, which harmoniously interact with their environment through coherent emotions and geometric laws. To bring the power of your auric body into harmony with Earth through your heart brings you into the web of life itself, and helps to activate your dormant DNA potentials.

The more resonant your auric field becomes with the earth's natural frequencies, the wider your aura spreads, bringing you into contact with many hidden realities, laws and communion with beings within nature. As the frequency of your spirit body comes into Resonance it interlocks with the earth grids, and your consciousness expands by becoming able to give and receive with Earth, thereby receiving more of the incoming photonic waves and information from outside our planet, which are transduced through the Earth Grids into us.

In birthing, when we tune into the Earths Hum and frequency, it allows us to surrender, to be guided into a field and frequency of innate harmony, to open to the primordial wave-forces of creation that our body viscerally engages in, and to enjoy the ride in bliss and peaceful power rather than fear and contraction.

MAGNETIC MEMORIES

Many of our deepest charged memories are held within the Earth's magnetic fields surrounding the sphere of our planet. The magnetic fields around the earth hold part of our emotional memories, emotional identity and emotional reference points in place.

NASA astronauts found that when they first left the earths orbit and magnetic fields, they became disorientated and confused because they lost connection to some of their magnetic field. NASA learnt from this, and now every astronaut has a magnetic attenuation box on their belt so they do not lose their emotional identity composed of their memories, reference points and sense of orientation.

Similarly, Researcher Valerie Hunt did experiments with people in special rooms where they removed ambient environmental electro-magnetic (EM) charge, or part of the earths electromagnetic field frequency. With this background field gone, people became deeply emotional for no reason. When the field was restored, people felt balanced and 'normal' again.

Women directly connect to Earth through their Yoni Lips and womb. In so doing, we open to the web of life, the web of interconnection, opening the door to access more of our memories. As one feels the emotions held here, you can welcome aspects of your soul back into the here and now, and in feeling them, presence-ing them, they can release the layers of memories around the soul so one can be present in the moment in a full body, sensual experience.

The magnetic flows of the Earths Grids are always in motion. As we connect into this magnetic flow, memories and blocks to this flow arise. All one has to do is activate this connection and stay with this magnetic flow. As we connect more into this flow, many dreams and experiences can arise.

For example, people in your life who may have died can come to your attention. This is because their spirits have remained trapped in the magnetic sphere of the earth's fields, because they are attached to the past, or fearful of moving beyond and letting go of earth-life. These souls are called earthbound spirits, and there are millions of them bound to earth because of their fear of other non-material planes of existence, their denial of them, their unknowing that they are actually dead, or their lack of knowledge that there is somewhere else to go to apart from earth upon their physical death.

In the past, Priestesses in Egypt, the Americas, India and Tibet helped move these earth-bound spirits on from their bondage to this plane of existence, as a sacred task of compassion and service. Today, the astral planes around earth and her fields are blocked with many spirits who cannot move on, and who lack the knowledge, courage and guidance to do so. This is a great astral pollution that affects us all psychically, as most of these spirits influence many humans alive today.

As we connect with our own emotional bodies more deeply in all that is held and mirrored in Earth's magnetic fields, we can reclaim pieces of our own self AND recognize our own embodiment through tending this living, breathing, matrix of life beyond the life that we 'see.'

THE EARTH HUM NOW

In June 2014, the Russian Space Observing System recorded a sharp increase in the Earth Hum frequency from 7.81Hz to 8.5 Hz. Since then, they have recorded days where the Schumann accelerated to 16.5 Hz, more than double the usual frequency. In 2020 and 2021 recordings were made of the frequency rising to as much as 120Hz!

The Earth frequency is speeding up. As this frequency is entrained with our brain wave states, specifically alpha/theta states, this acceleration can make us feel like time is speeding up: a whole day *now* can pass in what seems to be hours, and major events and changes in our lives are now happening more rapidly.

So, the frequency of Earth affects us, our evolution, our state of consciousness, our climate, and even our perception of time itself. Indigenous societies throughout the ages have tried to warn the western world about this, to steward and tend to Earth, yet few of these warnings have been heeded until it could be scientifically proven.

A 7.83 Hz frequency in the human brain is an alpha/theta state. This is a relaxed, lucid, between dimensions state of consciousness, where you feel dreamy, soft and open. In the 8.5 –16.5 Hz frequency range, one moves one out of the theta range into a calmer alpha state with faster, alert (almost like drinking coffee) beta frequencies. 12-15 Hz is a state of relaxed, focused equanimity and calm, similar to meditation, where we are calm yet focused and open. Our thought processes are quiet, clear, and "in the zone "or "in the flow," with intuitive access to wisdom, solutions and knowing.

As Earth shifts her vibrational frequency, so are we. With this acceleration, you may feel more tired, dizzy, depressed, and downright strange as you adapt your frequency to be "in tune" with the New Earth. You may also feel elated and joyful and have many memories, traumas and spontaneous breakdowns/breakthroughs occurring in your life because of these frequency shifts and the subsequent releases that come from them.

The fossil record and recent scientific tests show that that the electromagnetic field of earth has been decreasing for 4-5,000 years. Some speculate that the field decreases in advance of a magnetic field reversal or pole shift, from which a new field is created. 10 When the field reversal happens, it is speculated that this shifts, rewires and deletes two of the three electromagnetic fields of Earth which contain parts of the memories of the collective/racial consciousness of humanity. As the system reboots after being shifted, it recreates the fields in a new configuration or shield harmonic.

Our biology, our magnetic selves, our feelings and emotions, our DNA, our bodies and its hormonal/chemical reactions, rhythms and 'natural' cycles are connected to, and are mirrored by, the electromagnetic fields of Earth. We contain each other, and our evolution is intimately intertwined. We are partners, twins in the dance of life.

If Earth's fields were to change to a higher harmonic and geometry through sudden evolution or gradual evolution, it would directly affect us all on a profound level. Perhaps a genetic virus, the most efficient means of rapid genetic transformation on a mass scale, is stored in the depths of our junk DNA, and could be activated like a genetic trigger to initiate a cascading wave within us, reconnecting our junk DNA. Perhaps one person or many people could embody this new frequency, and this could happen suddenly, which is one of

---

10 The memories of Earth are connected to her magnetic fields, just like our human memories are connected to our own magnetic fields. Both intertwine.

the promises of the new children and the new species of homo luminous that they are heralding in.

BIRTHING A NEW PARADIGM

Earth is an important part of our Design in Birthing. She is a Foundation and a Living Being who herself is evolving into her next embodiment. She needs us and the New Children to do this, and we need her so we can evolve too. We are symbiotic beings birthing each other into our fullness.

Through stones such as Turquoise, a mainstay for the Native American and Tibetan peoples, and Pounamu or Nephrite Jade for the Waiteha and Maori peoples, we for millennia have communed with the Spirit of Earth, and slowed down into her heartbeat pulse. Connecting to her allows us to connect more with ourselves. Connecting to her electro magnetic flows allows us to deepen into our own electromagnetic flows.

Earth is the beginning and end, where we start and realize our Union. It is the alpha and the omega, the beginning and end of the human journey. We come to earth when we are born, and leave earth when we die. She is the ground for our own completion, our own embodiment, our own incarnation and karma to play out.

When you have fully connected to Earth and walked through this doorway, you can fully connect to all other dimensions and realms. Earth is the anchor and the gateway. Being fully grounded with her, being soul and spirit connected to your physical body and her Being, is the gateway for the Birth of the Divine Human. Earth is where the physical and spiritual meet. It is where we are born, and how we are re-born.

Earth is not in isolation from us or the rest of the universe. She is a living part of our Human Blueprint. It is vital to connect and ground yourself into your soul signature which embraces and includes the earth as part of itself. The action of the Divine happens on earth. In India there is a saying: 'God's work is done by God's servants, humans on earth'. God needs us to do this work here. Earth is our support, and we need to give and receive from the earth so we can both blossom.

The Divine Human living on the 5th Dimensional earth is being birthed NOW. The Fifth Dimension is a dimension of love, wisdom and non-duality that is our innate essence. It holds no judgment or conflict, and is the very substance of the peace of love. To embody this in birthing involves the communion of your physical body, your auric fields and your soul with Earth's physical body, her auric fields and her soul.

SOME SIMPLE WAYS TO COMMUNE WITH EARTH and THE ELEMENTS

Earth is the basis, the home for all the waters, the air we breathe, the earth we stand on, the fire we use and the space that contains it all. In pregnancy, birth and life itself, attuning to all these elements is crucial to allow us to embody ourselves, and for our child to embody.

- Walk, sit, lie barefoot on the earth daily for at least 15 minutes
- Spend time quietly in nature doing nothing
- Place your womb on the Earth and breathe into her core and back.
- Breathe through your womb and feet down into her, and back up from the womb of Earth into your feet and womb
- Bury yourself in the earth and sand, like you did when you were a child
- Attune yourself to Earth's Core/electromagnetic fields through meditations
- Bathe regularly in oceans, rivers or lakes
- Sun gaze, for the Sun is Earth's Partner
- Breath fresh air out in nature
- Moon bathe
- Rest in the spaciousness with your baby whilst you are on the earth.
- Work with sacred sites

Specific geographical locations or sacred sites are where fifth dimensional Earth is easily accessible, and these sites are potent multidimensional portals. These most potent of these sites are in nature, and have a particular quality of refined and full spectrum light to them that is unmistakably 5th dimensional.

OUR BODY, HER BODY: THE 7 GATES of the EARTH

As long as we inhabit our earthly bodies we are intimately connected to the body of the Earth, our Earthly home. In this Design, our spirits and our souls also intimately connect, feed and are nurtured by her. Both of us have chosen this as part of our mutual covenant.

The 7 Gates of Earth are Openings into Earth that mirror a woman's own 7 Gates (the gateways to her womb-soul) in her body. Just as we have chakras, meridians and leylines, so too does the earth. Our very own Feminine Body is mirrored on the earth.

Her 7 Gates are found all over the globe, in every continent, and have been a guarded secret in many Tantric and indigenous societies worldwide. They are found in some well known Goddess sites, and some lesser known places that only a handful of people have the responsibility to access. Like a woman, the entrance into her holy of holies, the Womb, is only granted to those who are truly loving, wise and sovereignly empowered.

Visiting these sites is an opportunity to give and receive love with her: not just to take and be nurtured, but also to give, to enter into the Sacred Hoop of Life, where we are the interface between the heavens and the earth through our bodies and souls. Earth is our anchor for the Sacred Hoop of the Web of Life, and in fully including her we also include a part of ourselves.

Connecting our Seven Gates (see Womb Consciousness section) to the Seven Gates of the Earth opens us into a template of wholeness. Just as Earth holds this Divine imprint for each of us, so do we hold it for her. Our Gates, when open, become keys for our own AND her awakening, expansion and fulfillment.

As we engage more through our Gates with our sexual energy, our emotions, our consciousness and our physical body in balance with the Earth, her field awakens and expands. This vital, living exchange co-creates harmony and abundance, fueling our own living interface with the Earth. This was regularly practiced in the past by our ancestors.

We belong to the web of life, in the very fabric of our beings, in the very spiraling of our DNA. Ways that we have forgotten and denied this spirit of interconnection, with our parents, families, our sexuality, our own passions, will show up as disconnections in our Yoni Lips: the web or ring will feel fragmented or broken.

Our First Gate of the Yoni Lips and for a man his Lingam Lips is a portal into the web of creation, and our interconnectedness with it. It is how we connect to the Web of Life magnetically, through sexual energy and emotions with our bodies. The strands of this Web are built, fortified, and maintained by the love we give and receive within all our relationships. When our Yoni Lips are healed, open, vitally sensitive and alive, we are more able to engage in a free flow of love through all our relationships that enables us to actualize our humanity.

Earth deeply loves us. Connecting to Earth's Gates is a way we open that channel with her, to more deeply give and receive love and embody ourselves. When we live in disconnect from Earth and this source of sustaining love, we cut ourselves off from much magnetic sustenance, for our bodies and souls. Sexuality wed with love, awareness and healing help repair the split between Earth and the masculine/feminine energies in each individual.

THE 7 WELLS of the EARTH

Holy Wells and Sacred Springs are natural interfaces to the earth's magnetic field. These ancient Wells were naturally formed, not man made. Returning to our innate connection through water allows us to conduct all parts of ourselves, especially our emotions, which are how our souls feel, operate and communicate on a causal level with others.

Holy Wells have long been known to be Oracles of The Goddess, of Earth, of Feminine Wisdom and Intelligences. Wells are portals into the consciousness of Earth and entrances into the various realms and inhabitants of earth. Wells reveal the conducting abilities of water and minerals, providing an interface to the Devic realms and their consciousness, support and intelligence.

Wells mark the 7 Gates of the Earth, just as each woman has 7 Gates in our own body. The 7 Gates mark stages of our journey into embodying the soul through opening fully to our magnetic, emotional, sexual self. The 7 Wells of Earth help connect us to the magnetic web of life. Each Well is a portal into all the Wells, for they are an interconnected Web of Life, Water and Magnetic Consciousness.

Each Well is twinned with a Celestial Stargate. They were created together, and are intimately intertwined. Stargates are doorways through dimensions of time and space. Specific wells are directly attuned to the frequencies and qualities of these stargates. Earth's field is a harmonic orchestration of all these frequencies mapped in the stars and on earth. Earth maps out the Galaxy in her body through her feeling waters.

Well and Stargate are One Consciousness. They provide essential polarities for each other, for Earth, and for humanity, to align themselves into magnetic consciousness, flow and feminine wisdom, nurturance, dimensional travel and healing. Well and Stargate can connect us to different parts of ourselves and the galaxy. In visiting an Earth Well we can connect to the Celestial Stargate and the vastness of the cosmos and ourselves. Well and Stargate are vortexes, and contain a center point. Where the waters emerge from the earth, a vortex is created with the stargate emanation.

Each Well has a female Guardian to protect the well, to give guidance as an Oracle to those who come to her, and to help us connect to Earth's magnetic consciousness through our own magnetic self. We may meet forgotten aspects of ourselves in these wells that may be fragmented, lost or wounded. Great wisdom and openings to your essential magnetic self can reveal in these Wells.

They can also stimulate and show us where we have neglected or over worked our electric, masculine self. The feminine magnetic fields of Earth have been tampered with, abused and over ridden in favor of the electric masculine fields, which have become emotionally imbalanced and rely too much on the mind, technology and industrial processes without consideration of the organic feminine or Earth herself. When we are too Yang, Yin retreats and becomes wounded.

Connecting to the 7 Wells of Earth and their pure magnetic field helps us feel our magnetic souls and Pure Feminine. One aspect of the 'Dark Goddess 'that needs reclaiming is how women throughout the ages have disconnected from their own magnetic selves through pain, fear, revenge and loss. Many spirits are stuck in these reoccurring patterns and limited possibilities, which create a specific grid matrix around the earth.

Staying in this grid removes us from a felt sense of where we have come from, our primordial origins and our celestial connections. Humility and causal wound healing stops this vicious cycle from perpetuating with men and in competition with other women.

Holy Wells have traditionally been used as communication portals between human, Earth, Devic, and Celestial. Their magnetic spheres of influence create a Sacred Hoop of Interconnection. There is one main Well that connects to the core of Earth in each continent, but through the holographic network you can connect to the core through any of the seven principal Wells.

When visiting a Well, sprinkle salt around it. Pass some salt through a candle flame; it helps to ionize/ trigger a response in the atmosphere around the Well. This will help make the connections, grounding and anchoring of your meditation or ceremony there more potent and available to you, the Devas there, and the Earth's field. This will generally take about 2 days to be absorbed into the earth's fields.

In Her Arms

When our circle is broken,
When we feel less than whole,
When the sadness is heavy
On our hearts and we
Can't seem to find lightness beyond the
Gravity of grief.

She Waits,
Whispers,
Watches....

"Come to me child. breathe in my bosom,
rest your body on my earth,
Fall apart in my arms,
Be whole-ed in my holding.
The pieces will come together,
of their own time,
their own knowing,
their own place,
but first you must
come undone.

It is here you are safe,
To dive down
to the bottom of your silent ocean
And remember the shiny piece of yourself,
You let drop,
A long time ago."

And somehow,
we are rearranged,
sorted,
strengthened,
lightened,
and blessed.
Before she raises us up from the depths,
to go on,
about our Way.

THE UNITY GRID of EARTH

We all have our own unique connections to the magnetic Grids of Earth, and each species also has its own unique Grid around Earth. In our own unique grid network or unique web of life within the Grids of Earth, we find our magnetic memories and unique affiliations, connections and recordings. Earth's Fields maintain intricate webs of billions of grids connecting to billions of beings. This incredible latticework helps guide all species on earth, during which time they will enter different grid works depending on their level of evolution.

Each of humanity's major emotions also has its own grid network within the larger Grids of Earth. For example, there is a Shame Grid, an Anger Grid, just as there is a Compassion Grid, a Joy Grid. Each of us cord into specific grids based on our own Law of Attraction, our conditioning, DNA and emotional states. Some of these grids are stronger than others: for example, the Fear Grid is fueled by more people than the Compassion Grid.

Each of these Grids have specific guardians to them, which are detailed in ancient texts such as The Tibetan Book of the Dead, The Egyptian Book of Living and Dying, and the Archons of the Gnostic Gospels. When we have felt and released these emotions from ourselves and de-corded from these Grids, we are free to create our life with a much broader spectrum of love, of possibility, of intimacy within the high frequency of the Unity Grid.

Our unique grid work determines which country and places we resonate with. We will intuitively know what this is for us, with the science of astro-cartography and our own physical travels around different places on Earth ascertaining the rest. Our unique grid work also weaves us into the solar system and Galaxy through our own unique series of filters and guideposts that determine our solar, galactic and universal orientation points and 'home' stars, or StarSeed Origins.

The Unity Grid is a specific high frequency geometric Grid that circles round Earth's Body. Its frequency and blueprint is compassion and love, and it is an access point to profound wisdom and our multidimensional self. The Unity Grid is the highest frequency field around Earth, with there being three different geometric fields or three different modulating harmonic layers to Earth's Grids, all of which contain information, knowledge and functions of differing degrees.

All 3 of Earth's Fields create a living, organic matrix of consciousness that we interact with. Each of these three layers hold specific functions, and resonate to different people at different times depending on their level of consciousness and their soul purpose. All three Grids are encased within one another. They expand and contract, they are alive, they 'breathe'. Each of the greater complex grid geometries contains the one below it.

Earth's Grids connect her to the Sun, the planets and the stars, modulating incoming waves of solar-galactic light, as well as sending out energies through her ley-line system. The

Grids are two-way conductors and transmitters. It aligns humanity to Earth, and as such is a golden Key for Communion with Earth and beyond.

The Unity Grid is increasing in frequency as the other magnetic fields weaken. In quantum physics, all of creation is simultaneously Field, Wave and Particle. In Earth's Field structure, the Wave are the energies coming into earth and leaving earth, connecting to the Wave of Light creating our Solar system, Galaxy and entire universe. This Wave that Earth is part of is part of One Wave of Shakti.

The Spirit of Earth, Shekinah, the Divine Mother, are all part of One Wave. They are not separate, as we have been led to believe. In this Union is where the solid ground for the birth of the Divine Human happens. This is the Queendom, where the actions of the Divine on earth happen. It feels like love in action.

This Feminine Trinity of Creation brings the magnetic waves of Creation into its right harmony into us, as particles of the Whole, through our bodies. We are one part of it, and all of it at the same time.

All three layers of Earth's Spirit Body or Auric Field are formed, created and emanated from Her spinning crystal core, Her womb. 11This is how our spirit-auric body operates, emanating from our soul, just on a different scale. She mirrors our own Design. Our auric body emanates from our soul, and is a direct reflection of the state of our soul. It is through our auric field that other people and creatures first feel and sense us, and how we feel and sense others initially.

Each layer of Earth's Grids have specific devas or guardians looking after them, with their own unique gifts and responsibilities. Some of these beings look after specific geographical locations and sacred sites, some monitor certain states of consciousness, others are here to regulate electromagnetic flows, others are Guardians to allow or bar people from entering or becoming aware of certain sites or knowledge. It is a vast, living system, and everything is moving and dynamic.

Many people mistake these individual beings for Earth herself. Earth's voice is vast and feeling and quite different to the voices of guardians devas. It is an innate feeling and Communion, deeper and more permeating on a core level than the other beings, and more natural. This is Communion more than communication, IF you are resonating soul-to-soul, rather than mind.

Our physical and spirit bodies contain, and are made from, the crystal and mineral frequencies of Earth. This has evolved over time due to natural DNA mutations created by the tangible substance of love found in the higher frequencies of the Unity Grid. Specific geometries and harmonics (which create the infrastructure of all vibrating forms) in the

---

[11] . *Throughout history, these Fields have also been modulated by advanced Beings who understood The Laws of Vibration and utilized them accordingly.*

Unity Grid are interwoven and encoded within our very own DNA. This gives us an innate access to the Unity Grids once we have cleared our own veils enough to do so.

In one sense, Earth is already within us.

Our own auric bodies, composed of our electro-magnetic fields, are innately and indivisibly twinned with Earth's Fields. Both twin sets of fields are affected by solar flare and cosmic ray activity, which affect and change the grid lines within Earth. With these increases in electro-magnetic activity, deeper clearing of genetic and ancestral distortions can occur, allowing healing to occur faster.

These changes are being made on a cellular level within the foundations of ALL matter, which means the vibratory rate of matter itself is rising, as seen in the increase in the frequency of the Schumann Resonance. This quickening of vibration within matter has been happening for many years, as initially embodied by Sri Aurobindo and his partner, The Mother.

These changes are preparing the way for a genetic mutation to occur within the human race, potentially raising us into a new species. This genetic mutation will occur because of our ever-deepening communion with Earth, that aspect of ourselves in form. Within us, these changes create an increase in "ascension' symptoms, emotional conflicts and health issues. This is why we need to focus, ground, connect and attune to the Grids to assist us in the assimilation process.

When we attune to the Grids on a deeper level, our electromagnetic field adjusts and our physical body tries to cope with this on a cellular level. By attuning to the Grids now, you will support this process, and heal by Embodying yourself here and now. If you clear your own mental and emotional veils, you can become fully connected with these Grids, and the incoming waves of photonic light that are modulated by the Grids around the planet so they can come to us safely.

If these fields were not there, we would be fried by the power of the many incoming energies. The Unity Grids step down energy so that we can safely and effectively use and work with it. They are a conductor.

BIOSPHERIC WAVE

The brain resonates with electrical frequencies that also occur in the differing energy fields of the planet.[12] The connection between Earth frequencies and our own Alpha brainwaves enable us to call the Earth "Mother" for the strands of vibration that interweave us both are like an umbilical cord.

---

[12] For more information see Elkingtons "In the name of the Gods."

Within this resonance is held memory – memory of all that has happened on Earth, as well as a communication wave that can be harnessed when we are in the heightened vibratory states of ecstasy and rapture, group consciousness, loving sexual union and divine love.

When we enact rites of connection and resonance in sacred sites in these heightened states, we can initiate a biospheric wave, whereby all participants enter a one pointed consciousness; when more than one person is gathered in the same focus. Our ancestors used this energy to maintain the living link between them, the Earth, and the Cosmos, enabling them to access resonant information about the nature of life itself. This information never needed to be written down, as it is (still) holographically stored in wavebands in the earths fields vibrating at a high frequency.

SACRED SITES

The easiest way to access this is to connect to the guardians of sacred sites and raise our vibration, for then doors of perception open into the naturally occurring webs and waves of vibration that compose our reality and Earth.13 There are many geographical sites on Earth that serve as nodes of the Unity Grids. These sacred sites hold concentrated levels of earth energy, crystalline energy, telluric energy, and are where multiple magnetic and electric ley-lines converge to form potent arenas of energy, wisdom and influence.

Sacred Feminine Earth sites will often have a deep connection to water through holy wells, underground reservoirs and streams. Certain sacred sites are portals where incoming solar and galactic rays intersect with Earths Fields in powerful ways, as NASA has recently discovered. For example, various 'Temples of the Sun' worldwide (Mexico, Bolivia, Egypt) were built on these sites and still exist today.

In these places lie the power stations of the Unity Grids. They hold massive energy fields that can span over 30kms in radius on the surface of the earth, and they support the Grid's Matrix on earth and the fields around the earth. These sacred sites have specific sacred geometries and electromagnetic properties, (male and female energies) which allow higher dimensional light, wisdom and energy to flow into the 3D reality, and for information from earth to flow out into the solar system and larger galaxy.

Sacred sites are the organic machinery of the Unity Grid, and when you visit these sites, you can align yourselves to the Grids, anchor yourself to its frequency, and powerfully activate your souls, spirit bodies and physical bodies. To do this correctly, you have to identify what the purpose of the sacred site is; contact its guardians; utilize it through the Laws of Vibration and specific Sound Codes; and fully give and fully receive love as the fuel for the Work you desire to do there.

Sacred Sites can greatly amplify our desires and intentions by focusing the energy of the Earth into a manageable focused form for us to use. When light amplifies, it becomes powerful, just as when love amplifies, it becomes powerful.

From the main power stations of Earth flow numerous channels, like veins that flow off from an artery. These channels branch off and create little power stations or supporting nodes that hold a high concentration of earth energy and light force. This Sacred Hoop, this hologram of creation, is a circuit between Source, Galactic Center, The Earth Grids, the Womb of the Earth and you: and then back again through the Earth Grids, the Womb of the Earth and back to Galactic Center. We are a conduit in this great game of light, and as human beings, we are in the middle of this cycle. We are conduits and bridges to this Grid, and back again.

---

[13] yet which we have forgotten about in our poor imitations of them, as seen in modern day versions of this like the World Wide Web for example

The clearer we are, the more empty we are, the more loving we are, the more we can just allow all these energies to just flow through us; and amazing things can be done through us. As human portals and radiators of this Grid, we can direct energy from the Grid to certain people, places and events. We can also be charged and re-charged with energy as we connect into the Grids and go about our work in the world.

The Grids hold the entire knowledge of the planet and the Living Template for The Fifth Dimensional Earth. We can become energy alchemists and masters of manifestation, unifying all the different parts of us. By connecting to the Grid daily and using this as a bridge into the New Earth Template and Reality, we can make accelerated impact upon our individual growth, earth, the new children and the awakening of ALL humanity.

How can we use the Unity Grids?

Higher dimensional intelligences of many kinds use the Grids because it is the most efficient way to communicate and travel across Earth, into Earth, and leave Earth. In the past this was quite common across the globe, with its vast networked system of sacred sites and buildings that spanned many countries and interconnected civilizations.

The Unity Grids are based solely on love, so you could only send a loving feeling or intention to another. If one were to receive a negative picture, feeling or thought, they would not receive it through the Unity Grids, but through other planes such as the lower astral plane. It could not go through the Unity Grids.

The Unity Grids are a transmittive, conducting and healing medium for feelings and intentions that supports the growth of the soul in love, truth and wisdom. In the Grids, we can instantly connect with other individuals and groups. For example: you can arrange at some point: "Hey, Michael, my friend in LA. Let's sit down at 10 o'clock your time, 6 o'clock my time. Let's meditate together through the Unity Grids and I will transmit to you a feeling, a sacred geometry, a picture, a sentence: whatever it is."

Try this. See what happens!
Then ring them on the phone and say "Hey, what happened for you?' And you will be able to see what you did.

Then, you can do it with groups as well. If your group wants to connect to another group to do something, it can be done through the organic mechanisms of the Unity Grids.

You can develop telepathic communication and skills of expanded consciousness into the fourth dimension, the fluid nature of time, and the fifth dimension, the activated heart soul. So, what this means is that you are extending your consciousness and you can play with that. You can refine and develop these skills if you want to. It is like the Internet, but you don't need anything external, you just sit down and go into your heart and the Grids: that is it.

To fully access the Grids usually takes training, healing, an increase in your personal vibration and an increase in the amount of love you are living and consciously holding. Specific spiritual technologies can quickly take one into Earth's Grids, yet once you are granted fuller access, one realizes it is a responsibility. This responsibility is not just for yourself but also for others: to not create any further distortion, and only to share and transmit what is good, holy, true and beautiful into the Grids.

Once you have clear communion and resonance in your body, soul and womb with Earth, and you trust it, communication with the Grids and Earth will become fast, even instant.

The Unity Grids can be used as entry and exit points for inter dimensional travel. Through the Grids, which hold all the wisdom of the planet, you can access any knowledge anytime, if you want. As you connect more into the Unity Grid, through meditation, prayer, infusions, healings, sacred site Communions, your vibration rises and you become more of whom you are.

To co-create with the Divine on Earth is the ultimate purpose for the Grids. All other purposes are steps to this original purpose: to feel this harmony and unconditional love.

THE EARTH HUMAN

Earth and her sacred sites are a Map of the stars carved onto Earth. As above, so below. Throughout history this has been widely acknowledged by different sacred cultures across the world, from the River Nile and Pyramids mapping out the Milky Way and Orion, to the Great Bear Constellation being mapped onto France and Spain, to myriads of other sacred sites worldwide mapping out the stars ON EARTH. They are a direct reflection of each other in holographic form.

As humans, we are a literal map of the stars. Earth and the Galaxy are contained within us. We are the Universal Human containing all the codes of life within us: all stars, all planets, all galaxies, all the life streams and life codes of DNA. Everything ever created lies within us in seed holographic form.

Earth is one of the pillars of this Wisdom, and how to practically experience it, utilize it and embody it. Indeed, we cannot access the fullness of Earth and our own Human Blueprint without having a Galactic Connection, and vice versa. We cannot fully access Galactic Intelligence without having profound communion with the Earth.

Earth is the centerpiece of this Galaxy, a Seed Point of Emanation and Creation. Within her Core or Womb she holds the holographic library databank of all Creation itself. She is Being and Doing far more than just working with humanity. Earth is far more important than just a home for a few earth bound species, as compared to the millions of species in our Galaxy ALONE. Many beings are here on earth not to have the human experience, but to work for their civilization, planet or Galaxy with their agendas and desire for growth or destruction.

Sacred geometry is the fabric of the Unity Grids higher dimensional consciousness, and the Grids contain the energy patterns of Life itself. All is contained right here. This is known to many civilizations in this Universe, who utilize Earth for this purpose. Her Core-Womb contains a quantum supercomputer: a place where all Programs for earth, humanity and all its timelines, all possibilities and all outcomes for humanity are held and stored.

Certain high frequency beings can enter her Womb Core and insert, release and even delete old programs. They can change timelines, alter outcomes, bring forth stored information to help others, seed new programs that will influence the entire body of humanity and this Galaxy, and even create new ways of Being.

A possibility held in Earth's Womb that has still not yet been realized is for groups of humans to co-create with Earth and Divine Intelligence new futures, new creations, new timelines, new outcomes and new ways of being. We can channel great flows of energy through prayer, focused meditation and synchronized ecstatic states to create powerful openings for the entire collective of humanity. When a whole high frequency group of humans goes into ecstasy with deep heartful desire and intention, this is when big things happen.

This is important, as the New Children arriving on earth will be able to do this, and will be able to access Earth's Core much more than present day humanity. They will need to, in order to anchor and ground themselves here, and help support humanity into its next octave of evolution.

Your own frequency is required to rise to enter into the Unity Grids. Each time you tap into the grids, it activates you and itself in the process. The more you use it, the better it is for you, the better it is for the planet, the better it is for all humanity, because it becomes more available for everyone; it is a win-win-win situation for everyone.

Understand that this is our Divine Human Blueprint. Through the Unity Grids, we can simultaneously activate ourselves and the Earth Brain, becoming loving, channeling columns of light, connecting in one synergetic field of ecstasy. Each conscious participant is a vortex, a pulsing, brilliant point of light shining forth, bursting light, co-creating the frequency of the New Earth for the highest good.

EARTH AND BIRTHING

When a soul can incarnate intact, meaning through the journey of conception, gestation and birth they assimilate the structure of their soul into their bodily form, they are born with a remembrance of Source and do not undergo so much of the amnesia of forgetting who they are and why they have come to Earth. Most of us were born unto this world in amnesia, meaning we had to move through years of healing, remembering, and regathering aspects of our soul to come to a place within us that could take responsibility for our choice to be here.

Many of the children incarnating at this time have the potential to incarnate intact, a process that is greatly aided by women who are healing and activating their magnetic, sensual, feminine selves and opening their wombs into embodiment, and by men who are heart and sexually connected, sensitive and wise enough to help guide this process.

The journey of a soul onto earth from Source is guided by a navigational system of stargates in our Galaxy to align baby's soul into the mother's womb onto earth. These stargates are held in stars such as Sirius, the Pleiades, Antares, Arcturus and many more.

The irresistible focus and magnetic center of attraction of baby's journey is Earth's magnetic core/womb and the magnetic core/womb of the human mother. The more open the magnetic channels are in a woman, the more she is connected to Earth, the more easily a soul can cohesively and fully arrive onto Earth.

In the moment of conception, sperm enters ovum, literally releasing a shower of sparks of light. (This has been recently filmed.) This is the moment we as a soul 'spark' our own freewill into physical individuation. It is our individuation that will lead us to at-one-ment in Love, the total return to Source.

Souls choose to come to earth to evolve, as Earth is an accelerated medium for evolution. The intensity and friction of opposites creates a perfect tension for rapid awakening. When we access this moment of freewill choice to incarnate on Earth, we become empowered. We embrace all the lessons and gifts earthly life is affording us, and we more efficiently heal and move toward enacting our soul's purpose.

For those choosing to consciously conceive through an open womb in connection to Earth and the Divine, we are offered a priceless opportunity for ourselves and our children to embody in this earthly realm firmly connected to soul's purpose, innate joy and love, and an expanded sense of identity beyond just the body.

A woman who has a strong connection to Earth and has her own magnetics activated will consciously communicate with the soul of her child early on in the gestation process, thus drawing aspects of her baby closer into form. Aspects of the soul will continue to arrive through various star gates as she moves closer to birth. The power and potency of the vortex her womb becomes amidst the rushes of labour becomes a superconductor that magnetizes the remaining aspects of baby's soul through her 7 Gates into her womb and Earth's Field's.

Earth holds the map or key for our total embodiment as a human soul. As a soul moves through these portals toward earth, they begin to attenuate to Earth's frequency. Each stargate provides an ordering geometric pattern for the incoming soul, a systematic framework for the organization of consciousness in your body and your child's body to birth itself blissfully on earth.

PRACTICE: THE WOMB EARTH PULSE

Earth's Womb, the crystalline Core Center of the earth, is innately connected to our own wombs and to the Galactic Center. When we lie on the earth and allow the magnetics of our own womb to connect to the magnetics of Earth and her womb, we connect into a matrix that anchors us beyond our personal struggles and stories into a larger context. In this connection we can let go of the tensions and accumulations that have taken us out of our innate flow. We can open and soften into the flow of life and love inherent in the moment.

The following practice is a way for women and men to align and connect to Earths core womb. In doing this we open ourselves as vessels for the Divine Feminine to express through us in a grounded and integrated way (in relationship to earthly form, through her). This helps seat us firmly in our womanhood, a bridge between heaven and earth.

1. Lay face down on the earth. Take a few deep breaths, breathing in the smell of the earth and allowing your breath to mingle with her smell, her touch, her taste, her feel, and her breath. Feel your womb/hara rest against her soft earth. Feel how she holds you. Rest, relax and deepen.

2. As you become more still, feel the pulse emanating from your womb/hara. Rest your awareness on this steady rhythm. Breathe out from your womb into her Core. Ask to synchronize your pulse with her pulse. Synchronize with her breath. Spend as long as you like in this space of deep connection.

3. Feel the magnetic connection between your center and hers. Once you are anchored in this synchronized womb/hara Earth pulse, breathe Earth's energy from her womb core deep into your womb/hara 12 times.

4. Breathe this energy from your womb into your heart 12 times.

5. *Beloved Divine Mother, I Love You. Please send me your love. Holy, Beloved, Blessed, Sacred Shekinah, I Love You. Please send me your love. Beloved Mother Earth, I Love You. Please send me Your Love. Beloved Mother, help me have compassion for all souls, as You do. Have compassion on me. Give me shelter and holy rest within You. Please help me be as heroically patient and radiantly kind as You. I love You. Please send me your love.*

6. Now breathe from Earth's Core into your womb-hara, heart, into your third eye 12 times. Stay in this flow as long as you feel.

7. Now, Breathe from your third eye down into the core of Earth. Rest in the flow of rejuvenation and deep resonant harmony for as long as you feel.

8. When you feel complete, extend your heart to the Earth, sending her your love, and thanking her for her love.

EARTH HEART CONNECTION

To Attune in Love to Earth in 2 minutes.

Feel, from your heart, a beautiful place in nature that is your sacred site and power spot, the place in nature you most resonate with: a river, a park, a forest, a sacred site, the one that comes to you immediately. Feel/ See the details: the beach, the ocean, trees, animals, birds, scenery and energy of the place itself.

Feel the love, the gratitude, the appreciation that you have for Mother Earth. Keep deepening this experience of love and say:
"Beloved Mother Earth, I love you, I love you!"

Once you feel this, send your love through your heart and womb directly down into the Womb of the Earth, and say:
"Beloved Mother Earth, please send me your Love."

Just wait for Mother Earth to send her love back to you. When you feel this love, let it move throughout your heart, your soul, your womb, your body.

Thank you to Drunvalo Melchizedek for the first part of this Meditation.

WOMB CONSCIOUSNESS

Womb consciousness holds the unified feminine embodied love, wisdom and power. It embodies the most tender and human to the most exalted and Divine. It is vastness, it is intimate. It is silent, it is sound. It is the space from which we are born and the ground to which we long to return. It is love, it is power, it is wisdom expressed through the feminine essence, body and soul.

The Womb harmonizes, heals, holds, harbors. It holds and births continual fractals and octaves of evolution. It is a container for alchemy, the vessel for Divine Embodiment. It is the black, velvety recess of nothingness that holds all of us.

It is a space within our own uterus, a spiraling array nested deep in our bellies. It is the means of continued evolution for our species. It is the gateway to our experience of life, and of awakening beyond time and space. It builds us into human form, and dissolves us into pure consciousness.

We are all birthed from the womb, yet it is one of the least known parts of ourselves. It holds the greatest power a woman possesses: the powers to nurture, grow, and create life, not just through physical birth *but on many other levels of consciousness as well.* The very power of creation, what gives birth to universes and children, planets and souls, is what each woman carries within her, yet she rarely accesses this, even in the process of giving physical birth.

Womb Consciousness is a state of being that births *us, and* that can birth a new reality. The womb is a woman's feminine core, the generator of tremendous creative potential, vitality, boundless well-being, sensual power, deeper consciousness and manifestation. It is the feminine foundation that enables the heart to flower and bloom open as a woman, not in a mans idea of it or a male pathway.

As women, we have become divorced from the womb, our primal center of gravity, and have forgotten who we are and how to live in alignment with our souls, our Earth, our Creator, and sexuality and our very feminine foundation. Instead, we try to compete on masculine terms to get by in the world of today. The flowering of the feminine rose has become dwarfed by the pillar of the masculine, instead of each exalting the other, side by side in harmony.

In this forgetting, men too have forgotten how to relate fully to the feminine and how to be truly human, building walls of denial, rationalization, intellectual abstraction, justification and anger around the wounds that have been created by this separation.

A woman's center is in her magnetic foundation of womb-heart, not her head. She lives on Earth, connected through relationship, not in an abstract concept of what life is. When a woman's center is in her head, she suffers and becomes disempowered, trying to compete with men, losing connection with her feminine essence.

As our center of gravity shifts to the womb, sadness, fear and pain well up within us as we emotionally Realize this. We start to shift our centers of gravity and resonance back to our primal center, the source of our joy and womanhood. This then allows the heart to flower, deeply and organically, flowing in spontaneity, emanating from the web of life, from all that nurtures and supports life.

All life benefits when we come to love our wombs and live from this truth. For the womb is the generator and keeper of Life, the source of full feminine expression. An awakened, soul conscious, and egalitarian society is built on the foundation of the womb that honors life in all its forms. The Soul's Design for Birthing is activated and manifested through the organic flowering of the womb and application of its wisdom and rhythms.

With enough open wombs, no wars would be fought, for the empowered, life-affirming woman shares the sustaining nurturing power of life. The strength and depth of the womb provides the security and foundation deep within you to be able to express yourself freely through the heart. The head and heart work within grounded foundations sunk deep within the womb. The head by itself cannot come into the heart. The womb is required for a woman, just as the hara is for a man, to bring down the mind into your center of gravity, to embody and be here now, *and then* the mind can act as a true servant of the heart.

The womb is autonomous, has a voice of its own, and can respond depending on what is required in each moment. The womb's voice is wise, powerful, and primordial. It is sunk deep into the tap roots of your feminine. *Womb holds, heart gives*. Heart's desire is to unify and bring things together—to end division. The womb holds the space, the container, the crucible for this to happen, for this to birth into manifestation.

Heart manifests womb, and womb holds heart in a safe, secure space, allowing the heart to go deeper into its layers rather than just being on the surface. The womb holds the steadiness, the trust, an unwavering center and ground, steady, still, reliable—a well of creation.

With this foundation the heart feels safe and secure, feeling its innate and natural ground to lean, rest and rely upon, a place to arise from in wisdom and strength, able to see clearly and give accordingly to what is the highest potential in the moment.

One can say that the womb is the banks of the river, and the heart *is* the river. The womb is the container for the alchemy of love and sacred union in relationship to occur. Mind is the servant of womb-heart, designed to carry out its orders.

The heart is incomplete without the maturity of the womb. The womb establishes itself deep within you as a feeling-voice of character, clarity and inner guidance, housing the ground upon which you may come to take solace and guidance throughout life. You have within you this reliable source, this inner guru. The Womb holds your original voice, the voice that will never betray you and will always lead you to the truth of love in action, the being of joy, and peace: The Voice of Life itself.

With the resurrection of the womb comes the resurrection of man. Man finds his timeless, primordial identity when he comes into harmony with the clear and activated womb-heart.

BECOMING WOMB CONSCIOUS: THE THRONE of YOUR WOMB

Your pelvic bowl holds your womb and magnetic foundation in place. Emotional blocks, past history, sexual armoring and numbness in a woman's womb and pelvic bowl determines whether or not she is in her body *emotionally and soulfully*. This determines the depth of loving sexual pleasure you can experience, which increases with loving emotion and sensation permeating the whole bowl.

When a woman releases the emotions and physical effects of these emotions stored in her womb-pelvic region and finds her magnetic ground again, she becomes powerful, open, soft, anchored and in her center, leading to more feeling, sensation and joy. An open, connected pelvic bowl in harmony with the womb makes a vibrant woman. The pelvic bowl is the ROOT PLACE in the female body, the grounding of your womb core.

Close your eyes and visualize your pelvic bowl. Place your fingertips on your pubic bone beneath your womb. Move your awareness here. Breathe deeply into here 5 times.

Feel the pubic bone connect to the triangular sacrum bone through the hammock of the perineum. Place one of your palms over your sacrum. Allow your pelvic bowl to settle into this support. Breathe deeply 5 times and feel here. Allow whatever physical sensations, emotions, thoughts, pictures, memories to arise.

Feel how the inner curve of your pelvis forms a supportive bowl under your womb, your centre. Rest here and breathe into, and all around, your bowl. Allow physical sensations, emotions, thoughts, pictures or memories to arise.

Sense the spaciousness within your bowl. Sense the energetic shape of what is inside your pelvic bowl. Your Womb! Start visualizing this, as you would hold a bowl in your hands. Breathe into this creative well in your core, which has a concentrated energy in the centre. Drop into this concentrated, dark, inviting centre of your gravity.

Sense, on either side of your womb, the radiance, light, warmth and power of your ovaries shining forth. Breathe red, then black, then white deeply into them.

Focus on the diamond base of your pelvis. It is outlined by the tip of your tailbone, pubic bone and the two sits bones on either side of the diamond. Nestled within the centre of this diamond lies your yoni passageway.

How does your yoni feel? What are you presently releasing or bringing in? Is there tension? Whatever comes up, acknowledge and release.

Picture the base and front of your bowl, your yoni lips. Towards the front of your body is your clitoris. Feel your clitoris.

Picture the back of your bowl. Toward the back of your root, below your yoni opening, lies your anus. Between these two openings is your perineum. Touch it. It immediately grounds you and connects your root to earth's energy. Is that dynamic point holding tension and grounding your root?

Locate your pubic bone and coccyx at the front and back of your pelvic ring. See a group of muscles covering this entire ring at the base of your pelvis.

This is your pelvic floor, supporting your magnetic center and magnetic foundation, your core, your sexual openness, sensation, feelings and pleasure. Your womb, yoni and anal openings all pass through your pelvic floor. Breathe deeply into it. What pictures, feelings come to the fore?

Find the top of your pubic bone in the front of your pelvis. Imagine a place just behind it that can be felt through your yoni. This is your G-spot. Breathe deeply into it a few times. The g-spot opens through a deep felt sense of gratitude. Can you feel gratitude for your womb, your life, the people in your life?

Take some deep breaths into your whole pelvic bowl. Visualize it filled with soft pink, orange and gold.

Imagine the golden warmth of sunlight touching, healing, energizing and filling your center.

HEALING THE WOMB

The womb woman is empowered, embodying her soul here and now with the body. This woman manifests her soul mission, and has intimate, fulfilling sacred relationships, engaged in the spontaneous joy of life. Without reservation or hesitation, without compromise, this woman uses her sexual energy and Shakti to dynamically fuel her evolution, health, service, relationships and lifestyle.

When one discovers the womb and what it does, it is a miraculous moment. Once this light switch is flicked on, there is no turning back because the womb leads us into the vast space of the feminine universe *within*.

It is the basis from which we relate to all life. It leads to clear, present, confident communication and interaction with others. It is an inner knowing and a clear feeling, a deep understanding of how things are.

The womb is each woman's own Grail, her own Oracle, her own Guru within her, steering us to answers, places and situations we could only have dreamed of before. It helps us rebirth ourselves into the truth and sovereign majesty of our being and what we are here to do in this life.

To have the womb open feels like a precious gift has been given you to treasure. A sacred fire reignites inside of you, a fire that brings power, creation, and passion into your life. It

makes one more able to discern people, places, and situations more clearly AND be more discerning with which man can enter into this, your most consecrated sacred space.
Having the womb open is like having a new stream of vitality pulsing through you. As a result of this newfound virginity and wisdom, a new maturity sprouts into being and one feels truly alive, fertile with possibility.

The womb allows truth to flow freely without attachment to outcome. Once the womb is discovered as an Oracle of truth, it is easy to impart truth without attachment or fear. Discovering this womb intelligence within provides a new way to navigate through life softly, which is a great strength.

A new sense of calmness, rootedness and confidence shines from you, with a knowingness that will scare boys, yet intrigue real men. Compassion and crystal clarity of perception allies with a deep sense of belonging and feeling comfortable in your own skin.

The womb is a cave of pure creativity where we are the creator. The womb is your inner council where you discover your doctor, adviser, confidant, sage, decision-maker and artist. It is so important to know that we can create from this center within us. Once the womb is discovered and embodied, we enter a sacred space of self-responsibility, which takes us from playing victim to playing creator, our true authentic self.

As the womb opens a sense of beauty and harmony is restored into one's being, a key to experiencing a beautiful inner reality that is not dependent on anyone else, that has always been innately yours.

Discovering the womb's power and voice, and taking the first steps to open its rich and fertile soil, is essential for every woman and man who want to have a child. The healed womb is the ideal container for your child to enter this world and for all of you to take your Rite of Passage Initiation into the deeper masculine and feminine.

Womb opening and connecting to the Heart is a discovering, an unveiling, and a Remembering. It is the true reference point and foundation for a woman to come from in all parts of her life. It gives a woman back her true house, her place of being, her *inner power spot*, so she may rise into the heart with strong-rooted foundations of deep safety, security and unbroken nourishment. It is the rock upon which women are built.

The womb holds deep silence, the sound knowledge of truth, and the loving embrace that holds a woman together. When all else fails in life, the womb remains as the pillar to lean against, the rock to hold on to, and arms to cry in.

To live with your womb open brings you a gift and state of being that was previously unknown. You feel beautiful, gorgeous, rich, and sensual without the "edge" of threat perceived from other women. You are non-threatening in your beauty and happiness within your body. You ooze nature, life, promise and joy.

Your womb is vast, full of a silence brimming and humming with the light of all creation. It includes the world, but is not of the world. It reaches all the way into the Galactic Center. It encompasses all living, birthing, and dying. Each woman has a precious window into the whole process of creation within her!

In the process of healing the womb, many emotions can come up, for She contains mother and child, birth and death, ancient and unborn. Without the open womb, life will only exist, not be lived. It simply has to be known, discovered, and entered. You do not know what you are missing until you have tasted it.

She creates cascading magnetic fields that regenerate yourself and your partner in love making, connecting you to the entire web of life. Imagine you do this and then Consciously Conceive! Moving through pregnancy and childbirth with an awakened womb amplifies the power and presence within your womb tenfold.

Womb sensitivity to feelings, psychic abilities, love, and deeper cosmic understanding and wisdom expand and are more accessible. It is from this cleared womb that your soul purpose will be born.

A vital facet of Womb Opening for parents is this: *a clear and open womb is the channel for the next species of humankind to come through, The New Children of Light.* Giving birth to these master souls here on earth is one of the surest ways to elevate yourself on your own path of growth, as well as all of humankind. Birthing through the open womb is extremely attractive, inviting and welcoming to these Children. Most of them will not choose to come onto earth in any other way.

Clearing and opening the womb is necessary not just for conception of these New Children, but for cocooning them in their early years as well. Once they have left the internal physical womb, they will be continually held and embraced by your womb consciousness energetically. This continued womb connection brings connection and safety to their experience, ensuring they can develop their highly attuned selves and manifest their sense of emotional wholeness without interruption.

Ultimately your womb leads you to the womb of all life, the Universal Womb, from where all life is birthed, and where all life dissolves back into. The Universal Womb is the beginning and end of all universes. It is the place which all life streams from. When you realize this, you can begin to create within the womb, placing heart's desires within it to be birthed through you into the world.

WOMB BREATHING

Womb breathing begins to bring conscious awareness, attention, breath and light into the womb, energizing and focusing her. This also works with men and their *haras*. Womb breathing requires gentle presence from you, done softly with clear intention to soothe and gently open the gateway into the womb. Womb breathing can also help you find answers to questions you may have.

Your womb is normally the size of a pear. Touching and massaging the womb helps you to focus on her. Feelings and emotions may begin to surface at different times in this practice, so be your allowing, open, receptive self and go wherever the practice takes you. Most of all, enjoy! This can be a pleasurable, sensual experience.

1. To begin, find a place and time where you will be undisturbed and feel safe to make sound or rest in silence. Sit comfortably on the floor with the soles of your feet together and your knees spread. This is an important posture that enables you to sit on your throne, centered in your power.

2. Close your eyes, rest your hands over the womb in an inverted triangle, and breathe down into her. Focus and meditate. You may choose to allow sounds from the womb to spontaneously express themselves. Just let go into it. You may be surprised at what she needs to share and say.

3. Lie on your back with feet on the floor and knees bent, as if you were giving birth. Make yourself comfortable with cushions to support your head. Place both hands over the womb and make conscious connection with yourself, your womb, and your breath. Be with your breath, and give it your undivided attention and focus.

4. Begin to bring your focus to your PC muscles (the area between your vagina and anus).

5. Take your time to find these muscles, and then contract them. On a slow rhythmic inhale, squeeze the PC muscles together and suck the breath into the womb. Feel and see the breath as light coming into the womb.
Treat the breath with a quality of preciousness. Imagine light flowing into the womb.

6. Hold the breath in the womb, while squeezing the PC muscles, (as if you were holding in from urinating), and with your hands make slow large circles, clockwise and counterclockwise. As you make circles, feel the light of the breath bathing and suffusing the whole womb. On the exhale, relax the PC muscles, pushing the breath through the PC. As you release the breath, feel the subtlety of the light flowing *out* of the yoni.

7. Feel as if you are making love with yourself and cleansing your womb with golden light. And then again inhale, pulling in the PC, holding the breath in the womb, making circles with your hands.

Do this for 10 minutes. How do you feel?

Now, with your focus and attention on your womb, gently holding her, ask her these questions:

Are you disease-free in your belly, womb, and sexual organs? Have you had any major surgery that involves your belly and womb?

What is your mother's story with her body and sexuality?

Do you suffer from PMS or hormonal imbalances?

Do you feel emotionally clear about your birth story? That is to say, were you born through a cesarean section, through the force of forceps, were you induced or premature, was the umbilical cord tied around your neck, was the birth traumatic, what drugs were used, was your mother in danger, were you adopted?

Do you feel any impact now from your birth story?
Did you ever have an opportunity to grieve an abortion, a miscarriage, or a stillbirth? Have you suffered sexual, emotional, or physical abuse in your life? Are you able to recognize how you may punish yourself by your internal dialogue or your actions?

Do you enjoy making love?
Are you completely open and receptive to being penetrated by a lover?
Do you hold back pleasure or sound when making love?
Are you able to love your body, your womanhood, in total acceptance?
Do you have orgasms? Are your orgasms full-bodied?
Do you trust the masculine totally?
Do you honor your gut feelings and intuition?
Do you get indigestion, stomach upsets, heartburn, period pain, bloating?
Where does fear live in your body? Where does power live in your body?
Do you know what your wounds sound like? Have you let sound out of the dark, hidden places inside? Do you want to?

What happened when you first began to bleed as a young woman? Was your period or moon time celebrated? How do you honor your rites of passage now with your daughters, friends? Do you participate in women's circles or ceremonies? Do you want to? Do you trust, or compete with, other women?

Do you maintain any spiritual practices that cultivate energy in your belly?
Do you breathe rhythmically and deeply? Do you need more energy?

How much bliss and joy do you allow yourself in your everyday activities?
Do you have a love for life on Earth?
What makes you passionate? What inspires you and brings you into the fullness of life?

OPENING THE WOMB

The opening of the womb is an ever-deepening self discovery and journey into growth, generation, creativity, and of birthing your our own wholeness. Embarking on this journey, you start to rediscover your own latent gifts and gain a deeper sensitivity, a deeper softness, a deeper knowing, of what you are here for.

There are many ways to open the womb, using the physical womb as the vehicle to connect to the emotional, and the soul. Raw foods and juices can help flush the womb and the whole system. David Wolfe and Queen Afua are some of the best people to look to for this.

Members of tantric societies used to drink their menstrual blood, boosting estrogen levels and hormones, increasing iron levels, and giving a rush of well-being and vitality. This blood, when combined with other hormones, could lead people to heightened states of consciousness, prophecy and spiritual powers. And it is known that pouring nitrogen-rich menstrual blood on plants helps them grow.

Open the womb and yoni to sunshine. Allow the vital energy of the sun inside you; it is greatly vitalizing. Simply find a private space, take off your underwear, and open your legs out to the sun, placing your hands on the womb to focus your attention there if needed. Just relax, and breathe the sun into your womb. Hands-on healing also works with someone you trust enough to allow to place their hands there.

Spend time in nature placing your womb next to the earth, just allowing yourself to embrace and be embraced by Mother Earth. This is so simple, but something we forget to do, and it only takes a few minutes to reconnect. In fact, it is quite enjoyable! The key is to place awareness on the womb rather than the head every day, as this will tune your awareness into that area.

One has to clear obstacles out of the way to carve more space for the light and life force to reside in your physical womb. As this occurs, your body becomes lighter and more fluid. We spiritualize the body by honoring it. As we honor it, we begin to identify more with the light and life force inherent in the womb and body.

THE PULSE OF THE WOMB

We start to connect more deeply into the womb by feeling the pulse of life force directly in her. Just as you have a heartbeat, so you have a womb beat. This womb–beat awakens when we direct our life force into her.

The heart-beat and womb-beat are the two pulses of a woman. Each needs the other in order for you to become a whole woman, uniting love and depth in your body. As both pulse beats unite, a life-affirming *yes!* pulses through you and a deep sense of comfort, of being held and nurtured by your own innate feminine.

Feeling the pulse of the womb allows that which you have been holding onto to release out of your system, as The Pulse brings to life that which has been stagnant and buried within you. The Pulse is a direct reconnection to your core, clearing negative electrical charges, emotions, memories, traumas, and shocks of the past.

In the past The Pulse was known as *the dragon energy*, the primordial serpent power, raw untamed feminine energy or Shakti, wild and free. Once this aliveness and sensual power is released, It floods the whole system with life flow.

"For most it is not possible to pass alone through this strong, deep, energy, to welcome it, to make love with it. You can't give birth without being in connection. You can't give birth in a state of seclusion, for to give birth means we stay completely in connection with All That Is, with the pain and the death, with the purest joy and love, with it all. When we welcome it, love it, and make love with all parts of being, then a great magic can come true. You can give birth to life "U. W.

Only the connection between the womb and the heart can make this primordial power really live again. Allowing the Pulse to activate and charge through us makes us fluid, able to flow with what is happening without story or belief. The charges dissolve, and blissful joy explodes within us, flooding and connecting our whole being. This is a potent and palpable experience, and really brings us home to the power of the womb and the joy contained within it.

THE ORACLE VOICE OF THE WOMB

The womb is a sanctified, precious space. In ancient times it was known as the *holy of holies*, the inner sanctum where only a True Man could enter to help activate the vast potential that lies within woman. The womb is the heart of the feminine temple, the heart of the feminine vision, the heart of the feminine prophecy and Oracle, guiding the way from darkness into light and from light into darkness.

The womb holds a soft feminine voice. As this voice wakes up from its ancient slumber, it is quiet, hardly recognizable as a voice; and then murmur by murmur, whisper by whisper, it increases in volume. It can be like the wise voice of your grandmother, and it is so familiar you feel "Oh it's me!" And it really is you, the real *you*!

The Oracle Voice of the open womb is a woman's Guru, sage, doctor, most trusted advisor and best friend. It is the womb that is your original voice, separate from the mind, a whole, unique voice, a distinct chord playing in the music that creates a woman's body and soul. It is this chord that holds together a woman; it is the interface, the connector.

Without being fully plugged into the womb there are parts of you that are fragmented, disconnected, and separate. Joining and uniting all the parts of your heart-womb through this focus, this lens, requires conscious effort on your behalf.

Be mindful of the womb as you rise, and as you go to sleep. Check on HER, and make sure she is clear and happy. Run the events, interactions and feelings of the day through the womb, and see what she says. She allows you to respond to life in an authentic, clear, life-enhancing manner.

The womb is a portal of wisdom and will, highly sensitive, a life and voice of its own, with a distinct, clear voice. In following this voice, a woman may initiate shifts, feeling guided into changing her spirituality along with her lifestyle, her diet, her home, changing all the relationships that do not serve her flowering and further unfolding.

The womb opens through Right Relationship. Right Relationship is about knowing who you are, where you are in your souls growth, what you need to grow, what are your strengths and weaknesses, what is your truth right now, and what people you desire to have in your life. In this process of knowing yourself, you learn discernment: you learn who your allies are, or who is feeding off your energy in an unhealthy way.

Energies, people, spirits and even places regularly plug into your womb, like an electrical plug, in many ways in which you have no conscious idea of. Old lovers, deceased people, parents, ancestors, friends, as well as people who wish you no good, can ALL attach to your womb and feed off your vital, life-giving, creative energy.

If we do not know what, and who, we are connecting to in our wombs, we cannot have appropriate boundaries as to what, and who, we connect to. This plugging into our wombs, our centre of life, happens largely subconsciously because we do not know our own womb self. Knowing thy womb is really what the Womb Mandala is about.

If you have Right Relationships, you will feel supported, nurtured, and nurturing in your daily life. You will have a clearer connection to the web of life and will be more able to manifest your heart's passion and desires in a tangible way.

THE OVARIES

The ovaries are biological light generators, giving us vitality, joyful exuberance, a soft yet strong, clear, female essence and life force energy. The ovaries are the essence of femininity.

The ovary energy is the spark of light, spark of life. They weave the nest of the womb, the energetic architecture of the magnetic ground. The womb is the gate way, the ovaries are the impulse, wave of energy that moves one through the experience.

The ovaries are the storehouse for all ancestral information. As our disharmonies and distortions are seen and healed within our entire human ancestry, we change the stored information held in our ovaries. This obviously impacts the genetic inheritance of incoming children.

The awake and alive ovaries feel like deep, warming red wine. They hold the energy of the heart in manifestation when the circuit is clear. They serve to embody and transmit the pure female principle of creation here in the body, here on earth. They allow the heart to fully bring its love and giving into manifestation through the body and DNA.

The ovaries complete the embodiment of the yoni principle in a woman. They revitalize, rejuvenate, and create the actual light body of the yoni. When the ovaries are fully active on all seven levels, then the embodied light that the female principle is, will fully embody the Divine Feminine on earth.

The ovaries, in their circuit of the Queen, generate the light force for the Queen to embody fully into her biology and genetics here on earth. This creation of the Grail Chalice principle on earth allows the feminine magnetics to rest, relax, and come into harmony, both within oneself and in the men surrounding her.

There is a dance between both ovaries. The left is more fire, the right is more white. Ruby and White. They have their different qualities, the fire and the light, and these two qualities have to totally mingle and merge and share all light information, resonances, vibrations, emotions, powers, qualities, wisdom and hormones between each other.

They are distinct, but you cannot separate them. Separating them leads to a great split between love and power, electro and magnetic, or male and female within. The most harmonious way is to work with both together. They will automatically perform their functions with the total circuit that includes the heart.

The whole circuit connected to the ovaries is what helps ground it within the body. It is a series of relationships to the ovaries, yoni lips, clitoris, heart and brain. Each movement or relationship helps ground and complete the other one. It is an internal alchemy.

The true ovary energy is one of vitality and embodied radiance. They hold the energy to attract people and resources into your life, by magnetizing what you desire to you. You become potent, alive, and your inner light shines forth from your body itself.

The true ovary energy is a spark, a transmission of your life force, to actualize in the world. The Ovaries transmit your soul mission ignited. It brings forth purpose, passion, and actualization. From here, we create new life, both with a baby and with other projects we wish to fulfill.

Our embodied soul purpose is carried forth through the true ovary energy, and is birthed into the world. They are transmitters of our true potency as a woman, transmitters of ourselves. They help to birth and embody US into the world. In the true ovary energy, we feel assured, strong yet soft and relaxed in our female identity. We feel proud of our yoni.

We truly appreciate and can freely praise, without ego, the beauty, strength, magnificence and love we have for our yoni, womb and feminine self. We can share this with intimate others without shame or trepidation.
The ovary energy is embodying and relaxing, allowing us to be natural, let down and let go into our pure, essence of womanhood. As the ovary energy is a biological light generator that fuels the heart and womb, it rejuvenates the cells with life force. The true ovary energy is pro life, all inclusive, and all that blocks it is anti life.

When the ovary energy is refined through emotional connection, release and vulnerability (not just chi orientated processes) it becomes a softness and a strength simultaneously. It becomes a fuel for light and innocence, a playfully innocent drive for soul growth. The stronger you become, the gentler you can be.

As a woman heals her ovaries and heart circuit, physical adjustments may happen in the pelvis and sacral area. Pains and aches may arise that no other form of bodywork can address fully. These pains are the false body-spirit attitude relaxing and releasing themselves, and asking for your attention to be placed into your sexual gates to accelerate the healing process.

In the ovary energy, we enjoy connecting more deeply and truthfully with friends, and soul sisters. A sense of true sisterhood helps this energy to bloom and root on earth, in the body, in the webs of interconnection and relationship that define us all.

The ovaries hold a fear of death as well as being generators of light and life. This is their essential polarity. As they are two in nature, the infinity loop between them allows both aspects to freely share with each other, like making love and exchanging your energies.

In this interplay, your latent seeds of creation are ignited, their information shared with the other, and then alchemised into wholeness through becoming integrated within you, through your circuit of heart, hara, amygdala and pineal. They are then transmitted and sent forth into the world. When the ovaries are connected to its circuit, their energy becomes a fuel for vitality, joy, life force and a clear and pure female essence to be exuded.

THE SHADOW of THE OVARIES

What blocks this in modern women? When we use our pure life force for survival, ambition, physical appearance, competitiveness, and pushing our personal agendas, this disrupts the flow from our ovaries. When we allow the deeper feminine aspects of ourselves to be expressed, such as sensuality, vibrancy, compassion, passion, intuition, and creativity to express, we support the healthy flow of energy in our ovaries.

Ovaries are life force generators, and they can be the fuel to sustain us and manifest our soul's purpose in the world. When we don't direct this energy into our passions and desires, and use it solely for 'getting life done,' we can step into the martyr and victim consciousness.

What blocks the ovaries? Deep emotions of jealousy, hatred, martyrdom, and victimhood stemming from unworthiness all block the life enhancing, soul embodying, joyful expression of the ovaries. Sexual abuse, miscarriages, abortions, [14]and painful intimate relationship breakdowns (that have not been resolved and healed in appreciation of the lessons learned and the path you have walked together) also deeply affect the ovaries.

Feelings of loss, grief, abandonment of a significant female or male partner, son or parent can be stored in either the ovaries. The yang ovary denotes the loss of a major male partner, son, or any male the person loved and bonded with. Rejection in the sexual arena is also stored here, and if not resolved feelings of shame and inadequacy and fear of intimacy with the opposite sex can result. The yin ovary indicates the loss of a major female friend, mother, daughter or any female the person was very fond of.

When the ovaries are blocked, our life force is blocked. Pride, fear, hatred of the opposite sex can arise. We may fall into roles of martyr and victim in the outside world, as we have not been a 'woman" in our inner world and in intimacy. Because we feel disconnected to our sensuality and femininity within, we may feel anger or jealousy toward other women who are in touch with this part of themselves.

We may become a slave to the matrix and conform to the sick, imbalanced cultural and relating ways of being accepted by modern society, becoming a people pleaser to try and fit into the disabled view of sex and relationships that are so prevalent amongst polite society today.

The benefit of releasing these emotions is that it helps restore your vitality and life force energies so you have space to flow, and to just be you. In this flow, all we authentically and sincerely desire from our souls can begin to be given to us. Being controlled or smothered by a dominating parent can be imprinted here, impacting the ovaries feeling link to the soul.

---

[14] Miscarriages and abortions also affect the man involved in colluding with the woman who had them.

This can diminish our essential vitality and joy, disembodying us, keeping us in a partial sense of our womanhood, and making us a servant to the opposite sex in order to get their love in a vain attempt to reclaim our own vitality. Fragments of our true feminine self arise here to be recollected in both action and feeling, as we feel into and release emotions of not feeling loved, protected, recognized or heard from childhood and from men.

Reactions in the ovaries vary from fearing men and staying away from intimacy with them, or staying in relationships where you remain in, and even enjoy a subservient position, manipulating the other through hidden resentment, a sense of revenge and guilt/shame.

Emotions and memories of sexual abuse, sex without love, sex with overt aggression and too much lust, as well as emotions of humiliation and shame
(particularly in the sexual arena) are recorded here, along with sadness, grief and emotions of loss and abandonment for the innocent self you once were and which you, somewhere, somehow, wish to reclaim again.

Emotions and drives are the way our reproductive organs guarantee the continuation of the species. When we 'fall in love', many times it has little to do with our heart; it has a lot however to do with the ovaries, and lessons to be learnt. The original illusion of our emotions is "The Other." As babies, we depend on our father "Other" for protection. Later, a similar dependency can be formed with a sexual partner.

PRACTICE: OVARIES CIRCUIT BREATHING

PART 1

Inhale glowing, iridescent, deep wine-red energy deep down into the seed of your ovaries. Do this 6 times. Your ovaries become glowing, iridescent, deep wine-red with each breath.

Inhale shining, glowing, iridescent fluid black energy deeply into the seed of your ovaries, and slowly exhale out, 6 times. Your ovaries become shining, glowing, iridescent fluid black.

Inhale radiant, glowing, iridescent, fluid white energy, and slowly inhale them deeply into the core and seed of your ovaries, then slowly exhale out, 6 times. Your ovaries become radiant, glowing, iridescent, fluid white.

Breathe these cycles of wine red, shining black, and radiant white, twice more.

Now, gently ask your ovaries the following questions. *If you feel any emotions arise, simply breathe and allow yourself to feel them fully.*

Do you ever feel threatened, exposed, and insecure? Do you deal with, and do you handle all the situations life throws at you on an emotional level, rather than just on a mental level? Are you uncomfortable, ashamed and unsure with your sexual expression? Do you hold onto guilt and anger?
Do you have difficulty forgiving, letting go and moving on from past emotional hurts from men? Do you make yourself small and overly 'serviceful' around men? Do you invalidate yourself with others? Do you try and please and placate others? Do you trust your feminine sensuality, vibrancy, intuition, power and gentleness? Are you scared and ashamed of being a powerful woman?

Say: *"Divine Healing Intelligence, I ask You to help me feel and release all feelings of my being ridiculed, humiliated, my shame, my mistrust of men, my fear of not living freely and fully as a woman, and my grief and sadness from my ovaries and soul."*

PART 2

Inhale glowing, iridescent, deep wine-red energy down into the seed of your ovaries 6 times. Inhale shining, glowing, iridescent fluid black energy deeply into the seed of your ovaries, and slowly exhale out, 6 times. Inhale radiant, glowing, iridescent, fluid white energy, deeply into the core of your ovaries, then slowly exhale out, 6 times.

Breathe these cycles of wine red, shining black, and radiant white, twice more.

1.Inhale, and direct the breath down to your ovaries. Exhaling releases accumulated wastes, and if done with prayer, desire and intent, can release emotions.

2. After a while a cool, tingling energy is felt inside the ovaries. Now, "sip" this into the void like fullness of the womb.

3. To move this energy totally, move the sacrum down and then pull it up. Rock your pelvis back and forth, this helps move the energy.

4. Now, breathe/ move this into the heart. Trace an infinity loop between both nipples to stimulate your magnetic circuitry. Ask for Divine Love.

Say: *"Divine Healing Intelligence, help me feel and release my unworthiness, my emotions of rejection, my hatred, anger and resentment towards men, all past hurts and pains with my father and my sexual partners, grief and sadness from my ovaries and soul."*

Breathe glowing, iridescent wine red energy slowly and deeply into the core of your ovaries, then slowly exhale out. Do this 3 times.

Say: *"Divine Healing Intelligence, please heal and regenerate my ovaries to their most emotional openness, their greatest power and vitality, good health and Divine Design. Beloved Divine Mother, send me Your Divine Love."*

Visualize a pure, radiant red-black-gold Sun in your ovaries, deeply, warmly bright. A radiant, shining, golden Divine Spirit arises. What does she want to say to you? What does she say you need to heal, release and open your ovaries fully? Ask whatever questions arise, naturally and spontaneously.

NB : Tibetan Pulsing for the Ovaries, and Sacred Sound Meditation for the Testes, complete this healing on all levels : physical, emotional, spiritual and soulful, into Divine Design.

YOUR MAGNETIC FOUNDATION

The magnetic foundation is found in the pelvic bowl and sexual gates of men and women. It gives us a felt sense of embodied safety, security, autonomy, sexual integrity, inner strength and independence to help create our own inner pillar.

This magnetic foundation allows us to flow with our emotions and sexuality. It allows us to have healthy emotional boundaries on a sexual, personal and emotional level. It helps us on a deep, pre verbal, subconscious and sexual level to feel whole within ourselves, in ways in which psychology and many spiritual healing techniques cannot touch, so deeply is it found within our very roots.

With a healthy and intact magnetic foundation, we can fully engage in intimate relationships. We can love ourselves and be sovereign, and therefore be totally open and vulnerable to others. Our sense of safety is intact within us on a core level, and therefore we have the right position within us to be able to relate to others from a place of desire rather than need.

Deeper surrender comes from knowing oneself and being individuated. The magnetic foundation provides a felt structure for resting in yourself on a physical-emotional-sexual level, uniting all three through a web matrix that bridges dimensions of experience, emotion and time, providing spaciousness for all to move, breathe, weave and come alive in harmony.

Surrender is a great act of strength, and is the final 'act' in becoming Soul Realized. Becoming sovereign involves surrender, and surrendering leads to ultimate sovereignty. Sovereignty is embodied physically and manifested through the magnetic floor, an embodiment that fully embraces polarity, sexual energy and the depth of our emotions in loving balance, passion and wisdom.

We acquire part of our magnetic foundation from both of our parents. The Masculine Pillar of a father helps to stabilize and anchor the magnetic foundation of his children. It is both parents role to help us develop this, to recognize it, to use it, from pregnancy to age twenty one. If the parents own magnetic foundation is under developed or damaged, this will affect the child deeply in many ways.

Sexological bodywork, Reichian de-armouring massage, prostate massage, pelvic massage can all help realign aspects of your magnetic foundation. Yet this does not go deep enough into the deep emotions and loss that is affected by not having your magnetic foundation in place. This is where the Journey through the Seven Gates into the Womb comes in, as the womb is the deepest seat of a woman's essence, the throne of her magnetic, deep feeling foundation.

To feel a depth of love in the womb united with power is the flowering of your magnetic foundation into all the magnetic circuits that flow throughout your body. The seat of our magnetic foundation is found in the womb and pelvic region, yet it spans out throughout our whole body and soul, touching all parts of you through pure feeling.

It is this reawakening of feeling in all parts of you that brings you into the embodiment of your soul. It is how your baby embodies onto earth intact and whole. Through the water element in gestation in mothers womb is where we first meet these deeper feelings, where they are formed and re formed, shaped by our own and our parents emotions. This is the start of our magnetic foundation, which translates in later life into our magnetic circuits: our feeling body, gateway to the soul.

TRUST AND INTIMACY

With an insecure magnetic foundation we do not trust ourselves, our deeper feminine voices, our partner or life fully. Not trusting also means we feel unsafe. This can haunt us our whole lives because of what happened in our childhood. If we had no siblings, arguing and violence between our parents, sexual abuse, or even an affair had by either parent, this will create an unstable ground within us for our future relationships.

Of course, we can hang out on the surface and have superficially happy or 'pleasurable' relationships, but as soon as we desire to experience deeper intimacy, wounds will arise.

Perhaps the biggest effect of this comes from trying to get safety or security from someone or something else, such as money and possessions to make up for this sense of lack and insecurity in our very core. Controlling ourselves to make us feel safe and secure, controlling our environment, controlling our emotions, controlling our needs and desires, controlling others allows us to feel this superficial and false safety. If you are a control freak in any way, you are hiding your true self and your true feelings.

The deepest cause of a weak magnetic floor comes from how you were treated in the womb and early childhood by your parents. Giving birth and having vaginal tearing affects your magnetic floor, as can severe physical trauma to the points of your Magnetic Ground Circuit. Abusive intimate relationships in later life and emotional severing or cutting in intimate relationships also deeply affect the magnetic floor.

If you were placed into an incubator, if your umbilical cord was cut prematurely, your mother shunned you and you were denied touch and presence, if you felt on any level your parents did not love you and were not there for you, this deeply affects your ability to trust, feel safe, and feel secure.

This will then play out in your intimate relationships, so that you will never feel you can drop down into your feminine core and rest, feel safe and secure, and truly open up and surrender into intimacy and deeper communication. In other words you will never have an authentically intimate relationship with anyone, including your own soul, until this wound is journeyed into and healed.

Not addressing this can then attract partners who act out this behavior, triggering more insecurity, an inability to feel safe, and inability to trust *within oneself*, which may get projected outwards into wanting this from another even more. This pattern will keep repeating until you reclaim your *magnetic ground*, or seat of inner trust, security, intimacy and sovereign authority within the soul and womb-yoni.

This reclaiming and restructuring of the magnetic ground naturally leads us to disconnecting from the "Godfather/GodMother Gestalt[15]" where we may unconsciously trade our inner power and authority for a false sense of outer security and safety, usually connected with a mother or father type figure.

A woman's magnetic ground opens and heals when:

She is held by her partner in a truly authentic Masculine Pillar
She engages with the masculine authentically, vulnerably and openly
She feels safe and loves herself as a sovereign being
She appreciates herself - She gives herself what she needs
She trusts herself and puts this confidently into action in her relationships
She is authentic and real in relationship with her soul, her wounds, Beloved and God
She has brought back her sacred sexual self and healed this into her body
She has healed her parental wounds and deep mistrust this engendered in her
She physically re aligns her yoni, pelvic floor and womb to its right place
She brings back feelings and sensitivity into her yoni, sexuality, heart and womb

As an effect of magnetic ground healing, a woman will attract the right partner. When this is in place, a woman can completely trust and let go, surrendering herself, allowing her Sacred Sexual Self to express. When this occurs, there is often a shuddering, shaking and pulsing in the yoni and womb. This is called *Spanda* – the sacred tremor of the life force, the pulse of creation and the goal of all Tantra.

If this shuddering, pulsing and shaking, if her male partner remains with her at this time in loving connection, touching and nesting within the womb and magnetic fields released during the pulsing and during orgasm, then both open up further.

Every woman wants to feel safe with the pillar of her man, so he can catch her, hold her, be there for her, and allow her to surrender. Every woman wants to surrender and open totally with her man, even if she does not know it yet. There is a deep urge and need to do so in every woman, just as there is for a man to feel totally embraced and dissolve into the Womb.

---

[15] Ambe Ray

DEEPER ASPECTS OF THE MAGNETIC FLOOR

The magnetic floor resonates with the mitochondrial DNA connection to our ancestors and future generations. The mitochondrial DNA is the feminine DNA which directly connects into the ovaries. The ovaries create the energy fluid that holds the magnetic foundation in place. If the ovaries are wounded or not operating at true capacity, then the magnetic floor will be weakened. This is true for many women.

The magnetic floor and the mitochondrial DNA connection is a direct line to the ancestral, both back in time and forwards in time. This is a rich source of wisdom and energy. The magnetic floor allows a woman to sit in herself, to be comfortable in herself, to know herself, have confidence in herself, to trust herself and her feminine intuition, her womb voice, her womb intuition, the voice of her yoni that will say yes or no to a man entering her or leaving her.

All these deeply intuitive, very sensitive voices of a woman are anchored through the magnetic foundation. The magnetic foundation holds a woman together in a very structural way.

The womb holds the essence of a woman and allows the heart to flower and is her direct connection to feminine source and feminine wisdom. The magnetic foundation is directly connected to this. The womb is the feminine throne, and a throne needs pillars that the throne sits on. These pillars are the magnetic foundation. The throne needs these parts to be stable.

The magnetic foundation gives the structural interface in the third and fourth dimensions to allow the womb to manifest. A key aspect of the magnetic foundation is the energy of time, as it is connected to the ancestral both past and future, and your genetics. It allows time to be mastered within the body.

The experience of time speeds up or slows down according to ones state of consciousness and ones absorption in the moment. This is anchored in the female body through the magnetic foundation and the womb, i.e., time itself can be stopped, and this leads into timelessness or the infinite where there is no sense of time and space. This is what the womb holds.

The womb holds this access point into timelessness, into the void and also into the sparks of conception, the sparks of creation. The magnetic foundation is a bridge between past, present and future. Knowing this, one can create a profound future, one can live in the present moment and one can live in deep feminine intuition, wisdom and Shakti flow.

The magnetic foundation is the key bridge to the full soul embodiment of a woman. One can heal the past, the wounds of incarnation, and anchor it into your structure so it becomes fully embodied. The healed and open magnetic foundation allows the toroidal spiral of creation, the torus spiral coming in and coming out of all creation, coming in and out of you, constantly circulating in perpetuity the sacred hoop of life that is the movement of the web of life,. The magnetic foundation allows the toroidal spiral to fully come into you and fully exit from you, keeping you in harmony with all life.

For a woman this happens through crown, heart, womb and magnetic foundation united. This connects one into the web of life, into the web of interconnection and living relationship that determines how we move and operate in life. There is strong connection to the spirit body or auric field in the magnetic foundation.

One should always connect to this part of the spirit body when doing deep work on the magnetic foundation. Visualize your spirit body in front of you, in whatever condition it is in, and breathe and desire that connection after doing deep work on the magnetic foundation in the physical, sexual or emotional realms.

Anchoring the spirit body in this way will strengthen your bridge from time into timelessness, allowing you to hold that and be held in this. When you feel held in this, then the mind can become quieter because your center of gravity is established in its correct place. The mind can become quieter, the body becomes more relaxed, the shakti can flow in a different way, lovemaking will become deeper, stiller, slower and more embodied.

The sensitivity and the bridge is there to allow deeper feeling to occur once other aspects of healing have happened. A woman can become more still and enjoy the more delicious, slow sensations that occur in true lovemaking. Because she is in her seat she has established in herself, the voices of her different aspects are coagulating and moving together. She can truly drop and enjoy.

The magnetic foundation is also about pleasure and enjoyment. This is what truly takes you out of time if you are embodied. You go into that zone of the pleasure of love, of enjoyment, and time flies by quickly. If you are making love, time can stop. When the magnetic foundation is established and its obstacles embraced and released, ones experience of joy and vital engagement in daily life and ones experience of sensual pleasure increases and deepens. Ones engagement with the masculine, with oneself, will also expand its capacity and widen.

A solid, clear and strong magnetic foundation helps you to fully embrace anything. Embrace yourself, hold yourself, embrace and hold your man, embrace others and your children. The more you are centered in your true self, the more you can freely embrace others unconditionally. The magnetic foundation is a key part of this with the womb and heart. It allows that full embrace, not just as a mother, lover, sister or friend, but beyond all labels, roles, definitions and aspects.

There lies a deeper embrace that is beyond all these roles. It cannot be called anything in truth, it is just a total embrace that has no identity. Magnetic foundation in alliance with womb and heart allows this to be embodied and palpably, viscerally and tangibly felt by both man and woman and anyone else who is involved in this embrace. This is a key part of the feminine consciousness: embrace and surrender.

Embrace and surrender are the final, deepest gateways to total love, to total union with soul and God as one evolves. By having these bridges established, one can feel safe enough and trust enough in ones own connection to the divine, in ones own connection to the body, Shakti, feminine wisdom and soul voice. All these aspects are underpinned by the magnetic foundation. In Egypt this was the djed pillar of Osiris, the pillar of masculine. The magnetic foundation is the 'pillar' or seat of the feminine.

The physical symptoms of a disconnected or damaged magnetic foundation are the inability to walk your talk. This may seem emotional, but is actually very physical because trust is engendered in and felt in the body, if one is on a path of embodiment.

Other symptoms include: having intentions but not following through, not completing things. Having ideas but never putting them into action. The magnetic foundation is very much about, "by their actions they are known". It is a holding place, but also a dynamic action place. If women have had a negative experience with father, or father has not been there, it will deeply impact magnetic foundation.

Other symptoms are mental disorganization or scatteredness, psychological holes, lack of psycho-somatic integration and logic, un-groundedness, over playing feminine roles and facades, the shadow feminine, an over reliance on others or external objects for a sense of security and stability, and promiscuity.

A tendency to inwardly collapse or not be able to withstand certain energies or forces. Inability to dynamically engage with life, dynamically move forward in life, to move into the future. Inability to be truly present with emotions and drop down fully into the cause of them. People circling in their emotions rather than dropping into the cause.

This will also deeply impact your ability to have a meaningful and sustainable intimate relationship. Bonding is not possible with a damaged magnetic floor, for one can not authentically, emotionally, intimately bond with an adult if your magnetic floor is weak or damaged. (It is different with a child.) There is no place to hold oneself within the dynamic of relationship. If you look at the figure 8 infinity loop, this is what true relationship is about; but you both need to be whole and yet connected.

With a damaged magnetic ground, one is not fully whole in self and therefore cannot fully connect to another adult. Of course you can create relationships with another where they also cannot connect to you too. With a damaged magnetic ground this is what you will create through the law of attraction. Through healing this, you can then manifest a relationship inside you to then mirror it outside you.

With the foundation of the magnetic ground in place, you can be intimate with yourself, your deeper feelings, deeper emotions, the more painful parts within you, where you have not dared to go. This becomes more accessible and safe. It is not as scary or as daunting or as taboo. Everything becomes more available and nothing is as scary as it once may have been.

Because women have wombs and are generally in their bodies more, this becomes more of a major issue for a woman than a man. She needs to feel this trust in her body to really open. The magnetic foundation allows the full blooming of the womb heart and full integration of such. If a woman has had a weak or largely absent father and then has had relationships with weak men as a consequence, this will hold the damaged foundation in its abnormal pattern. It will fix the erratic geometry into position.

Often to repair the magnetic ground will require that dysfunctional wounded relatings end so that the energy can be withdrawn from the abnormal, wounded position. Then the deeper healing can occur from an inner sovereign place so the woman can get to know herself as she is, without interference or without being drawn outside of herself in an unhealthy way.

The magnetic foundation allows a clarity of feeling and of thought because the mind is quieter and more established in the silence and depth of womb space. There is a greater clarity of direction of thought and deeper accessibility availability of emotions. A wider palate of emotions becomes available because you feel safe enough to open upto the unknown more.

Your sexual engagement, making love, will go to another level of intimacy and pleasure and true connection within yourself and with your partner. One of the pathways to the womb and magnetic foundation is through the anus. If this is done in a loving and gentle way, this can also help to relax and release some of the tension or abnormal positions within the magnetic foundation, in that area of the body.

The magnetic foundation in birth is important. Tearing happens in birth process if magnetic foundation is not established. If the magnetic foundation is weak or damaged there is a much higher likelihood of c-section and medical interventions. Magnetic foundation is the basis for a blissful birth. It also seats the spine into its optimum alignment.

MAGNETIC PULSE PRACTICE

Start with OVARY BREATHING for 11 minutes

Inhale glowing, iridescent, deep wine-red energy deep down into the seed of your testes/ovaries. Do this 6 times. They become glowing, iridescent, deep wine-red with each breath. Inhale shining, glowing, iridescent fluid black energy deeply into the seed of your testes/ovaries, and slowly exhale out, 6 times. They become shining, glowing, iridescent fluid black. Breathe these cycles of wine red, shining black, and radiant white, twice more.

Say: *"Beloved Divine Father, Divine Mother, send me 8000% Red Ray of Spiritual Warrior to charge my ovaries/ testes now. Beloved Divine Mother, send me 4000% Black Ray to anchor my ovaries/ testes now. Beloved Divine Father, send me 6000% White Ray to cleanse my ovaries/ testes now.'*

This exercise works to reactivate the circuitry of the magnetic floor and the corresponding connections in the two hemispheres of the brain.

1. Lie down comfortably on your back, legs spread wide open in abandon.
2. Connect your womb and heart to the Earth.
3. With your right hand, insert your middle finger into your g-spot, and allow your ring finger of that hand to rest on your anus.
4. With your left hand firmly touch the base of your spine with middle and ring fingers.
5. Begin a pulsing movement with the fingers of both hands, steady at the rate of one pulse per second. Continue breathing while doing this.

THE SEVEN GATES of THE WOMB:
EMBODYING SOUL ON EARTH

Womb Wisdom is an intimate internal journey through your sacred sexual self, your magnetic foundation, your ancestors and the Divine.

The 7 Gates are a journey in relating with your Beloved man, your ways of making and expressing love in the qualities of the gates, and your ways of relating to your man outside the bedroom. If your daily way of life is suffused with the feeling qualities of the Gates, for example trust, pleasure and purity, and you are relating to your partner in this way, you are embodying the Gates. Inside and outside become One, and here lies Heaven.

The 7 Gates and Womb becomes a way of relating and connecting to all life. Through giving and receiving love we commune with all beings, all intelligences and all life forms. In the 7 Gates and Womb we experience Keys to become part of the living rhythmic intelligence of the web of life, the feminine dance of creation.

The 7 Gates are biological and emotional guardians that open the doorway into our physical womb space as well as Womb Consciousness. These Gates hold a powerful pathway to a magnetic-feminine truth, a soulful and biological foundation for spirit and matter, soul and body, to manifest.

The Seven Gates are a series of doorways that open the Way into the Womb. They form rivers of magnetic flow uniting your body and soul, coursing through the yoni lips to the G-spot, moving to the Red Rose of the clitoris, flowing through the cervix into the womb, and then the spaciousness of the Cosmic Womb.

The seven gates hold a great key for a woman to become fully embodied in the essence of her true feminine nature here on earth, in her body. These seven gateways hold a powerful pathway to feminine truth, a pathway that is now being remembered again.

The seven gates were most recently practiced by the Priestesses of Isis in the Middle East, Near East and France, and were used to empower and guide women into experiencing and using their full Shakti through the crucible of the womb and heart united.

This enabled them to empower men into the essence of the true masculine, to initiate men into many aspects of life, from lovemaking, sacred union and conception-pregnancy-birthing, to earth mysteries and co-creation together through the balance between male and female, amongst many other subjects. To initiate a man into this Presence required that he enter a fully open womb through the seven gates.

The womb is the crucible of creation. Each woman holds this loving power to create and manifest from her own womb, which becomes the portal to the Cosmic Womb from which all creation springs, and into which all dissolves back. This has been known and used in cultures such as the Mayan, Tibetan, Indian, Gnostic Christian, and Egyptian, amongst others.

When healed, nourished, remembered, and honored as sacred, these seven gates become a royal road into the Grail of the Womb: they become the keys to manifestation of the holy, sacred and joyfully embodied loving feminine. Keys to Creation itself.

Each gate opens as you progressively heal each part of the yoni and womb, making them sacred portals once again. As each gate opens, one by one, the level of openness and ability to experience love, embrace and surrender also deepens. This deepening occurs in direct relationship to what you are able to let *in*, to the extent that you are able to be physically, emotionally, and spiritually vulnerable.

The seven gates stir memories of the feminine fire and power within you. Integration of these emotional essences and memories is a key to opening and crossing each threshold. Allowing yourself to be penetrated by a male consciousness is another key to opening *all* the gates *if* you are in a physical relationship.

However, many female mystics have opened some of the gates through surrendering to God in a personal form, such as a lover of Krishna (a gopi) would, or like female Christian mystics who asked for, and were penetrated by, the Holy Spirit. However, in today's world, and for most normal people, the embodiment process of vulnerability and intimacy is usually accessed through an intimate and committed relationship between man and woman.

The womb's wounds, which have made her shut down, are comprised of the memories and emotions that have created a deep mistrust of life and others. Many of these emotions come from our unloving and unconscious sexual interactions with men.

These wounds impair a woman's level of creativity, inspiration, stability, success in loving relationships, and fertility. Allowing these deep wellsprings of grief and pain, the masks of hardness, indifference, and the veneers of cynicism and fragility to melt through vulnerability with your self and with your partner, are key steps in healing and opening the womb.

This initial thawing affects every aspect of life, but in particular we notice it through our lovemaking and sexual expression. In the beginning of the opening of the womb and the seven gates, you may find it difficult to experience full orgasm. You may feel a sense of holding back, of pain or sadness arising, of frustration, of superficial pleasure, of not being totally present, of feeling unfulfilled but not speaking up.

You may even enjoy the act of making love but feel that it has reached its apex and that the experience tends to feel the same. Something else is beckoning to you, an ancient memory deep within your core, a whisper of something beyond your present experience, but something you know intimately.

When the womb is clear and free from restrictions, a new discovery of orgasm is experienced as a natural release of free expression. These could be orgasms of vaginal release, or full-body orgasms that are felt as rushes of bliss coursing throughout the whole being, or orgasms felt in the womb, heart, and subtle bodies. There are as many different types of orgasms as there are stars in the sky. They cannot be limited by definition or comparison to other women.

Yet, there is a distinct orgasm that happens in the womb. The *wombgasm* occurs when the womb itself starts to experience deep, distinct orgasmic pulses, bursts, or waves, different from vaginal or full-body orgasms.

When the womb receives consistent attention, nurturance, and unconditional love, the womb starts to stir, flower, and come alive, beginning to attune to its vastness and its energetic subtleties. If the woman is attentive to its presence, new and amazingly unique sensations can be experienced.

The womb becomes exquisitely sensitive to tastes, feelings and sensations, responding to loving touch with openness, delight, and deep pleasure. This pleasurable feeling can literally be felt in the womb as bliss and joy. Explosions or bursts of palpable loving energy spontaneously erupt, felt as orgasms in the womb itself.

This orgasmic feeling is rich in essence and can bring a woman into extra ordinary depths and heights of love. It is truly a blessing and a miraculous gift for a woman to feel this mysteriously awesome, beautiful sensation occurring in her womb.

The yoni, and womb become highly sensitive instruments, able to receive and transmit nonphysical information to a partner. These pleasurable feelings are felt in the womb as bursts of palpable loving energy, feelings beyond comprehension which are experienced uniquely by each woman.

They can be orgasmic, magical, ripe, holy, pleasurable, passionate, and blissful. For a woman to feel these feelings in her womb is a blessing and a gift, for it is from here that the womb becomes the holiest of shrines, a sacred space where bliss, life, and joy are birthed.

WOMAN AND MAN

The immune system relies on being supported and fed by your sexual energy, 90 percent of which feeds directly into our immunity. So in essence, without a thriving, vital flow of sexual energy, your immune defense system will be undernourished, leaving you prone to sickness, weakness, and depression. An orgasm, when flushed throughout the entire body-mind, has the sustenance to bring in a complete healing state. Try this next time you are ill and see what happens.

The inviting of the masculine essence to come deep into your most sacred place of the womb requires that you become totally vulnerable, opening, embracing, surrendering to, and receiving the male essence in its totality. The question that arises here, again and again, is how deeply do you trust the masculine?

When the womb and gates open, you can let a man deep into your feminine essence, fully into the womb consciousness, which has enormous benefits for both of you. This letting in, of course, can only happen through deep mutual intimacy and surrender to the other. When enough sexual, emotional, and heart healing has been done by both partners—both alone and in the mirror of relationship—then this penetration and surrender can occur, organically unfolding the gates.

The level of mutual love, trust, commitment, and willingness to grow are key factors in this, as well as the ability of the man to be able to support the woman, to be the safe pillar for the woman, therefore letting her go deeper into her own essential feminine nature and womb consciousness, taking the masculine with her.

As the womb opens, one starts to make love in a different way on the subtle planes and goes deeper into bliss. The man becomes swallowed in the vastness of the womb and surrenders to this drawing inward into the depths where all men wish to go, back to the source of life and original innocence.

The man becomes humbled and empowered in a new manner, and the woman rests in ease and a deep, felt majesty of her own true nature, born from the connecting and opening of womb and heart. True Feminine and True Masculine are born, for a real woman is birthed through the masculine, and a real man is born through the feminine.

To align to these movements of the womb requires that you become fluid. When you are fully fluid, you can experience any feeling whatsoever at any time, at will. However, the less you can summon feelings, the more you are frightened of them, the more you are at their mercy.

Conversely, the more you allow yourself to experience feelings, the less you can be enslaved by them. If you allow them to pass through you, you become transparent, without holding on to anything or anybody. Thus you learn to move the body, emotions, feelings, and mind, so that spirit can move you. In this flow, you feel you are in sync with everything within and around you. The world and your relation to it seems different . . . it is as if you are involved with the process of creation, instant by instant. You are creating it as it is creating you; it is always there, you just have been too busy to notice it.

In preconception, we can bring our awareness and loving touch to awaken and open our gates, making them sacred portals again. As each gate opens, the level of openness and ability to experience love, embrace and surrender, sexually, emotionally and transcendentally, also deepens. This also applies to the man as well.

In conscious conception we journey through the gates with our partner with the intent to receive an incoming soul. Here we can join in sacred union and move more deeply into the gifts and sanctity held within the deeper aspects of the womb.

In pregnancy, the qualities and voices of the different gates are highlighted during different stages, allowing a woman to more deeply embody these soul qualities. In birth, the gates reveal the very processes of creation, inviting deeper awe, wonder, understanding and embodiment for mother, child, and father.

THE SEVEN GATES: JOURNEY INTO THE WOMB

1. Praise, Appreciation, Connection to the Web of Life
2. Gratitude and Giving of oneself to the other
3. Compassion and Beauty of Purity and Power
4. Humility, Trust and Self/ self awareness
5. Black Hole Dissolving of self
6. Gaia-Galactic Centre
7. Embody Soul here and now in Physical body manifested in Physical World

These qualities are shared and felt by both man and woman in the process of sexual healing, intimacy, communication and love making. Simply put, these seven are qualities of love and feeling, and the initiations both man and woman move through in the journey through the seven gates and the depths of the soul. When one has experienced and integrated these seven gates within ones own self, one can embody their True Self in the physical world.

The Journey through the Seven Gates is what Yeshua and Mary Magdalene, amongst other couples, have done here on earth as the culmination of their spiritual path: the embodiment of the divine feminine and divine masculine soul on earth.

Great pathways of pain, and bliss, lie carved in the bodies of women. In forgetting the legacy of women's power, you have suffered the pain of being separated from parts of yourself you are no longer taught to honour, and whose wisdom you no longer heed. The power is within you, and you are being called now to find and reclaim this.

To do this, you must first go into the darkness, discover all the ways you have repressed yourself and have been repressed, all the ways in which you have abandoned and forgotten your true nature. It is all stored in your body as a gateway to your soul.

Your journey through the seven gates will take you into that darkness to bring you out into light, a light that is reached through your own soulful vulnerability, humility, wild feminine self and deep care. This is the gift that awaits. Each of these gates has a voice to express. Each has its own nature and way of feeling.

The Journey into the Gates begins with the first gate, found at the opening of the yoni lips, and culminates in the seventh gate of the fully open womb. With gentle focus on each gate, touching it with your breath, feel the sparking of life force at each threshold. Love and bathe each gate with conscious Presence, so the true feeling and purpose of your sacred sexuality can come alive.

Praise and Appreciation for each other, for Gaia and the Divine is the opening of the first gate, the lips of the yoni, the royal road to the womb grail. In being praised and adored, the yoni opens, and just as God is appreciated and adored, so God too opens to you, and just as Gaia is appreciated, she opens herself more to you. The labia, the Lips of Love, form the entrance to the yoni. They are guardians not just of the body and sexuality, but also of soul. They are the flowering sentinels who serve your sacred well and life force, and whose message is "I honor myself." Touching the Lips of Love—the First Gate at the threshold of the yoni—and massaging them into fullness, opens the pathway to the Second Gate.

This Gate, when activated through pleasure, appreciation and gratitude, is Known as the G-spot or Gratitude Spot. This is a fountain of erotic pleasure that gives both partners the gifts of a woman's arousal. Bathed in love, its sensuality amplifies and readies you for the Third Gate, the blooming Red Rose of the clitoris, velvet to the touch, the pleasure of true love and the deep sensitivity to loving, and being loved.

Gratitude for being loved, gratitude for being loving, gratitude to God for the blessing of intimacy with self, other and God and gratitude for Gods Love all culminate in the visceral giving of oneself to another and to God. This all occurs as the second gate opens and blooms. Gratitude to Gaia for all her gifts of abundance and life.

The Beauty of Purity in the Third Gate arises when two souls make love giving oneself wholly to the other, with God in the bedroom, invited to complete the Holy Trinity here on earth. Lovemaking becomes light, yet passionate, with purity becoming the ultimate turn on for the pure soul, and beauty being the result of two souls engaged in the holy desire for Union with Self and with God.

In the third gate, a woman becomes both the purity and the dynamism, the virgin and the whore, who delights in her orgasmic, natural, blissful high frequency self AND is totally pure and innocent.

The Red Rose, a symbol of the Grail and of Magdalene, opens in the purity, freshness and virginity of pure love. This Rose leads you into a deep surrender to the river flowing into the Fourth Gate of the cervix. This is the portal to the womb, a star gate, a sacred diamond opening.

The Gateway to the Womb of the Fourth Gate involves both man and woman becoming totally humble to their own wounds, owning them completely, and being totally vulnerable with the other. This is the deepest heart opening and revelation of your wounded self to the other, and the full embrace of yours, and the others, shadow. This process will bring forth the foundation of the deepest trust you can ever have with another human soul, and your own deeper self awareness

The gates become more like energetic veils of emotion and love when one reaches the fourth gate and beyond, which is the opening into the womb of pure space and infinite potential. At this point, you start to access the subtler energies of the womb and the unmanifest.

Crossing through this portal into the vastness of womb, you can feel the peace and Remember. In this knowing, you journey through Gates five, six and seven, to the source of being: the Grail within.

The Fifth Gate of Union opens when both of you enter the womb space. Here, you both lose your previous sense of self in profound experiences that then need to be integrated into your daily life through aligning to the Self and pure soul you are, individually.

The Sixth Gate involves connecting to Gaia and Galactic Centre from having dissolved your previous sense of self identity and reference points which you used to navigate your way though life. This initiation is accessed through the Core of the Earth, which leads into the Galactic Centre.

The Seventh Gate is cosmic consciousness, inter-dimensional travel and connection, and Communion with God. It leads to the full embodiment of the pure soul here on earth in the physical body, and the full embodiment of God by both partners here on earth.

THE FIRST GATE: THE LIPS OF LOVE

"To understand the vagina properly is to realize that it is not only coextensive with the female brain, but is also, essentially, part of the female soul. Female sexual pleasure serves as a medium of female self-knowledge, female creativity and courage; female focus and initiative; female bliss and transcendence; and as medium of a sensibility that feels very much like freedom."
Naomi Wolff

One enters the First Gate with praise and appreciation. Praise, from self and others, begins to heal you of your own subjective, inner experiences of life, sexuality, and men you have sexually connected with.

The First Gate is a foundation for love, as appreciation leads to true gratitude and the ability to see the beauty in all beings. Praise, the gatekeeper of the First Gate, allows us to let go of limiting habits of self-judgment and condemnation, and awakens us to the beauty of others, and ourselves.

As the First Gate is cherished, she adorns you. When in her essence, she throbs with fragrance and her full lips bloom, sweet and inviting. To receive the fullness of her hidden gifts, pause and reflect.

The more reverence and gratitude you feel and give for this wonderful present, the sweeter the gifts you will receive in return. In approaching the yoni with a sense of being honoured by a great presence, rather than being out to "get" something, you open into deeper possibilities of emotional experience and rapture.

Praise brings you into emotionally appreciating and feeling the beauty of another, and of your Self. Honoring and appreciating are the basis for kindness and gratitude, the basis for love. Without praising, without appreciating, we shrink and wilt into our ego, allowing it to be the master with the soul as servant.

Vulnerability and humility open the doorway to love and intimacy. Without vulnerability and humility, appreciation and devotion, the gates can never fully open, and the Grail womb cannot be entered. In giving these qualities, we receive them.

The First Gate helps to open us into deeper trust. Trust yourself, and what it is you are letting into you, or keeping out. The wounds women carry here, both personal and collective, revolve around this issue of trust. For men to come fully into the First Gate they must approach it with praise, honest integrity, and purity of heart and intent, fully honoring this sacred portal into the feminine.

For a woman to surrender into this space of trust she must respect her own sanctity and feel respect and praise from the man she is with. The nature of relationship today has led to a deep forgetting of this sacred path, and most women hold a great unconscious sadness at the loss of their connection to the True Feminine, which is accessed through this First Gate.

This sadness arises because of the deeply felt loss of communion/ wholeness that comes from fully honoring, and being honored by, yourself and your partner. Being loved and loving oneself and fully giving and receiving love with another intimately, are vital keys to the fullness of our humanity.

Unworthiness stands in the way. True praise and appreciation allows this small self to fall away. It is this small self's fear that in praise it will be giving away its power, love, and beauty to something outside itself. There is nothing outside itself. In praise you feel the beauty and perfection of another welling up inside yourself, and you speak it out to the other person—to honor the gift of that person's existence.

To see, feel, and honor another's presence fully, whether human or Divine, allows the gift you perceive in another into your own heart, body, and soul. In fully giving your appreciation to another you feel the depth to which he/she is a reflection of your self.

To be devoted means to be committed to giving to your partner, to your soul purpose, to your healing, and to God. These qualities enable all the Gates to open and flower. Devotion is serving the flowering of love, allied with the appreciation of another's efforts, struggles, or endeavors that can give that person the impetus to continue, persist, push on, especially when he or she struggles to do so.

Devotion is gratitude—for something that touches you emotionally, for someone else's struggles or efforts, for the wonderful gifts of life that creation surrounds us with.

The first gate is our welcome. It is how we welcome others into our energy, and it opens when we feel welcomed by another. An open first gate is vibrant and full of presence. This enables a co-creation with the energy that enters, instead of a rape or channeling by allowing something in with out meeting it with the fullness of ourselves.

The first gate is our direct connection into the web of life, of Gaia's magnetic fields and the grid matrices of the earth. The more open and connected we are to our first gate, the more in harmony we are with all of life.

The word *yoni,* from Sanskrit, is an honoring, sacred and truly appropriate word for this sacred space from which all life emerges. It means the divine passage, the holder, the matrix of generation, the origin or primal source of all being, the birthplace of the universe. In astrology, each child is considered to be born from a yoni of stars—constellations that prevailed during the child's birth.

The yoni is a temple where the pure essence of a woman can be connected with. It is a gateway to the infinite, rising through the six other gates into the open womb, the birth space for all life. The First Gate is where a woman learns true self-love and self-respect by only allowing into her that which is loving and honoring of her essence.

PRACTICE: HEALING THE FIRST GATE THROUGH YONI GAZING

A practice for starting to heal the first gate is yoni gazing. This requires a sacred intent on behalf of both partners to be vulnerable, open and honest with their emotions and experiences.

To begin this practice, the sacred woman takes off her clothes, lies down and spreads her legs wide open, in birthing position, knees up.

The sacred man lies between her legs, and looks at her yoni intently, with a relaxed focus. This can take the man into an alpha state of meditation, and bring the woman into different feelings of insecurity and shame. The urge to giggle may arise, which is fine, as it provides a release of energy hidden behind embarrassment and shame. Just do not use it as an excuse to stop going deeper.

Remember to keep breathing and allow the process. This practice is remarkably healing and insightful for men as well as women; it enables them to honor the feminine and also to hear all the judgments they have ever held about women's bodies. It enables a woman also to feel all her insecurities and self judgments. Eventually a shared intimacy, openness, peace and healing will arise.

Just allow it all and do not forget to express your experience with each other after the practice is complete. The yoni gazing can last for up to 45 minutes. If you treat it as a sacred healing practice, it will become one. In addition, you can reverse the process, with the woman doing lingam gazing.

A SACRED DOORWAY

The First Gate is the sacred doorway into your holy of places. Many women have forgotten this, and have allowed energies to enter them in many ways, that do not respect or honor them. In essence, women have disrespected themselves by allowing these energies in. We now each have the power to demand that those who enter us do so with love and honor.

Many people find anger, pain, betrayal and mistrust stored in the First Gate. These emotions come from screams not expressed, from anger and hatred toward men for their ignorance in putting women down. Here is stored rage at the disrespect shown to children who have been molested, those who have been sold into sex slavery and shut themselves off from feeling any other emotion just to survive the pain.

Here is heard the cries of these children, "Where is my protector, where is my dad, my mom?" Sadness and loss of trust from having been violated and unable to protect oneself reside in this First Gate.

What affects one woman affects all women in the web of life, and through feeling the emotions of the collective psyche of women in the First Gate—the First Gate of all women-that you can be healed of them. As these emotions release from being held within you, the web of life becomes that much brighter for all women, and all beings.

Sexually entering a woman and just "going for it" without respect for the yoni, without loving connection and 'foreplay'—just shoving the penis in for the man's own pleasure and self-gratification—is where sex becomes violence, ownership, conquering, and animal aggression.

By allowing these actions, women lose their sense of beauty and sanctity, their sense of being cherished. Gradually their feminine power begins to slip and fade away. The sense of safety, trust, and vulnerability recedes as numbness sets in. The lips become desensitized to true intimacy, and many women have little or no feeling beyond this Gate.

This Gate holds sadness—for the loss of sanctity, all the ways you have been violated and forgotten. Yet you are not a victim! When this Gate and its attendant pains and sorrows are cleared, a woman is able to more fully trust her own being and be more Sovereign.

She holds herself and her sexuality as sacred, and knows when to surrender, when to be open, and also when to exert discernment and create boundaries. She does not trust blindly—she respects and knows her own intuition, and does not give this power away. She is a woman who knows her own worth and grants entrance only to those who are deserving and appreciative of her.

THE SECOND GATE: THE GRATITUDE SPOT

It has been said that gratitude is the attitude of enlightenment. Flowing naturally in the wake of praise, gratitude begins to neutralize the judgments we have around sexuality, our bodies, our selves, around others, and with the world around us. Gratitude enables us to have an open mind. As the judgments we hold in these areas dissolve, we reconnect with ourselves and the world *as it is*, rather than the world as we think it to be.

Gratitude is deeply magnetic. It draws all the events, aspects, and ingredients of our lives intimately close to us, where we can embrace them beyond judgement. This dissolves layers of separation and invites more flow, more love into our bodies, our beings.

When gratitude is showered into the G-spot, it opens. Then Shakti herself wells up in her fullness, beaming with exuberance, ready to share her gifts and knowledge. In her gratitude, Shakti wants to pour outward in even greater amounts, knowing that as she gives, she receives.

Gratitude results in a desire to give constantly; the circular flow of giving and receiving, the sacred hoop, builds upon itself, which allows a continuous outpouring of love to flow from the soul filled with Shakti. She builds trust and then expands into her essence, letting you fall into a river of bliss. In her gratitude for being acknowledged, she lets you fall in love with her, and shows you your greatest potentials.

If you thank all things in your life, you gain a deeper understanding of your power as creator. You see that you truly have created everything that is happening to you, and that, in your magnificence, you have done so in order to learn ever-deeper lessons about compassion and love. This starts with your own love for yourself, and compassion for what you have put yourself through in order to learn and remember.

If you bless and thank all occurrences and people in your life, you spiritualize your whole experience, down to the most mundane events. Everything becomes an opportunity to grow deeper into humility and deeper feeling of all your own pains; everything becomes an opportunity to bring loving wisdom into your everyday life.

When you thank everything, no matter what it is, your heart can break open, again and again and again. The more you thank the deeper lessons that darkness and fear present to you, the more you see their purpose, and the more humble you become to the beauty and soulful orchestration of life as it is occurring to you now, in the present.

Kindness and gratitude are interlinked. In gratitude one realizes that you cannot *get* love, you can only receive it, and you can only fully receive it by giving it away. To have all, give all. To be truly happy is to live in gratitude. Living in gratitude *and in grace* means accepting whatever comes one's way, both good and bad, with thankfulness. There is no exception to what one can be thankful for, as gratitude wears down our resistance to conflicts, humbles us, and brings us into joy.

Try this: Thank all the painful and beautiful occurrences that happen to you today, and see how you feel. In the conflicts that arise, in the "unfortunate" circumstances that happen, there is a lesson that your soul has created in order to open your heart a littler bit more, even if that opening is upsetting, painful or annoying. This heart makes all things full by thanking them, and in the process empties itself of any resentment, frustration, or thoughts of harm.

This openness leads to beauty, which arises from the clarity of our own perception. Beauty is not about how a person, place, or object looks; it is about how you, who are looking, feel. The beauty that you experience "out there" is a direct reflection of the beauty that is happening inside you. When you are in a state of joy and feel uplifted, everything appears beautiful to you.

What we often describe as beautiful is an interpretation, a view that has been taught to us—a perception that one thing is beautiful, and another is ugly. Where we do not see beauty, we can see where our mind still judges and misunderstands.

To see beauty is to see with the heart, to see things as they are, and to appreciate them and connect with them in a heart-centered way. When we truly see reality it is beautiful, as it involves no judgment, no naming or identifying with things, no boxes, labels, categories or ideas, no past history of what we once felt was beautiful.

Without the mind's judgment and commentary, we can see the beauty in a rotting pile of dung lying on the street. If you have no judgment about the value of something, then you can appreciate the nature, and use, *of all things*. In true beauty we do not exclude anything, but embrace it all.

THE WELL OF DARKNESS

The Second Gate is a great power generator of the yoni, and as such may harbor rage at all the ways women have been disempowered, and have disempowered themselves. Women's collective memories of being repressed, tied up, shut up, shut down, raped, savaged—of playing small, of giving their power away, of feeling violated and impotent—all are seething here in the Second Gate.

The rage comes from feeling powerless at the hands of aggression, both blatant violence and all the passive acts of aggression that have become acceptable in our society. This rage and self-punishment is something women direct at themselves for having silenced their own expression. This is the place where women have turned all these acts of sexual violence and unconsciousness against themselves, and have cut themselves off from their own bodies and sexuality.

The Second Gate is a well of suffering in the collective consciousness, where rivers of rage and shame manifest. Imagine that every minute of every day somewhere in the world, there is a woman curled up in the fetal position, rocking herself into cathartic slumber. Having been raped, abused, or routinely taken for granted, she thinks it is her fault, and has cut herself off from herself and from everyone else. She withdraws from life, disengages from the life force, and suppresses her rage at her loss of power. She feels physically helpless to do anything, and her self-worth plummets.

PRACTICE: HEALING THE SECOND GATE

The feelings of isolation generated here can be healed by connection to the sweet balms of gratitude and pleasure. As we gift and share our pleasure, appreciation and gratitude with others, we begin to feel loved and appreciated, building deep, felt, physically embodied feelings of trust and safety that enable the first Two Gates to open. This is not something just to do in the bedroom: this is a way of life, a lifestyle, a way of being, acting and feeling. *Gratitude is the attitude of enlightenment.*

Rub your hands together slowly until they are warm. Place the palm of your hand gently and lovingly, with conscious attention, on your lower pelvic area, where the G Spot is inside you. Simply feel here and drop your feeling heart consciousness down into the G Spot. Rest and breathe a pink red colour down into your Gratitude Spot.

Now, ask her the following questions. If you feel any emotions arise around these questions, simply breathe into them and allow yourself to feel them fully. In feeling, you begin the process of releasing. Feel to heal.

> *Are you holding onto any past hurts, especially with men?*
> *Do you invalidate yourself?*
> *Do you reject your femininity and feminine nature?*
> *Do you allow yourself to enjoy your loving sensuality and womanhood?*
> *Have you ever suffered or given sexual abuse? Do you have any shame?*
> *Did you lose your sexual innocence and virginity without love?*
> *Do you love your body as it is? Do you accept yourself as you are?*
> *Do you have rage and anger? Are you scared of becoming nobody?*
> *Are you over sensitive, especially with men and your partner?*

Say, from your heart: *"Beloved Divine Mother, please help me feel and release my mistrust of men, my feelings of shame, my fear, my humiliation, my anger and my bitterness from my G-spot and soul."*

Repeat the word CLEAR until you feel a shift occur.

> *Are you able to give freely in intimacy, especially to a man?*
> *Are you able to surrender, especially with a man?*
> *Are you transparent, honest, vulnerable and expressive with all your feelings to your partner?*
> *Are you grateful every day, or not?*
> *Do you repress expressing any of your feelings and emotions for any reason whatsoever?*
> *Do you experience isolation or loneliness?*
> *Do you feel disconnected in a cold or harsh way from any part of you, or anyone else?*

Say, from your heart: "*Beloved Divine Mother, please help me feel and release my feelings of isolation, loneliness, repression and unwillingness to speak out, my feelings of unworthiness, my feelings of being used, my sadness from my G-spot and soul.*"

Repeat the word CLEAR until you feel a shift occur.

Visualize your G Spot encased in a pink-red ball of softly glowing light. Breathe gently into it through pursed lips, and as you do, see the pink red light intensify with each breath. Do this for a few minutes.

Now, feel into your G Spot: has she ever felt loved, thanked and admired, by you or by another? Have you ever felt gratitude to a man whilst making love? Can you remember and feel this feeling right now? Give and send thanks to any soul who has shared real love, appreciation and thanks for your G Spot and yoni.

Say: "*Beloved Divine Mother, please flood my G Spot and my soul with 6000% Pink ray of tender, unconditional love. Please flood my emotions, my G Spot and my soul with 6000% Red ray of honor, courage and cleansing. Please help me feel and experience my true value. Please awaken my feeling of giving thanks to others. Please Revive my inner strength and courage to share my vulnerability and feelings. Thank you.*"

Feel the greatest, most powerful feeling memory of gratitude you have ever felt in your life, to any person or to the Divine. Allow this feeling to swell in you. Breathe it in, and direct it into your G Spot. Keep breathing this in.

Say: "*Thank you for being a part of me. I love you. From now on, I only allow love into me. My G Spot: you are a valuable part of me and my soul: I honor you now from the depths of my heart as part of my loving, sensual, sacred self. Thank you, thank you, thank you!*'

Visualize a pure white sea shell, with a radiant, shining white Goddess arising from your G Spot and yoni. What does she say you need to heal, release and open your G Spot fully? Ask whatever questions arise from your heart.

THE THIRD GATE

Compassion and giving are a natural response of a life lived in appreciation and gratitude. As one's consciousness naturally expands, neutrality and compassion replaces judgment. When a woman feels the spirit of devotion being lavished upon her, she starts to come into contact with the essence of the Third Gate and her Red Rose blossoms.

When the Third Gate of the clitoris is lovingly stimulated, it creates waves of resonance that nourish the central nervous system, feeding our intuitive and psychic abilities. When clitoral stimulation is accompanied by gratitude, appreciation, care and enjoyment, our bodies create more of these same qualities. As this occurs, nerves along the spine recalibrate and retune.

We journey into a deeper embrace of those parts of ourselves that are lost and isolated. This embrace allows us to heal abuses and feelings of disconnection and numbness from our bodies, emotions and sexuality.

As we soften our armor, we soften what is rigid within—the protection and the disconnection, the pain and numbness felt in our emotional body and clitoris—to allow ecstasy to reawaken and reconnect us. As this Gate heals, purity and innocence merges with a feeling of holiness and sensual pleasure together.

The Third Gate is a vortex where the nervous system and the twin channels of Kundalini that rise up the spine into the brain connect. The more sensual aspects of the Third Gate allow a woman to bring forth her magnetic foundation (as has been built in the previous two gates) and emanate it, pour it into the vessel that she is. This pouring forth starts to affect the womb and Fifth Gate.

The Third Gate allows the draining out of the womb. This is a paradox: the womb cup is being filled, but all that is not appropriate in the womb starts to be drained out. Is the cup half empty or half full? Nevertheless, this draining out from the womb of emotional and electromagnetic debris brings a further element of trust, safety and a fertile magnetic ground, all of which creates a space for feminine essence to embody and be shared.

As the Third Gate circuit unfolds, the anus too is affected and involved as part of this release mechanism. The clitoris and the anus come into resonance, and this allows the master of the body, the anus, to feel welcomed and to properly do her job, which is to release all that does not serve her biology, her health, her flowering as a soul.

The Third Gate is very much about regenerating and revivifying the nervous system, bringing pleasure and delight to help your body come into the moment. Not just your mind or your soul, but your body, your biology, your DNA has to come into the moment. As your body does this, it relaxes, because the body goes into deep trust. And in this deepening trust, all that is not trusted releases from the nervous system, soul and physical body.

The Third Gate helps to build and activate neural pathways in the brain, heart and the brain in the gut. It serves to align these three nerve centers in the biology and nervous system. All of this is necessary to allow the soul to embody through these clarified centers. When this happens, you can sit deeply and comfortably in your body and nervous system and enjoy it. Then the soul can gracefully embody.

Once the human biology and nervous system are connected through the Seven Gates with Gaia, the mind relaxes and comes into its right synchronic flow. The mind cannot ever really generate or understand the pleasure of being in the moment. It will try to understand, it will try to create events, people and situations to help itself with its avowed purpose to be in the moment. Yet, being in the moment is a soulful and biological event for a woman in particular. It is a full body feeling, knowing and sensing. This is what embodies this now moment.

In the now moment of awe and wonder, bliss and pleasure, sublime love and creative flow, one finds the meeting of the twin channels of kundalini energy. This moment can be still and internal, it can be when making love, allowing a deep surrender of enjoyment and love, or surrender of giving spontaneously.

In this there is a vibrancy, a freshness, a purity, because nothing else is in that moment, there is only That. It is, it is, it is. This is purity, this is virginity. This was part of the understanding about the Virgin Mary. If a woman has this gate fully activated then she ''re becomes 'virginal. All of the memories, recorded emotions, have all been released and forgiven from her body, soul and nervous system.

The essence of this gate is connected to virginal qualities. Making love to a woman who embodies this gate can be like making love to a virgin. This is the entry point that the vestal virgins and priestesses in Greece, Palestine, Egypt and other countries used, to access lovemaking and immaculate conception. This is all possible, every woman can become like a virgin again, to live in the fresh now moment in body and soul.

In a committed relationship, both woman and man can constantly renew themselves through the Third Gate, and in this renewal, lovemaking can always be fresh, new and different.

This will sustain, nurture and water the sensual, intimately emotional soul unfolding of a relationship, and can lead out of the bedroom into the rest of your life, so you can be fresh and spontaneous with each other. You can always discover more about the person you have been with, even if you have spent a lot of time with them, for there are always new facets found in the moment that are delightful, undiscovered and a joy to behold and share in.

The Third Gate is crucial for intimate relationships. The clitoris becomes a spark of light that emanates and sparks, and this light goes outward and inward, nourishing the nervous system, nourishing the pelvic bowl, and allowing ones magnetic foundation to drop down, for you to sit more securely and comfortably in your inner throne.

In the Third Gate we find the blooming of birthing consciousness. In birthing a child, the Third Gate circuit allows one to navigate through all the realms in the birthing process. It is an innate guidance or navigation system that helps connect you and your child's spirit and soul throughout all the Gates down into physical birth in this world.

This is an intuitive and innate mechanism of Knowing within the connected nervous system and soul of the mother. The Third Gate is vital in this. True birthing only happens in the immediacy and freshness of the moment, allowing orgasmic birth to take place when a woman is connected in her seat, her throne, in pleasure.

All the emotions that are hindering this innate knowing within a woman's biology have to be cleared out first. Once it is anchored in a woman, she becomes more of a woman. She becomes both the purity and the dynamism, the virgin and the whore, who delights in her orgasmic, natural, blissful high frequency self AND is totally pure and innocent.

This is the way to give birth, for as you make love, so you can give birth. It can be a similar journey once the Gates are open - similar in an internal sense, not an external sense.

One woman shares the Voice of the Third Gate: "Ahh, what sweetness there is in connection. I take such pleasure in closeness, in feeling another's tenderness. When open, I am your center of joy and excitement, transforming all things back into their pure nature. I leap outward in joy, exuberance, and embrace. All life is beauty to me. When open, I am your own heart's compassion.

Treat me with greatest appreciation, and I will return you to innocence. With this healing process and this great gift of appreciation you have shown me, you will find in the circle of giving and receiving my own gifts back to you.

Like the full rose with all its petals opening out to the sun, all of my cells accessible to the atmosphere, I become more sensitive to all the energies passing over me; the slightest breeze, shift in sunlight, or fall of mist upon my petals sends ripples to my core. The more you receive it, the more you give joy back to me, and I continue to heal and clear deep within my being. (A.T.)

In the shadow of the Third Gate lies the mutilation of clitoral cutting, and the shame of all the people involved in these ceremonies found in many religious cultures. Here is stored numbness, a pain so intense that it leads to the switching off of emotion, so deep is the grief and sadness. Here is stored the clitoral shock at being touched and fondled un-lovingly and inappropriately, and not knowing what to do with these unexpressed emotions. Here lies the neglect and lack of appreciation of the clitoris.

Because our bodies and souls intuitively know what is right and sacred, and what is not, we subconsciously protect ourselves from disrespectful and dishonoring stimulation and penetration. This protection can feel like heavy, thick energy sitting in our bodies, or in the space around us, manifesting as extra physical weight, as lethargy, as dullness of thought, or lack of motivation.

A woman who feels emotionally and physically violated here may also disappear into her mind, "tuning out" and going numb in an attempt to avoid being present, as well as becoming overly mental, overly masculine or even overly feminine in attempts to compensate for this pain.

She is unable to describe her behavior as she is too used to this treatment. She knows no better and has been programmed to think this is normal. She lives in a man's world and is used to man's instant gratification with no depth of emotion or meaning. She may even fool herself into thinking that she is enjoying herself, finding sensory pleasure alone.

The clitoris feels this suppression at the level of the soul. Women store this in their cellular memories and energetic patterning. These emotional veils build up over time and eventually crust over, until the clitoris is desensitized and disconnected.

Physical stimulation of the clitoris for titillating pleasure, rather than for love, only adds to the abuse of a holy yoni. Any person who watches a pornographic film knows how to physically stimulate a clitoris, but to devotedly love a soul and clitoris is another matter that requires gratitude, appreciation, respect, joy, a good heart and purity of intention, as well as a choice to leave lust alone and refine oneself into loving devotion.

PRACTICE: HEALING THE THIRD GATE

Place a finger pad gently and lovingly on your clitoris. Feel and visualize your clitoris as a blooming red rose, feeling and touching this red rose, feeling her energetic and physical texture. Introduce yourself to her from your hearts voice, and await her welcome. What does she emanate to you as a feeling *from* her?

Now ask her these questions. *If you feel any emotions arise around these questions, simply breathe into them and allow yourself to feel them fully.*

> *Are you holding onto hurts from past partners and your father?*
> *Have past partners hurt the tender red rose of your clitoris, or used it in unloving ways?*
> *Do you have a deep mistrust of men?*
> *Have you ever felt the pure innocence of your sensual, feminine nature?*
> *Have you suffered, or given, sexual abuse?*
> *Do you feel you have lost your sexual purity, given it away or had it taken somehow?*
> *Do you feel dirty, ashamed, used and abused under the surface?*
> *Did you lose your virginity without love?*
> *Have you, and do you still, have sex without love, appreciation, gratitude and affection?*
> *Do you have an inability to have longer term intimate relationships?*
> *Do you avoid partnerships or conflicts?*
> *Do you have deeply Encoded fear?*
> *Do you feel dullness, lethargy, numbness, disconnection, cut off, low energy, de sensitized, armoring and protection in your clitoris?*
> *Do you, and have you ever, felt loveless, lustful and animalistic whilst having sex?*
> *Are you over weight?*
> *Are you spirit possessed or influenced by negative sexual spirits feeding off your life force?*

Say: *"Beloved Divine Mother, please help me feel and release my mistrust of men, my deep feelings of fear, shame, my desperation to please, my feelings of pain, my dullness, my lust, my bitterness, my loneliness, my deep feelings of grief, sadness and control from my clitoris and soul."* Repeat the word CLEAR until you feel a shift occur.

Visualize the red rose of your clitoris encased in a pink-gold-red sphere of softly glowing light. Breathe gently into her and this sphere of light through pursed lips, and see the light intensify with each breath. Do this for a few minutes until it is a radiant pink gold-red sphere of light totally encasing your clitoris.

Say: *"Beloved Divine Mother, Divine Healing Intelligence, please flood my clitoris and my soul with 6000% Pink Ray of tender, unconditional love. Please help me to feel love and forgiveness here. Please flood my clitoris and my soul with 4000% Red Ray of honour, passion and cleansing. Revive my inner strength and courage to share my total vulnerability and all my feelings. Allow me to feel and experience my true worth and value. Beloved Mother God, please flood my clitoris and my soul with 5000% of the Gold Ray of Christ. Please help me feel compassion here. Thank you."*

When you have felt and released the emotions held in your soul that are focalized though the clitoris, feelings of innocence and sweet freshness, borne from gratitude, appreciation, and compassion, arise. This Gate can be worked on alone or with a partner, yet it is harder to clear this gate without knowing what you are doing, and without going into both the light and dark of her. However, the alchemy of love between two committed people will surely heal this Gate if both partners are emotionally aware and open.

When the first Three Gates are connected and healed, both personally and collectively, the yoni becomes a portal to the womb.

"Being touched with praise, my yoni lips quiver in rhythmic, pulsing breath. Gentle remembering, feeling the honoring, the gratitude within the looping love flowing between us touches my Second Gate. As the blooming rose of my Third Gate is touched by compassion, the breath of my being is felt in a soft presence on the surface.

The river of fury, unleashed moments earlier, is felt below the surface, molten lava that will not be controlled in its collapsing of the surface illusion of peace and harmony. To create anew, the old must be destroyed. True peace and harmony will arise within the balancing, the reharmonizing of our instruments." (C.O.)

You have to feel your own healing in order for the yoni channel to become a gateway into the womb. This is the way it has always been done, and always will be done. What affects one woman affects all women in the web of life and interconnection that we all live in.

THE FOURTH GATE: ENTERING THE GRAIL WOMB

The Fourth Gate is the cervix, entrance to the holy of holies—the womb Grail. Magdalene is known as the Grail for carrying the bloodline of Christ, yet she herself knew, and taught, that the opening to the Grail, the opening to Womb Consciousness, lies through the Fourth Gate in each and every woman.

The Fourth Gate is a diamond doorway, a star gate: the opening into your womb is an opening into space. This diamond shape is similar to the outer layer of the sacred geometrical figure known as the Sri Yantra. The Sri Yantra is the Pattern of Creation, a creation held in seed form within the wombs of all women.

Most neo-tantric sexual healing focuses on the personal healing only, neglecting the deeper, larger picture of the collective feminine consciousness that must be experienced in order to transform the vessel of the yoni into the holy of holies: the Grail Womb.

This means you travel through these arenas and cultivate a deeper empathy, a deeper compassion, a deeper opening within you that blesses and sanctifies your yoni for sacred union, the alchemy of co-creation. To have this open yoni, to enter the Grail Womb, means we travel into the darkest depths and the highest heights, with commitment, devotion, sincerity, and dedication to transmute what is held there.

THE DWELLER ON THE THRESHOLD

The Fourth Gate is known alchemically as the Dweller on the Threshold. This is a vital place for all women to enter, and is the greatest barrier, and guardian, to the womb's mysteries. It is here that the reversal of roles happens: where the soul becomes master of the ego, instead of the ego being master of the soul. As the soul is made of love-wisdom-power derived from humility and holy desire in greater and greater degrees, this is what you have to be living, to some degree, to enter the womb.

As the Fourth Gate opens, many voices of fear, conflict, projection, judgment and resistance arise, for many issues are stored here on the most primordial levels. Here is where many of your deepest healings lie, where some of your deepest causal wounds and deep seated emotional pains of your soul lie.

It takes true courage, trust, and deep vulnerability, to enter this gateway. You have to be prepared to let go of everything you know, and have learnt, to enter this space. To be able to heal this (with your partner) takes true commitment, for it is the gateway to your deepest sadness, your deepest love, your most profound separation, and your most profound union between your inner male and female.

The Fourth Gate is a portal to many dimensions of experience: when you enter it, your life will change. For a man to enter this Gate, a woman must trust him completely, surrender completely, and be totally vulnerable on a preverbal, primal level beyond words and thoughts.

As he is allowed into the womb through the portals of appreciation, love, and trust, a man's consciousness enters pure space, and he feels the immense power of creation, as well as the power to create, accompanied by loving bliss and the sheer beauty of love that is painful and heartbreaking in its clarity, purity and intensity. This has to be experienced to be believed; it is how sacred sexual union occurs between souls, not just between bodies and minds.

One can have glimpses of this opening into the Fourth Gate, but to integrate it is another matter. To integrate it means journeying to the Fifth gate inside the womb: unifying your inner male and female. This is a journey both within you and outside you (in your outer relationships) and it requires all of you to participate; your sexual energy, your emotions, your body, your mind, and your soul all have to come together and express themselves in order to unify.

To be strong in sovereign Self-love is a key to entering the Fifth Gate. As a woman opens up even further from a place of strength, self-empowerment and independence, she can become more vulnerable, as now she understands this not as weakness, but as strength.

It is a feminine strength to be receptive and whole, and to allow your chosen man deep within you. This may take some time, as after the initial opening of the Fourth Gate, many healing issues arise in order to be integrated into self-empowerment.

For the Fourth Gate to open, you leave your comfort zones. The arts of Tantra and sacred relationship take on whole new dimensions, and become deeper and richer on many more levels of awareness. Indeed, the whole union of man and woman becomes possible through the opening of the seven gates, as the woman becomes open to the cosmic womb, drawing the man within this womb, which in turn dissolves them both.

The womb is the source of great healing. Once we return to it, having healed all that happened on our journey away from it, we become whole. The womb first awakens as we bring her the gifts of Presence, devotion, deep respect, appreciation, and the feeling qualities of love and adoration. This begins the birthing phase. The womb will then begin to speak of her needs and desires. Only the purified heart will hear, only the courageous will respond.

The womb speaks the language of love. Nothing else will nurture and nourish her, or provide her the safety she needs to flower. She drinks in radiating light, the sweetness of conscious breath, the sounds and vibrations of harmony.
The womb does not understand the intellect and the ways of the world. She does not hear or respond to voices of fear or judgment. She will not expose herself to the impure, and she will not trust to bare her fruit for the foolish. One must be prepared to take great risks and rise to challenges, and be tested in unexpected ways.

The jewel of an open womb is not for the meek and half-hearted. It is for the brave and the strong-willed, for the heroes and heroines among you. For the womb to reveal herself, she needs to feel a genuine loyalty, and a love that surpasses all worldly desires. Only then can she begin to allow herself to be unveiled, and reveal the secrets of creation and the mysteries of life.

The womb's desire is to feel the warmth of love and support from the feminine and masculine, which are both necessary for her to open and expand. The womb desires to attune to the masculine to feel his strength, protection and love. The feminine must embody the womb in all its innocence and power, and the male must act according to her wisdom and guidance.

A deep love between inner man and inner woman creates a resonant vibration of sacred union where birth can be manifest in its fullest potential. When two share and melt into the flames of love, the womb is ignited. All separate desires and individual agendas must be surrendered to the wisdom the womb holds. This is bringing Heaven to Earth, spirit into matter, love into form.

The womb is where the un-manifest is brought into manifestation—where beauty and joy are birthed into life as a juicy, orgasmic, tangible experience. When love is anchored into form, into reality, into a direct lived experience.

Total respect and humility is offered for this voice to come forth. This voice is recognizable as a soft, powerful clarity. It is the voice of the feminine—pure, gentle, and graceful, yet powerful, direct, and deep. It does not compromise or search for approval. It does not speak of duality nor fear and doubt. It remains calm and precise, knowing exactly what is required in each moment.

At this stage, the voice of the ego will likely emerge, fearful of its own death and trying to reassert control over the heart in order to stay alive. The ego has been the driving force for so long that it will not be put to rest easily. This is where vigilance and discernment are of utmost importance: the way to distinguish truth from illusion, the voice of ego from the voice of the womb, is by the quality of its tone.

The ego's voice is hurried and will cause disturbance to the flow of breath. It will talk in an unrefined harshness that will try to persuade, argue, defend, project, belittle, or manipulate. This language is foreign to the reality of our being.

The womb will soothe, invite, inspire, and will, more often than not, surprise in what it has to share. A portal to wisdom, the womb has a unique point of view separate from the mind's. She will share her own unerring insight in such a distinct voice that it will be impossible to ignore.

The womb has to become the master, for it is the voice of wisdom. This authority must be respected and acted upon. When the womb receives consistent nurturance and unconditional love, it starts to come alive, and begins to attune to its vastness and energetic subtleties. If a woman is attentive to the awakening presence of her womb, she will experience new and unique sensations.

PRACTICE: TRAVELING THROUGH THE FOURTH GATE

Breathe. CentER. Drop your consciousness down into your womb space, holding the yoni mudra over your womb, the size of a pear. Visualize the diamond shape at the opening to your cervix. Breathe into it.

Through this neck of your womb—the thick band of muscles that paves the way for new life to come into the world—you can also travel *toward* the womb, to the Grail within. Bring your attention to your cervix, and try to isolate it, just focusing on that one area. Breathe here and ask yourself lovingly, "Can I feel this entry gate?"

If not, you may want to physically feel your cervix and allow your finger to just rest there. Bring breath and presence into it. Now that you can feel it ..

What do you feel here?
Do you see any colors, feel any sensations, emotions, do any memories arise?

What does she want to say to you?
What specifically does she want from you to open, and how can you best connect to her, and to your womb?
How does she want you to recognize and honor her?

THE FIFTH GATE

The body and sexuality are tools through which we can experience duality/separation and unity/love. Sexual union, practiced as a rite and an art, is a bridge to the Divine and to other dimensions. In this union, intercourse becomes a living bliss, love and joy.

As this union occurs, dimensional doorways are opened between you and your partner. In this union, your evolution will accelerate exponentially, each of you receiving the deepest lesson/energy you need from the other to complete the wholeness of yourself.

The Fifth Gate circuit consolidates and integrates an essential part of the human journey with sexuality, soul, Earth and Divine. The Fifth Gate circuit creates a platform and foundation for a true meeting, a true sacred union, to occur within you, and your relationships. The Fifth Gate allows a beginning and an ending, a dissolution and a building of a foundation, the ending of one story, one choice or one path, and the beginning of another pathway and a fresh choice now unhindered by conditioning.

It is from this basis, bowl or chalice of choice, free, un-channeled and unhindered, that a form of sacred union can occur within the bridal chamber of the heart-womb. The Fifth Gate is a coalescing of many different parts into a new stream of coherent, unified light and consciousness. There are many forms of sacred union we engage in, found in the different inter relationships and polarities within you on the Tree of Life. This sacred union in the Fifth Gate is the fuller connection of love and power within you.

This can be deeply internal for a woman, for this place once reached is inviolate. The woman becomes a virgin again, pure and free in her sexuality, but also loyal and committed. All the imprints, encodements, memories, experiences, partners that influenced and coated your sexuality in the past, dissolve in the field of the Fifth Gate. We are left with the pure felt sense of our own Self.

In the Fifth Gate, the light soul and dark shadow waves of yourself (or the red and white male and female streams) have come together from the Fourth Gate. The field created by their coming together is the Fifth Gate. It is from this space that the womb can open, because these trinities of field, wave, and particle, the second trinity of your soul, body and spirit, the third trinity of you, Creator and your partner, and the fourth trinity of you, Earth, and Creator can all be felt now.

All these trinities can now actualize in your individuated form. All your webs of relationship are now solid, clear and in integrity, and more than that in love, Shakti, and the flow of life.

In the field that is the Fifth Gate, dissolution leads to regeneration. In this field are held many possibilities, potentials and choices. Even within this field you may still be attracted or tempted by certain avenues, pathways or choices that may seem reasonable and were part of your past. The most loving choice one can make here is to go for the 'one 'in everything that you do. It is here that new choices can be made, and they will be presented to you in this field of the Fifth Gate. [16]

The Fifth Gate is accessed in its entirety by those who have healed their wounds of incarnation, by those who have a single minded focus, heart-full surrender and dedication woven together through the fabric of soul and the Earth.

In the Fifth Gate, we find the completing of separation from attachments and lustful sensuality from the soul. As we grow in the purity of the soul, previous 'pleasures 'become a hindrance.

As this occurs, woman starts to emanate and live in a Magnetic Silence, a warm, inviting, enticing field with a centre of silence. When a woman is living in this receptive, attractive silence, transmitted through her open magnetic body and self, she invites man in, effortlessly, gracefully.

She is a pulsating beacon of velvety attraction that attracts a man from his very essence, beyond the mind and subconscious, from the roots of his soul. It draws him in without question, without thought, without hesitation, magnetizing him back to the source and womb of creation.

Back into the depths of warm, vast, all Comforting Silence he goes, letting go of the mind that has made him a man, into Divine Man. In all he sees and feels, attraction is innate, effortless. Bliss is what she attains, and becomes.

The field that is created around the Fourth Gate, the entrance to your womb, is the Fifth Gate, the abyss, the void, the womb, portal, or Da'ath. Within the field of the Fifth Gate lies the dissolution of the tension between one set of our inner polarities, where electromagnetic male and female dissolve. It is not a true meeting, it is actually a dissolution.

The Fifth Gate is a guardian. You have to move through, heal, learn from and successfully release distorted polarities within you. This is not a linear process. It is a multidimensional, spatial process. It may not happen all at one time, for there are different aspects of you being resolved here, and bit by bit, piece by piece, the old self can surrender and let go into this unknown abyss.

In the Fifth Gate, you can be greatly helped in your purpose if you are sufficiently cohesive to enter here fully and come out with the wisdom, integration and release of your old sense of polarity/duality. Here, an aspect of your old form drops away or lets go. It is not destructive or a death, it is a releasing, a letting go, dissolving, dropping away, like you are wearing a coat and you let it drop off your shoulders to the floor.

---

[16] This field is also connected to Preconception, found in the Tree of Life in Binah, where preconception occurs both in human and universal forms.

This can work in many ways. If you are interested in tantra or relationship, it will be the dropping of old ideas or needs around sexual love or sexual relating. Up to this point, you may be very interested in certain forms of relating, and after this you won't be interested in those forms of relating.

In the Fifth Gate, the geo-genetic template of Gaia as a living part of our Divine Blueprint is more embodied as a balance of love and power. The Fifth Gate is a Well where our previous sense of male/female is neutralized and releases by staying in this space between spaces. Many parts of you can come together, and in this coming together there is dissolution, OR when much dissolves, then many parts of you can come together.

BIOLOGICAL CHANGES IN THE HEALING OF THE WOMB

Awakening is a physical and neurobiological phenomenon, as brain, spine, chakras, and organs change their frequency. The same occurs to a womb. New cell configurations and geometries, birthing pains, cramps, actual physical expansion of the womb, womb discharges, and other phenomena arise.

Chemicals and hormones change their flow, brain patterns change, and your cells start to separate out from each other, revealing more and more space within, a space that allows more love to manifest and be felt. As this happens, you gain another ability, that of being able to transmute with the womb.

The womb has the facility to be able to contain and transmute negative or harming energies, stripping away the orientation of the negativity into a pure state of neutrality. This stage of working with the womb comes only after it has been cleared and with the guidance of a womb teacher.

Womb healing is also a physical phenomenon. Our physical bodies are the last stop for disharmony and dis-ease to reveal and heal. It is not uncommon for cancers, physical cysts to actually show up during the healing process as the causal level is releasing. Often things get worse before they get better. Many occurrences can take place that can be detected by the medical profession. It is a biological change as well as a consciousness shift. I noticed that some of these shifts included:

- bleeding constantly for months, and/or irregular menstrual cycles
  a polyp, or growth inside the yoni/womb
- precancerous cells at dangerous levels as emotions and toxins release
- actual physical muscular sensation, painful at times, of the womb and pelvis stretching and expanding
- feeling of blocks/old numbness dissolving and being felt while making love
- the carving open of spaces within the yoni and womb physically, emotionally, and spiritually
- seeing and experiencing different aspects of my womanly self being found, discovered, excavated, and opened

- random points of sharp, electrical pain in the ovaries as opposed to the deep, dull ache of the womb as it heals and releases
- lower back pain in the space behind the womb in deep, throbbing aches
- increased physical and emotional sensitivity to anyone approaching the womb and wanting something from me
- sadness at anyone apart from the beloved touching your most precious, open, and innocent space
- actual physical birthing contractions felt from within, similar to birthing a baby
- All of these can happen when the womb opens, ignites, and becomes alive. It is a mark of womb consciousness becoming integrated with the soul and body-mind.

THE SIXTH GATE

"In the space between the fifth and sixth gates, a woman, like the Dakinis and priestesses of ancient tradition, can open herself in service to any man and bring a healing and transformation for him."

To activate and manifest the sixth gate fully requires surrender. Surrendering to the power of Shakti as it is comes through you means you are open to life, regeneration, and the laws and beauty of nature. Surrendering to love means you love the other as you are loved by the Divine. You actually totally embrace the other person without charge or resistance, loving them unconditionally in exactly the same way God loves each and every soul created. This is the greatest Gift of Sacred Union, and its goal. Surrender is the final feminine wisdom key to awakening.

In this process of surrendering to what is presented to you in life, in your relating, within yourself, rises up your deepest resistance, your deepest shadows. Everything in the basement of your subconscious, every voice within you that says no to love, no to peace, no to joy, no to what IS, arises, and fights. This fight takes you deeper and deeper, and wears you out, wears out the fight in you, the resistances of the small self, until you break down.

In this breaking down lies the opening to the softness and gentling of love. Surrender dismantles every part of you, and remakes you in love's image, but only when you have sincerely asked for love to enter your life.

Surrender softens what is rigid within. It gentles us. Surrender is a process, a continual experience that happens every day. It is never done or completed, never a statement. One is always surrendering.

Surrender leads to true vulnerability, which cleanses the heart and releases fear. Letting go of fear we are able to expand into more love, which in turn leads to more vulnerability and more fears arising . . . until all that is left is a pure heart as a conduit for love to flow through—life as a moment-by-moment surrender. You move when the palpable living force of love moves you, because you have become so available, so present, that you live by what you know to be true, because it is happening right now.

In this trust, nothing matters because everything changes every moment. All your sense of reason and planning collapses. Everything that is needed right now might be completely different from what was needed in the previous moment, and in the next moment. Love responds in the now, and there is no teaching, laws, or rules for this. Love is the whole of the law.

In surrender all things are given through you. You have to completely release the little self and the dream of "getting" in order to be open, and in this release you become quite attractive—a magnet that draws to you ten times what you have given.

You do what you need to do, with care, with full attention, and then move on to the next thing to do, which unfolds organically. This step-by-step approach allows the full death of the previous moment in order to create space for the next new moment, where we know nothing about the future, and have forgotten about the past. This involves deep trust that whatever is needed will come, that the unfolding will take you wherever you need to go.

Everything is included in surrender, and nothing is left out. Everything has to go, and you have to leave no back door, no escape route, no way for the small self to come back.

Surrender is the last quality to master you before you live the surrendered life. Living a surrendered life, there are few thoughts arising within you. You may not know the words that will come out of your mouth in any moment, and have no need to remember what they are, or what the actions are that flow through your bodymind and speech. You learn by what comes through you. There is great delight and joy in this, for in this allowing of ourselves to be nobody, we become able to relate with anybody, in any moment.

Surrender is the portal through which love and Shakti flow. The acceptance and allowance of everything that is happening to you right now leads, by extension, to an acceptance of everything that is happening in the world around you, locally and globally. This surrender does not lead to passivity, but to an ever-present thread of contentment, a state of fluid peace that is the basis for awakened and radical action in the world.

Whereas surrender is the source of harmony, contention is the root of discord. When one is in contention, one is not in surrender. Surrender is recognizing the difference between the presence of flow and the absence of flow. Life lives through us, love masters us, and the adventure of life carries us along, moment by magical moment.

"I am the gravity of blackness, the essence of the void. I am velvety nothingness, the silence that absorbs all. I am nothingness and in me all dissolves and returns to stillness. I am the void, I am the black light. I am space of transition."

The Sixth Gate is the silent, deep primordial center, a richly fertile field of tremendous depth where we are ready to fully incarnate, to embody and individualize, and be without fear, judgment, grief or residue from the past.

The sixth gate is the meeting of personal womb and Gaia's womb. It is in the sixth gate that a woman really feels her womb's connection with Gaia and her innate resting place in Gaia's crystalline core. The sixth gate is the void from which all creation emerges, first into essence in the fifth gate, then more into form in the lower gates.

It connects to the fifth gate magnetic field around the physical womb space that connects directly into the magnetics of Gaia's core which opens the gateway for a woman to access this multidimensional space. It is the direct entry point into galactic center.

The Sixth Gate is accessed through an upwards spiraling movement from the womb into the pineal that opens into the vastness of void. The teeming movement within the silence, stillness and vastness of the void lies here encapsulated. The Sixth Gate is one of absorption into bliss. You arrive more into your feminine embodiment in a graceful, Self understood, deeply loving and self evident way.

This deep, soft movement into the Sixth Gate is feminine, strong and centered. It is not about holding and embracing the other here; it is where both male and female are in this space in union. This is a space of mutuality. The love we feel for the other, the love we feel inside, all merges into one love.

As we take full responsibility for our fulfillment, we become whole—no longer demanding that the context of our lives provide us happiness, or hoping to view our wholeness through anyone else's eyes.

This aloneness creates spaciousness, depth, and genuineness, because you no longer feel a need to look or act in any way shaped by your ancestry or the world. You no longer value what the world thinks. Paradoxically, such aloneness allows you to become closer to every person, and allows every person to feel closer to you. You have dismantled any barriers to closeness and people can feel that; it speaks to their hearts and attracts them.

Fluidity dissolves all rules, allowing you to express and embody the highest potential in any moment. This is resting in the heart of harmony. This resting, this abiding, is natural and graceful, and cannot be forced.

For a woman to fully embody this, they need the Divine Masculine to provide the grid or Divine Matrix for these unformed energies to clothe themselves into form, into manifestation: to bring all your soul into embodiment. One could say this is the structure of a vacuum, where the idea of form and the vast expanse of emptiness co-exist: one known, one unknown.

This is the final stargate before birth that a child's soul has to come through. For two or three weeks before birth, at the time of the "Braxton Hicks" contractions, is an ideal time to connect to the core of the Earth with mother, father and child.[17] In communing at this time with the spirit child ready to be born in labour, mother father and child can enable the final adjustments to occur.

The Sixth Gate requires that you have integrated the previous Five Gates in your lived, embodied experience. A solo practitioner not in a Beloved relationship can reach the Sixth and Seventh Gate, but will not be able to embody it. It is the Tantrics like Padmasambhava and Yeshe Tsogyal, Christ and Mary, and other couples known and unknown throughout history, who have managed to go all the way and BE this on earth, in relationship.

---

[17] This can be simple using a practice for communicating with your unborn baby. Just insert 'core of Earth', into the circuit and the breath practice. Ideally also Yabyum, but that is not vital.

The original and pure DNA blueprint for humanity is held here. To ignite this blueprint takes the sexual energy to be sublimated in Divine Relating, the mutual honoring and weaving of the Gates between man and woman. The blueprint of male female union is the basis for a harmonious, God inspired loving materialization of Earth's Dreaming held in the core of the Earth, a flowing infinity loop between your Sixth Gate, Gaia, God and your partners Sixth Gate.

The Sixth Gate is the *active reunion* with the first primordial pair of polarities; they are already wed, they are unity in duality. They are vibrating stillness at the heart of all duality. Man and woman embody, re-connect, remember, re-awaken within them this primordial unity IN duality, and live it in, and between them.

As you travel through the Sixth Gate, you embody more and more, deepening into living the consummation of Divinity on Earth. Many couples will come to this through a clear understanding of womb awakening, beyond healing or a reactionary paradigm, into a true, Clear Seeing.

The Sixth and Seventh Gates are about Awakening. Duality and electromagnetic distortions are not here. This is a realm for soulful, Divinely inspired tantric beloveds. One Key for this are the seed codes of light held in The Beloved Lords Prayer in Aramaic, which delineate the journey from Seventh Gate to First Gate. Immersing in this living light prayer, before, during and after lovemaking will help this carving open of the infinite light that stretches through all creation.

From the Seventh Gate this infinite light wave of *Ha Shem* courses through the womb of the Earth flowing through the womb of woman into the world, into Earth's fields, into Cosmos, Void and Source. This infinite wave Ha Shem is coursing in all creation, and is brought to a manifested, focalized point through the womb. This living light of perpetual birthing, of perpetual consummation, of eternal unfolding, never ceasing and never born, never dying, is always unfolding.

THE SEVENTH GATE

'I have no form no shape, I am infinite consciousness. I am all that exists before and after. You cannot find me because I come to you. I am infinite creation. Infinite embrace. Infinite wisdom. Pure presence. Through me you enter into God creation, infinite Love.

I am being constantly creating, forming, shaping, I hold the universe as much as I am part of it. I am pure creation before and after. In me you find all connections, all that is, all that ever was, all that ever will be. If you can hold me in my expanse, in one place, this is the access of the seventh gate.

I am the ultimate space of healing that women are. All exists here, every question, every answer, every form, every formless. Being in this means everything finds its place within creation, in all layers and all levels of the human physical, emotional, spiritual, and soulful. Everything has its place and all connections can be made with alignment of freewill and time. When all is connected and all has its place and all is seen, there is a wholeness, everything is healed on all levels within your being.

I am breath with out breath. I am the cosmos in its utter stillness and total vibration in its fullest vibration."

The 7th Gate encompasses every single circuit, structure, aspect within our body and soul consciousness. It IS everything alive and connected. When the pelvic bowl, spine, alta major, crown and pineal are fully open and connected, this creates the skeleton of energetic circuitry that allows the 7th Gate Consciousness to awaken.

This consciousness in intimately woven into Earth and through Earth into galactic center and beyond.

There is an innate safety built into this consciousness that when entered with a question in a certain way, unfolding occurs in that moment. It is totally known in this moment, and at the same time the way is not accessible outside of this moment.

The seventh gate is so vast, you can take a whole planet into it. It is deeply connected to Divine Will, the deep innate emanation of a woman embodying unconditional love. This is why it is so nourishing and sustaining.

It is God creation, that infinite place of creation. When we as women come into this place and offer a piece to manifest, everything can come and be held in this field. This holding is effortless, there is no action in it. It is an awareness of consciousness, a holding in being. As it is held here, it is nourished, held in unconditional love, in God creation. Everything that it needs is in that infinite space and through the conscious awareness of the woman being it, it finds its place.

THE INFINITE WELL AND THE GRAIL

Within the seventh gate lies the power of transformation on a core level. The Grail is the Black Light, the light that washes you clean of your small self, that washes you into the eternal, that brings you the experience of the infinite from deep within your body-mind.

It is in the seventh gate that female Samadhi happens: the breath within the womb stops, the mind stops, the fear of death stops, and you are left totally present, totally natural. You become unadorned simplicity, able to sit in the moment where all creation starts, and stops.

It is here that you go within for your fuel, the limitless flow in the swelling river of being. It is here that eternity lies, from which all is birthed, from which Shakti flows—the doorway to the great Central Sun, to Source. As above, so below: the great Central Sun at the center of our galaxy, the Great Womb prophesied by the Mayans as meeting us in 2012, lies within you right now. Not in the future, but here and now. Why wait for it when it is here now?

As you traveled through the sixth gate, you learned how to use all the aspects of the eighteen pathways, and how to transmute the blockages that stop you from venturing deeper into your feminine essence. It demanded tremendous courage to pass through here, for we can only go as far as our longing can reach: our longing, our passion, and our desire for the Ultimate.

The silence of the seventh gate is accessed as we find light in the heart of darkness to lead us to our core. To get there, we are required to travel far from ordinary experience. Here there is nothing familiar, no matrix world, and no realm of dreams—just silence. Here lies what is ignored or glossed over by most humans.

PRACTICE: THE SEVEN GATES FLOW MEDITATION

Womb consciousness is the weaving of all aspects of feminine awakening consciousness into our experience, in all dimensions. Each of the gates, the feminine portals into soul awareness, brings an aspect of the hologram of womb consciousness that is an ever expanding, infinite, and all-encompassing way of being-ness. The more deeply a woman inhabits all of her gates, the more she anchors in this way of being.

1. Interlace your fingers at the base of your skull. Tilt your head forward to stretch and open your Alta Major, where the head connects to the first vertebrae of spine. Take some deep breaths into this, opening, cleansing, feeling and releasing any tension or density held here. Spend five minutes breathing and opening this portal, the mouth of the Goddess where Shakti enters a woman's body.

    Pray from the seed of your heart: Beloved Divine Mother, I love You. I open my Alta Major, my body, my soul, to receive more of You.

2. Release your hands and place them gently on your kidneys. Invite the warmth and energy from your Alta Major down to your kidneys. The kidneys are key to feminine embodiment, bringing us down out of our mental energy and stored fear into our fluid feeling body. Breathe deeply into your kidneys for five minutes.

    Pray from the seed of your heart: Beloved Divine Mother, I love You. Please open and soften my kidneys to receive more of your Divine Shakti, your Divine Love.

3. Release your hand from your kidneys and place a finger against your anus, and your other hand under your perineum like a hammock. Breathe the warmth, the flow, the love from your kidneys down to your entire pelvic floor for five minutes.

    Pray from the seed of your heart: Beloved Divine Mother, I love You. Please soften and open my anus and my magnetic ground, so that I may rest more deeply in my true seat, my sovereign self.

4. From your anus, breathe all this energy into your ovaries until you feel them tingle. Continue breathing here for 5 minutes.

    Pray from the seed of your heart: Beloved Mother Gaia, I Love You. Please connect my ovaries more directly to your body. Please ground my ovaries more deeply into your grids.

5. First Gate, Yoni Lips:
    The first gate is the entrance to our most sacred space. It opens when we feel trust, welcoming, respect, safety and appreciation. Our first gate is deeply connected to the magnetic current that runs throughout the entire Web of Life. It holds the innate intelligence of what energies are 'right 'to welcome deeper into our lives, our hearts, our more intimate spaces.

From your ovaries, breathe all this energy into your yoni lips. *Touch your Yoni Lips. Hold them.* Gently, softly, sensually breathe into your yoni lips. Feel their contact with the surface you are sitting on. Feel their magnetic pull toward Gaia. Breathe deeply into this connection.

Pray: Beloved Divine Mother. I love You. I welcome your love. I deeply trust your guidance. Feel the warmth and softness move into your yoni lips.

What do you feel here? What colors, sensations, feelings are here?
What does she want to say to you?
What specifically does she want from you to open and connect to the other gates?
How does she want you to recognize and honor her?

6. Third Gate, Clitoris:
From the yoni lips our energy organically flows into the clitoris. The clitoris holds a depth of dynamic vitality, purity and pleasure. The radiating joy that emanates from the clitoris is contagious and energizing. When Shakti moves through our third gate unhindered we feel a freshness and excitement about all that we engage in, bringing a lightness, a playful engagement and motivating energy.

Bring your breath from your yoni lips into your clitoris. If she feels tight and tucked away, touch her gently with your finger, allowing the warmth of your hand to soften and invite her out of hiding. If you feel sexual energy building here, allow it to move through you, without grasping or directing it. The third gate holds tremendous pleasure that can become orgasmic and undulating through out our whole body and being if we surrender with out grasping to its flow.

Pray from the seed of your heart: Beloved Divine Mother. I love You. I feel You. Help me to feel my sweet innocence and purity. Help me to open to my pure Shakti vitality and flow. Help me to trust the wisdom of pleasure and surrender.

What do you feel here? What colors, sensations, feelings are here?
What does she want to say to you?
What specifically does she want from you to open and connect to the other gates?
How does she want you to recognize and honor her?

7. Second Gate, G-Spot:
The second gate or G-spot is a powerful magnetic center deep in a woman's yoni and body. It anchors her into part of her magnetic floor, bringing a certain sovereignty and trust that allows her to open to the enlightening flow of gratitude. The magnetism generated in this gratitude attracts resources, relationships, and opportunities for a woman to express her soul and Shakti in her life and relationships. The pleasure generated here is woven into a tremendous power that can open deeper energy centers all along the central channel of the spine.

Breathe all the light, energy and warmth from your clitoris through your yoni to the cave of your G-spot. Allow it to pool here, perhaps you will feel a pulse or strong magnetic current. Keep breathing deeper and deeper into this place and feel your magnetic floor begin to relax into a more settled anchoring of your essence deep in your pelvic bowl.

Pray from the seed of your heart: *Beloved Divine Mother. I love You. Please help me surrender more deeply. Thank you for your love. Thank you for my life, thank you for all the gifts and people You bring me. I give you all the power, all the glory, all the honour. Thank you, thank you, thank you!*

Visualize a streaming blue waterfall, wild and free.
What is its sound? What do you feel here?
What colors, sensations, feelings are here?
What does she want to say to you?
What specifically does she want from you to open and connect to the other gates?
How does she want you to recognize and honor her?

8. Fourth Gate, Cervix:
The fourth gate is the threshold to the womb. It is the meeting place of our deepest polarities, male/female, light/dark, dynamic/still. We cannot enter through the fourth gate without deep reconciliation with our shadow. When we have seen, felt, and embraced our darkness we open to power and sovereignty. The fourth gate holds deep wounding and also the keys to our greatest evolution through womb consciousness. When these imprints are unearthed, unraveled and brought back into love, we are invited into the powers and mystery of womb space.

Breathe all the energy from your G-spot into your cervix. Feel around the collagenous ring of your cervix for any tensions or densities. Breath into these places with curiosity and love. Allow any feeling to arise.

Pray from the seed of your heart: *Beloved Divine Father, I love you. Please penetrate my fourth gate with your love. Please illuminate all the darkness within me, so that I may bring it back into love. Please help me unify all parts of me. Please help me anchor more deeply in my internal pillar and knowing of Your Divine Will.*

Visualize a diamond opening, the star gate of your cervix. This is the opening into your womb, and an opening into infinite space.
What do you feel here? What colors, sensations, feelings are here?
What does she want to say to you?
What specifically does she want from you to open, and connect to her, and the womb?
How does she want you to recognize and honor her?

9. Fifth Gate, Field of the Womb:
   The fifth gate is the field that surrounds the womb. It is a space that invites a deeper and softer dissolution of who we thought we were, a space of sacred union with self, with God, with partner, where we disrobe and merge into the pulse of unity.

   Pray from the seed of your heart: *Beloved Divine Mother, Beloved Divine Father. I love You. I want to merge all of me into You. Beloved Mother Earth, please take my womb deeper into your crystalline spinning core. I AM LOVE. I AM LOVE. I AM LOVE.*

   Enter pure, vast space. Visualize the Yab-Yum or Sacred Marriage, the union between the inner male and female aspects of yourself. Breathe gently into this space.

10. Sixth Gate, Void:
    The sixth gate is the deep, vast darkness of void space. It is our direct connection to galactic center, and the womb-heart of our Beloved Divine Mother. The sixth gate holds keys for transmutation and healing of energies both personal and collective. It is both the entry and exit point for all creations entering and exiting the field of manifestation.

    From the field of the fifth gate, gently breathe and allow yourself to drop deeper into the center of gravity deep in the core of your womb. Allow all the mists of the fifth gate to condense and collapse into the very center of your womb space.

    Pray, from the seed of your heart: *Beloved Mother God, I love You. I feel You. Please move me, please move all of me deeper into your core. Please take me deeper into galactic center, the seed of your sacred womb-heart. I love You, I love You, I love You.*

    Visualize a cross within a Vesica Piscis. Relax, and be silent to whatever arises within you.

11. The Seventh Gate, The Creating:
    The Seventh Gate is the pure infinite light of Source that weaves throughout all creation.

    From the deep void space of your sixth gate, allow yourself to release any sense of gravity or depth, and dissolve into the expansion of light emerging from deep within this void. Feel see this Light going in all directions, creating everything in this universe. Rest in this as long as you feel.

LIVING FROM WOMB-HEART

Once your center of gravity has dropped down from your mind into your magnetic ground of womb-heart, you are living Feminine Essence. This is the feminine pillar, a meeting point of reference between the physical body and soul of a woman. Dropping your sense of identity, reaction and response down into the womb is a more silent, still place than the mind.

It is important to integrate your psychological state, your feelings, your womb and your body awareness to create a bridge of expression between them that can emanate and communicate outwards as well as inwards. Many times we can leave out the mind and a piece of our embodiment from our feminine, that is we leave out a part of our masculine. This needs to be tended to, recognized and integrated with the womb-heart, and the best place to do this is in intimate relationship.

During the day, become aware of which center you are speaking from, thinking from, feeling from. Do you feel from the mind, do you feel from the heart, do you feel from the womb? Be aware of these movements within you every day. The more you are aware of this, the more your attention can descend down into the quiet, still, peaceful strength of the womb heart with the mind as the servant of this, included and integrated.

Living from the womb-heart is living from a balanced place of love and power. In connecting with the womb-heart, two aspects of the soul harmonize and, work together to discover the visceral knowing of what is necessary to conceive high vibration children.

It is the combination of power and love, womb and heart merged and surrendered to Divine source, that creates the gateway, the spark of light to which these New Children are drawn. To develop and Remember your innate consciousness of the unified womb heart within you requires focusing on your heart and womb, and breathing there every day.

PART 3:
BIRTHING

CONSCIOUS CONCEPTION

CONSCIOUS CONCEPTION

The Soul's Design for Birthing happens when you are conceived in the wedding of love, Shakti, joy and bliss: you are conceived within a Sacred Relating. In ecstatic mutually orgasmic conception, these waves create a rich field container for the fertilized egg, providing photonic nutrients of light beyond the standard biological processes that create the newly fertilized egg. These powerful sexual, magnetic, bio-photonic and electric energy fields transmit many codes of information that influence DNA.

These codes can be activated in many different ways depending on the loving, or not, fuel that activates the pairing of genetic codes. The many variations that can happen, similar to the tumbling locks of a safe or a Rubiks Cube, are guided by the amount of life force, love and sensual presence present at the moment of conception.

In the Soul's Design for Birthing you are grown and genetically coded in the womb to freely give and receive love, which is greatly facilitated by you being conceived in pleasure and love. Sacred Relationship and its love-making brings forth Conscious Conception.

Three months before you actually conceive your child, all your childs information and potentials are already being formed, informed by your felt relationship with your partner. In research done by Dr Bruce Lipton, many of our potentials are created due to our parents mutual (or not) bonding. This partially determines which genetic codes will be released, and which ones will lie dormant.

Studies on Genomic Imprinting show that even before the egg and sperm cells are released in conception, the nature of both parents has already specified a specific set of gene characteristics to be activated upon conception.18 This understanding underlines the importance of healing our emotional or causal wounds in pre-conception: before we even conceive our children. The potential of our child's genetics becomes hindered or helped by the character and nature of our relationship with our partner, which of course is determined by our own emotional and spiritual state of consciousness.

In order to raise our state of consciousness and improve our ability to consciously conceive with our partner, we must venture into deep emotional territory. Your emotions often cover your pure feelings such as compassion, joy, and love. Emotions include trauma imprints, wounds and sadness, anger, fear, unworthiness and any emotional pains we try and avoid. In this avoidance, we build walls of beliefs and create our own programs about what reality is.

---

[18] Cellular Echoes DVD: Journey From Womb to World

The five main keys to having a conscious conception and rite of passage birth process are:
- Parental healing
- Birth trauma healing: abortions, miscarriages,
- Healing your own personal birth story, healing what happened to you in your mother's pregnancy, conception and labour
- Sexual healing and re connection
- Emotional healing

The traumas we carry from our own births, the deep memories of the time in your mother's womb, and the traumatic experiences of our childhoods are all part of the factors that subconsciously flow in your life and stand in the way of your relationships. These emotions can arise full force when we are pregnant, surfacing in strong sets of emotions along with fears, anxieties and stresses.

In pre-conception before a conscious conception, many of our own pains, imprints and residues should be recognized, explored and felt in order to be released. If not, it is common during pregnancy to be faced with these wounds and patterns. The deep imprints of 'family,' come down to what was, or was not, given to you as a child, and the ways you felt separate from love in your own gestation and childhood.

If these issues are not addressed pre-conception, then in pregnancy lies a beautiful opportunity to 'mother' yourself home, bringing love to all these untouched layers. This will clear the template for your emerging family, to build relationships based on what is present now between you. Your future possibilities and timelines change when you address these layers of wounding.

To know these underlying wounds are there is the first step. For them to be healed and dissolved is the next. The energetic shocks to the nervous system and emotional/ancestral imprints children receive from their parents during conception, gestation and birth become emotional and biological flows of energy in them. In time, some of these wounds twist into knots of energy in the nervous system and spine, becoming future seeds of some of their soul's lessons. Each of these knots contains a 'seed,' from which the 'tree' of karma arises. The branches of this tree are patterns held in the physical as false body posture, disease, emotional traumas, breath disorders and illness of various kinds.

Most spiritual work is based on releasing and embracing, one by one, the branches of this tree until we reach the seed. In this process, we learn our lessons and heal our wounds. But, these knots can be lessened, and dissolved, with wisdom and devotion to a conscious pre-conception process, a soulful pregnancy, and a blissful birth initiation, for child and parents.

THE IMPACT OF CONCEPTION

Many of us were not conceived in intimate ecstatic love making by our parents. Many of us were conceived out of lust, out of obligation for sex, out of a need for security, out of insecurity, out of boredom, to stave off loneliness, out of fear, out of raw, basic biological need, out of primal ancestral urges and genetic impulses.

In the moment of Conception, all these forces and emotions impact and imprint upon our emotional body, DNA and soul. Part of our capacity to give and receive love freely is imprinted in this moment. From here, a default program for behavior is established for our entire life, a whole belief system around what love is, and what love is not.
This directly affects our self-worth, our self-love and our ability to have satisfying relationships later in life, as well as the ability to fulfil our own soul. We are conditioned to the experience of what love is through the filter of conception, pregnancy, birth, ancestors, mother and father. And as we know, the actual pregnancy and birth experience itself can be highly traumatic.

Some traditions share that our karmas from previous lives all manifest in the womb and gestation process. We are not victims of our ancestors or parents: rather, we have attracted these experiences as reflections of our own soul condition, for us to see ourselves and heal ourselves. We have created these circumstances and events because of our own previous actions, and they are here now to show us who we are and what we have to do to become whole.

If we are conceived in loving joy, bliss and heartfelt tenderness, this becomes our introduction to the world, giving us a felt reference point to navigate through life, through our lessons, through whatever pains and pleasures we may experience later in life. We will always have this origin point Remembered within us in some way, even in our darkest times.

If we are conceived in a true union of energies by two people who genuinely love each other, enjoy each other and want to share themselves fully in all ways with each other, then the child borne from this union will have this imprint active within them already. This is not something unusual: this is our innate design.

If both parents are committed to each other in a grounded, safe and sacred container, are open and true friends of the heart, integrated with their own father and mother, then their child will have this already installed within them, a reference point already available, not a million miles away or thousands of hours of healing away. They will then attract this type of relating, will want it, and will not settle for anything else.

The child will be secure, centered, able to fully enjoy life, and perhaps most importantly will be able to think for themselves, will be able to feel deeply, and will be able to express their gifts and soul purpose easily. They will be living in their true nature more. They will be natural, not artificial.

Authentic sacred relationship is the imprint your child needs with his/her conception. It is what you both as parents need too! This will establish the child's inner emotional security, well-being and genius, enabling them to be all they can be, to be who they truly are as an individual, and more easily have an opportunity for a healthy sacred relationship later in their life.

Pre-Conception is where a healthy sacred relationship is formed, tested, and its container created. A balanced child feels loved and nurtured, safe, cared for, supported and honored. The Inner Child Self we all have is the consciousness of unconditioned love and innocence, where each moment is trusted and love can flow freely.

CONCEIVING A CHILD

A Conscious Conception is much about preparation, as shared above. It is also an invitation, and a meditational ceremony that consciously connects both would-be parents to the incoming soul who wishes to be their child. This creates a mutual path of communication and readiness between all three souls in a fertile, welcoming field. This is how many sacred cultures used to bring in their children before physical conception.

We consciously conceive when both man and woman agree to invite another soul to incarnate through them through making love in joy, care, giving to each other, pleasure borne from this, and a mutual sharing of souls with each other. To connect to a child's soul at this time with the desire to Conceive and bring his/ her spirit into a woman's body is Conscious Conception, where aspects of all three souls come into manifestation together for the good of all.

In this meeting of conception, a shower of sparks of light release. (This has recently been filmed by scientists) A couple Consciously Conceiving knows when this moment happens and has prepared for it, understanding that these sparks of life are heralding an incoming soul bonding with the soul in the fetus.

In this moment of mutual orgasm in lovemaking, the feeling qualities of love, bliss and joy, the highest frequencies in creation, imprint onto your child's soul. This will then become a benchmark for your child's life, as it is his/her origin and starting point.

What greater gift can you give to your child?

All souls come to earth to have the experience of being human. A major goal of the human experience from a soul perspective is being able to fully and freely be able to give and receive love. The extent of this capacity is partially determined in the pivotal moments of conception, gestation and birth. All these emotions are remembered as a baseline for future experiences in the limbic imprint recorded deep in the reptilian brain, beyond cognitive thought.

It is from this record, this unseen reference point deep in your subconscious, that many lessons and patterns in life happen again and again, until they are learned. By healing ourselves and choosing to conceive AND birth in love, we are creating a sound foundation for our own AND our children's capacity to experience love.

In Conceiving a Child, we enter into the field of Conscious and Aligned Conception. You attract a Child to you through your own frequency and the amount of love you are holding or have recognized and embodied within you. Aligned Conception is aligning to a baby whose frequency is the next octave beyond your frequency. You can ask for such a Child to come through you if you so desire and are ready for this.

For example, if you visualize yourself from above your body, you will see a certain quality of light around you. It may be bright, it may be colorful, it may be one color or it may be many colors. You will see yourself as a vibrational dancing field, not just as a form and body.

This is what the soul of your child will see, and it will be attracted by the light around you, the intensity, quality and flavors of it. The more love you hold, the more the child will recognize it and feel drawn to it. It feels comfortable for them.

If a couple undergoes soulful sexual and emotional healing Pre-Conception, this will help attract a New Child. You will be clearer, softer and more loving to yourself and others, there will be more light in you, you will be expressing your soul purpose and gifts: this is all highly attractive and enticing to a New Child. If you are situated more in your soul, that is THE most attractive thing for a New Child of light.

ACTIVATING and OPENING to CONCEIVE

For a woman, conception happens in a deeply receptive, magnetic space. The more deeply she opens to receive all of her partner on every level of her physical, emotional and spiritual self, the more powerful the union of their magnetic and electric polarities is, igniting a powerful spark of light, life force, and love.

In order for a woman to open to this most receptive place, she needs to feel safe and trust her man. This alchemy happens throughout the ebbs and flows of an intimate relationship, and as it does this drops her deeper into her feminine core, her deepest magnetic self. Safety and trust are emotional qualities, reflected in the physical anatomy of her magnetic floor, especially the span between anus and womb. Her magnetic floor relaxes with her man when she feels a palpable respect, commitment, and presence in him, when he has shown his love and proved his trustworthiness. By bringing his loving touch to her pelvic floor, he can help support these feelings.

PRACTICE: RELAXING THE MAGNETIC FLOOR

Take some deep breaths and drop into your open, vulnerable hearts. Your man stands behind you, wrapping his arms around your front and embracing your womb, fingers pointed down toward the public bone. Allow yourself to lean your weight back into him, the back of your heart supported by the front of your heart, so you feel the strength of your physical frame and the support of his hands encircling your womb.

Man: Gently, rhythmically, massage her womb in wave like motions, undulating from your fingertips to your wrists. Continue for about 5 minutes, then cross the hands, wrapping them round either side of her womb, and draw them together, giving her womb a hug. This will feel relaxing and supportive for her.

Next, invite her to lie face down, unclothed. Use some oil, and beginning on the back of her thighs just below her buttocks, firmly slide your hands up and over her buttocks and near the sacrum. Circle your hands round to the sides of her pelvis.

Do this sweeping motion 5-10 times, with increasing slowness and depth.

Now, place your thumbs on either side of her tailbone and your fingers out toward the side of her hips. Rhythmically press the thumbs in on either side of the spine, and slowly work your way up to the base of her skull. Then reverse, and return to the tailbone.

Now, wrap your fingers underneath the sides of her pelvis, grab the handles of the prominent bone, and rock her pelvis from side to side. Encourage her to breathe deeply into her pelvis while you do this.

Finally, invite her to roll onto her back, and bending her knees, drop them out to the side. Honoring the vulnerability of this position, using oil, slide your hands up the inside of the knees and thighs, past the groin, gently over her pubic bone and then connect with her womb.

From here, slide your hands around the back of her buttocks and draw them down to the back of her knees. Continue this circular motion until you feel her relax.

This is a beautiful time to lie in a silent embrace together.

PRACTICE: EMBRACING YOUR UNBORN CHILD

Perhaps the most important thing for a child to know is whether it is wanted, or not. He or she can feel this, so our responsibility as parents begins at the moment of our conscious knowledge of conception. We may feel panic, dismay or uncertainty at this moment, or joy, celebration and happiness, but this moment is a grand opportunity to radiate a welcome and acceptance of this new soul.

This is the first great blessing we can offer our child, the first spiritual gift we can give. If this first gift is well given, it establishes a pattern for the giving of everything else. [19] So give thanks that you have been blessed with such a Child, and give thanks to the Child that he/she has chosen to incarnate through you.

The souls transition into the physical plane is made easier if they know that their parents are doing all that they can to make their souls full manifestation possible. For example, when you go to visit a friend or a relative how do you view the upcoming visit? If you know that you will be given a real welcome, that everything possible will be done by the ones who receive you to make you feel at home, you will look forward to it.

If you know they will be grumpy and preoccupied, unwelcoming and invasive, you will likely view the coming visit as an ordeal. The same thing is true on the soul level. If we make the spirit of our baby feel welcomed, it will effect the entire incarnation. This is why, in the instant of consciously knowing that conception has occurred, roll out the welcome mat! [20]

This embrace is about welcoming your child, feeling your child, and inviting him/her forth to you as soon as you know you have conceived. Your unborn child WILL feel this, as they are sensitive to the nuances of the soul and your emotions towards them.

Do this hug five minutes a day, really attuning yourself, inviting and reaching out to the spirit and soul of your unborn child. This 'etheric hugging' will help massage your fields. These blooming and expanding fields can be tangibly felt and experienced.

Stand with your legs hip width apart, and your knees slightly bent.

With your hands at your sides, inhale deeply into your perineum, down through the soles of your feet into the earth. Exhale, drawing the energy from the core of the earth back through the soles of your feet and perineum into your heart.

Continue for a few minutes until you feel connected in your heart and body to the earth's support and energy.

---

[19] Even if this welcome is muted or sombre at the time, it can be healed later.
[20] Communing with the Spirit of your Unborn Child by Dawson Church.

Now from your heart, on the inhale, breathe out through your crown to reach the Source of the Divine. Exhale from this awareness back through your crown to your heart. Continue for a few breaths, then combine this with the first breath and do them simultaneously.

Once you feel connected and aligned to the earth, to Source, draw your arms up to make a circle in front of your breast line. From the seed of your heart, invite the spirit and soul of your incoming child to be with you. Inhale and slowly draw your hands into your heart, embracing the energy of their spirit.

With this hug, you are welcoming the child's soul and spirit to you. Do this slowly, and with your feeling.

Exhale, and release your hands outwards back into a circle, allowing space for more of their spirit and soul to arrive. Inhale again, drawing them into your heart, and exhale, opening your arms to allow and welcome more of their fullness.

Continue this motion with the inhale and exhale, staying centered in the seed of your heart.

Father is corded to baby, and is receiving a lot of this cording from the mother. So it is important that their communication is flowing. In the pre conception and pregnancy period, this is how father will receive a lot of the child's spirit and soul.

THE CONTAINER

Container: A crucible and sound structure to allow energies to alchemize. A shared field matrix that allows gestation of new evolutionary expressions.

Pregnancy, the gestation period for an incoming soul to arrive on earth, is held within four concentric containers of womb, family, a woman's seven gates, and a home. The containers purpose is to "hold" them all together. Mutual presence, love and support creates a loving container for the combined energies of your shared intent, purpose and soul agreements to flow into, and take form.

All processes in creation need a container to bring the formless into form. This is the womb and heart in union, the container for life. A soul can embody more if consciously aided by the parents providing the right vibratory container in which he or she can Be and do its work.

Many New Children, part of the next evolutionary leap, have not been on earth before. They need to feel the solid container of you, their mother. As mother, your belly and being becomes the bowl for your incoming child. You are the grail for this child to land, body, spirit and soul onto earth.

This grail must be carefully prepared and harmonized. Because your whole being is the container and bowl, this means all aspects of you must be included, inculcated into this pregnancy. Your body, your spirit, your soul, your sexuality, your wisdom, your stillness, your love, your strength, your vulnerability, your womb, all must find their way into this container. The more a Child feels this container of you, the more he/she will want to be here.

Another aspect of maintaining harmony in the container of the womb is connecting to Earth. Simply by laying your body down on the Earth, breathing her in, allowing your body to let go and be totally supported by her ground, we can open more deeply to our innate resting place.

Just as our heart has our pulse, so does our womb. Allowing our womb pulse to align with Earth's pulse is deeply grounding and centering, bringing more parts of yourself into the here and now.

PRACTICE: WOMB EARTH PULSE PRACTICE

This allows your womb-heart to receive Earth's pulse. Fathers can do this practice with the hara.

1. Lie face down on the earth with your third eye, heart and womb/hara pressed against the earth. (This is a great exercise to do on a ley line!) Breathe deeply, allowing the smell of the earth to come into your nostrils, your head, your lungs; breathe deeply into your womb/hara. Tune into your womb beat and then your heart beat. Ask to connect with the beat of placenta, with baby's heart beat as well. Allow all beats to synchronize. Feel.

2. Say -Feel: "Beloved Mother Earth, I love you. Please send me your love.' x7

Connect the heart and womb together in a golden infinity loop with this love, vision and gentle breath.

3. Now bring your awareness to your pineal gland or third eye. Through your third eye, look through the layers of the earths crust, into the core crystalline center. Once at the earth's center, feel her pulse, and draw-breathe this energy through your yoni into your womb.

You may feel a light as the pulse ignites your womb. Breathe it into your heart, and then up to your third eye so the circuit is completed. Rest in this position on the earth as long as you feel to, letting the circuit of energy flow from you, into Earth, and back into you.

'The first time I felt Earths's pulse, I felt an overwhelming light surge move up through my yoni into my womb and literally pulse, sending a wave throughout my entire body. A few moments later I felt my heart beat synchronize to the beat in my womb, and my third eye began pulsing in sync as well. I felt very grounded and connected, and it lasted a long time, a deep synchronization with a timing and flow where I was a part of a wave of movement much larger than me or my immediate surroundings. ''S.Z.

THE CONTAINER of FAMILY

In the co creation of a child between your partner and the Divine comes the unifying of sexual energy with your soul's emotions and feelings. This unifying includes every aspect of human expression.

An emotionally integrated and soulfully bonded family emerges with the full and conscious engagement of father and mother in the entire birth process, from pre-conception to pregnancy, birth and raising their child. In so doing, they embody and embrace more of their essential femininity and masculinity.

Their joint and mutual effort becomes the foundation for their own integration of the masculine and feminine through the Rite of passage of Birth and Parenthood, as well as a healthy soulful childhood for their child.

The roles of mother and father are unique, different and both crucial to the whole process. Both have to be fully engaged with the process. By becoming a pillar of strength, trust, masculine care and solidity the father-to-be creates a sound container for the safe, sacred and soulful guidance of his partner and child.

In this space, the mother-to-be can soften and surrender to the deeper currents of magnetic presence, wisdom, nurturance and love that brings wholeness to her family, taking her deeper into her feminine essence.

We are dependent on our children to become parents. Our children are dependent on us as parents, to be children. In this relationship, we discover aspects of love that we will not authentically encounter in any other relationship or practice. When the relationship between mother and father is based on unconditioned love, respect, honor and trust, there is a sound foundation for family and society as a whole to blossom.

The first trimester is crucial for creating a container within yourself, between you and your partner, and with your and your child. Time needs to be spent alone just with you three in a conscious and engaged manner through singing, holding your belly, speaking to your child (both of you), and through physical nurturance.

Part of the journey of moving into 'family' entails stepping away from your life before as you knew it, and letting go, spending more time and energy in this new container. There then arises a natural weaving together of the 3 of you, and a letting go of many threads of your previous life. This means completing any unfinished issues and relationships, bringing your relationships into harmony, and fully acknowledging you are on a new sacred journey.

It is time to fully honor this journey and set your self apart from old ways of being and doing. In a way, part of you has to die for another part to arise and take full responsibility. In this way, you create more space for you to grow into your role, and who you are becoming, opening to the lessons that will unfold motherhood and fatherhood within you.

Pregnancy and the container of family offers us an opportunity to go to the next deeper layer of intimacy and healing. Before pregnancy you may have thought and even felt you had dealt with and healed much, but pregnancy will bring up the next layer asking to be embraced. All healing happens in a spiral, and we keep revisiting the same wounds in deeper octaves until we have released them entirely.

What moves, touches and inspires you in your depths? Experiencing our feelings in the crucible of pregnancy, embracing and healing them, or denying and projecting them, allows us to recognize our soul in ways few other situations and events can. Family relationships show us where we are deceiving ourselves as to our true soul condition, our true state of evolution.

Many times we misunderstand, deny and try to prematurely transcend our emotions and souls in favor of a lifestyle that sees emotions as something to be witnessed and glossed over, rather than embrace through humility and vulnerability. This glossing over becomes quite impossible to do in pregnancy and in raising a child, as any parent can tell you!

What makes a safe and loving container in pregnancy for these emotions to be felt safe to release? The quality of love, integrity, honor, self-responsibility and communication on a soul level between the parents.

PRACTICE: DRAWING THE SACRED CIRCLE of YOUR FAMILY COCOON

As soon as you are aware mother is pregnant, a cocoon needs to be weaved energetically, physically, and emotionally around all three souls. A sacred circle of love, protection and power needs to be drawn around the holy trinity of mother, father, and child.

This is a powerful Protector Prayer from St Joseph, the father of Yeshua and husband to Mother Mary. He is renowned as being a protector of children, the helpless, the undefended, and can help assist in creating a safe, strong, gentle container for birth to happen.

Beloved Father-Mother God, please keep me in Your Divine Love and Divine Infinite Truth Light every moment of this day and night.

O Glorious Brother St. Joseph, father of Christ Yeshua, we choose you as our protector and our counselor of our family. Please become a guardian of our three souls! Please become a guardian of my child. Please accept all three of us within the folds of your Holy, Alchemical, Protector Cloak! Thank you Beloved Brother Joseph!

Please Dismiss all obstacles and difficulties standing in my way, my baby's way, my partners way: defend us from negative spirits, visible and invisible, who wish to interfere with all three of us. Protect our family as we set forth to give birth to a beautiful child of light.

We do this for the benefit of all beings, past, present and future. Please grant our family your unique blessings to bring us into a blissful, happy and safe birth, as God Designed it to Be. Amen.

THE CONTAINER OF HOME

Even in the first trimester we may be feeling the impending approach of birth. It is important even at this stage to begin tuning into what you and your child want and need for birth, for plans for where you need to be, who needs to be there and what needs to happen have to be made ahead of time.

Home birth is our natural way to give birth, and is a sacred birthright for parents and children. Many women share that giving birth at home, and being able to embody this process as a rite of passage, was the most profound and empowering experience of their life.

Our home is our place of refuge, a place of safety, comfort, play, ease and communion with ourselves, our families, our source, and the place that nurtures us away from the world. Alchemy can only happen within the security of a sound container. The integrity and clarity of the home container creates a foundation for that which is born through it.

Home allows us to surrender more deeply into ourself. We can relax beyond the tugs and demands of the world and tune into the deeper urges and whispers of our souls. When we maintain and protect the sanctity and privacy of our home, we allow ourselves to bloom.

Birth is a natural, sacred family affair. To birth blissfully, a woman needs to feel safe, relaxed, at ease and comfortable. Your home is the most natural place for this to happen. When a child is born in the quiet, safe and gentle container of a home, birth is allowed its natural sacredness, bonding and bliss. This deeply imprints mother, father and child and initiates them into more closeness as a family.

The first trimester of pregnancy opens an opportunity to consolidate life before birth. Consolidation brings together and resolves the previous aspects of life before pregnancy. It sounds a Call to gather fragments of yourself together into a 'new you', letting go of that which will not serve your blooming. From this consolidation a couple can bring consciousness and attention into the honoring and building of their containers: womb, family and home. Once this framework is in place, they can deepen more into the pregnancy journey.

Pregnancy and labour are not a sickness. Birth is not a disease, it is a natural process facilitated by the calm, serenity and level of comfort found in one's own home and ones own self. Hospitals are for sick people, and homes are for family. Birth is not an emergency, it is a natural family affair.

Being at home with a loving partner uninterrupted allows both parents to comfortably do what they need to. Life, love and home create the container. In home birth, there is no pressure to "perform" for the doctors and nurses. Many women cannot fully relax and birth without the comfort of home, with no interruptions, no strangers, no sterile walls, blinking lights and bleeping machines.

At home, one is more able to follow the natural rhythms of the birthing process, wherever and however it happens, with the parents in control, not the doctor. The parents are in charge and can step up into full self-responsibility, having intimacy in a familiar setting.

We are designed to have babies in a natural, intimate setting. This allows the male partner to truly participate in birth and have the moment where he can be his partner's hero and live the masculine legend and archetype. It is said that if men were present at their sons' births, there would be less war.

It is only when we let fear cloud our judgment that we think about the hospital, where fear will end up controlling the birth. A natural process, if going well, needs only natural nurturing, with back up of friends or midwives. Many parents do not want to put their newborn in a car and drive. It is wise to slow down and be grounded for baby's arrival and not go anywhere for days before or after.

Home births encourages the mother within the safe container of home and relationship to step into her power through fully experiencing this rite of passage. This rite of passage has to come from a relaxed, caring and safe place within both mother and father. When the intention for a home birth is held in your awareness from the beginning, the container of home is strengthened and clarified.

There are three aspects to the container of home: Divine, Devic/Earthly, and Human. When our home is in alignment with Cosmic Harmony, it is a sanctuary, a place of communion. It is natural and easy for us to connect to Source in a gentle and supportive environment that invites a soulful existence.

The Devic connection with our home comes from Earth and the devic spirits living on the land. When we take time to connect and commune with them, we enable a harmony to exist between ourselves and these nature spirits around us. They often will have guidance or insights to offer us relative to healing or birth. These spirits are very eager to assist if they are asked!

The Earthly connection to our home, or connection to the soul of the earth, enables a deep magnetic settling within the body. Earth has a way of holding us and supporting us in a way nothing else can do, and the more a woman is connected to this the more her mind, soul and body can feel held throughout pregnancy and birth.

The human aspect of our home includes cleanliness on all levels, physical, bodily and energetic. When our home is clear of clutter, smudged regularly, and we tend to and care for our bodies internally and externally, the environment is clean and energy can flow smoothly. Having a professional Feng Shui clearing and resetting of the home environment in accordance with laws of harmonic flow and proportion can be very helpful. The human aspect in our homes also speaks to the communication, care, love and respect shared between the parents.
.

PRACTICE: THE CIRCLE of GIVING and RECEIVING LOVE

There is a mutual giving and receiving between parent and child. This is the beauty, the mutuality of it. It is not just the parent being the teacher or the child being the teacher. We are all here to give and receive, and children are no different. This mutual giving and receiving, learning and sharing, is a dance and a dynamic relationship that is mutually enhancing and satisfying, supporting all of you.

Any obstacles the parents have to fully giving and receiving love with each other will arise in pregnancy, before birth. This is a key foundational premise that is vital for your child.

Draw a circle around you, your partner, and close ones who know you and are close to your soul. An Ideal Circle is: mother, father, baby, 2 mutual soul friends, and the Divine. Sit in it for a moment together, close your eyes, breathe, connect, and hold hands.

Start the circle with a prayer: Beloved Divine Mother, Divine Father, how am I blocking the full giving and receiving of love with my partner, my child, and my friends? One person at a time asks this. Every other person prays for that person as well, at the same time. As answers and insights arise, speak them out. You may be surprised!

Speak to each other about how you feel about your ability to give and receive love. Each of you in the circle will hold a key for the other person that can lead to concrete actions.

This circle can be convened in pregnancy, in pre-conception, and afterwards in raising a child. You may want to do it three times as this can be a deep, profound question that can lead to much healing.

If you do it three times, you will find three different perspectives and three different courses of action and healing that each person may undertake to remove the obstacles for giving and receiving love and truly enjoying each other, their child and their friends.

EMBODIED PREGNANCY

Becoming pregnant is more than a physiological shift and process within our body. Our exaggerated nipples, swollen breasts and fits of nausea are all symptoms of a much deeper impregnation within our psyche, spirit and soul.

What does it mean to become pregnant with soul? When we open our wombs to an essence other than our own, we begin to feel the qualities of this seed of a soul that is choosing to incarnate through us. This is one of the most intimate meetings between souls, that feeling of another deep in the innermost folds of our body.

A conscious mother knows the soul essence of her child better than anyone else, as she "in-bodied" it for the nine months of pregnancy. The more she is present in feeling and embracing this essence of her gestating child, the more she will gracefully transition through pregnancy and birth into motherhood. Her magnetic presence supports her child in embodying more fully.

Simultaneously, in this deep presence-ing, she should guide herself and be guided to become more grounded and oriented in her rightful place in earth's magnetic fields. The more mother and child attune and open to each other, even in this early meeting, the more embodied both can become.

Pregnancy is more about being than doing. It is an opportunity to enjoy the increased elasticity of our beings that opens old densities and patterns to be released. It is an invitation to discover, play with and express new, unknown energies. It is a gravitational deepening into the richness of a blooming family.

Pregnancy is a gift of being and becoming in a graceful organic unfolding. Many deep emotions from your childhood, your gestational time, your parents and ancestors deep patterns that warrant release before the actual birth, will surface. These deep imprints of 'family,' come down to what was, or was not, given to you as a child, and the ways you felt separate from love in your own gestation and childhood. There is much assistance and support for a woman to be able to feel and release these emotions in this time.

Pregnancy is a beautiful opportunity to 'mother' your self home, bringing love to all those dark and untouched layers. This will clear the template for your emerging family, to build relationships based on what is present now in the love between you. From here, you are able to open more to the new life within you, and YOUR new life as it is unfolding.

This new life brings new responsibilities, new openings of spirit, soul and body, a new lifestyle, a new attitude to inculcate, a new way of being that is lying dormant within you. Pregnancy offers a profound time for a woman to deepen in connection with her womb, heart and soul and take more time for herself to do this. In the innate and natural design for birth, she becomes softer and stronger in her own vessel.

PREGNANCY AND BIRTH IS A RITE OF PASSAGE

There is an innate theme to every pregnancy. This theme is born of the character of your incoming child and specific gifts you will need in order to rear him or her in love and truth.

I remember with my daughter that I was continually asked to use, trust and strengthen my intuition. With my son, the journey was more about surrender. Both of those qualities have been cornerstones in my navigating unique ways of parenting for each of them. The unique theme for your child will naturally emerge as a mother moves through the organic unfolding of each trimester.

Pregnancy is designed to be an initiation.

When a woman undergoes the Rite of Passage of pregnancy and birth, she will reap many gifts and capacities. However as with all rites of passage or shamanic journeys, it is important for her to have an integration period upon her Return from the journey in the 4th trimester for the 3 trimester journey to be digested, understood, and for her to adapt to her new frequency and role of Mother.

The difference between a rite of passage and a trauma is the Return. Without the Return the soul and body, whilst in such an expanded state, is suddenly led crashing down into the mundane world. This can lead to the woman becoming fragmented, and the nervous system becoming frozen in a disconnected loop.

Birth in our Soul's Design is made to be a caring rite of passage with proper rest afterwards to integrate the birth initiation, ideally for 40 Days. Yet too often in today's world, after-birth and the Return from the shamans journey of pregnancy and birth becomes an experience of disconnection and disempowerment.

RITE OF PASSAGE BIRTH STORY

My first pregnancy and birth was a journey into the unknown. I took my cues from my connection with the natural world, and a bit of guidance from my midwife. I refused to read any birth stories or books, as I didn't want to be influenced or dictated by other perceptions on birth. It was a journey in trusting my instincts and intuition, and the deep scripted knowing of birth in my female body.

Early on in my pregnancy my daughter suggested through dreams that she wanted to be born in the ocean. Her father started looking into where this would be possible. After finding a midwife on the Big Island of Hawaii who would support us in our attempt at an ocean birth, we moved there.

The Big Island is powerful, Shakti-filled and raw; it was exactly the energy for me to delve into in my third trimester to harness and dance in the deeper energies of the land, the fiery volcanoes, and the powerful forces of the cosmos coming through with little interruption from cities or matrix. I would spend hours with my bare feet in the grass, spiraling my hips, just allowing the life, the sheer force of Shakti and primal Earth, to play her way through me.

For weeks I scoured the western shoreline to find the exact place she wanted to be born. I found a small tide pool protected from the big waves by massive black lava guardian rocks. The pool was cleansed with gentle rushes of fresh ocean water intermittently between waves, and the waters were warmed by the baking sun radiating off the black lava surrounding the pool and the soft sandy bottom. The pool was on a remote peninsula removed from traffic, and the moment I stumbled upon it and sank my toes into the sand, my womb gave me a resounding "YES!" This was the place.

For the next 40 days I woke early to swim with the dolphins in this bay. I would spend hours twirling, playing, silently swimming and floating with them. A few in the pod took special interest in me and my belly, sometimes coming up underneath me and rubbing belly to belly. The moment I submerged my head in the water and heard the dolphins, my daughter began to kick! She too communed with her friends.

These mornings were ecstatic for me, the rising slant of golden sun filtering through the turquoise waters and the joyful exchange with these loving and joyful beings filled my heart. Soft undulating waves held me suspended while I released any remaining fear of the unknown surrounding birth. The dolphins and the ocean were an ever-beckoning invitation for me to relax into the joy of pregnancy and birth.

One morning I began feeling rushes while I was a good ways out from shore with the dolphins. I broke off from the pod and swam my way back into shore flanked by two guardian dolphins. They accompanied me until I safely reached the shallows. Once upon land I sat down to catch my breath and sink deeper into the rhythmic intensity building within me.

After I dried in the sun, my daughter's father came in from his swim and escorted me to a small clearing in the nearby jungle. We had come prepared (just in case) with plenty of water and food, and it was here that I labored all day long. With each oncoming rush I would reach for the strong stringy vines off the trees and hang, spiraling my hips in wider and wider circles. I was danced, totally losing myself in the energy, with Gaia, and she with me. I danced in between the veils, the threads of movement, laughter and bliss my constant companions.

As I watched the brilliant orange sun drop below the horizon, the rushes intensified. My energy dropped even deeper inward, into my womb and the yawning portal of the blackness of beyond. All around me was a soft hue of purple light. We felt our way to the edge of the water near the tide pool and set up a thick pad on the lava rock.

I surrendered on all fours, rocking and moving. The intensity of energy within me was building and it felt more than I could hold. As soon as I recognized the tiny torch of my Midwife and could magnetically feel her walking toward me from the distance, my pelvis relaxed. She wordlessly put her hand on my sacrum and helped the energy move through.

I surrendered to the human support of her hands and of my partner's frame. This lasted not long, until I felt the vortex of energies from above and below. I needed to be held by something far vaster. I suddenly felt like a caged animal between the midwife and my daughter's father. I could hear and feel their thoughts, doubts, fears and anticipations.

I told them it was time for me to get into the water. He heard me, and somewhere recognized not only what I needed, but also my capacity. They both supported me over the jagged rocks into the pool. I sat down in the soft sand, and felt the cool water gather around me, like a welcoming and silent hug, relaxing my whole body. The moon shone its silvery light down into the pool bringing a surreal luminescence.

The ocean waves reached high for the moon, and crashed down in a spectacular show just beyond the guardian lava rocks of my protected tide pool. My womb resounded dancing, reaching, expanding and contracting. Not long after, my daughter emerged into the Pacific Ocean, into my midwife's hands amidst tiny fish and crabs in the soft, sandy bottomed tide pool.

The power of this first birth experience blew me wide open. I fully surrendered to my inner guidance, and the guidance of the natural world. This strengthened my trust and empowered me. I found the true Womb Shaman within. I experienced the interconnection and one-ness that I had only conceptually understood before. In the birthing moments, I was held by mother ocean and could open my yoni, womb, and heart to a further reach of my soul.

However, this was not sustainable for me, beyond those moments. There was no structure in place for my 'return.' My life outside the birthing tide pool did not support me. As soon as I left these safe and sacred waters and walked on the rocky land, I felt the jagged sharpness of the lava rock underneath my feet and the harsh reality of a loveless relationship and no community of loved ones to welcome me home.

I had done everything to insure my daughter would be born in the right place, but I had done nothing to set up the support I needed to return home from the experience. Though I was connected to my body and intuition, I was not very conscious, had no real connection to God, no community, no real love with my daughter's father, and no means to communicate the experience to anyone else.

Something so beautiful had become a trauma to my soul and nervous system because I had not known the means to call myself home. I had not set up the container, and neither had my partner, to hold myself and my child upon her emergence and my re-emergence.

The three years following were depressive and painful. This birth only became a rite of passage for me when I become pregnant with my next child, and could re-gather the fragments of my split soul in a sound container with a truly loving partner.

FATHER'S ROLE IN PREGNANCY

Pregnancy is actually becoming pregnant with soul. The woman becomes pregnant with her own blooming soul, and enters into a process of becoming pregnant with the soul and spirit of her child. The child's soul and spirit starts to come into her emotional fields through her magnetic and sexual circuitry and her magnetic foundation shifts, with all the effects this has on her nervous system and chakras. Her biology changes within her womb and hormones. Her soul starts to intertwine with her childs soul.

There is a soul pregnancy for the father as well. This is an essential point. He is now no longer just his own, for fathers soul and spirit are now intertwining with baby and mother. In his electromagnetic body, father is working more electrically whereas mother is working more magnetically. As this happens, the fields around the father start to change, adapt, include and open to allow increased communion and communication between him, his partner AND his child.

Being pregnant is actually becoming pregnant with bodt, spirit and soul. It is from this perspective that everything must be seen, for the physical effects are caused by the soul and spirit. As a mother's spirit and soul becomes permeated, more pliable and more open to the spirit and soul of child, so does a fathers in his way, and thus the three-way bond between mother, father and baby grows.

Father, through connecting with mother AND by consciously communicating and feeling the spirit of the unborn child, becomes activated. In this activation will arise his learning's and emotions. If he follows this and is emotionally sensitive, the embodiment process will deepen for him throughout pregnancy, labour, physical birth and in the process of raising a child.

This embodiment process is a continual deepening on multiple levels of consciousness. If father is aware, enjoying his child, and soulfully growing, he and his child will complete one cycle of this mutual embodiment by the time the child is twenty-seven months old.

The father maintains the cohesion and balance of physical, emotional and spiritual energies in the nine months of pregnancy, ensuring the processes move forward at their own pace and not by an external clock or external people. Other people's presence causes ripples in the delicate fabric of labour and pregnancy, so you need to be aware of this.

Only have the right people there for your child, even if they are not your previous closest friends, or even your own parents. The direct clarity and strength of the masculine is good for discerning this and putting clear boundaries into action.

Part of a father's soul role with his child is:

- To be an emotionally clear, calm, reassuring strength and pillar of the masculine
- To engender and deepen trust and respect through his own integrity, right guidance and actions
- To withstand and process adversity in the whirlwind of emotions that often arise in pregnancy and after. To be self-responsible and humble, knowing his emotions are his own and processing them without lashing out
- To play, sing, do movement and care for the child
- To consciously communicate with his child in pregnancy and start to share spiritual energies, mantras, prayers and healing energies through his hands and voice to the child.
- To encourage the Remembrance of soul Presence for the child, Reminding the child of its own pure presence of light in pregnancy, birth and in raising a child. To engage with the child soul to soul, understanding what he needs from the masculine – and sharing a depth of interaction and stillness from this space. For example, for a father to openly cry in front of mother and child gives the child permission to also be open and vulnerable about their feelings and emotions, which is a priceless gateway to the soul.
- To imprint the loving, strong, gentle and vulnerable masculine into his child through his actions and emotions
- To create a degree of discipline and healthy emotional boundaries for all
- To become conscious of and remember his own soul agreement with the child, and why the child has chosen him. To cognize his own learnings and growth with the child, and why he has chosen the child to be with him. To remember the child's own learning and growth with him, and why the child has chosen him, and to then put this into conscious action and create the environments, people, resources and educational opportunities that are right for his child. What do you both need to learn from and with each other?
- To help create a safe, strong emotional and spiritual container for physical and soulful growth.

Often, the father is more in the background, but this does not mean his role is any less important. Both male and female are necessary for the child to be balanced.

A father's role during pregnancy, and for years afterwards, is to look after and care for the mother in all ways. This includes helping her get on track with her soul purpose, which may have changed during the pregnancy and birth process, and to encourage the blooming of her own individual soul gifts, to ensure she grows as an individual.

Too many times, mother's deeper soul growth is subordinated and even forgotten in looking after the child. Motherhood is part of a spiritual path, not the whole of it. Mother still has to continue to evolve within herself as an individual, as well as being stimulated into growth by loving and supporting the child. It is important to not be a martyr to the demands of motherhood and fatherhood. Balance is key.

The father also has his worldly role in taking care of, and providing, things like money, a home, a support network, feeding mama when she is tired or cannot look after herself properly, and looking out for mama in the ways she forgets to look after herself because of the child. This is an automatic response, coming from care and love. If it is felt out of obligation, if it annoys the father or the mother feels this is not right in any way, there are deeper emotions to be felt into, inquired into and released.

PRACTICE: QUESTIONS FOR FATHER TO BE

Ask yourself: did your father give you all of this?

Do you trust in the birth process?
Do you feel fear about birth?
Do you trust your partner's guidance in birth?
Do you feel the need to control your woman at times?
Do you trust your intuition?
Do you know the story of your own birth?

Do feel unresolved anger or frustration with your father?
What didn't he provide for you that you wish he had?
Do you take time to truly process your emotions?
Do you feel resistance to your partner's emotions?
Where does your guidance come from?

Can you express the truth even if it is hard for others to hear?
Can you draw strong boundaries for your child and partner even if it means turning loved ones away?
Do you have clear boundaries in your relationships?
Do you exercise authority in your life and your relationships?
Are you honest with yourself and your partner?

YOUR GUARDIAN ANGEL GUIDE

Every journey of soul consequence begins at a doorway, face to face with a guardian or test. Sacred vows and a sincere commitment are needed before you can enter this doorway, and once you make that commitment you must have the bravery to step into the unknown, even though it may be frightening. You will go through the fire, and encounter a deeper, intuitive knowing about the worlds that lies beyond he appearances of the third dimension.

This bridge into a vaster reality occurs through pregnancy and birth, and is helped by your guardian angel or daimon. Originally, angels were called daimons, with 'guardian' angels coming from the Greek notion of us all having a personal daimon. The daimon is your inner friend or guide, your guardian angel. It is found in all traditions as the Roman genius, the Arabic genie or jinn, the shaman's spirit helper, or the Christian's guardian angel.

It manifests as a voice within, and will protect you, but only the real, essential "You" who serves the plan for your true Self. Daimons are intermediary spirits, guides and spiritual advisors often portrayed as angelic beings or as animal/devic spirits, and serve as inspiration. They act as a reminder of the voice of the soul, and sometimes manifest as feelings of unrest that may force us into the unknown, where we can discover ourselves and can transform ourselves.

Daimons are different from what are called angels today; they are powers of transformation that speak through dreams, symbols, meetings, inner voices and events in our lives. They are messengers, dwelling in the place where light and dark, angels and demons, meet. They are beyond the duality of good and evil, and use either polarity at any time in order to make you whole, through the rich mine of spiritual wealth known as the "golden shadow"—where our highest potential lies. In this, the daimon inspires our true imagination and creative potential, not only soothing us, but provoking us in order to liberate us into our highest potential.

We are assigned a daimon at birth to help govern and direct our lives. They act as a force of fate and an accompanying guide who Remembers your soul mission and Calling, even when you may forget. The daimon motivates, protects, and persists, resisting soul compromise, often engineering situations that turn our lives upside down when we are off track.

Each of us has a soul purpose that demands our commitment and focus. The challenge in following our daimon is that it will urge us, at times, in the direction of our fears and what we do not want to do or feel as a means of overcoming these selfsame fears and pains, in order to fulfill your soul purpose.

The daimonic force is unorthodox, a guiding maturation of your soul through the unification of opposing forces within you. The daimonic force sees both polarities coming from the same source: the power of our highest potential. Its source lies where the Self roots in natural forces. The daimon is the incorrigible Will to fulfill and achieve our humanity through this natural innate force, which we are all born with, but which many forget. Your daimon has the "right" answers for you, regardless of whether that information makes 'logical' sense.

Birth and the daimon serve one goal: Soul Embodiment, living your Highest Potential, bringing all aspects of your soul into the present, into your body, onto Earth, now. It is an experiential living in the present designed to weave every part of you into the fabric of life.

We each have a responsibility to follow our soul purpose and not give up on it. In order to live our purpose, we must abandon many conditioned ideas of right and wrong, of what makes "sense" and what does not, and step into the intuitive imagination. Following our soul's purpose and "going for it" is a requirement of happiness. You might establish a level of contentment without it, but that is not true happiness.

Whatever level we live in the spirals of evolution, the next one above serves as our daimon. This is a fundamental law of energy; we cannot solve problems by working at the same level of energy where the problem is. We have to go to the next octave in order to resolve the issue. Daimons are not fixed, but unfold in relation to our own spiritual development, changing their faces and roles over time as we transform and evolve.

Those who become aware of their daimon will eventually become aware of their true Self, as the daimon is a portal to this. Having a daimon does not make you immune to suffering, but rather it accelerates the lessons in our lives. What our daimon teaches us is not to always be seeking a cure for our suffering, but rather to seek a use for it, a channel to direct this force into, so we may create something of it.

Our daimons hold keys to our own personal shadow pillar, our personal archetype, which we play out and live into over the course of our lives. This voice calls us to our vocation, for the daimon is your partner in a relating to fulfill your soul.

The daimon's face differs for each of us. For those who are lovers, it takes the face of the beloved. For those who prefer service to the world and family as their main practice, it could appear as Divine Mother. For those on the path of high wisdom, it is the inner mentor. For artists, it is the Muse of inspiration who pushes them past their creative limits.

Pregnancy and birth are a rite of passage. If we engage in this process with humility and openness to our learning and all aspects of the journey and the Return, it is an initiation leading to a deeper embodiment of the soul. The daimon can be a guiding force in your conception and pregnancy.

There are many possible rituals and meditations to help you connect with your Daimon or Guardian Angel. The daimon differs from the guardian angel energy in that it spans more dimensions than just the astral plane, where many find a diluted or partial version of their guardian angel. Finding your guardian angel and establishing communication with it is a good first step; aligning with your daimon takes the whole process into deep alchemy and soul transformation.

Our Daimon is our primordial guardian, the one who is a helpful connector to our embodying our true Self. The Daimon helps bring you to your next big step in your soul's evolution. This is the Daimon's purpose, and what this unique spirit who has been entrusted to you, is for.

The Daimon works and communicates through many ways, imagination, intuition, synchronicities and worldly events. Anything and everything can be used to guide you into your next octave of evolution. This is what the Daimon is primarily concerned with, so address this first and foremost. Ask, 'what do I need to do to go to my next level of evolution?'

Have another 5 questions prepared before doing the following practice. The following meditation is from the Christ Lineage.

PRACTICE: CONNECTING TO YOUR GUARDIAN ANGEL DAIMON

Sit down and draw a circle around you physically and with your hands around your body energetically.

Draw the pentagram of Venus around you in blue or white, so your head and the arms are the top 3 arms of the pentagram, and your legs are the bottom 2 arms of the pentagram. You are now in the pentagram. Rest in this feeling, knowing, sensing that this pentagram is your body AND the reflection of the body of Venus in the sky. Feel this.

In this understanding, breathe deeply into your womb/hara, breathing in deeply this pentagram of Venus. Visualize it around you with every deep breath, so you become encased within the pentagram. Breathe it through your womb up into your heart and into your whole body.

Pray: Beloved Divine Mother Father, beloved watchers of my soul, beloved guardians of my spirit, beloved Devas of this world, I call you forth, I call you forth, I call you forth.

I call forth the ONE Daimon who is assigned to me to watch over me. I call forth the one assigned to me who is here to guard me, guide me, protect me and lead me into my soul. I call forth the one who is assigned to me to please show me what I need to do to go to my next level of evolution.

I call forth the one assigned to me to bring me into my fullness as a soul. I call forth the one assigned to me and my child to be with us now, to surround us, to protect us, to guide us into the ever increasing love bounty and alchemy that I am about to embark upon, with my family, my partner, my child in my pregnancy and birth.

I call forth my Daimon, divinely assigned.
I call you forth NOW x3. Be here with me now.

After doing this invocation, Sit silently and allow whatever impressions, intuitions, pictures and guidance to arise. Then, Ask your questions. Rest in this space, staying quiet so your

Daimon can inform you. If you feel you are not psychically or spiritually open to commune, it will use other means to communicate with you.

Complete and thank your Daimon. Breathe in the entire pentagram again connecting to Venus, into your body. This will seal the connection with your Daimon and Venus.

THREE TRIMESTERS of SOULFUL PREGNANCY

During pregnancy, your estrogen and progesterone levels rise, creating changes in your body that boosts libido, increases vaginal lubrication and heightens sensitivity in your breasts and nipples. This can be quite arousing and fascinating to explore!

But the same hormones can also turn you off sex, especially in the beginning when nausea and fatigue arise as you become used to the changes in your body. And towards the end of pregnancy, you may just feel big, unwieldy and unattractive anymore. This is where a responsive and loving man comes in! 21

Just as every woman's pregnancy is unique, so is every pregnant woman's sex drive. Use your intuition. You may feel like making love at different times of the day and night than you did before. You may feel like making love more: you may feel like making love less. Express all these feelings to your partner.

In making love in pregnancy some women experience bleeding, especially in the first trimester. This is caused by the swelling of capillaries in the cervix which can burst when irritated during sex. While such spotting or bleeding is generally nothing to worry about, still mention it to your doctor or midwife.

There is little chance of hurting baby during love making because the amniotic fluid and womb protect baby. The only caution is during oral sex, when your partner should not blow air into your yoni, as this can cause air bubbles to block a blood vessel.

Making love in pregnancy is beautiful when both partners are committed to each other, love each other, and want each other. All these feelings get tested throughout pregnancy as emotions flare, misunderstandings arise and tiredness sets in. Making love in pregnancy brings both partners together. It can be very sweet when you feel baby moving and can even touch baby when you are together!

Biologically, the hormones, orgasmic highs and happiness released in connected, loving love-making benefits baby's emotional and physical well being and growth, and can bring all three of you together emotionally. Making love in pregnancy allows the womb to relax, and the woman's gates to open, making labour easier and more pleasurable.

Making love in pregnancy allows a deeper magnetic bonding between all three of you. Why? After making love, when you are lying together, a series of concentric circular magnetic fields enclose you both, a series of fields within fields that bond you together physically, electromagnetically and in the cranial pulse and flows of your nervous system. This is why we feel so close, and wish to snuggle and cuddle each other after making love, as these magnetic fields arising from the womb and the male gates feel good!

It is important to cuddle together quietly in deep feeling after you make love, just feeling each other without words. This allows the magnetic fields to go deeper. (Because many

---

[21] Months four to six are often called the "honeymoon" trimester.

men are not attuned to their magnetic, feminine sides they go to sleep and miss out on the deeper feeling of their feminine side.)

For man and woman to do this with baby in the womb brings baby into these fields too. Baby will feel this love, bliss and joy and will be electromagnetically imprinted and bonded with mother and father, especially if the love making is loving, blissful, caring and conscious.[22] Through this imprinting, baby will feel inclined in later life to having sex with love and joy, and will feel something is amiss if these emotions are not there. Of course, baby's potential for intimate fulfilling relationships will also be heightened.

If sex is lustful, rough, short and uncaring, baby too will have this imprint within them, and will be more inclined to unconscious sex when it grows up, as its first experience of sex will be this. Baby's potential for intimate fulfilling relationships will be diminished. This is another reason why it is important for the parents sexual and emotional healing happens pre conception, and if not, during pregnancy.

Making love in pregnancy is wonderful for baby on all levels. After six months, one has to be more careful with the positions, yet as always, the woman has to use her intuition and common sense to determine what is good for her. Making love in the spooning position, from behind, woman sitting on top (i.e any position not putting pressure on belly or the woman lying on her belly) are all good provided the woman can control the movements and able to express when it is not comfortable, or if she starts to bleed.

Some parents do not like making love during pregnancy. The man can feel turned off by his partners appearance and new found bumps, curves, tiredness and emotional ups and downs. Mother can simply not feel like it sometimes. Yet, this time is a wonderful opportunity for sexual exploration, healing and growth.

We may not feel like making love during pregnancy because sexual abuse, harm and hurt may arise from the past. Miscarriage and abortion traumas may arise. Painful past relatings, past occasions of having had sex without love, father and mother traumas and deep unresolved needs for love can all arise in the sexual journey of pregnancy.

Becoming aware of these issues, and reaching out for love and support to heal them, can be immensely bonding for mother and father. Taking responsibility for these issues, vulnerably and honestly sharing and discussing them, taking steps to heal them together, can bring the sexual part of ourselves fully into the heart. When this is shared with your partner, a deeper bond, care, support and togetherness arises, that baby will also feel and appreciate.

Remember, your baby feels everything. All the healing you do in pregnancy, and for the first seven to fourteen years of baby's life, will deeply impact baby, and will help heal baby too.

---

[22] Passion works too! although after six months of pregnancy this has to be reigned in a little.

Making love and exploring sacred sexuality with your partner is one way to explore the seven gates during pregnancy, helping you both to deepen in the felt understanding of these portals into the different aspects of feminine consciousness.

Just as each trimester of pregnancy holds a different energy and theme, so are certain gates more present or accessible in each phase. For example, the fifth gate or the field of the womb is very active throughout all of pregnancy. This essence is experienced as a misty field of softness, life force and love. The fifth gate in its essence, IS the energy of pregnancy.

THE FIRST TRIMESTER: ESTABLISHING THE CONTAINER

At first the 'presence' of our incoming child can be felt in our wombs as a dense quality of light. When we invite our womb and heart to soften to this essence, we can tune into the subtler frequencies and flavors of this other soul. Already you can learn much about this soul essence, what it exalts or challenges within you, and how you feel yourself responding to it.

Morning sickness can be a subtle layer of resistance to this new being and presence within our womb. When we feel these symptoms arising, we can ask what aspects of us are resisting? How can we open more to our child and recalibrate our systems and our souls to resonate at a harmonious frequency together? Time with your womb on earth, dancing, singing while connecting to your womb, being held by your partner: all invite an entrainment between you and your incoming child.

Imagine how you feel when you invite a new friend into your home, your intimate space. Sometimes it takes time to acclimate to their energy, find the way your energies harmonize. It is similar with the presence of a new being in our wombs.

This is a time of joy, excitement, the opening into something new. In allowing this spirit to flow through you, you open to more of your femininity. It is important to continually tune into this new flow that is emerging through you, as it will allow you to open more gracefully to the process that is happening within and to you.

YOUR SPIRIT BODY AURIC FIELD

Our spirit body or auric field is an electromagnetic field located around our physical body, and is our direct connector into the web of life. It is through the web of life that our spirit bodies receive replenishment, nourishment, and connection to the life force that connects all things. It is the vehicle through which we access the web of life and come into connection with the auric fields of all other sentient beings. Our spirit bodies are the moving vehicles of our souls, our essence, just as our physical bodies are the moving vehicles of our spirit.

The auric field of a woman changes in her first trimester. Your child's auric field merges with your auric field, a phenomenon that will continue in various degrees until the child reaches seven years old when he or she develops their own unique auric field. This merging of fields enables direct feeling and sensing communication between mother and child, as well as establishing the reality that the child is directly influenced by mother's thoughts, emotions and immediate environments.

Because your auric field changes with the inclusion of your child, it is helpful to become more intimately aware of your auric field, and how it is interfacing with your child. You can begin to see and recognize any blocks or areas of resistance in you, and between you and your baby. 'Tuning in' this way will strengthen your increasing sensitivity and intuition and help you to see and feel baby more clearly in new and exciting ways.

PRACTICE: VISUALIZING YOUR SPIRIT BODY AURIC FIELD

Sit down, and take a few deep breaths into your belly. Center yourself and clear your mind. Close your eyes.

Directly in front of you, visualize your spirit body sitting opposite you. It looks exactly like you but is transparent and crystalline. Look at it. Notice its lines and contours, its colours and flows, and any rips, tears or black spots within it. What is it doing? What is it showing you?

Now look at it more closely. Zoom into its belly area. Can you see the presence of your child, can you sense it's spirit body within you, and where you are merged? Is the relationship between your two spirit bodies harmonious? Is there a disturbance such as red lines, spots or shadows? Do you see the difference in your spirit body and how it looks with your child now; how does it feel, and what is happening?

Dialoguing with your spirit body is important, as it holds much information for you. As the spirit body of your child develops, an extra layer is added to your spirit body form. You are deeply influenced by your child, and the emanations you begin transmitting are different to your solo frequency.

This extra layer in the spirit body also acts to set you apart from others because you are now entering your own cocoon. This is happening with every mother and child in the first trimester. The more conscious you make it, the more the spirit of your unborn child will come to rest and come into more active communication with you because he/she will feel welcomed, honored, received and included by you, not just as a biological entity but as a breathing, living person.

It is helpful and supportive to be around other conscious mothers in the first trimester whose auric fields have also changed and shifted.

THE OVARIES IN PREGNANCY

The ovaries are the light generators of the feminine body and spirit. They house the essence of pure femininity, the seed essences of all our potential creations from children to soul purpose projects, as well as sexual wounding and ancestral patterns. Ovaries are an indispensable source of energy for women, especially during pregnancy when we have excessive demands on our physiological systems to grow a baby.

Because our ovaries are powerful light generators of the female body, generating about 40% of a woman's daily energy, they directly influence our spirit body, which is our direct connection to the Earth. The more we keep these lines of connection open, through our ovaries, spirit bodies and Earth's energy field, the more we can be directly nourished, energized in a feminine way, and sustained.

PRACTICE: OPENING TO GAIA and THE SUN

As we open and connect to our First Gate of yoni lips and align it with the Earth, we enliven the magnetic web that exists between ourselves and Her. The First Gate is a means of transmission and communication, a Beacon, an avenue through which we receive and give magnetic impulses, drawing in and inviting those that are aligned. When we allow ourselves to fully give and receive love, enacting our sacred desires and moving from this impulse, we help enliven the collective web of the First Gate of creation.

When we directly connect our First Gate to the feminine and masculine energies of Earth and Sun, we can feel the love, warmth, energization, relaxation and nurturing of our natural and intimate connection to our Earth Mother and Father Sun. We can ground and nurture our First Gate into blooming, vitality, and new life.

1. Find a quiet, soft, grassy spot in nature. Before sitting down, look around you, appreciate the beauty and life you see and feel. Open your heart to the Earth, and let her know you see and recognize her beauty. Feel your praise, appreciation of her. Thank her.

2. Sit down and let your naked yoni lips rest on the Earth. Breathe deeply into your yoni lips, and feel the sensation of the pure earth against your lips. Wait to feel Earth's response to your pure, vulnerable yoni entrance. When you feel her, invite her into your yoni through your lips.

3. You may begin to feel an exchange, between the lips of your yoni and the earth. You may feel a tingling, a warmth, a softening as you recognize and remember the living being that is touching you.

4. From the deep sincerity of your heart, and from the warmth of your yoni lips, ask for Earth to help you connect more deeply to your First Gate, and to the interconnected web of life accessed through this portal.

5. Breathe into this connection, soften into it, and invite her to share with you, as she wills. You can ask her specifically what you need to do to further open your First Gate, what relationships need tending, what aspects of yourself need to be embraced.

6. Sit with her, in this First Gate Kiss, for as long as you feel. When you feel complete, lie back on the grass and rest. When you feel ready, open your legs and yoni lips to the Sun.

7. Feel the warmth of the sun on your yoni, feel the penetrating heat, the steady, strong rays of warmth touching you. Breathe into this, allow your lips to open and receive this energy.

8. When you feel touched by this loving force of the Sun, ask the Sun to penetrate your First Gate. Surrender to this presence, allow your lips and yoni to melt and let down.

9. Lie here for as long as you feel. Feel any emotion that arises as you deeply receive this benevolent energy. This love, this warmth is always here for you, when you open to receive it.

10. Now, feeling the connection between Earth, your yoni lips, and the Sun, breathe into your heart. Feel the perfect love that is available to you, through your Earthly Mother, your Fatherly Sun. Feel the appreciation and recognition they have for you.

11. Inhale the love, from Earth and the Sun through your yoni lips into your heart. Exhale, release the love you feel for Earth and the Sun out through your yoni lips. Continue to breath this breath of love through your yoni lips, until you feel complete.

Now: Offer this prayer in deep sincerity from your wombs voice, through the seed of your heart. Really feel the truth or distance from truth as you say each sentence. Allow space to sit with any emotions that arise from this practice. In feeling and releasing them, you will come more into alignment with the truth of this prayer.

I love you mother. Please send me your love. I love you father. Please send me your love. I love you my partner xxx. Please send me your love. I love you my child xxx. Please send me your love. I love you Mother Earth. Please send me your love. I love you Father Sun. Please send me your love.

I feel safe with my mother. I feel safe with my father. I feel safe with my partner. I feel safe on Earth. I feel safe within me. I feel safe with all beings. I feel safe in life. I trust myself. I trust my partner. I trust my father. I trust my mother. I trust the Beloved. I trust life. I trust in the purity of all beings. I trust earth. I trust the Sun.

I welcome my partner. I welcome my learnings with my mother. I welcome my learnings with my father. I welcome my family. I welcome all parts of myself. I welcome life! I welcome Earth. I welcome the Sun.

I feel and receive support. I feel and receive support from my partner. I feel and receive support from my mother. I feel and receive support from my father. I feel and receive support from my family. I feel and receive support from others. I feel and receive support from life. I feel and receive support from Earth. I feel and receive support from the Sun.

PRACTICE: WOMB BREATHING

Pregnancy is a very emotional time with increased sensitivity and hormone levels. This provides incredible opportunity to release many deeper held emotions quickly as mother opens to the vaster flow of life force moving through her body and her being.

The more space a woman can allow for these emotions to surface, be felt, and be released, the more present, magnetic and fluid she becomes. The more relaxed and fluid mother is, the happier baby and father will be as well.

1. Lie down on your back with your knees up. Place your hands on your lower belly and womb.

2. Feel your womb, and from your heart, offer her your love.

3. On your next inhale bring your breath to the edge of your womb, and wait for her to open to receive it. When you feel her open, when she is ready, offer your breath to her.

4. Exhale from your womb out through your mouth any tension, pain, or heaviness.

5. Inhale again bringing the breath to the edge of your womb, and allow her to begin breathing with you when she is ready.

6. Continue to inhale and exhale with her. Allow her to guide your breath. Allow your breath to fill and nourish her, and surround baby. Continue to exhale out anything you no longer need.

7. Continue this breath for 15 minutes.

THE SECOND TRIMESTER: COMMUNICATION and CONNECTION

The second trimester is a time of enjoyment, bonding, communion and pleasure. I is often called the honeymoon trimester. Having nurtured the growing flow of life and Shakti moving through your being in the first trimester, you are emerging into a new way of being. You may carry a curiosity, excitement, contentment and joy around all that is presenting.

You may find a deeper feminine sense of gravity borne of your womb and soul, and the changing dance of this expression. You start to enjoy the flow of hormones, the bump in your belly and the sensuality of your ripening form. There becomes a magnetic, deepening closeness between you and your partner. There is a deeper element of nurture for mother, child, and father with each other.

Making love in this trimester can be particularly heart opening. It also allows a deepening of the bonding between all three of you. Making love also helps to regulate your hormones and relax the body with the new found weight and burgeoning presence of your child.

During this time, the magnetic fields of the womb are creating subtle fields within fields like a series of concentric circles. These circles naturally emanate outwards. The magnetic fields emanating from a pregnant woman's belly can be felt by many. Some people may see a glow, others may feel the radiant energy and goodness of life from you as an all attractive, beckoning emanation to them.

A lot of men will help a pregnant woman as their own magnetics are triggered to care for and nurture the pregnant woman and her child. Your partners capacity to nurture and care for you and baby will increase as his magnetics grow in this period. If this doesn't happen, it is because the man has some emotions to feel and release.

These magnetic fields within fields also allow the child to connect more deeply to both parents and the Earth. Earth is a living being. When we allow an open energy exchange with her, we receive her deep grounding nurturance, and she receives the awakened connectivity of our presence.

Aspects of Earth's magnetic fields hold aspects of our own souls, that may have fragmented off during painful periods in our lives. The more we reconnect with her through our hearts and wombs, the more we welcome ourselves home. (see Earth resonance section)

When a mother connects through these magnetic fields more deeply to Earth, it enables a child to truly relax and receive input from Earth. The child will also give out toward Earth's fields and nurture Earth herself. The pregnancy and birthing process is good for our Earthly Mother too, as her energy both thrives on and supports this journey. We are all one interconnected organism.

CONNECTING TO YOUR CHILD
THE POINT OF ORIGIN and SEED OF LIGHT

The child at this stage is already starting to develop certain sensory perceptions. They are awakening to their feeling bodies and electromagnetic fields around them that are nourishing their preverbal sense of self.

Imagine a blooming white rose, with the bulb of the fetus at the very center, and the opening petals the outer edges of this magnetic bowl. The fetus can feel the surrounding layers of warm soft radiance.

Within these blooming fields is a focal point of light. When a mother spends time consciously connecting and aligning to this light source, she will come into deeper communion with her child, strengthen the container of her womb, and bloom these magnetic fields more fully.

All magnetic fields come from a Source center point. When this Source point is connected to and through the mother and to Earth, Children can experience another layer of a strong and soft cocoon of refuge for their physical bodies, spirits, and incoming souls.

Honoring the soul of your unborn child is an expression of your desire to honor your own soul. One of the first steps in this process is to make contact with the unborn child whilst he/she is in the womb, and communicate soul to soul. This will deepen the understanding and awareness of the parents about their child, *and themselves.*

Do you want the Light of the Divine to shine through your child?

If so, the parent that wants this has a direct responsibility. The Light that shines through the child will also shine through the pure heart and mind of the parent.

The following exercise can be used before, during, and after birth to consciously merge your energetic field with your child's. Over time it can build a foundation for soulful communication, before the use of language. It can also be used to speed up labor by aligning the energy of mother and child.

The following meditation can be done alone or with mother AND father. If this is practiced for ten minutes a day, it will strengthen the capacity for child to be held in earth's magnetic fields while staying connected to it's origin of light.

This practice is later reinforced through the daily Running the Light Practice which also connects child to Earth and his-her original seed of light. This is a beautiful meditation to do early in the morning when the slant of the sun can be received deep in the pineal gland.

PRACTICE: THE POINT OF ORIGIN and SEED OF LIGHT MEDITATION

1. Find a still quiet place and take a few deep breaths into your belly.

    With your eyes closed, gaze gently up at your third eye. Breathe deeply from here into the center of your brain, inviting the light of the sun, the light of the cosmos to enter. Set the intention and desire to connect with your child's Seed of Light.

2. Connect with your own Seed of Light by placing your fingers in the center of your chest where the ribs come together in a point. Relax. Breathe DEEPLY and slowly. Imagine that your breath is moving in, and out, of this point. Focus on this point until you feel your Seed of Light respond.

3. The sensation may be warmth, tingling, a sense of connection. Be aware of any images, memories, or possibilities that surface. This is your inner wisdom, your inner voice, your inner knowing. Enjoy this, and stay with it for a while.

4. Say: 'I ask my God Self I AM to be present here now. My Beloved Divine Mother-Father, please send me your Divine Love.'
    Feel this source of light connect with your own inner seed of light, located just below your heart center. Keep asking. Feel that they are connected and exchanging love, warmth, energy. Rest in this as long as you feel.

5. Now become aware of your child's seed of light, deep in your womb in the center of the baby's body. Visualize this seed of light just outside your body in a small energy field. Feel this connection. Invite this seed to join in the exchange from Source with your own. " I ask my God Self I AM to be present here now. My Beloved Divine Mother-Father, please send me your Divine Love.'
    Stay with this communion for a few minutes.

6. Send an arc of light from your Seed to your child's Seed. Now send a golden thread to your child. Weave this thread back and forth between your Seeds, joining them together.
    Strengthen your bond through the golden thread, weaving it back and forth in feeling and breath. As you do this may feel a sensation, quickening, or warmth. You may feel the connection in your heart, your Seed of Light, or in your body.

There is no specific way this has to happen. Take your time. Just enjoy the merging of your energetic fields. Get to know each other. Very gently receive impressions. When you feel complete, rest in the beautiful field you have created together. Take a deep breath and let the visualization subside.

Father is welcome to join in too, making this a group meditation time. Father brings in more of an electric presence, and this helps make baby feel safe, held, connected and part of a family in an innate and instinctual way. It is intimate and beautiful to silently commune with each other through a single point of light. This is an experience of bonding, origin and Source. This time can strengthen your individual connections to soul, and harmonize and bond the three of you on a deep preverbal level. It becomes a weaving from Source together between all three of you.

The second trimester is a time of deep communion, with Earth, with Source, with each other. In this opening comes a deeper bonding based on an unconditional foundation. From this can arise an organic dance of joy and pleasure, opening natural channels of nurturance necessary for all of you at this time.

Meditation from 'Honoring Your Child's Spirit,' by Flo Aeveia Magdalena.

PRACTICE: COMMUNICATING WITH YOUR SPIRIT BABY
From 'Spirit Babies,' by Walter Makichen

The following meditation connects with your child in the womb, enabling detailed communication. It contains three parts: firstly, calling your spirit baby, then attuning your energy to create a nurturing environment that will amplify your child's communication, and then establishing a direct line of communication.

I. Calling to your Spirit Baby

1. Sit with your spine straight and your feet flat on the floor. Place your left hand palm up on our left thigh and your right hand palm up on your right thigh. The fingers of both hands should be facing each other. Close your eyes and listen to your breath.

2. After you are settled, imagine that as you inhale, your breath is being pulled down through the top of your head to the base of your spine. As you exhale, imagine the breath flowing down your legs into the earth. Repeat this pattern for three or four minutes or until you feel ready to continue.

3. Focus on the center of your chest. Imagine yourself as a parent calling your child home for the evening.

4. Chant "OH, NAH, MAY, AH, SAH, NAH, CHA, OH, NAY, AH."

5. Continue to chant for five minutes or until you feel complete.

6. After you have finished chanting, keep your eyes closed—and relax until you are ready to go to the next part of the meditation.

II. Attuning Yourself to Your Spirit Baby

1. Close your eyes. Imagine you can breathe a bright red energy in through the top of your head. Let your inhalation draw the energy all the way down to the soles of your feet. As you exhale, imagine your entire body flowing a bright red.

2. Repeat this breath two more times. With each breath let the red glow of your body extend father into the space around you.

3. Repeat this process with the following colors: orange, yellow, green, blue, purple, and white. Allow three breaths for each color.

4. After you have finished, keep your eyes closed. Take a few moments and listen to your breath.

5. Ask yourself what color felt the most right, the most comfortable. Let your inhalation draw this color in through the top of your head, and fill your body with it. Let your exhalation extend the flow of this color into the space around you. Repeat this breath eight more times or until or feel ready to go on to the next meditation.

III. Direct Communication

1. Focus on the center of your chest and listen to your breath for a minute or so.

2. Imagine your spirit baby as a green oval floating in space about three feet in front of you.

3. Chant *"OH, AH, OH, AH, OH, AH, OM."*

   As you chant, imagine the OHs vibrating in the center of your chest, the AHs vibrating the spirit baby oval, and the OM vibrating in the space between you. Repeat the chant ten times. You may do it longer if you wish.

   After you have asked your question, pay attention and wait for an answer. Simple direct questions are best. Sometimes your baby will respond and sometimes they will not. Each time you call you are creating a loving nurturing energy that supports their growth, so there is always benefit.)

Some suggested questions to ask your baby:

- Have we known each other before?
- Why did you choose me as a parent?
- What are our lessons together? What do I need to learn from you, and what do you need to learn from me? What can I give you?
- Is there anything I can do to facilitate your conception or birth?
- Do you know of any problems that will impact your pregnancy or birth?
- What do you know of your destiny and soul purpose?
- How can we best prepare for your life with us?

- How can we make you feel at home with us?
- What do I and my partner need to eat that will serve the needs of your growing body?
- What sort of physical environment does my body need in order to nurture yours?
- What sort of mental environment must I maintain in order to nurture yours?
- What sort of emotional climate do I need to maintain in order to nurture yours?
- What physical habits do I have that obstruct your growth and function?
- What mental habits do I have that obstruct your growth and function?
- What habits in my relationship with my partner do I have that obstruct your growth? What sorts of people do you want around you while you are an infant?
- What physical place would best serve your growth?
- What is your primary purpose in coming to Earth?
- What are some of your secondary purposes? How can I help you with those?
- What is our soul contract? How can you help me with these?
- What is your name?
- Do you have any closely related souls incarnating around this same time?
- Are there any books you would like me to read?
- Are there any people you would like me to talk to?
- What style of birthing would you most prefer? Who would you like as a (midwife, nurse, doctor)? Which friends and relatives, if any, would you like at the birth?
- How can I minimize stress for you after birth?
- How can I minimize stress for myself after your birth?
- How can I minimize stress for my partner after your birth?
- What else should I know before your birth?
- What is the most important thing you would like me to remember after your birth?
- What else would you like to tell me?

It is important to say "I love you," with feeling and depth at the end and beginning.

SECOND TRIMESTER: SECOND AND THIRD GATES

The second trimester is a time of bonding and deepening between mother and father and between each individual parent and the Divine. To deepen takes trust, as when we viscerally trust, our bodies and souls relax, expand and move more freely into the new spaces that await you both.

The magnetic floor of a woman is her seat of trust. Any unhealed emotions held in the magnetic floor, the g-spot and anus will arise in birth as those tissues are intensely stretched and sensitized. The more she inhabits and embodies this area *now*, the more orgasmic her birth can be.

Her magnetic floor can be accessed through the perineum, anus, g-spot and cervix. The anus is an entry point into the back of her womb space. Gentle, sensual anal massage to help her relax, open, feel any suppressed fear or shame, will enable her to settle more in herself, into pregnancy and into the relationship with father. This massage is a beautiful way to open her inhibitions as well, which brings the potential for more freedom and bliss into birth.

The second gate or G-spot is a powerful point that can bring cascading pleasure to a woman. When this energy is invited and guided to flow through womb into heart it brings a woman into more love, abundance and connection to her experience. When the energy is further guided into her brain and third eye, it becomes a communion point with the Divine.

The cave of the g-spot is hollow and deep. If she has not released the density of emotion held here, she can still be harboring resentment and hatred toward her man, toward all men, which keeps her from dropping deeper into her feminine center, and has her acting from an unbalanced or manipulative place of control.

When she has released anger, hatred and shame from her g-spot, the magnetic flow can release unhindered. She becomes deep, settled, sensual, and alluring.

PRACTICE: MAGNETIC FLOOR PULSE

This is a powerful exercise to further open and activate the magnetic floor of a woman, and deepen her into her g-spot. A woman can do this with herself or can receive it from her partner. The more present she is in her g-spot before birth, the more easily and pleasurably she will birth, *and* recover after birth. *This exercise should not be done after the second trimester.*

1. Place the middle finger of your right hand inside your yoni on g-spot. Place the ring finger of this same hand gently on your anus.

2. Begin a slow and rhythmic pulse, like a conversation back and forth, one spot then the other.

3. Breath into this pulsing, feeling into any numbness, any emotion that may arise.

4. Place the left hand with fingertips on the tip of the tailbone, this creates a grounding point for the energy.

5. After a few minutes, synchronize the pulses so they happen at the same time. Keep breathing, keep softening all of your awareness and presence into your magnetic floor. Keep feeling all that is activated and awakening here.

6. You may feel sexual energy arise, try not to 'do' anything with it. Surrender to the natural emanation into your magnetic floor, opening the places that were shut down. Keep softening and allowing.

7. When you feel complete release your hands and roll into a fetal position on your left side. Embrace yourself, embrace any parts of you that feel vulnerable or needy. Breathe the energy from your magnetic floor up into your heart and back again a few times until all feels smooth and integrated.

For man and woman, exploring the second gates of g-spot and prostate during the second trimester of pregnancy can bring a deeper, felt bond of gratitude and trust between all three souls that anchors them all more physically into the body. The focus here is not so much on sexual energy, but soulful vulnerability and connection.

The anchor of the G Spot second gate, and the opening spiraling vortexes of energy along the spine that initiate in the opening of the clitoris third gate, create a direct access point in the human body between sexuality, soul and the Divine. When Shakti flowing through these gates is invited into the heart and pineal, a profound space for communion is opened.

This takes meditation and prayer deeper into the sensual circuitry of a woman's sexuality, and palpably brings that energy into her growing baby's experience. Through mirror neurons, each time she opens herself to prayer, opens herself to receive energy and love from the Divine, her child will be receiving it too.

I remember being pregnant with my son, and each time I would drop into prayer, I would feel his heart ignite, and my own prayer intensified. I felt blessed, as Yeshua shared, "When two or more are gathered in my name, there I AM." *Carrying my son in my womb, I was 'two or more' at all times.*

With the thinner veils of perception and heightened sensitivity in pregnancy it becomes a potent time for Divine connection, communication and communion. By the second trimester baby is entrained to mother's meditations and prayers, and when she surrenders more into her second and third gates, she can more viscerally feel the channel open to the Divine.

It is essential for her to make space and have times of solitude in this time for marinating in Divine energy, receiving clear guidance, and sensitizing herself to the movements and expressions of all the currents within her. It is here she will begin to receive more guidance on her deeper fulfillment, and the recognition of her true blueprint.

THIRD TRIMESTER: COMMUNING with CREATION

The third trimester is the time for your inner Womb Shaman to arise. It is time to reconvene with the powers of Creation. This connection can be natural at this stage. By spending time in wild nature, a mother will more easily be able to tune into and allow the raw powers of Earth, the raw powers of her own body, Shakti and spirit, to flow. Surrendering to this flow brings a deep reclamation of power.

This feminine power is exactly what she will need to navigate her own birthing journey and her ways of stepping into the world in her authentic soul's expression. This is an opportunity for her to raise the Womb Shaman within.

What is a Shaman? A Shaman is one who wields, navigates and harnesses the forces of existence. A Shaman is one who can navigate through different worlds and bring forth medicine, wisdom, healing and (re) connection. A Shaman is one who can harness the forces flowing from the Heavens down through her transparent vessel and back again. A Shaman is one who can harness the forces flowing from Earth through her transparent vessel and back again.

A Shaman is a bridge between this dimension and many other dimensions. With one foot in this world and one foot in others, she is a transparent conduit of many forces. She plays a co-creative role in directing these forces toward love, evolution, change, and the breaking of illusions. A Shaman is one who allows her self to be carved open in this process, beyond any personal identity or agenda, into surrender to the very breath of Creation. These forces flow into her and they also emerge from her, for they are the living breath of her essence.

This is training for birth *and* this is training for life. This is the very energy her New Child needs to feel within her, to help lay the foundation for what she and the child have come to Earth to actualize.

Get your drum out. Move your hips. Become the wild woman! Dip into your inner witch. Go on a vision quest. It is time for you to spend more time alone. Time to tune into an even deeper listening, a deeper presence-ing, a deeper dance and awareness of the powerful life force that is moving through you. Spend more time in your womb space, go on more inner travels and deep journeying.

Reap the benefits of this fantastic fertile time. The veils between you and your innate capacities of 'seeing and feeling 'are wide open. It is time to explore and navigate through the different fields of the Earth and the different dimensions of reality. It is time to see and commune more deeply with your guides.

All of these doorways open to you now. The gifts and treasures you gather on your journeys will play a part in the latter expression of your soul's purpose and manifestation here on Earth. Use this time, go deep, gather all that you can, for the harvest will feed your parenting, your purpose and your passion.

If it is not natural for you to access these inner spaces, it only takes a bit of desire from you to ask for guidance from an authentic Shaman or Guide whom you feel drawn to and has long standing experience in these realms. Yet this is a time of reclamation of power, not giving it away, so if you ask someone else to help you open these channels, take command of it. Simply ask them to help you open the way. Trust that opening up and journeying into these different dimensions with guidance will connect you more to your way of accessing these innate capacities within yourself.

During my third trimester with my son, I was doing many psychic Readings for others. My ability to 'See 'clearly had opened up so much, I could read other's physical bodies, spirits and souls very clearly. This gift has remained after my pregnancy, partially because I utilized and strengthened it every day.

As the cauldron of hormones and energies of your biology have changed and mutated to a degree, this is a ripe and rich time to develop these visionary gifts and powers. They will stand you in good stead for the birth navigation and afterwards in your life. This will also be important for your child.

Mother needs to be a visionary and a Womb Shaman, able to sense, feel and see the web and flows of connection, to manifest, move, and magnetize the people and resources to serve the family as you all grow. As a mother accesses this space between dimensions, she can consciously attract what is best for her and her child. She can explore and begin to deeply understand the process of manifestation. She can create bridges to these unseen realms that can guide her and which she can access instantly, even amidst the busy dance of being a mother.

The visionary capacities found within solitude, found within the blooming womb, found within the bond between mother and fetus, allows one to perceive reality in the third dimension in a different way. This is a great opening, gift and initiation of being a mother. Being able to perceive the world in a different way as a mother, as a Womb Shaman, means she can choose *how* to show up and *be* in the world, how to alchemize the present energies to create an environment of love, truth and beauty.

This initiation and embodiment into the mother part of the feminine marked mothers out in the old times. Mothers were more revered in the past because they had these qualities inculcated during pregnancy. They were more respected because they lived using these awakened powers.

Once a woman has her Shamanic connection from the depths and roots of her primordial feminine self, once she has wielded her feminine power throughout the most primordial of feminine initiations in birth, then she becomes deeply embodied. This can be felt just upon meeting her.

The latent part of her that has bloomed throughout pregnancy becomes fully anchored and activated in all the different streams of her self. She becomes a light unto herself. In this sovereignty she is more resilient, more empowered, and also able to be more vulnerable and open to the greatest gift: the capacity to fully give and receive love from a magnetic feeling place.

She has this foundational primordial power within her, of primordial consciousness, of the ability to bridge realities and embody it here and now. She can now be in full alignment with these energies, and they will accompany her beyond birth, so that she can draw on them at any time.

For the New Children this shamanic energy is particularly important, as they will need to feel this power to feel safe on Earth. Yes, they need to feel welcomed and loved and held, as there is great grounding for their being that happens through these magnetic qualities. Yet the power of primordial, instinctual, fertile energy moving through their embodied mother will root them in their natural alignment between heaven and earth, and root them in their bodies.

In this, they are connected to the very power that birthed the stars, that birthed the universe. They are innately connected to *Spanda*-the humming vibration within everything, and *Eon*--the magical power of transformation that lies in the heart of all sentient beings. When they are truly rooted in this as Mother and has embodied this to a degree, they will always have this reference point.

A man cannot birth or manifest in this way. Only a woman holds this innate capacity to embody, live, create and manifest from this infinite well of existence.

Being aligned to the vibration within all things allows these New Children to feel safe. They will come to subconsciously recognize this vibration in all things and will resonate and play with this. This will make them feel truly grounded and connected *within themselves*.

The true connection we all seek is to the vibrating essence of all things, which is also within us. These New Children already have that innate within them, and coming to Earth will give them a different experience of that. When mother has integrated and grounded herself in this primordial fertility and resonance, then baby can be inculcated into this in the third trimester, and will be able to embody more parts of themselves. This will alleviate many of the problems or symptoms Star Children currently struggle with in adapting to Earth life.

PRACTICE: CONNECTING WITH SPANDA

This exercise is best done outside, immersed in nature. Choose a place that resonates with you, as this is the entry vibration you are seeking to open you up more deeply to the movements of life. It may be helpful to listen to some instrumental music that is slow with a rhythmic repetitive beat. Use your intuition and tune into what your body is telling you to do.

1. Stand firmly on the ground, feet bare and hip distance apart. Place your hands around your womb, in a comfortable position. Feel the temperature of the Earth on the soles of your feet, feel her texture between your toes, sense her essence emanating from her living expression beneath you.

2. On your inhale, open the soles of your feet, like eyes to the earth, and draw her energy up into your womb. Exhale, release the energy and allow gravity to move through you as you rest your weight heavily on the earth. Keep breathing like this.

3. As you engage more deeply with Earth's essence, in your womb feel the tendency to begin to move your hips. Allow this to happen, gently, organically, rhythmically.

4. Allow yourself to breathe, stretch, sigh, moan, whatever sound wants to emerge. Keep the movement happening, allow your body to translate the energy that is emerging between you and the earth. Let yourself be moved by her, co-create the dance with her.

5. If there are emotions that arise, let them move through you. This intent is not about healing in particular, just being moved and connected to that wave of life force within all things. This is bound to touch the places within that are stuck or resistant. Allow these places to dissolve into the dance.

6. There may come a point when your sense of your own boundaries, your skin, your magnetic field, begins to blur with that of Earth, of life around you. Allow this, feel yourself at the center of this, yet allow your container to expand, breathe, be moved by life itself.

7. Breathe, Breathe, Breathe, move, dance, delight, go where you are moved to go.

8. When you feel yourself coming to completion with this time, make your way onto the ground. With knees wide rest in child's pose with your forehead on the Earth. Thank Earth, thank Beloved Divine Mother, thank yourself, thank your child for this dance, this connection, this experience of creation moving and expressing through your being and form.

This is a beautiful exercise in and of itself, and can also be an invitation to allow you to open up to more ways of movement and expression that will emerge in birth.

OPENNESS and THE CERVIX

The third trimester invites us to the threshold of birth. In the final stages before birth the cervix or fourth gate begins softening, melting and opening to make way for the blooming of baby through yoni into the world. As this happens, the veils between worlds become thin, and the solidity of old structures and ways of navigating in the outer and inner worlds begin to dissolve.

We become more sensitized and open to everything. Openness is vulnerability, transparency and total honesty. Total honesty requires you share what you feel and think, even if you think your partner may not like it! This does not mean being rude, arrogant or unkind. It means you are honest and are not concealing your real emotions from your partner. Taking self responsibility for these emotions and thoughts, and sharing them in a gentle, open way allows real dialogue and exploration to occur.

When you express something, you can also release it. Just through expressing yourself about touchy topics, the energy unfolds and can resolve more gracefully. The pent-up energy of anxiety, stress and emotions can unwind and release, enabling you to feel unburdened, clear and free.

'My Grace is sufficient for you for my power is made perfect in weakness.'
2: Cor 12:9

Expression is the medium for transparency. Deeper expression allows yourself to be known. Becoming known means there are no more secrets, places to hide in or retreat to. In the revealing lies a softness, a gentling. All that is rigid can melt and open.

Expressing intimately with another allows you to know more of yourself. Knowing yourself means you realize your fullest potential and become happy. Be intimate today, share your deepest secrets and unsaid feelings with another. You may be pleasantly surprised.

This expression leads to a weakening of the armored, forgotten parts within us; in our keenly felt humanity we open the door to our divinity. Vulnerability is an open doorway to the divine, for the divine to enter us.

You sublimely transform as you consciously allow yourself to be known by your partner nakedly, allowing your partner into every nook and cranny of your body and soul, willingly, humbly, gratefully.

Vulnerability is part of humility. Vulnerability allows all the secret places in our heart, all we are scared of, all we are ashamed of and hide in dark, secret places within us, to come out to the light. Whenever we are truly vulnerable, the other always feels this, and is drawn to you, to comfort, hug and hold you. Vulnerability is a great attractor and inspires support. Vulnerability brings us all closer together, and allows someone else to be at your side.

When we are not vulnerable, we push others away, and stop ourselves from receiving what we truly want: love. Vulnerability brings us the loving balm that our souls needs to grow, and when we live into this in our daily lives with transparency and honesty we become open.

Openness means we are open to whatever life brings us, knowing that it is ultimately for our good. Openness is the end of attachment to any outcome. We may still have preferences, but we are not attached to them. Openness is true flow, where we become like water, able to flow into any situation and environment. We can be speaking to a beggar one moment and a king the next, and we are equally open with them both, meeting them where they are, sharing what is needed to be shared in the moment.

Openness has no dogma, creed or religion, no special jargon or language. It resonates and speaks to everyone wherever they are at, without you losing your centre or pretending to be something you are not. Openness brings us directly into the flow of life, the flow of synchronicity, the flow of the Law of Attraction. Openness shares everything we feel without self-judgment, blame, self-punishment or unworthiness.

Openness is a blank canvas that has infinite possibilities and infinite choices, none of which are good or bad. There is no good or bad in openness, no duality, as everything is seen as equal. What is good for you one moment may be bad for you the next, what is not good for you today may be the best thing in your life tomorrow.

True openness comes from your soul, as the soul is naturally free and open. In openness, there is an emotional intelligence, strength and softness that comes from transparency, vulnerability and honesty. You can access all these qualities in any moment, and there is no negativity, shame or worry about it. Openness is a consolidation of all these qualities to bring a solid but fluid centre, a core within you that is supple, strong yet flexible and open to change.

Having this foundation of openness means we are open to the greatest changes and transformations. We can flow with whatever comes, secure in our emotional centre. Openness brings us all we ever wanted as we can now receive it without barrier or block. The universe is always conspiring to bring us our souls desires: *can you be open enough to receive it?*

Prayer
'Beloved Divine Mother Father God, please help me open myself to Your Love and Your Will. Please help me open myself to my deeper emotions, hidden away inside me. Please help me open myself to all that life wants to give me, teach me, and share with me. Please help me open myself more to my partner. Help me be more vulnerable, honest and sharing of all that is within me. Amen.'

NOW: Tell your partner 5 things you have never told them before. Maybe you did not tell them out of fear, out of being polite or because you were ashamed to say it. Try it today. Be vulnerable, honest, transparent and brave. What happens?

In the cervical experience and its opening up of the light and dark sides of our primordial self, we find our purity and our passion, our shadow and wild woman, our wounded self and tender loving self. We need to draw forth from our inner well and unknown depths more of this womb shaman in the third trimester. This trimester can be deeply emotional, with the rollercoaster of hormones regulating, readying and radically altering mothers biology.

It is at this time she especially needs the strength and support of her man. If she feels the safety, solidarity and trustworthiness of his pillar with her, if she feels his emotional presence, his care, his seen and unseen support, if she feels his increased responsibility and care for her and baby, she can surrender and emerge into a new way of being. If she does not feel safe, she can become out of control emotionally, creating havoc for partner, baby and herself.

At this time, it is important for mother to take more time alone, to have the space and sanctity to nest more deeply with her baby, with herself, and with her home space she will be birthing in. This is because we are so open at this time, physically, emotionally and psychically, that the influence and energy of other people's emotions and thoughts becomes much harder to filter out from yourself: you become much more empathic and open to every vibration around you.

Father here needs to step up and guard these boundaries for his partner and his child. It is in this time that the clear expression and presencing of truths from mother can enable her to remember her centre and release any emotional blocks within her, leading to deeper surrender. These blocks are the final pieces arising to be released before birth.

When she can embrace and surrender, she can begin to enter the vast void space of her womb or sixth gate where the early tuning movements of labour begin. A pregnant woman in her sixth gate has a far-away look in her eyes. She has a depth of presence that is straddling 3-dimensional reality and yet rooted in something far beyond. She is present and here, but also deeply internal.

In this deep womb space, we become a bridging infinity loop for aspects of the child's soul to travel through remaining star gates into manifestation. The more a woman can allow space and time to deeply drop into these spontaneous meditations that open to her, the more she is consciously involved in the process of her child's incarnation and assisting him-her to bring all pieces of themselves into the body.

I remember with my son that the entry into my womb and sixth gate brought me into a deeper experiential understanding of the movements of creation. It was here that I could surrender to literally feel his emanating spark emerging from the deep blackness of space. I understood how our experience on earth is a non-linear convergence of our soul frequency to enable a density of experience for learning. It is the crucible to inhabit and test the truth of our evolution. When we embody in our sixth gate, we utilize time and space as a forum to execute our unique emanation of Divine Will. This expression brings us more deeply into embodiment or individuation.

The sixth gate is an infinity loop, crossing in 3-dimensional time/space. As I moved throughout this infinity loop, I felt the perfection in the orchestration of 'timing 'in a larger cosmic alignment, a harmony far beyond what is seen in our 3D world. When a soul can emerge into this world in this larger sense of timing and harmony, their life is 'graced,' meaning there is a fluidity of connection and integration beyond a separate self.

This is the deep wisdom of the Divine Feminine...the cycles and rhythms of time that creates and decays all life. It is the sixth gate that weaves a woman deeper into this.

Most women in their ninth month of pregnancy move through impatience and being 'over ready 'for baby to come. Yet when we allow ourselves the gift of dropping into our womb in the final hours of pregnancy, we understand the importance of allowing baby to emerge, not of our own agenda, but in "Divine Timing."

After baby is born, her sixth gate enables her to commune with parts of baby's soul that are still moving into being. Coagulating a soul into 3-dimensional form is not something that happens in a moment; it happens magnetically throughout the journey of pregnancy and birth.

Embodiment is a spectrum of experience that continues unhindered if the environment is fertile and allowing. Once the momentum is instigated, by surrendering to our Souls Design for birth, it becomes a way of living for mother, father and child.

THE FATHER IN THE THIRD TRIMESTER

The father by this time needs to be embodied in softness, strength and service as the pillar. To be this, he too will need his alone time, and will need to be supporting his testes, the generator of light for his body and the fuel for his masculine energy, through good male companionship, exercise and through breathing into the testes regularly.

Father in the third trimester needs to step into fully supporting his partner physically, emotionally, spiritually and soulfully. He has to be prepared to give up a part of his old life, more so than ever before in the previous six months, and devote himself *and* more of his time to serving his family. This has to be done in alliance with him nurturing himself and doing the unique things he needs to do at this time, which will be different for every man.

The biological portal to a man's soul lies through his testes. The testes are the biological light generators of the male physical body, like the ovaries are for the feminine form. The testes give a man vitality, exuberance, a soft yet strong, clear male essence and life force energy. Testes are the fuel for the embodying essence of masculinity.

Testosterone is not just an athletic, aggressive, macho, bravado way of being. This is just the most basic aspect of the testes energy. The awake and alive testes feel like deep, warming, velvety-soft red wine. They hold the energy of the heart in manifestation. They serve to embody and transmit the pure male principle of creation here in the body, here on earth. They connect to and empower the heart to bring love and giving into manifestation through the male body.

When a man is embodied in his testes, this power and presence is deeply felt by mother and child, and allows them both to relax and surrender more into the container partially held by him. This is especially important during birth.

The testes energize and complete the embodiment of the lingam principle in a man, the most fundamental identity a man has. The testes revitalize, rejuvenate, and create the light body of the lingam, "the wand of light." When the testes are fully active on all seven levels, ranging from the first level of physical power and macho testosterone to the seventh level of pure light, then the pillar of light of the male principle embodies within the male form.

The testes generate the light force for a King to embody fully into his biology here on earth. *This energy is very attractive for a woman.* This pure masculine pillar (as demonstrated by the Shiva lingam in India) allows the feminine magnetics to rest, relax, come into harmony, feel safe and surrender, both within the man *and* in the women surrounding him.

The true testes energy is vitality, grounded safety, trust, peace and embodied radiance. They hold the energy to attract people and resources into your life. You become potent, alive, and your inner light shines forth from your body itself. The Testes transmit your soul mission ignited. It brings forth purpose, passion, and actualization. From here, we create new life, both with a baby and with other projects we wish to fulfill. They are transmitters of the true potency of a man, and help to embody a man into the world.

In the true testes energy, we feel assured, strong, yet soft and relaxed in our identity. We feel proud of our lingam. We truly appreciate and can freely praise, without ego, the beauty, strength, magnificence and love of our lingam and masculinity. We enjoy our masculinity without reservation and can share this with others without shame, ego or trepidation.

The testes energy is embodying and relaxing, allowing us to be natural, and to let go into our pure essence of manhood. The true testes energy is a light generator that fuels heart and hara; it rejuvenates the cells on a deeply felt level with life force. The true testes energy is pro-life, all inclusive, and all that blocks it is anti-life.

Testosterone produces drive, aggression, bravery and power, and when this is refined through emotional connection, release and vulnerability (not just chi orientated processes) it becomes a softness and a strength simultaneously. It becomes a fuel for light and innocence, a playfully innocent drive. The stronger you become, the gentler you can be.

As a man's heals his testes circuit and steps more into his Kingship, physical adjustments happen in the pelvis, prostate and sacral area. Pains and aches may arise that no other form of bodywork can address fully. These pains are the false masculine body-spirit attitude relaxing and releasing themselves, asking for your attention to be placed into your Gates to accelerate the healing process.

In the true testes energy, we enjoy connecting more deeply and truthfully with male friends and soul brothers. A sense of male kinship, of male bonding, of male play, of male camaraderie, of male connection, of true brotherhood, helps the testes energy to bloom and root on earth, in the body, in your masculinity.

What blocks this in modern man? The sole use of the testes energy without deeper emotional content and feeling connection with the heart. This exhausts the testes, and the firing of testosterone without magnetic connection, *solely* for vitality, ambition, athletic prowess, physical appearance, competitiveness, power gone amok with war and conflict, and the alpha male syndrome is debilitating for the soul.

These are aspects of the testes that are designed to be connected into the courage and strength of the spiritual warrior connected to his heart, vulnerability and humility, NOT left disconnected. Yet, there is nothing wrong with using the testes for vitality, ambition, athletic prowess, physical appearance at times. It also needs to be connected into the spiritual warrior *as well.*

What blocks the testes? Emotions of humiliation, shame, ridicule and unworthiness all block the life enhancing power and presence of the testes. Sexual abuse, sex without love, sex with overt aggression, miscarriages, abortions,[23] and painful intimate relationship breakdowns (that have not been resolved and healed in appreciation of the lessons learned) deeply affect the testes.

---

[23] Miscarriages and abortions also affect the man involved in colluding with the woman who had them.

Feelings of loss, grief, abandonment of a significant female or male partner, son, daughter, mother or father can be stored here. Rejection in the sexual arena is also stored here, and if not resolved, feelings of impotence, powerlessness and fear of intimacy with the opposite sex can result. Ancestral woundings, abuses and inherited emotions also impact the testes ability to fully connect to the heart.

When the testes are blocked, our life force is blocked. Pride, inferiority, fear and even hatred of the opposite sex can arise. We may feel the need to prove ourselves in the material world, as we have not been a 'man" in our inner world and in intimacy. Because we feel powerless and impotent within, we may feel the need to achieve, obtain, and get power and material wealth from others and the material world through reliance on and manipulation of the mind.

We may become a slave to the matrix, wanting to be accepted by society, wanting to be rich, powerful, famous to prove our worth and to prove we are a real man. We can become a people pleaser to try and fit into the distorted view of masculinity, sexuality and relationships so prevalent in our wounded society. Releasing these emotions and beliefs helps restore your vitality and life force energies so you have space to flow, and to just be yourself.

Being controlled, abandoned or smothered by a dominating parent can be imprinted in the testes, impacting the testes feeling link to the heart. This can diminish our essential vitality and joy, disembodying us, keeping us in a partial sense of our manhood, and making us a servant to the opposite sex in order to get their love in a vain attempt to reclaim our own self. Here, we can feel into and release emotions of not feeling loved, nurtured, tended to or heard, from childhood and from women.

Reactions in the testes vary from fearing women and staying away from intimacy, or staying in relationships where you remain in a subservient position, manipulating the other through hidden resentment, a sense of revenge and guilt/shame.

Instinctual drives and their attendant emotions are the way our reproductive organs guarantee the continuation of the species. When we 'fall in love', many times it has little to do with our heart; it has a lot however to do with the testes and lessons to be learnt. The original illusion of our emotions is "The Other." As babies, we depend on the mother "Other" for survival. Later, a similar dependency can be formed with a sexual partner.

Both partners project their needs on the "Other," substituting the other for real love, but these needs can never be fulfilled from the outside. A true love affair is not about the survival of a wound pattern, but our instincts give us this message, which is why many relationships end in disillusionment. A man may end up martyring, sacrificing and offering part of his life to try and get back someone, or something, who has gone from his life.

PRACTICE: TESTES HEALING

Inhale glowing, iridescent, deep wine-red energy deep down into the seed of your testes for 6 seconds, so they rise up; as you exhale out, your balls fall back down. Do this 6 times. Your balls become glowing, iridescent, deep wine-red with each breath.
Pray: "Beloved Divine Father, send me 8000% Red Ray of Spiritual Warrior to charge my testes now."

Inhale shining, glowing, iridescent fluid black energy deeply into the seed of your testes for 6 seconds, and slowly exhale out, 6 times. Your balls become shining, glowing, iridescent fluid black.
Pray: 'Beloved Divine Mother, send me 4000% Black Ray to anchor my testes now."

Inhale radiant, glowing, iridescent, fluid white energy, and slowly inhale them deeply into the core and seed of your testes for 6 seconds, then slowly exhale out, 6 times. Your balls become radiant, glowing, iridescent, fluid white.
Pray: 'Beloved Divine Father , send me 6000% White Ray to cleanse my testes now.'

Breathe these cycles of wine red, shining black, and radiant white, twice more.

Now, gently ask your testes the following questions. *If you feel any emotions arise, simply breathe and allow yourself to feel them fully.*

Do you ever feel threatened, exposed, and insecure? Do you handle the situations life throws at you on an emotional level, or just on a mental level? Are you unsure, uncomfortable, ashamed with your sexual expression? Do you hold onto guilt and anger? Do you have difficulty forgiving, letting go and moving on from past emotional hurts from women?

Do you make yourself small and overly 'serviceful' around women? Do you invalidate yourself with others? Do you try and please and placate others? Do you trust your masculine drive, power, gentleness and intuition? Are you scared and ashamed of being a powerful man? Are you scared and ashamed of being a soft, tender man?

Pray: *"Beloved Divine Father, I ask You, please help me feel and release all my emotions of being ridiculed, of being humiliated, all my deep shame, my mistrust of women, my fear of not living freely, and my grief and sadness from my testes and soul."*
Repeat the word "CLEAR" until you feel a shift occur.

As Pure Consciousness, the masculine essence is naturally suited to being alone, all-one, content in the depths of his Self. Deep feelings of aloneness, or all-one-ness, arise in the depths of the Testes Circuit, opening to a detachment to what is playing out on the 'outside'. This is a deep, soft, self-contained loving fullness, a contentment and organic feeling within oneSelf, as you settle more into yourself. It is not an unfeeling mental detachment from yourself and others.

The stillness and self-contained nature of this wholeness and aloneness allows one to Be, simply. A man desires to be alone and rest in his cave- this is valuable and necessary. The Testes allows one to rest within masculine essence, and allows a man to be himself, without need for anyone or anything.

No need comes from a soft, deep wholeness within you, not a cold, mental observation. A wish to be alone and stay in this nourishing, natural space is natural. Deeper relating with others occurs from this space, this deep, soft anchoring in Self. A lightness and depth of heart opens with an engagement from this place with others.

In this inner stillness, one can also feel where your masculine essence is still not fulfilled. Any sadness within you can arise in emotions, pangs and the cut of loneliness and separation from parts of yourself which you may project onto your partner. *Feel into what this is, and how to fulfill it within yourself.*

The softness, depth and wholeness of YOU is found here, in a direct way. So far removed from the common perception of the masculine, the testes and testosterone help fuel peace, not war, help fuel silence, not chatter, help fuel aloneness in order to relate better, and help fuel Being, not doing.

All is allowed to Be what It Is. Just Be Yourself. Yang comes full circle into Himself.

YOUR CHILD IN THE THIRD TRIMESTER

From your baby's perspective, the magnetic fields encasing them in the womb are getting tighter and closer. The fields are rotating faster. The point of light nestled within the magnetic folds of the womb is getting bigger in their awareness. When mother can allow herself to drop into this space, she can gently join in with this point of light. This will be an important focal point for both of them during birth. In the meantime, do not focus too intently on this point because it may trigger movement into birth in the third trimester.

In the third trimester, the child will be traveling through different dimensions and aligning more and more to this point of light amidst these ever-contracting magnetic fields. The birthing journey of labours rushes begins the moment the magnetic fields completely collapse, leaving only the source point of light.

In this moment, your child will have no choice but to move, as the magnetic container around them is dissolving into a single point of light. When mother is aware of this, she can entrain more deeply with her child's emergence in body and soul. In this process, mother also reclaims or inhabits another part of herself as part of her own Rite of Passage.

In this time of the third trimester remember to stay in frequent contact with your child and allow your child to share with you what they need. This can be intuitive; you may not have to ask in a direct way, you may just know. However, if you need direction there are three questions you can ask:

How do you feel now?
What is happening for you now?
What do you need?

Each child is unique and will require different things, different foods, different emotions, even different sounds and dialogues. These three questions will guide you to more awareness and practical information to help you support your New Child

In connecting with your child, the best focal points are the seeds of light found in the womb, heart and pineal. In meditation, begin to automatically tune into the interplay between these points. Surrender your awareness to them and focus on them. This will help align and adjust you and your baby to the shifting frequencies and energies as birth approaches.

Changes in hormones are an effect of these points of light aligning. The womb light will become especially predominant in the last 28 days of pregnancy, and will become your child's primary focus as a gateway to this world.

PRACTICE: UNCOVERING BELIEFS THAT SHAPE PREGNANCY AND BIRTH QUESTIONS FOR YOUR PARENTS

Did you know that the 3 trimesters of pregnancy reflect the physical, emotional and spiritual aspects of the child until they are 21? And any diseases or problems the child may have?

Ask your parents:
Can you remember what happened to you, and how you were feeling, in those 3 cycles when you were pregnant with me? .
Were you:
arguing or fighting with your partner, blaming / projecting each other,
frustrated, resentful, unhealthy, sick,
happy, contented, calm,
searching, enquiring, lonely,
feeling fear, shame, guilt, unworthiness, anger,
in denial, feeling betrayed, untrusting of ash or life,
stressed,
feeling separated or alone,
judged,
abandoned?

Did you feel powerless and helpless? Sad? Grieving?
Did you try and deny and avoid deeper feelings? Did you control these feelings?
Did you feel, at any time, without help and hope?
Did you create strategies and controls, substitutes to deal with this?
Did you go for help in these times to Source, or to someone else? Did you have a shoulder to cry on or talk to about these things?

Did you have friends, or emotionally open and fulfilling contact?

Did you agree, enjoy each-other's company, and love truly?

Were you healthy physically?
If not, what illnesses and ailments did you have that were unusual for a pregnant woman?

Were you spiritually connecting to anything or anybody? God, Krishna, Buddha, Christ, Mohammed, Mary etc?
Were you praying, meditating, reading spiritual books, feeling the peace?
Did you have any kind of spiritual relating or conversing with your partner?

Did you speak to me whilst I was in your womb?
Did you feel me, or take the time to do so? Did your partner?

BIRTH BELIEFS

Birth beliefs held in our subconscious mind and emotional body from our own births, our mothers birth and some of our ancestor's births can play out in our experiences of giving birth. The more these beliefs are uncovered and the emotions forming them are felt and released before birth, the more freedom and joy we can experience in birth.

What were you told about birth as a child?
What do you know about your own birth?
What was your family's attitude toward birth?
Was it ever talked about, and if so, in what way?

What, if any, education did you have about reproduction, birth and pregnancy at school?

What is your experience of birth via the media?

SUPPORT BELIEFS

Asking for and receiving support is vital in pregnancy and birth, and can lead to deeper humility and love. Below are some questions to stimulate self-inquiry about your ability to give and receive support.

How do you support your friends and your partner?

How do you feel about being supported?
Do you consider yourself well supported in your life currently?

What kind of support works best for you?

Are you comfortable with asking for help?

Do you feel hassled when asked for lots of support from one particular person, and if so, how do you deal with that?

SOUND IN BIRTHING

Our bodies form through the Earth Element, and are a symphony of harmony that connects to all life everywhere. Our bodies contain our genetic blueprints woven together in an exquisite dance of wave vibration that connects into the web of life.

We can access this in many ways. One way is when we slow down, ground and rest in a different way: we enjoy the simple things more and we do less. We appreciate and rejuvenate, drinking from the well of Earth's bountiful nurturance and abundance. We become more still, more patient, more allowing, so other parts of us can grow.

In this art of being, and doing less, more actually happens, paradoxically enough! Science has shown that spending 72 hours in nature without distraction or technology actually changes our brainwave patterns from 'doing' into 'being'. We begin to appreciate the small wonders of life, we slow down to immerse in and appreciate the life flow that surrounds us. We become a more conscious part of it all.

The Earth Element forms our bodies and sustains them. Throughout pregnancy, as our bodies develop and grow from heart and tongue to mouth, anus, limbs and organs, the vibrations and sounds echoing and undulating through the watery resonating chamber of the womb combine with the background pulse of mother's heartbeat to create a throbbing, humming, frequency rich environment. This sonic bath in mothers living waters of the womb is a key part in the forming of life itself.

Sound in water moves differently, sounds different, and even looks different to how sound operates in the earth element. As shown through Dr Emoto's Water Crystal Photography, sound imprints us more deeply in water (which our bodies are mainly composed of) than sound moving in the air element or earth element.

In the womb, (just as dolphins and whales perceive sound) sounds resonate and echo in a simultaneous surround sound effect, 'originating' from all seven directions at once. The receiver, your child, attunes itself to these vibrations, imprinting, informing and guiding it as these vibrations wash through and resonate the womb fluid chamber. These vibrations guide the growth process itself, not just for baby but for all life's growth processes throughout the universe.

Shamanic traditions throughout history have used rhythm and sounds to try and recreate this Womb Symphony and rich sound bath in caves, sound chambers and sacred sites across the world. From Native American Kivas and Celtic Sound Chambers, to the Pyramids in Egypt, to modern cathedrals and acoustically attuned caves, we have attempted to recreate the Sounds of the Womb to return to the source of creation, to refresh and renew our vital connection to life itself.

Some of these shamanic sounds and rhythms are patterned and recognizable: some are designed to create a certain resonant dissonance to allow other states of awareness to arise. The Mother Kali religion in India specializes in the cognitive dissonance approach to sound in order to awaken dormant faculties within us, and when it is done correctly it shifts your consciousness into the luminous. [24]

MOTHERS VOICE

In modern times, it has been observed that our mother's unique pattern of speaking in pitches and rhythms, her tonality and her emotional voice spectrum, form part of our early musical journey in the womb. Her tone, mind-set, vocal register and emotional depths and tonality expresses her emotional spectrum, and research by Dr. Truby shows that by age 30 weeks we can accurately reproduce our mother's exact voice spectrum.

From our time in our mother's womb we can remember *and* distinguish the voices of our parents and others who are consistently around them. We remember the songs, tones and words spoken to us in the womb, and they can imprint us for life.

We can feel the levels of vibration coming from our mother and father's sounds and words. The most important for the baby is the emotional imprint that our voices carry, which are a direct reflection of our soul.

Did your parents speak caringly, softly and gently to you? Did they send their love to you through their voices? Did they feel and say they love you? Did they sing to you? Did they sing mantras, hymns, sacred songs to you? Did they pray aloud? What was the vibration of their words and conversations between each other? Was there shouting and conflict sounds?

Did they reach out to you? Did they make the effort? Did they feel you and reassure you? Did they feel you when you were feeling unsafe and scared? Did they ask you what you needed? Did your parents commune with you without words? Did they send you pictures and feelings? Did they read to you? Did they reach out with their feeling and emotions to you? Did they apologise to you and reassure you when they were upset and angry?

In understanding this, we can begin to appreciate that our fathers and mother's 'missing notes,' i.e the gaps in their emotional spectrum and vibrational resonances, allied with what they didn't say to us, can become our own 'missing notes' as we grow up, as our voice and emotional spectrum partially mirrors theirs to a degree. This is rectified in indigenous traditions by parents sharing baby's own unique Soul Song to the baby whilst baby is still in the womb.

When a mother is deeply tuned into her own Soul Song, she can expand and deepen her vibrational spectrum, her voice, her feelings and her emotional spectrum *to include more of baby's tones.* In this way, she is stimulated to embody new aspects of her own Soul Song, her own soul, her own voice, thus allowing baby to more fully feel their own identity. She and baby bond deeper, commune and communicate, and baby receives a complete welcome to the earth experience, their own body world, and the soul.

---

[24] Transformation also lies in the spaces between the rhythms and sounds, which may not be considered 'beautiful" by an ear used to pop music and syncopated computer driven patterns.

THE VOICE OF THE WOMB

By using certain sounds and sounding them from the womb space, we can resonate and feel the depths and richness of our own womb centre. These sounds can become foundational in the birthing journey, as well as throughout pregnancy, to more deeply connect with our child and our own primordial being.

The sounds of the womb focus on your individual messages of power that spring from your center. This form of deep, primal chanting can express that which may seem inexpressible, that which you have felt deep within but have not been able to articulate, voice, or give sound to. These universal, primal sounds help to unlock wisdom we have not allowed ourselves to know, or have been too scared to let ourselves approach and immerse into.

Sound creates life, and life is born from sound. By sounding the womb, from where all life arises from and passes away into, we can begin to enter this space of birthing and dying.

AH - Opening to Create

AH is the first sound of creating, the opening of the creative flow of life from the void. It is one of the first sounds of orgasm, the sound of pleasure and bliss. *AH!* It releases and opens yourself to higher potentials, and is a sound that is present in all life. If you simply stop and rest for a moment, you can hear the sound of *AH* in nature, in your body, and all around you.

Many cultures use this sound meditation to tune in to the sound behind all life, and by using this sound you too can relax into a deeper state of consciousness. Tibetan monks have used this sound to leave their bodies at will.

Use this sound in labour to open yourself up more, and in times you wish to deepen in pregnancy. It is meant to be pronounced effortlessly –simply open your mouth wide and let *AH* come out, without any effort on your part.

OH—Opening the womb

OH is the sound of the Well, the deep dark depths within you. It breathes in life force, and brings you into your centre when sounded from and into the womb.

OH is a naturally deep sound that draws you inwards. It creates a tunnel or vortex within you that you can use to travel deeper into the womb. *OH* is a sound that leads you through your inner well into your inner shaman. *OH and UU* combine together to take you into this space. *OH* is the forming of creation after *AH*.

OH is one of the main sounds of orgasm. "Oh, oh, oh!" as when a woman is being penetrated; this is the sound that naturally arises in all women regardless of race or country. *OH* dominates words meaning either the whole or a void, such as womb, dome, hole and OM.

Try sounding OH deep into your belly x12. Travel with it. Allow yourself to bring the sound deep into you, and then sound OH from this deep womb space within you.
What happens?

Use this sound in labour to deepen into the primordial energies running through you, and in times you wish to deepen in communion with your womb and child during pregnancy.

OM MA OM – The Hum of Birthing

OM is the background sound vibration or "hum" of the universe. It is a primordial sound of creating, used to attune us to the sound vibration that underlies all life.

MA is the sound of the mother found in all languages. It is one of the first sounds a baby makes and is the sound that most of us relate to when we call out for help, for love, for comfort. *MA* is the sound of the heart yearning, calling out to the universe, the most common sound found in all cultures, which we all instinctively identify with.

MA loves us all, no matter what we do and who we are. It can only love and support, for that is its very nature—it cannot do anything else. Together the mantra *OM MA OM* swirling deep inside the womb evokes the mother of love resonating with the sound behind all creation.

A PRACTICE: OM MA OM

This is a deep sounding of the womb chamber, to be done whilst focusing on the womb. Try and keep the sound as continuous as possible. Magic will happen!

Stop everything for a moment. Take a few deep breaths. Now sound the mantra *OM MA OM* aloud twelve times, at your keynote, the pitch and frequency you find most comfortable.

Now whisper it twelve times.

Now take this current of energy you have created and repeat *OM MA OM* twelve times in your womb silently.

Now let go of the sound, and relax into the current of energy created by the sound. Relax and let go of the repetition of the words. Focus solely on the current of energy weaving its way through your womb-brain consciousness. Follow it loosely, and relax into its pathway.
What happens?

Note: you can do each repetition 24 times to help you go deeper.

YOUR SOUL SONG

Your Soul Song, as it is known in many indigenous traditions, holds your pure soul frequency and vibrational spectrum. It is the unique frequency you were created in by The Creator. To Remember it is to Remember your True Sovereign Self, your soul spark.

When your soul was created, there was a spark, and that spark is a pure seed of light. With this creation of your seed spark, there was incredible joy. There was reveling, exalting, and celebrating of this creation of your soul, in delight, mirth and great gales of laughter! Overflowing with happiness with how you were created, the whole universe resounded with this booming, celebration of laughter and joy.

In the Vedas, India's most ancient sacred scriptures, it is said that the universe and ourselves were created simply for joy, delight and Self-expression. No other reason. Life is a game, because everything began with this laughter. Laughter is the best medicine and true joy is healing, because it brings you back to the moment of the very conception and creation of your soul, and the very creation of the universe as well. To mirror this in our human conception in sacred lovemaking is the Souls Design for Birth.

This is truly who you are. Joy for no reason, laughter for no reason, the feeling that you are loved totally, that you love totally, that you are this love; and all has been created in this incredible way. Sovereignty comes back to this essence of feeling, and flowing from this point of how your soul was created. Here you find the 'real you.' Healing happens when you are in your soul center.

As science has now discovered, the music of sound and language organizes our brain development. 'In the beginning was the Word' – sound vibration emerging from the Void Womb, echoing and pulsing in our own wombs. Whilst we are in the womb we react to chants, songs, and music we love, and when people speak directly with joyful feeling to us.

We most directly resonate to the *sacred languages*, the roots of most present-day languages, such as Sanskrit and Aramaic. These languages resonate with us on a primal feeling level of consciousness, whereas most modern-day languages resonate more with the surface layers of our conditioned awareness. For example, Hindi derives from Sanskrit, its root. English is an agglomeration of many different languages. Most modern-day languages are a dilution of the more powerful vibrations of sacred languages, yet still hold aspects of them in modern day words.

Each child will resonate more with specific sacred languages, just as you do with certain chants that you like and listen to. Do you like Sanskrit or Tibetan chants? Perhaps Hebrew or Arabic touches something deep in you? Or maybe even Hawaiian or South American healing songs?

Each person is different, and your child may have different tastes to you. Use your intuition and try out different languages to sing to him/her. You will be able to feel which language or chants your baby resonates with.

PEOPLE ARE MUSIC

We constantly generate forms and patterns from sound. Whilst it may seem that sound vibration is an aspect of life, life may well be an aspect of sound vibration. Life itself is triggered, moulded, composed of and shaped by frequencies, known in sacred traditions as the Creator's 'voice,' or "Word." Our voice has the power to connect us with this Creator through the vibrational frequencies and waves of creation.

We are all made up of patterns of sounds that intermingle to create a harmony, a coherent structure. When sounds come together in this way, music is created. It can be said that each person is a symphony, a collection of individual notes playing together in a self-contained harmony.

Some people know their theme, and can play it clearly and dynamically. As these people know themselves well and are able to express freely, they can attract their desires and others to their music. They have come to know some of the vibrational spectrum of their soul song, and have many of these notes to play with; they may be easy to connect to, as they can share a resonant sympathetic chord with our own music. When you are in your own soul song, it is easier to connect with others.

Other people are complex, deep, and unable to understand immediately as they share different chord structures to our own. These are people you might have to spend some time with before you can 'catch onto" or groove with their music.

The ways a song can vary are almost infinite, so each time we meet a new being who is playing their own music at their own rhythm, we experience how our music harmonises with theirs. We feel others music instantly, at first sight; we feel whether the person feels resonant to us, whether we feel attracted or repelled to that person, whether they groove with and organically fit into our own symphony.

We can also recognise people when they are being true to their own vibration and are playing it without disguise or added notes; without pretence or faking it.

As we are music, we have to work out how to play our theme. What is your key note, what is your resonant chord? What tempos, what rhythms do you move to? What is your soul song? Perhaps some people have more complicated melodies, and it might be harder for them to find their groove and play it to its highest potential. Maybe some people find it easier to play what other people want to hear from them, as they have not yet discovered their own music.

One purpose of life is to syncopate, to tune into, the resonant vibrations of our own soul song. When we get stuck in our life, attached or caught in a negative pattern, it is because one or more of our chords, notes or sounds is not being heard, because it is frozen within us, a frozen music that is not alive, not expressed. Here, we are not tuning into our resonance, our truth.

For Communication is not just what happens when two people speak to each other. In every moment of our lives we are immersed in a 'living landscape' of vibrations which are all actively communicating to us. Whether you are walking down a busy urban street, sitting in the quiet cool depths of a forest, or are within the sanctuary of your home, you are always in a vitalized field of communicating vibration.

Each object, each person, every event which transpires in life, is part of a continuous, unbroken stream of vibrational creating, perpetually happening afresh in every moment. It is but for us to be open to receive and commune with. Every intelligence in creation is available to communicate with us, and many actively desire to do so with us, from the devas of the earth realm, to other humans, to Gaia and stellar intelligences.

Songs in indigenous traditions do something similar to this, as their songs are maps, libraries and cores of knowledge for them. Both Mojave and Aboriginal creation songs encode knowledge of how to reach sacred sites for ceremony, how to get water and physical sustenance along the way, what route to take, what to avoid, as well as spiritual lessons and secret knowledge.

Song is a precursor to speech: song minus music is speech, and song minus speech is music. Song unites, as many people who do not speak the same language can all join together in song. Music is a Universal Language, for any good musician can play with another instantly, despite differences in tradition, training or language, as they share the common language of music and can dynamically 'jam' with others soul expression.

Many spiritual teachers, like Guru Nanak (who founded Sikhism) used to answer questions in song, singing back his replies, bringing the questioner into the state of song and consciousness that dissolves all questions. Similarly, in the last weeks of the life of St Francis of Assisi he sang constantly in a state of joy and rapture, for God was his Soul Song.

When we are living in our own soul song we are in sync with everything within and around us. The world and our relation to it feels different – our connection to all we perceive is vivid and undeniable. This rhythmic intelligence easily translates from one octave of vibration to the next. In discovering and sharing our rhythms with others, we come to a state of communion beyond words, situated in the present moment. This is most commonly felt in making love, and singing and chanting together.

When you discover your own soul song, your own chords, your own frequency, then you will be able to hear the soul song of your baby. Then, you can literally 'sing' the soul of your child into form, in a grand welcome and resonance that will bond you all together in a true soul to soul bonding.

The soul song within each of us holds the potential of what the soul came to earth to embody, discover, learn and complete. It is the person's inner rhythm, what he or she goes by, what their tune is.

In indigenous cultures, the Soul Song is sung after the baby is conceived, when the baby is in the womb during pregnancy, when the baby is born in the ecstatic throes of labour. It is sung when baby is growing up and when baby has grown up and is going through major life transitions such as puberty and marriage, when they themselves have children, and when they lose their direction and soul purpose in life: when they have lost their groove, when they have forgotten who they are in the distractions and demands of earthly life.

In all cases, the Soul Song is sung to remind the soul of who they really are. Finally, the soul song is sung as the person dies and enters the spirit worlds.

You may have certain pieces of music you really resonate to, that deeply touch you and bring you to tears, that bring you to triumph, that bring you into deep sadness or devotion: these songs play one of the chords of your soul song. A song made or played by another person, no matter how touching and beautiful it is, can never truly replicate the beauty of your own soul song, but merely reflect parts of it.

PRACTICE: DISCOVERING YOUR SOUL SONG

Spiritual teachers throughout time have given their students names, just as you will with your baby. Ideally you will have asked your baby what his or her name is through communion with baby in the womb.

However, when you are in a sacred site, or deep in ceremony, your original name can arise more quickly. When you sing spontaneously in abandoned connection with the currents of creation, when you let go of yourself, then this sound, your soul song, can arise. The purest sound you can make is this song of your soul.

Make discovering your Soul Song a ceremony with your partner. Set a clear intention with your partner that you will now discover your soul song. Sit down and clear your mind. Forget about anything else. Do whatever you need to do to connect to your soul through your heart. Take a few deep breaths into your heart and womb/hara. Centre yourself here.

Now sound these nine vowel sounds out loud. *Which ones most resonate with you?*

AH
A
E
I
OH
UU
AI
AU
AHM

Play with the vowels and place them into an order that feels right for you.
Do you feel to add any consonants between the spaces? Play with this for a while.
Now sound these vowels and consonants in different pitches, up and down the scale. Have fun with the sounds in different pitches, lengths, durations, and timings. Some sounds can be shorter or longer, faster or slower; even different accents can be fun.

Deep bass sounds and high-pitched sounds can also resonate. What sound goes with what pitch? What pitch feels best overall to you? This pitch is your keynote, where your resonant frequency lies, the frequency you are most comfortable with and able to create the most from.

Play with and discover your SoulSong!

THE NAME of YOUR CHILD

Name is vibration. Vibration creates form. The moment we name something, be it a person, place or object, we give it a form. Names define objects through their vibration. Without names, there are no thoughts, no objects, no language, and no way of communicating in the third dimension. Without names, our worldly reality and everything we do every-day would literally cease to exist as we know it.

As soon as you Name something, you bring forth *all* the associations you have created in your life about that person. It is all there in that moment, the whole field of energy connected to the experiences of that person.

We first experience the power of sound through our own Name and its resonance to us. We are usually named by our parents, who may name us after their parents or grandparents evoking cultural and ancestral connection, or we are named after a famous person because it had meaning to our parents, or people they like and admire, a cultural or religious icon, or simply out of whimsy and passing fancy. It is no wonder so many people change their name when they become old enough, to reflect more of who they really are.

When parents pick names, they dream about the child they would like to have. But is this the child that is really here? Often it is not, and with the influx of new children arriving onto this planet, and their enhanced sensitivity to vibration, sound and light, their true soul Name will provide a sound foundation and platform for the child to be comfortable in their skin and align to who they really are.

Your soul Name is important, and the more it is repeated by others and by yourself, the more the vibrational connection grows. Inherent within this connection are the levels of meaning each word has. In sacred languages like Sanskrit, Hebrew and Tibetan, there are seven layers of meaning to each word: each layer reveals deeper meanings and energies that can transport your consciousness into the essence of that person.

The seventh layer or 'secret name' embodies the spiritual essence of the individual. It is a being's Name that contains its uniqueness and distinction, setting it apart from others while providing the means to express itself in the world as an entity unto itself AND connect more into the entire web of life.

Your name helps to define your relationship to the world. It connects you with your ancestry, and soul family. When you Name something, you bring it into being. Conversely, when something is unnamed it can be a mystery.

Your true soul Name is the name that you resonate with most: the frequency essence of your soul. This Name leads you forward into embodying who you are and what you are here to do. It is a reminder of your essence when you forget it. It is the sound of your soul, your God-given Name that creates resonance each time it is said, and that holds great power once you know what it is, and how to use it.

Mantras connected to your real Name hold great power for you, and remembering your soul Name and Soul Song anchors and helps to bring forth your soul purpose, grounding you into your true heart's desires and the reason you are here on earth.

Spiritual teachers throughout time have given their students their soul Names based on their "reading" of your soul essence. How many people change their name from John to VamaDeva, from Claire to Luna Shakti? Yet, in our Souls Design we have this name from before birth, and it is the unborn child, still in its untainted soul purity, who can share its true name with its parents before they are brought into this world.

All names, with their meanings and sounds help shape and create your reality. This also highlights the ways in which we are creating, manipulating, and veiling deeper realities through the indiscriminate use of sound, name, and meaning.

I remember the first time we had contact with our child in my womb. About four months into the pregnancy we were lying together in bed, and his father spontaneously connected with him on a soul level. For the next few months we both had communication with him, which began to reveal more and more of his soul nature.

At about 7 months, we did a formal meditation (see the previous meditation, where you can also ask your child his name) using sound and colour visualization to contact the soul of our child. In this conversation, we asked him his name and what he wanted to be called. He revealed it to us, (it was similar to what we had been calling him) but the meaning and vibration he imparted to us was different.

We asked all the questions we could come up with relative to his remaining time in the womb, his birth and beyond. He revealed very distinct answers about preparation for the birth, from practical 3D matters to spiritual matters. He gave details about the birth: who was to be there, and who was not, who was to be notified when labour began, and even certain things for us to do and roles to play during labor.

He told us his soul purpose, and where he came from. He illuminated the essence of our individual relationships with him as mother and father, where we knew him from, our soul agreements with him, and much more. Anything we asked, we received an answer, and he knew much about us that both surprised and informed us about ourselves. He even shared aspects about the connection between myself and his father. It was all very revealing!

At the end of this particular conversation we expressed and emanated our love for him, and our desire to receive and nurture him fully throughout his whole life. This was a profound meeting for all three of us. It resonated deep truth, and opened us more to the love, beauty and connection of the 'design' of our coming together.

His father wrote down his name, and the meanings associated with it. Over the next few months, as we called him by his true soul name, he felt more and more tangible to us…his essence, his expression, his way of being, his character. The more we called him by his name, the more we drew closer to him, and he to us, *and the more comfortable he was in being himself without any veils.* The more I used his name, the more dimensions it took on, beyond sound and syllable, into feeling and energy.

In this way, I began knowing my son, and in using his name, would feel aspects of my own soul drawn out and expressed. I remember feeling shy at first about pronouncing it, and then I found a place of power within me where I could truly resonate with him and his name from a place of love, that was my own expression of his resonance.

This was a beautiful precursor for my expansion into motherhood that his soul would demand of me: stepping more into my power, and speaking and acting on the strength of my own deep, inner knowing. He was catalysing my growth too!

This is the beauty of the Souls Design. As he was growing and developing in my womb, his being was shaping me into the mother he needed, which necessitated my own growth. Our children call forth the dormant aspects of ourselves to be developed. Thus just as we are raising them, they are raising us.

In the last month of pregnancy, we noticed he was quieter when we contacted him. This felt natural as he was embodying more, his essence condensing into his form. We still made the effort to connect, and share our love for him, and he responded, albeit less so.

After he was born, we spoke his full name to him many times a day. Each and every time he felt this resonance, there was recognition expressed through his tiny body…a softening, an expanding, a stillness, a widening of his eyes and a recognition through his eyes, a sound. Most often, he would completely stop whatever he was doing, drop into stillness, and gaze at us intently.

This Sounding of his soul Name helped him Remember who he was, as he entered the density of the physical plane, where much is usually forgotten in the onrush of biological growth. For example, when he cries in physical discomfort, often by saying his name the resonance penetrates through his physical experience and he stops crying, recognizing he is larger than his physical body and this world.

In birthing consciously, we prepare for our children's transition to this earthly plane to allow the Remembrance of their soul's blueprint. Incarnating with one's soul memory intact is an ongoing process, well beyond pregnancy and the moment of birth.

PRACTICE: A PORTAL TO INNOCENCE
'Be ye like a child, and ye shall enter the Kingdom of God."

As soon as you name a person, you bring forth to you *all* the associations and memories you have made in your entire life about that person. It is an honour, privilege and responsibility to name another soul, and this is best done by asking that soul what their name is, not what you wish or need it to be.

Yet, the only way to truly and purely experience that person is to see them in innocence, without name. Like a child.

Imagine: there is no such thing as language. Imagine, there are no words to describe objects around you, other people, and your thoughts. Imagine there is no language for your thoughts ...you are totally innocent.

Now look at an object right in front of you. Just gaze at it, without any labeling of what it is, what you have thought it to be, or even what it could be. Look at it like you have never seen it before, like there are no words to describe it, like it is completely new. Gaze at it like it is the very first time you have ever seen it.

Stay like this for a few minutes. What happens?

When we take away the labels from our perceptions, whole new levels open up. As one begins to dissolve layers of name and meanings that create the forms and perceptions of your world, the value you have given them starts to fade too.

Everything, and every event that occurs, is neutral. What you observe around you and within you is neutral until you make a decision as to what it will mean for you. You give the event a name and value, usually good or bad, helpful or not helpful. To stand back and see this process, of naming and defining what values and associations you give to that object or person, allows you to let go of what you think, allowing you to be truly Present with the person.

The idea of 'you 'is removed from your ideas, attachments and judgments about what that person is. Without attaching any meaning toward these thoughts or people, your mind becomes a blank canvas, an empty page.

You can experience this. Try this practice with your partner or baby. Sit quietly, center yourself, and follow your breath. Open your eyes, the windows to the soul, and truly gaze at your partner/baby/ eye to eye: you will see, as you do every day, that they have a form, a face, a body.

Keep gazing and you will see them blurring, becoming indistinct, a mass of shapes, faces, forms and vibrating patterns. As you keep gazing and concentrating, going deeper, you will eventually come to see that he/she is a blank canvas, an empty space. They disappear into a white empty canvas.

Witnessing this, what is already and always here, allows you the direct perception of reality behind any and all appearances. When you experience this, and literally see another person dissolve right in front of you, how real can this body-mind, this reality, be?

BLISSFUL BIRTH

In the journey of baby's emergence onto earth in the profound openings of pregnancy, labour and birth, an awakening experience to the most primordial powers of creation occurs. The intensity of birth draws us directly into the Power of Now and the Present Moment when we meet it with our breath, our heart, our Shakti and our surrender.

When we allow ourselves to surrender into the torrents of life force energy Shakti moving through us in the ecstatic throes of labour, we soften and expand the tissues of our yoni and womb, releasing the limitations in our mind of what is possible. Here, we can be overtaken by rhythmic waves of bliss, pleasure, spiraling sensuality and feminine power.

When pain or complication arises in birth, it is usually due to fear, unhealed emotions, past sexual issues recorded in the yoni and womb, or fears and emotions held in the field of those present at the birth. When both partners have done enough inner work to heal their own birth experiences, their sexuality and their causal wounds, and both genuinely love, honour and support each other, pain or complication does not occur. If pain, fear or complications do occur in a conscious birth, it can be quickly released in the moment by both man and woman working together to allow the birthing energy to continue into manifestation.

Birth is an opportunity for woman and man, regardless of past experiences, to choose love over fear. Love's field allows the natural blooming expression of a woman's body to deliver her child into the world. This is how birth has been naturally designed to be.

The final aspect of blissful birth is the natural honoring of the umbilical cord and placenta. Our connection to the placenta has profound physical and spiritual implications. When the umbilical cord from baby to mother is kept connected until it naturally drops away a few days after birth, there is very little emotional and physical separation felt by baby. In addition, when the umbilical cord's connection from baby to both mother and father is energetically reconnected after birth in sacred ceremony, there is no deep emotional imprint of separation for mother, father or child.

PLEASURE IN BIRTH

'When love, not fear, is an integral part of the birthing field, a woman has access to the power of creation that is working through her. The more power there is in her field, the less force she will need to use, because love is a highly coherent field.'
Elena Tonetti-Vladimirova

There is a growing movement of women reclaiming the power and pleasure of the birthing process. Birth is innately designed to be ecstatic, orgasmic and blissful, with many sublime moments of pure consciousness and union with all of creation in the process as well. To achieve this asks for intimacy with ourselves, our bodies and our deeper emotions, and every single woman can do if they desire to.

Orgasmic birth is our birthright. Orgasmic birth happens when we have healed enough to surrender to the potent flows of creative energy coursing through all parts of us. Orgasmic birth occurs by being surrendered to the possibility of being blown wide open, beyond our recognition of ourselves, into that which is greater than ourself. It is the allowance of the flowering dance of Shakti calling us to meet her in all her intensity, and asking us to open. Orgasmic birth occurs when we open to being palpably breathed by creation, moving, flowing and rising with the wave that originated us.

It is no wonder breath is an essential part of birth! It connects inner and outer, spirit and matter. It is through breath we build a bridge between conscious and sub conscious, releasing stress, old memories, emotions, and reactive tendencies. The life force is breath. Without breath, there is no life. The rhythms of our breath connect us to the breath of the Divine that is Shakti. When united, the breath runs throughout your body and mind as a wave moves through an ocean, changing and connecting all it touches.

As we inhale, spiraling rhythms of breath radiate outward from every cell and atom—as we exhale, we spiral inward into rest. Like breath, birth is a spiral. The muscles of the womb contract in rhythmic spirals in the ratio of harmonious perfection known as The Golden Mean, spinning baby towards emergence. Surrendering to the spirals of birth allows this primordial intensity and power to move through us. We become the spiral torus, inside and out, dancing in a circling continuum.

This continuum bridges heaven and earth, spirit and form. Riding the spiral and surrendering to it is the key to move beyond pain to harness the intensity and sensation into the bliss of birth. Orgasmic birth invites all parts of us to pulse in pleasure, love, and the power of fear transformed into bliss. It is the orgasming of our wombs, our yoni, our hearts and our auric field that opens us into this wave of possibility.

OUR BIRTHRIGHT

How did one of the most sacred, blissful and intimate initiations for a woman and her family become a scheduled, institutionalized, robotic and traumatic event? Somewhere along the way, woman allowed herself to be stripped of the sacredness of yoni and womb. Man allowed himself to be knocked down from his innate stance as protector and soulful pillar, and become reduced to being merely a monetary provider for his family.

She gave up her intuitive wisdom and wild shamanic power to the statistical forecast of machines and the 'safe 'opinions of minds in white lab coats. He surrendered the vulnerability of his vision and deep masculine presence to the grid of technology and fear.

She stuttered in the unpredictability of the unknown that most are scared of and try to stave away at every opportunity, letting her mind be numbed by a due date, pain killers and a 'safe' environment. She forgot her soul and traded it for a false safety, losing the sovereignty and empowerment that comes from navigating the unknown and feeling into the feminine power that is unleashed from the primordial, with the deep emotional openings into her soul gained by this surrender. She lost the deep feminine wisdom that emerges from being in the Present moment.

He gave into an external structure of perceived safety when he couldn't navigate his woman's emotional chaos. He became scared of what he couldnt control or understand. He aborted his mission to guide the impulse of creation into form, giving this power away because he couldn't claim it. He forgot that herein lies some of his deepest embodiment as a man through selfless action, inspired guidance and having the chance to be a true hero. She contracted and became small, subdued and scared. He retracted and became disengaged, busy, and an observer to his own creation.

For a woman, primal birthing energy deeply anchors her into her feminine self and her embodying of the authentic feminine power. It is rooted, circular, without doubt, powerful, expressive, sensual and surrendered. For a man this birthing energy draws forth his total presence of action, his attuned and sensitized consciousness, his joy, and his selfless movement forwards. It invokes his gentle power and grounded passion to move him beyond the confines of what is possible. It expands his capacity to hold all that is entrusted to him in fierce protection and love.

For both woman and man the intensity of birth draws us directly into the Present Moment, as we meet it with our breath, our presence, our heart and our soul. This is the only way to navigate the throes of labour and birth in its natural design. This takes responsibility and courage, to be present with all that is arising within us, and release it in the moment. In this we open wider and further to the present moment, where all the currents of creation flow. Both parents thus open to the deeper expressions of the primordial masculine and feminine selves.

Strength and surrender are aspects of love: to 'be with' 'let go' and 'take action' simultaneously. The intensity of a soulful, blissful birth gives us one of the clearest, most palpable and direct opportunities in our lives to choose love over fear. When we call upon our strength and courage to be with and feel the intensity of sensation and emotion in birth, we arrive in a palpable, potent presence of embrace and action simultaneously. This is our innate design for birth, our initiation through birth, anchoring us deeply in our bodies and souls. Holding a field of love and total giving is the man's role, surrender and total openness are the woman's.

BIRTH

*From seamless light, we are breathed by silent depth
into rhythm, pulse and beat,
intensity converging into the Vesica Piscis
emerging, dividing, shapes of polarities
that through their tensions
we become manifest in the third dimensional density
that invites the amnesia of forgetting.*

*Through the fog we see the beckoning lighthouse in the distance,
activating our journey of remembrance,
of what we came to do, with whom and why.
We make a choice:
to play our part in the resonant hum of harmony of the whole.*

*Ours is the bliss, the ecstasy, the wonder and the pleasure,
but not the product.
We are merely the conceiver and the vessel,
the impulse through which something else becomes.
And in this, we are forged deeper into our innate formation.
And deeper into love.
And then it is done.*

*And we choose, to come undone
from persona, purpose, and particulars that defined us
so as to execute the Divine Design into form.*

*Like a mounting wave dissolving itself back into the vast ocean,
we release our grasp on this theatrical plane,
and move into the unseen realms
that orchestrate this birthing consciousness from primordial presence,
Again and again and again into our next octave of creation.*

MY SON'S BIRTH

The first evening my ''Braxton Hicks'' or initial rushes began that mark the opening of the Seventh Gate, the rushes came on fast and intense. We lay down on the bed and with each rush were overcome with laughter and joy, with some traces of residual sadness from the past. This continued for a few hours, and my partner shared with me all the visions he was seeing for possible future creations.

Soon after this, we fell into a soft blanket of slumber. We were being readied, with my son becoming deeply adjusted into the right position in my womb. All three of us were being adjusted to a new aspect of our blooming selves, and we all palpably felt it. For the next few days, rushes would begin late afternoon and I would dance, move and sway as my womb moved my son deeper into position, readying him for his final journey.

On Tuesday early evening, the rushes started coming on more intensely, and I went into the bedroom to dance and move to music. His Papa began weaving a cocoon, with music, with prayer, with movement, with chants, with incense, with a fire, adjusting and readying the physical and spiritual environments, creating a field. He put on some music with a good beat, and I swung from the beams like a monkey, laughing and moving with each rush, readying my son for his emergence.

As Papa moved in and out of the room, making preparations and tending to my every need, he would erupt in spontaneous and infectious laughter as he felt me in my rushes, and I would catch it, transporting me further into joy. We were making each other ecstatic! He was feeling my ecstasy and Shakti, and fed it back to me so I felt it even more in his reflection. Papa burned Frankincense and played ancient chants, transporting my consciousness further. The scent carried me on a golden thread into the cosmos where I felt the love of my Source. I began to weave my heart more into my son's heart, aligning our energies to work together.

As I returned, another rush came on. I moved with the intensity and spilled my laughter as joy, spiraling my hips downward and feeling a simultaneous spiral moving up through my heart and out through my crown. I felt Celestial beings circling around us: Mary Magdalene, Yeshua, Mother Mary. I could feel their love for the three of us. The soft Aramaic chanting playing in the background sent my heart upward into a spiral of prayer and my womb spiraled downward to the Galactic Center, anchoring me, opening me to the soft sweet darkness from which my son was emerging.

Papa called the midwives, and when they arrived the rushes were in full swing! They checked my son's heartbeat and my dilation. Suddenly something felt stuck, and not progressing, I felt a bubble of fear rise up, and saw two roads in front of me. One led toward fear, hospitalization, giving up my power. The other led to trust, surrender, strength and perseverance. I felt and released this fear by talking to Papa for guidance, who received me and confirmed me. I made some physical adjustments with my cervix and hips, and with the next rush prayed to surrender.

The pain dissolved into intensity and I engaged in the dance again. I met the sensation full on with all of my body and all of my soul, welcoming it, welcoming him, feeling pushed to open beyond what I felt I could. There was a short reprieve, then the next rush came, asking me to surrender deeper, and yet stay strong with my presence. I was a cat both rolling onto my back surrendering to a belly rub, and roaring like a lion to meet the oncoming rush…softening and meeting, softening and meeting.

These moments of being fully immersed in the rushes, without turning away or resisting, took me deeper into my power, and fuller into my softness. My heart and womb, his heart, were my reference point, a place to return after each journey of spiraling. From here, the infinity loops and spirals emanated, from form and movement into light, connecting me to Source, to earth, to the field of love surrounding us woven by his father and the Celestial Guides.

Intensity was building, and the forces felt more than my body could hold. I moved into the warm waters of the tub. The water helped me relax and I felt held. I connected the infinity loop between my womb, heart and third eye again. There was no turning back, for my son was wending his way down to the gate of my yoni, with the fire and fullness of his soul's desire to arrive here on earth.

As each rush came I met it from my depths with a resounding "RAAAAAAAAAAA!" Being drawn into the downward spiral of his birth took me through more laughter, more intensity, and a brief reprieve from the overwhelming powers flowing through me.

This power was more than I could hold, be with, channel on my own. I asked his Papa to get into the tub of water with me. Feeling his warmth and holding container, the solid strength of his body and soul behind me, allowed me to melt even deeper. He was strong and loving, and whispered soulful encouragements in my ear. This simple fuel was enough to gather up my strength, connect my heart again to my son, and for us all to travel the last leg of the journey together.

With the next rush I let go of all effort, and rode the wave of movement and power coursing through me. *I did not push*, I allowed through breath and surrender. I reached down to my yawning yoni lips and could feel his soft skull. He was almost here.

His Papa brought his hand down too, to feel him, to welcome him. And, as if drawn by the love and gravity of our touch, two rushes later he emerged into our hands, carrying all the intensity and raw power of these final moments into the water, where all dissolved into peace, clarity and contented awe.

Papa softly sang the sounds of his Soul Song as he gently took our son out from my yoni and into the water. He brought him to my chest, and he took his time, still in between worlds, to take his first breath. A few tiny coughs, and the room fell silent. I gently rubbed his back. Soul and body, we held him at both ends, and his spirit arrived with his first human breath.

We made our way to the bedroom and collapsed on the bed together to enjoy and bond with our son in his 'golden hour.' The placenta emerged shortly afterwards to be salted and coated with dried lavender and rosemary, and we brought it into our bubble of love and light on the bed. Our son was surrounded by womb mother, earth mother and father, and Divine Love.

For two days I nursed him in the cocoon of our bed. His father looked after us both beautifully, bringing drinks, food, cuddles, being in awe of his son, as well as news from friends and family. Several spirit guides, male and female, came to visit as well, checking all was well and confirming he was indeed here. His placenta sat at my side, still connected to his tiny body. I would put my hand on it and feel the energy, gentle, loving and pure. In these days I received a slow, steady transmission of her essence guiding me into a fuller capacity of 'Mother.'

After the second day the energy had left from the placenta, and we both felt and knew it was time for the Placenta Ceremony. I spoke with the midwives and his father about the birth, gathering the pieces of the experience together and weaving them into this, my son's birth story. In doing so, I felt aspects of myself stabilizing. The experience had been so intense, so profound and so vast, that I needed to process all that happened to integrate it.

The Placenta Ceremony was profoundly moving and joyful for all three of us in the bathroom together. I held Sunyam in the tub while Papa stood over us, singing chants in sacred languages and praying powerfully. Sunyam was so at peace, and afterward made deep eye contact with both of us. He felt much more embodied after the honoring and release of the umbilical cord and placenta, and the deeper reconnection of the energetic cord between us three. We parents both felt blissful, light and joyous – a good sign for the success of any venture!

My initiation with my son's birth journey was surrender. Surrendering to what is presented in life, moment by moment, brings up our deepest resistances, our deepest shadows. Everything in the basement of our subconscious, every voice within us that says no to love, no to flow, no to joy, no to what IS, arises. This fight takes us deeper and wears us out, wears out the fight, the resistances of the small self, until we break down. In this breaking down lies the opening to the softness, the power and the gentling of love.

During my pregnancy, I began to deeply accept the love and support from my son's father. I allowed myself to truly be seen, in my vulnerability and tenderness. For the first time in my life, I let a man support me…financially, emotionally, spiritually and soulfully. This container opened some of my deepest wounds, which could dissolve and release in the gentle harmony between us. By the time I entered my third trimester, I was opened to a new degree of softness and femininity.

Just as feeling and releasing our wounds is an act of embrace and surrender, so is birth. I felt strongly during the most intense rushes of birth that my 'practice' of feeling emotions arise, and bringing my complete loving presence to them to release them, trained me to handle the intensity of the strongest rushes to bring them into bliss.

Some people call birth painful. And I did have about fifteen minutes of pain, in a seven hour stretch of otherwise blissful, joyful, laughing 'labour'. The pain happened when I felt fear, and for a moment, I let my mind run with it. When I harnessed my mind, addressed external circumstances to make myself more comfortable, communicated to Papa what was happening, and brought my full presence back into the overwhelming power of the moment, I could meet the intensity of rushes with the roar of passion, bliss and love that I AM.

We all have moments where we doubt, when we tire, when our habit of mind kicks in and overrides a deeper wisdom of presence. For me, in that moment I called upon the surrender that I had been cultivating over nine months and found the way through. For me, the key was in understanding that surrender is not passively giving in. There is an embrace and engagement with all that IS happening that takes tremendous strength.

My guides led me through many layers of surrender, to Source, to my son's father, to my own soul's bliss and love. For me the birth was a culmination of surrender, for in seven hours I journeyed through each of these doorways again, as if to seal the experiences into the fabric of my body, womb and soul.

Yet the initiation only truly became embodied for me when it was integrated. The experience of the birth was so powerful that it was only in the recounting of it with others present that I could remember. I wrote down the birth story, which felt like a gathering of all aspects of myself which had become so powerfully expanded in birth, and wove them into a new wholeness.

From here, I could take the gifts gleaned of this initiation and share them with others, laying a foundation of expression for my soul's purpose. This was only possible within the sound internal and external containers built by me and my son's father, and the external avenues generated and supported by his father.

BIRTH STORY THROUGH HIS FATHER'S EYES

During my son's birth I was completely present and engaged constantly in a whirlwind of activity, support and energetic presence for the entire seven hours, weaving and holding the container for my son and his mother. My 'I' or self was completely gone, consumed with everything that was happening and all that needed to be done. I did not have thoughts or worries about what needed to be done – I just did it.

My mind was gone in total flow, in total surrender, in total service and complete undivided giving presence for every single need and wish of my incoming son and Kat. Much of what they needed was unsaid, yet I picked up on it and gave them what they needed. This was always met with gratitude and recognition by Kat. They were all there was. Seven hours went by in minutes.

As time progressed, I cleansed the house physically and energetically to welcome my son's spirit and his guides, fetched water, made snacks, and constantly checked in on Kat and whatever she needed, rang the midwives, played music, sang, and created a billowing frankincense cloud to soothe and raise the vibrational frequency of the house. As I did all of this, I felt many spirit guides come to help us all and I briefly communicated with them.

I was in almost constant movement for the seven hours of labour, coming to and fro, linking everything together, much of which I cannot remember as I was totally present. When you are totally present with anything, the mind is totally subordinated to being a servant of the soul. In this presence of the moment, you do exactly what is needed to be done.

As time went on, I felt the container become more solid and clear, and I realized that everything I was doing was for one purpose, and one purpose alone: *to solidify the container for all three of us to be fully Present*. This would allow Kat and my sons spirit, soul and physical body to be birthed in his entirety, and would allow as much of him in all dimensions to come through intact, happy, connected, unhurt and as whole as possible.

This is the essence of being birthed: to allow the birth to happen through both parents …to be birthed into who we are. This is total presence.

During the birthing process I would feel overwhelming bursts of laughter and joy as I saw Kat hanging off the rafters in her bedroom, swinging from the beams deep in her birthing flow, travelling through her primordial ecstatic self, stretching and flowing with the movements of her Shakti, *not holding anything back*.

I would feel rushes of her magnetic bliss that were palpably emanating from her, triggering waves of ecstatic laughter from me that washed over us both. I would laugh and laugh and laugh, sometimes very raucous and primal, sometimes quieter, but each time deeply felt. My laughter became infectious and contagious, and then she would erupt into laughter! We ended up rolling around in laughter, until she had another rush and moved her body deeper into that with her breath. This happened many times throughout the evening. We both really enjoyed this, and were totally together in these waves of bliss.

Both midwives witnessed this, and one of them really enjoyed us and laughed with us, feeling the truth of it. The other midwife was a bit shocked and perturbed, thinking I was laughing at Kat's apparent pain and misfortune! (which she was used to witnessing from previous births.) The first midwife understood the bliss of birth, and explained this to the other one, who eventually got over her preconceived conditioning and began to enter more into the spirit of the party!

I had to protect the container from everyone, including my mother who was in the house to help us. As the birth started, she started to go through some of her own unfelt emotions, and I had to put up a clear boundary to stop her interfering with Kat and the baby. I made sure she stayed out of the birthing room, away from Kat, and in her own bubble in the house.

I even had to stop her complaining to the midwives about a totally unrelated topic at 1am in the morning, as her strident voice could be heard in the bedroom! I shushed her up and out, and continued holding the container.

It is very important for father to not give his power or intuitive knowing away to his mother, his partner's mother, doctors, nurses or midwives. He, and he alone, knows the mother of his child best at this moment IF they have a genuine love relationship, and he and mother know baby best. Father knows his baby far more than nurses, doctors, midwives and other parents ever will. Father has to be open to advice, but has to, at all times, follow his own souls knowing, even in the face of being contradicted. In his quiet, assured self-assertion in the face of 'authority' figures, he and he alone protects the container.

This is to be clearly understood by the father, and any interfering or negative energy has to be stopped by him in its tracks, swiftly and cleanly, to maintain the integrity of the birth container. People may have to be shushed or removed from the room: this is fine, even if they demand to be there.

Your single priority, in all dimensions, is to help mother and incoming baby feel totally safe, totally loved, totally nurtured and cared for, and totally not judged in any way whatsoever by anyone, including yourself!

The balance of energies in the birthing process is too fine, too delicate, to allow interference. The New Children are *very* refined, and interference at this stage is magnified. Of course, it can all be dealt with, and if you are prepared, all will go well. If some interference does happen, deal with it quickly, and ensure mother is settled back into a safe, secure and restful inner space afterwards.

For me, the whole birth was a whirlwind of activity, motion, serving and holding. The seven hours went by in a blink of an eye, and the container was only complete at 6am when I had the 'golden hour' time with my son and Kat on the bed. Before then, because I was so focused on them both, I did not feel any overwhelming emotions until 6am, about four hours after the physical birth. This was the time when everything had settled down, the midwives had left, and we were in the Golden Hour Cocoon.

I sat, holding my tiny new born son, just relaxing and letting go of the immense space I had been holding. Suddenly, I felt this overwhelming love arise from my heart, erupting for my son; it was incredibly beautiful, beyond words. I cried like a baby for many minutes as my heart burst and cracked wider open in my love for him. This was the culmination for me of the birth process. Love.

I had been so totally selfless for the previous 7+ hours, so present for Kat and my son, that finally now I could let down, and let go of everything. Then, and only then, could I go to sleep, and wake up to a new day, becoming a new man and a father.

The Container created during birth is an actual golden sphere. This is how I palpably felt and saw it throughout labour around Kat and in the bedroom, as I, as father, helped co-create it with my guides. In Aramaic, the language of Christ, they call this golden sphere *"Lehmeskanee"* literally meaning "the golden sphere surrounding you that connects you to all life," or "the luminous field of living energy suffusing creation." It was only a few months after the birth that I remembered this Aramaic term, confirming what I had already experienced and co-created intuitively in the birth process.

When both parents have created a loving container before birth, they become more emotionally intelligent. This allows birth to be blissful and loving, with your child becoming enabled to bring more of themselves into this world right from the beginning. This is a great gift for all souls involved, and a felt Blessing for us as parents.

THE MASCULINE PILLAR IN BIRTH

THE ROLE OF FATHER AT THE BIRTH OF HIS CHILD

Many men do not know how they fit in during the childbearing none months. In the past, almost all men have been excluded or chosen to opt out of the whole child bearing process, making the entire male collective consciousness on the planet feel that they were an unneeded and unwanted presence. It is now a known scientific fact that one-on-one contact from the man in the child bearing none months helps create a more caring, integrated, safer, more blissful container for mother and child, with far fewer birth interventions and mishaps occurring.

Why? Well fathers, it is because your woman needs you! You are her best friend, her confidante. This powerful connection of security and trust in a sound and nurtured container are key elements to a loving relationship, pregnancy and birth. Father knows mother better than anyone else. He is her advocate, her physical and emotional support, and her constant reminder that she is not alone. Birth is a team effort, with both parents being kind to one another, proud of the other and excited about the baby.

As a father, you play a vital role in pregnancy and birth. You have been responsible for getting the baby in, so you are also a major support and responsible for getting the baby out! Such is the design of nature.

A father weaves a safe, strong and sound physical, emotional and spiritual container for the whole nine months and beyond. When the labouring mother feels this, she can descend into the depths of the process in her womb. Father can create this sound container in labour through clearing the space physically and energetically, setting boundaries for others involved in the birth, lighting sage, incense and candles, playing the right music, tending to and nurturing mother and baby, communicating with the spirit of his child, guiding the mother, and affectionately and soulfully engaging with his love: the mother.

A father helps mother achieve deep relaxation by comforting, massaging, holding, being soft when needed, ecstatic and joyful when this is felt, and present and guiding her when she is lost in her process at other times. He listens to her and also anticipates what she needs. He is totally present in selfless service, in devotion, to his family.

In this way, father and mother engage in labour together, as partners. Though the father's role is less immediate in the early stages of labour, he is the power behind the throne. Later in labour, the father's presence moves more to the forefront alongside the mother, and he is as important as the mother. His familiar resonance is a comforting beacon inviting the child into the world of form.

Father is needed in birth, for just when you 'think' you know what you are doing, you will be shown otherwise! Birth keeps you humble and present, beyond ideas and concepts, and is designed for both male and female forms of power, wisdom and love to come together, to complete each other, in order to have a whole birth. This union of male and female creates a gateway, a portal, through which more of the soul of the child, not just the body, can come into this world.

Fathers are their partner's lover, and their most important role is one they do every day without classes, books, or practices: loving the mother. Fathers need to relax and simply be themselves. Fathers: just love your partner. It is YOU she wants at the birth. And the result of this is all three of you dancing your way through birth in a way that is uniquely your own.

Each father is as unique as each labouring woman. *Fathers go through labour too!* Fathers have their own emotional process in birth and in pregnancy, and go through many similar shifts like mother does. Throughout the process, father needs to be present in a way that is true to himself, being honest to himself and the mother, knowing his own strengths and weaknesses. In this expression, all three souls benefit, even if the father is scared to share something to mother. This is because respect is engendered by honesty, and respect creates trust.

Mother needs to feel comfortable when having a baby. They need to feel held, nurtured and safe in a secure environment. They need to palpably feel the trust and respect from the father as an emotional bedrock and touchstone for them. His presence, love and support helps create a loving birth for all three souls involved.

Every birth is different, every baby is different, and every woman and man is different. We are all unique. No one will know your child better than both of you. We all have our roles, and this is why the child has chosen both of you.

For example, the man is usually the protector of the family, designed to be present emotionally, physically and spiritually. But remember: he is birthing, too, and needs the space to experience his birth in his way. Not all fathers make good birth coaches, although that is a part of their role, because of course they are in labour, too. But they can be a gatekeeper for a mother in labour.

Father is best disposed to support the mother, often times without verbal prompting, yet also by the mother telling him what she needs, AND by his own intuitive reading and feeling of the situation, without his own beliefs clouding the way. Therefore, fathers sometimes need to take charge and lead the way because father knows mother the best!

In the true masculine, the father becomes a pillar for the mother to lean on and confide in, a source of strength and depth ever present and reliable. This honorable masculine is there for mother and child no matter what, living in an integrity that would do anything for his loved ones, the pillar of strength they can rely on, and always come back to.

For example, at the onset of transition labour just before birth itself, a woman will often say, "I can't!" This is when the father moves in close, holds her hands, looks in her eyes and lends her his strength. This allowa the expectant mother to move into his space, and to share his strength, his solidity, his unmoving pillar, which inspires her to keep going and travel deeper into herself and into baby. He too benefits because he connects more deeply to the primordial flow of the birthing energies: he joins in energetically with the process.

'As I entered transition labour, I felt undercurrents of defeat, physical and emotional exhaustion. I told him I needed him in the tub with me, and without hesitation, he climbed in. He situated himself behind me, and feeling the strength in his physical frame, the warmth of his body, and the softness of his gentle embrace, allowed me to completely relax. His gentle words of encouragement quenched me. The deep resonance of his encouraging voice called me home to my womb, my soul. This momentary exchange and connection enabled me to re-engage with the dance of birth, in love and power.

I reached down to my yoni and felt the soft hair on my child's head. I encouraged him to do the same, and at first he hesitated. I knew this was what our son needed, to physically feel both of us. Two rushes later, with both our hands on his crown, our son emerged into our hands. The gravity of our touch together drew him into this world."

The power of a woman giving birth is awe-inspiring and amazing. When a father joins in with these energies he is further awe struck and humbled into the noble masculine soul essence. Any father who has not seen, supported and helped his partner give birth has an incomplete emotional and soulful perspective of what it means to be a mother, has an incomplete emotional and soulful perspective of what it means to be a father, and he will not instinctively know, feel and appreciate the roles he has of being a father.

As the pregnancy evolves and birth becomes imminent, your woman will lean on you. Her needs and wants will become the fathers guide on how to be, and in this process the father will also learn what his own roles are. With good communication, everything falls into place. This communication is both verbal and preverbal in the sense that father has to read the energies of mother and baby and anticipate what is happening before it happens in many cases, which occurs by him being fully present and connected to the Shakti of mother and baby in the birthing process.

The male pillar anchors and grounds the container for birth, a 'bubble' that surrounds mother and child as they open up to the primal powers and alchemical forces of creation that are unleashed in birth. This 'bubble' is vital to maintain the integrity, alchemy and safety of what is being created, for all processes in creation needs a container to bring the formless into form.

A loving and present male partner provides (better than a midwife, mother, sister, girlfriend, doula) the ideal 'grounding' for the mother emotionally, soulfully and physically. Pregnancy is such a swirl of hormones and things to do that the mother can often forget and become overwhelmed in the emotions and 'rush' of it all. The man, solid, steady, true, brings a certain simplicity to the dance of pregnancy, bringing her back to her own centre point of what is true. He brings her balance, bringing everything into perspective, helping her with the larger context.

He helps ground her emotional body and soul by being unconditionally loving, helping her to return to her souls truth, passion and purpose when she is caught up in the swirls of her own process. He brings her back to the solid container of trust, bringing her back to the structures for relaxation, creating routines and rhythms that help her settle down into a natural rhythm.

Father holds the 'big picture,' allowing mother to find her own flow, and when necessary to express herself and return to the bigger picture.

The father solidly and unashamedly being masculine, being who he is (soulfully not egoically) is perhaps the greatest thing of all for mother. For this is why she chose to have a child with him in the first place. This becomes a reference point for her to return to from the swings of hormones, emotions and stress. Father is the reminder, the balance point in the middle of it all.

Father too has to speak truth to his partner at the right times, and when she is overly emotional, it is his job to be firm and clear with her. Father guides the overall energy of the container, organizing time, ensuring they all take time out to do fun and adventurous things together. Father keeps an even flow of energy ticking over and expanding throughout the pregnancy.

Grounding means we embody our soul here on earth now with our physical body being the anchor point for our spirits, souls and the Divine. A well balanced and soulful natural pregnancy and birth will help both mother and father woman embody their own souls here on earth in a profound way.

This can lead to a further activation of our own Self-expression here and now. This could mean many things; we create a new website, a book, a shop, a new career, a new lifestyle, home environment, or new relationships to complement our own evolution so we can manifest our full potential. Whatever it takes, is what we have to do.

It may also mean leaving behind many habits, people, jobs and relationships, and also changing your relationship with your own biological parents to reflect the new, more embodied you.

The father needs to recognize his role as supporter, as the rock, the pillar, the one the mother can rely on both internally and externally when her whole world changes and parts of it come crashing down. This also entails fluidity, gentleness and humility.

Father is available to support mother and baby and hold space as protector, lover and advocate, AND he is in his own process, his own labour and whirlwind of thoughts and emotions, which are a transition for him into his role. The birth process solidifies this.

Friendship between mother and father means we share our good times and bad times with each other. We open up honestly and express our vulnerabilities, releasing our secret burdens of having to be exclusively there for others alone, and excluding our own selves.

We bond through sharing the common thread of **all** that we experience, and we come together in this empathy to care for and love each other. In this, mother and father bond deeply and get to know each other AND their own selves' better, providing baby with a resonant, felt platform to be born into this world from.

The feminine provides us with great, enduring strength, great because it is soft and enduring. A man could never do what a woman does in labour. A mother is soft as she is strong; her strength comes from her softness, and this softness can endure for far longer periods of time than the masculine power or yang quality. Soft as it is strong, it is fluid and accepting of all.

In feeling, honouring and being naturally in awe of the soft, sustained, enduring strength of the feminine, men can evolve and deepen into their true nature. The wonder of labour, birth and the feminine strength, AND what women do consistently after birth in tending to the child patiently and lovingly, is something few men can do, or are designed to do.

The Souls Design for Birth shares that the qualities necessary to be a parent are *naturally transferred to the father during the conscious, soulful pregnancy and birth process*: the nine months are designed for the man to grow up into being a soulful and ready father, acquiring all the skills, intuitive capacities and embodied consciousness necessary to be a father in this time, just as the nine months are there for the woman to grow into being a soulful and ready mother.

At the beginning of the nine months, he is just a man: after birth, all going well, he will have brought forth and activated part of his dormant innate masculinity, that of the father, to bloom into his life, his spirit and his soul. This newly activated quality then has to come into a new relationship with the feminine.

Trusting the feminine qualities of feeling and sharing non verbally and emotionally have to be balanced with the active doing qualities of the masculine. The imbalances of feminine yin and masculine yang, of receptivity and being versus outwards looking power and direction, are the hallmarks of modern culture: achieving, doing, celebrating our busyness and how great we are in our doing.

We may measure our sense of self-worth, or how little self-worth we have, through how busy we are, how many 'friends'' we have, and how much we can do. As a whole, inaction or being is seen as weak and ineffective by modern day western society in 'getting ahead' in life.

This leads to self-destruction and depletion, for yang is limited. It needs constant replenishing by being harmonized with yin, which regenerates, restores and fortifies it. Imbalance is destructive on a body-mind level as well as being destructive on a global level with the destruction of the environment, war and conflict. True Yin would never initiate a war or sustain one; only yang versus yang can create that, and true yin would never deplete itself through outward action – as its innate nature is inwardness and receptivity.

It is yin that allows space and time in our schedules to be empty– not needing to fill in the gaps in our busy lives. Rest allows wellbeing, self-care, self-love, and from this arises the right, and most efficient activities that will most benefit you and others. Without this, we enter imbalance and stress related illnesses arise, as the body mind is not built to remain in yang action mode for long periods of time.

If we do, we become depleted, irritated, tired and stressed, which leads to us becoming stuck, inflexible and paradoxically unable to do things. The body mind **is** built to remain in harmony between yin and yang for indefinite periods of time. We can do this by spending more time in self-care, self-love, looking after ourselves and doing what we enjoy. This all increases our innate sense of wellbeing, and sometimes doing nothing is the most productive thing to do! Take time to relax in a yin way throughout your day, rest together with mother and baby, and be receptive and gentle with your child and yourself.

FATHER IN LABOUR

The most important thing you and your partner can do is to heal some of your own birth and ancestral traumas before engaging in the birth process.

Over half of all births are considered to be deeply traumatic. Hundreds of millions of people hold deeply buried emotional, genetic, and neuro-biological shock memories of what happened to them in conception, pregnancy and birth. As soon as a person enters into the heightened hormonal and emotional fields of pregnancy and labour, these memories will activate through your DNA and the part of the brain known as the Amygdala.[25]

These memories and shocks are not just from your own birthing process. Aspects of your parent's process will be in there, as will your ancestors, as will your own childhood memories and hurts. Everything will arise to be felt.

The Souls Design for Birthing is a private and intimate journey. Love blooms away from the prying eyes of the world, as Rumi once said. Birthing is a Holy Trinity of mother, father and child coming together, bonding deeply, and embodying their own male and female sides within a loving container. The deeper the embodiment of each of the parent's souls in this process, the more of the child's soul comes into its body when it is born.

Father has to become a Protector during pregnancy and birth, so no harm or interference either physically or psychically comes to partner and baby. Since your partner and baby are fully immersed in the birth itself and the powerful vortex of forces unleashed in labour, it is upto you to protect them and preserve the sanctity of the birth environment.

Do whatever you can to bring your full power into the birthing field and stand strong in your intention to keep your partner and child safe from others thoughts, emotions and unnecessary interventions. Whatever it takes to protect the birth environment of your partner and child – DO IT. Your courage and power to speak out and stand up to authority

---

[25] See Amygdala meditation for help in clearing this

is important, so that your partner and child feel safe and can trust you are strong enough to protect them and keep them from harm.

This allows mother to let go into the immense power of the birthing process. When she can let go physically and emotionally, with spirit and soul, she will respect you immensely and trust you even more. Trust is the foundation of intimacy.

It is important to remember that your partner's womb and yoni are sacred. They are the doorways through which you entered her to create your baby, and they are the doorways through which your child enters this dimension. Here, literally, is the beginning and end of all births!

Take special care of this sacred space and portal. Do not allow anyone to poke her repeatedly. Protect your partner's integrity (and your intimate relationship) by insisting all doctors, midwives, nurses and any others keep their hands off her unless there is an emergency or they are checking the dilation of the yoni in a respectful way. Do not give your power and knowing away to anyone else.

Sing to your child as soon as he or she starts to crown and come out of the yoni. We are vibrational beings, and the first sound your child hears has an impact on them.

Make loving, joyful eye contact with your baby immediately at birth. On a primal human level, the first thing babies need to see in this world are your love-filled eyes, the windows into your soul and the windows into their soul. What a welcome this is, to come onto earth and to be greeted by a radiant soul. Let this be the first experience of this world for your child.

Similarly, place your baby on yours and your partner's body immediately after birth. The other medical checks can wait for a while, as can the placenta cord. This skin-to-skin contact will make your baby feel safe, secure and welcomed on a profound, preverbal and subconscious level.

This feeling of bonding and trust then allows love to bloom and open in the delicate flower that your child is, producing a positive imprint of well-being that will last a lifetime. *Father's job is to remind mother of all these things, and look after her at this time.*

Do not allow your baby's umbilical cord to be cut. When babies first emerge from the womb, they are not breathing. They receive oxygen from the placental blood as it pulses through the umbilical cord into their little bodies. When their umbilical cord is immediately clamped or cut, baby's oxygen supply is abruptly cut off, forcing him/her to gasp for breath in fear for their life.

The blood pulsing through your baby's umbilical cord contains vital nutrients to help baby create a strong immune system. Your baby will be denied these nutrients if the umbilical cord is cut too soon. There is no medical reason why they cannot wait to cut your baby's umbilical cord. If they try to do this too soon, step in and protect your child.

Additionally, baby's emotional connection to mother is abruptly and violently severed at a time when baby is extremely vulnerable. This creates a long-lasting imprint of emotional trauma for your child and his/her emotional health.

THE GOLDEN SPIRAL IN BIRTH

Manifestation is a marriage of movement and fluid structure. The seed impulse and movement of Creation is Delight, Self-Expression and Love. The architecture of manifestation is the Golden Spiral, also known as The Golden Mean, often called the Ratio of Perfection and Harmony. The numbers of The Golden Mean 1.618 never end: they continue into infinity.

The Golden Spiral is seen in the architecture of many sacred buildings such as the Great Pyramids and the Parthenon, as well as many other temples worldwide. The Golden Spiral is found in the perfect proportions of the human body and DNA, how plants grow, and many works of art. It is the most universally binding of all mathematical relationships, and the pattern that life adheres to in creation.

In birth, the Golden Spiral and its spiraling movement maps *the dance of our rhythmically contracting-expanding wombs. This is the souls design for birth: to move in total harmony with the natural and potentially infinite forces of creation.*

When we attune to the Golden Spiral Harmony, we give and receive love deeply. The Golden Spiral is intertwined with the Earths frequency, intelligence and presence, and moves us through these interlinked frequency oscillations woven into our hearts and DNA. When the frequency of our DNA entrains more with the Golden Spiral our experience of time changes.

The more deeply you move into these frequencies, the more magnetic you become, able to flow, let go into, and trust the natural unfoldings and cycles of life. The natural harmony of the Golden Phi Spiral is the foundation for the Law of Attraction – the universal law that draws towards you that which serves your growth and reflects the state of your soul, be it relationships, teachings, events or resources. Until you resonate with the Golden Spiral, the Grace of this law is not fully realized in your life.

When our hips begin tracing the natural geometry of birth found in the Golden Spiral, we naturally birth in a harmonious expression. An interruption in the freedom of the spiral expression, an impingement on the movement of the emerging impulse, can compromise the adaptation of essence into integrated form.

This interruption can occur through our own unhealed emotions, in our inhibitions to open and move during birth, or our fears in allowing birth its natural timing. It can occur as interruptions in the birthing field such as fear, or external agendas. When these obstacles are released, removed or resolved, there is freedom again for the spiral to express its pure blueprint into being.

In labour the muscles of the uterus synchronize clockwise and counter clockwise spiraling movements, initiating a vortex of spiralling energy both upward and downwards, creating a bridge between dimensions This initiates the child's movement from the womb through the cervix, yoni and into the world. The more integrated and uninterrupted this spiral bridge is, the easier the child will transition to earth remaining connected to its soul. All souls are naturally connected to the Golden Spiral.

When a woman is connected through her womb-heart to the earth's core and through her pineal to Source, she becomes an expansive yet rooted stable axis for the primordial power of birth's Golden Spiral to move through her unhindered. It is here she is supported and can fully surrender to experience the full pleasure, power, and transformational Rite of Passage that birth is, and her child's soul can be safely and soundly delivered into form intact.

PRACTICE: PREPARING TO BIRTH WITH THE GOLDEN MEAN

One way of tuning into the Golden Spiral is through the infinity symbol, the figure eight symbol on its side that connects all things together. The infinity symbol shows two interconnected whole beings in relationship. Each individual circle is whole by itself, and intimately connected with the other in the dance of life and relationship.

This Meditation to harmonize with the Golden Phi Spiral can be done during Pre Conception, any time during pregnancy, during Labour and after Birth.

Take some deep breaths into your belly. Sit comfortably and relax. Go inwards. Take some deep breaths into the base of your spine. Draw, in light, the infinity symbol/ figure eight on its side, and keep looping it around with your inhale and exhale. Find a rhythm of drawing the symbol and breathing it in and around at the same time. Do this for a minute or two.

Now begin to move your hips in an infinity loop motion, again using your breath to loop the symbol into rhythm. Start with very small movements and allow them to organically get larger and larger. Do this for a minute or two.

Now do this same motion with your neck, physically looping it around in a figure eight. Do this for a minute or two, and then allow the energy-vibration to run through you. Take a deep breath of it down into the seed of your heart, and hold the breath for seven at the heart. Exhale.

Now draw the figure eight in the heart, and with each exhale expand it outwards. Keep drawing and breathing the figure eight spiral until everything becomes a sea of spirals flowing around you, within you.

Draw, with a deep breath, all of this into the seed of your heart, and hold the breath for six. Exhale.

Place your hands on your heart and womb. Now, breathe a connecting figure eight spiral between your heart and womb for a minute or two. Inhale into both heart and womb, and hold the breath for seven. Exhale.
How do you feel?

BIRTH and THE SEVEN GATES

Birth is the journey of a child from womb to world, and an initiatory journey of a woman into a deeper expression of her femininity. It begins at the first hint of a rush and ends after the honoring of the Placenta. This journey through a woman's seven gates of womb and yoni culminates in the incarnation of a child and deeper soul embodiment for a woman. This is our innate design.

The Seven Gates are biological and feeling portals of our yonis and wombs. They are where our emotions, our sexuality, our souls and the divine meet in our bodies. When entered into through labia lips, G-spot, clitoris, cervix, and the three spaces of the womb, they can lead to deep union within ourselves, another, and with Source. When they are accessed beginning from the womb and moving into emergence from the yoni lips, they are the journey of creation, of manifestation, of birth.

The Gates offer the structure for moving through the birth journey, and deepen the bonding between mother and father when journeyed through in love making, where the yoni lips are the beginning and the womb is the end. This strengthens the love, respect, trust and surrender together so necessary for raising their child, and bringing the seeds of purpose into manifestation from the birthing process.

All birthing journeys have the capacity to bring seeds of the parent's soul purpose into manifestation, along with their children. A solid foundation of family is an important anchor to ground more of the Divine evolutionary plan into expression.

In birthing we palpably travel through the Gates. The process of creation initiates from cosmic consciousness womb space and culminates in the world of form through our yoni lips. During birth we have the opportunity to travel with our child, and at times our partner, through the different stages of creation into manifestation. In doing so, we are also birthed into a new aspect or octave of our own Being.

7TH GATE: Cosmic Womb Consciousness
6TH GATE Womb: Galactic Center: *Emerging Spark*
5TH GATE Womb Field: Male-Female-Union: *Pulse*
4TH GATE Cervix: Crossing the Threshold: *Engaging in the Dance of Polarities*
3RD GATE Clitoris: Purity of Bliss: *Opening into Pure Pleasure*
2ND GATE G Spot: Gratitude: *Harnessing Power*
1ST GATE Yoni Lips: Celebration and Praise: *Let Go and Let God*

The opening of the Seventh Gate deep within the core of the womb initiates the birthing process. Physically, this occurs with the first rush (or Braxton Hicks rushes).[26] This is the time when a woman's womb connection with the core of her womb and the Galactic Center, the Womb Source for our Galaxy, is potent and expanding. The physical alignment through the rushes sync with her soul's alignment with Source. She becomes the toroidal vortex that unites heaven and earth.

---

[26] At this time, baby is moving more deeply into the right position to descend through the birth canal.

The time between the opening of the Seventh Gate and active labour is an opportunity for inner communion and exploration. It is a time to surrender to the natural timing of your child's emergence and enter inner doorways that are opening. Later, these experiences can be harvested into wisdom and expression. It may take months, even years to decipher and articulate the gems offered in this time.

The movement through the Sixth Gate brings deep stillness, the calm before the storm. It is here that we remember the void, the darkness of eternity, our orientation to Source. The void is beyond the experiences of time and space.

From this wholeness emerges a spark, entirely unique in its geometry of light. It carries a fractal of the wholeness from which it emerged, and moves toward manifestation to complete the outer reflection of the inner perfection. When we feel the rhythm in this journey of the spark, we cross into the Fifth Gate. The spark moved by the precursor of desire undulates and begins to pulse into form.

When we fully allow the experience of the Fifth Gate, we surrender to the innate, natural timing of birth. In the original impulse from source is the complete blueprint for the manifestation of this perfect being. Any interference with this organic rhythm and timing means cloaking this pure expression with our own agenda, ideas, beliefs, emotions, impatience or expectation. Trusting this intelligence in our bodies *and* the process opens us to more authentically actualize our own blueprint.

The opening of the Fourth Gate Cervix in birth is palpable and potent. The burning of the opening cervix draws us immediately into the choice for either pleasure or pain. It is here we choose to dance and engage into form, or shrink and become victim. Presence, breath, tenderness and movement all soften us into the Fourth Gate.

The labour process becomes more personal at this point. The physical intensity is building and there is no turning back. How will you walk through your Fourth Gate? Will you engage with your full power, surrender and love in the dance? Or will you resist and feed fear, trying to crawl away from your own body and the direct emergence happening through you?

This is a call to *bring all of you into the moment*, to meet each crashing wave of rushes with your full soul, spirit and form, surrendering to the expression emerging through you. All the emotions that hinder this innate knowing within a woman's biology are touched, and have to be released. This is intuitive and innate within the nervous system and soul of the mother.

True birthing happens in the immediacy and freshness of the moment. Orgasmic birth occurs when a woman is connected to her seat and her throne in pleasure, her clitoris fully alive, enjoying. *As you make love, so you can give birth. It can be a similar journey once the Gates are open.*

As the head of baby pressures the Third Gate clitoris, waves of pleasure, intensity and bliss can flow. This activates an internal guidance system that further connects mother and child to allow the organic movement of birth. Just as in orgasm our dancing womb and yoni undulate involuntarily, we are invited even more deeply to surrender to the waves of birth happening through us. When we do this without pushing or controlling we allow ourselves to dissolve into the birthing process, beyond agenda or control.

In this 'being' rather than 'doing' we surrender to the wisdom and pleasure of the Third Gate. This insures that no imprint of effort or straining are left in our yoni and in our child's first memory of emerging on earth. This release triggers the opening of the Second Gate of the G Spot with gratitude, power and reverence. As these qualities surge with rushes of life-force and Shakti, we rise into our power and truly harness the energy of birth.

Our focus allows us to stay present with the climax of intensity. The fine line between harnessing and controlling becomes evident again in the Second Gate. We can channel the power where it is warranted, or push to get through the process more quickly, *out of our discomfort*. In the essence of gratitude, the attitude of the Second Gate, there is an allowing and embracing of all that has been given to us in a moment. This relaxes us into a deeper, subtler power beyond force.

In one final surrender, our yoni lips First Gate bloom the crown of our child into the world. This is where we truly let go and let God. Celebration and appreciation innately flow forth from our First Gate, ushering our manifested child into our arms. The moments after birth, of bonding and connection, establish the healthy magnetics to help anchor our child here on earth, and also help to soothe and heal our yoni lips.

As we rest in the oxytocin rich love bubble generated by birth in 'The Golden Hour', the deep weaving of ourselves and our child together through our Gates happens, through our magnetic, welcoming love and embrace.

BIRTH IN IT'S MOVEMENTS

The entirety of the birth journey intelligently prepares and readies a family on all levels of body, spirit, and soul. The emergence of your baby from your yoni lips into your hands is a profound moment in the orchestral symphony of birthing.

The opening and deepening of my Seventh Gate in the days before true labour began was all consuming and spontaneous. I would have intermittent physical rushes, and then moments later I would drop into a profound vast stillness inside my womb where I lost all reference points, all sense of myself as a separate being, all recognition of anything beyond stillness; and yet I was here, present, encompassing all and nothing simultaneously.

I was taken to this place numerous times in the days leading up to my son's birth. I would feel it coming on, and I would surrender, put down the laundry, my computer, a conversation, and retreat to my room to be with the vast experience in silence, to immerse in it, with every aspect of my being. Sometimes I would sit for hours.

One day, while sitting in this deep stillness, I spontaneously began rocking. The rhythm came from so deep within me, beyond me, through me. I felt an image of a spark emanating out of the deep darkness from where I had been sitting, and the spark had a rhythm that propelled it forth into contrast against the black emptiness.

I rode the spark. I completely surrendered to its rhythm. All it's intelligence was contained within it. All I had to do was surrender, allow it to move through me, allow myself to ride it, and the gifts it carried would be revealed in it's own wise timing. All I had to do was surrender to this movement through me, from beyond.

I rocked and rocked. *I was being rocked.* Allowing the rocking, I began to dance with the rocking. I felt its innate rhythm at my center and I moved around it, improvising, harmonizing, joyously engaging. This carried me to the threshold of the Fourth Gate Cervix, where I was aware of myself and a rhythm outside of me, and I could move, dance and engage with it.

My experience in the Fourth Gate continued intermittently for the final days before birth. Rushes would shift my son deeper into position, and as each rush arrived I was faced with a choice: how would I engage? Would I tap into the joy and aliveness moving through me and dance and sway my hips through this rhythm, or would I become a victim, resist and turn the experience to pain?

I danced. I met each rush as it crashed upon me, with an opening of my heart and being. I spiraled my hips, I sang, I moaned, I laughed, feeling the penetration of sheer life force moving through me. This polarity, this force meeting me, brought me alive and I surrendered to the dance with my entirety.
As the intensity increased, I could feel my Third Gate Clitoris being physically stretched. Waves of Golden Spirals moved through me and around me, orgasmically circling me down, down, down. I roared, I smiled, I sang, I laughed. This was fully body bliss and beyond!

God, my partner, my baby, all laughed with me. A golden symphony of light moved through and around me, in harmony and joy! I could feel the absolute purity of my soul distilling into a magnetic center amidst it all. This magnetic center was my Second Gate G Spot.

1. EARLY LABOUR: THE THRESHOLD

Early labour begins physically when the spiraling muscles of the womb begin their initial sporadic rushes. Imagine the instruments in an orchestra tuning and warming up to perform a symphony. The first few intermittent rushes may happen over a few weeks or a few days before the 'main event'. This tuning gently positions your baby deeper into the pelvis, encouraging the relaxing and opening of the cervix, and stimulating the emotions.

These rushes are an opportunity for a woman to begin working with the energies of labour. Spiraling hips as the rushes come is a way of actively engaging in the dance. In this way, the energy can be directed into a joyous expression of movement and sound. Rushes without active engagement from the mother can become painful and overwhelming.

With the thinning of the cervix comes a heightened intuition and sensitivity. This serves on a biological level to warn the mother of any external threats or danger that would interfere with birth. On a spiritual level, this expansion in consciousness allows mother the capacity to tune in deeply to her own soul, her baby, and to Source.

In moving through the portal of her cervix she may meet deep subconscious emotions that are limiting her. In birth, we can die to ourselves and an old construct of who we thought we were. It is here that the Pillar Presence of a man affords a woman the trust to completely let go into the dissolution of her known self, and not to be concerned with anything else or the external world. She can drop and let go.

Once naked in this way, she can walk through the Fourth Gate doorway of the womb into becoming the vessel to manifest the will, body and love of the soul incarnating. This embodiment sanctifies the birth chamber as well as stabilizing the foundation for her child.

Spiritually, as the veils between levels of consciousness become thinner and awareness becomes more expanded and sensitized, she can tune in more accurately and directly with her baby. Through the seed of her heart, she can connect with her baby's spirit and receive/share images and feelings about their upcoming journey and the joy and love that awaits them.

Though part of me was experiencing impatience in waiting for my son to arrive, I understood on a soul level the importance of allowing the natural timing for his journey. In the process of honoring this journey, I was evolving. If I had acted from my ego need for control and induced his birth even in a small way, I would have interrupted the integrity of this natural process, and distorted his own journey, as well as stopping myself from taking my own Rite of Passage by surrendering to something far greater than I could have imagined. I was opening to more trust, more love and more wisdom beyond myself, beyond who I thought I was, beyond what I believed my capacities to be.

2. ACTIVE LABOUR: THE SPIRAL

Active labour is the beginning of consistent, rhythmic rushes. When a woman is uninhibited and free to flow with the intense amount of Shakti moving through her, this stage can be sensual, dynamic, expressive and ecstatic. Dance, play, laughter, sounding, toning and cuddling all help to ground the increased amounts of energy. The more a woman stays rooted in her body, the more connected she is to the innate wisdom that guides her into the correct positioning and adjustments for birth.

When physical pain arises during labour, it is a sign. Pain is constriction, resistance. When we surrender to emotion arising through breath and prayer, and release resistance, pain dissolves into sensation and intensity. This intensity can then be transformed into orgasmic sensation, *for it is just life force wanting to express*. This opening is enabled on a soul level by joy and bliss, and on a physical level by the combined hormones of DMT and Oxytocin.

OXYTOCIN and ADRENALINE

All complications in the birthing process, including hospitalization, arise from unfelt and unhealed emotions within you or your partner (who is in the birthing field). Emotions are the cause, and the physical is the effect. To understand this from a physiological perspective, it is important to know the function of two hormones: oxytocin and adrenaline.

Oxytocin release from the pineal gland is stimulated by the senses: dim and natural lighting, essential oils, relaxing music, sensual stimulation, massage, warm water, and most powerfully, prayer and love. It is especially stimulated in orgasm and breast feeding (which is one reason why nipple stimulation is helpful during labour).

Oxytocin emits endorphins that give us feelings of wellbeing, relaxation, connection, openness and joy. It releases opiates that decrease pain. It also stimulates rhythmic uterine rushes, present in both orgasm and labour. When a woman is held in an oxytocin rich environment, her physiology naturally unfolds and blooms into a blissful birth process. In essence, oxytocin is the hormone of being-ness, bonding, and love.

On the other hand, adrenaline is the hormone of doing, and basic survival fight, flight and fear responses. Adrenaline is released from the adrenal glands when our nervous system perceives a threat, or needs extra stimulus to respond to a need for action. Adrenaline cancels the effects of oxytocin, sending us into fight-flight-freeze mode.

In the heightened adrenaline state, pain is more intense, the primal survival mind is activated (to make quick decisions) blood is drained from the womb, muscles tense in anticipation, breathing quickens and becomes shallower. This state of fear, tension and pain is not conducive to the necessary softening and opening of birth.

Adrenaline can be activated in the birth process in many ways. Firstly, if the container or field set for the birth is intruded upon, the mother will feel a compromised safety. This is why it is so important for the father to maintain the sanctity of the birthing space physically, emotionally, and spiritually.

When the woman viscerally feels the soundness of the masculine pillar and its protection, her mammalian brain is activated, bringing relaxation, creativity, and intuition. Here, she is totally attentive to the messages from her baby and her body, and she can focus on her role in birthing, and what she needs to do.

This is one reason hospital births can be more traumatic. The moment a couple leaves the safe and comforting home environment, the process of disconnecting a woman from her innate connection to her womb and birth has begun. Quick decisions, panic, the unknown, rushed transport and bright lights all stimulate the frontal brain or neo-cortex, pulling a woman out of her instinctual nature.

The hospital initiates a downward cycle of artificial intervention in a natural process, and heightens the alienation of a woman from her body, her emotions, her loved ones supporting her, and thus her birth.

Adrenaline may also be released in the birthing process if a woman has a history of sexual abuse or sexually affected surgery. Any trauma or block still held in the cervix, womb or yoni will be stimulated by the intense sensations and stretching in the birthing process. The physical triggering of these emotions buried in the subconscious can trigger a response in the brain to stimulate a 'fight-flight-freeze' reaction, which releases adrenaline into the bloodstream.

Ideally, these emotions will be addressed in pre-conception and pregnancy. However, if they do arise in the labour process, they can be addressed quickly with breath, prayer, and strong desire to feel and release the underlying causal emotions. It is helpful for you to tell your birthing partner what is happening, and for him to recognize what is happening, in order to hold a caring and safe container for your emotions.

Oxytocin and adrenaline are contagious frequencies and emotional states. When a woman is in an oxytocin state, she is open, soft, radiant and blooming, palpably evoking feelings of devotion, appreciation and love from her man. If he shares these feelings with her in soulful words, loving touch and eye contact, more oxytocin is released, resulting in more womb rushes, more love, and more relaxing and flowering of the yoni and womb wider open.

Consequently, when a man sees fear or pain on his woman's face during labour, this can easily stimulate his own fear response. If he acts from this place, instead of stabilizing the container and supporting his woman selflessly in her process, it increases the undertone of fear in the room. The woman will feel less safe, and her body will tighten and become rigid, slowing down or stopping the birth progress.

Birth will inevitably bring up your next layer of emotions to be healed, no matter how evolved you think you are. Indeed, the more healed we are, the more humble, emotionally aware and emotionally sensitive we become. This creates a stronger container of authenticity, love and truth between both parents, and this means that both parents can more easily flow through the emotions that arise, as both parents feel supported and connected. *Vulnerability brings us all home.*

In rare cases, it is necessary to have assistance from the hospital for mother and child to be physically safe. If this is the case, the man can still provide a solid container through his presence, support, and advocacy in navigating through the hospital system. It is possible to create a softer environment in the hospital by dimming lights, sniffing essential oils, music, and throwing scarves over machines. Taking time to connect with baby and explain what is happening during a hospital birth can make it a less traumatic experience for everyone.

Active labour is an important time for a woman to establish the connection through her heart seed between herself and her child. When mother and child are synchronized in this way, labour is shorter. Communicating through images, pictures and feelings can help prepare a child and mother for the intense journey they are embarking upon.

3. TRANSITION and BIRTH

Towards the end of Active Labour, rushes are continual and intense. It is often at this time that a woman reaches her threshold and feels she cannot handle any more intensity. If the mind or emotional wound takes hold at this point, the sensation can turn to pain, and even fear. If the woman stays centered in her breath, body, shakti and prayer, she will surrender to new horizons of openness in body and soul.

The G-Spot (Gratitude Spot Second Gate) is intensely stimulated with the stretching of the yoni as baby's head descends. By bringing breath and shakti to the G Spot, a woman can release resistance here, and as resistance melts in a felt sense of relief and new relaxed flow, she can soften, deepen and open further with her gratitude.

Gratitude for the process, gratitude for the good things in her life, gratitude for her own self, gratitude to her partner, gratitude for her parents, gratitude for her midwives, gratitude for her lineage, gratitude for Earth, gratitude to God, gratitude for all the beautiful support and help in her life. Summoning forth and remembering a profound gratitude experience you have had previously in your life can help here.

The space in between her rushes allows her to settle, soften and integrate the opening of her tissues and the opening in her heart. Sharing eye contact or loving words at this point helps her bridge her inner and outer experiences.

Towards the end of transition, baby's head will engage with the clitoris or third gate. The yoni begins to breathe, drawing the crown of the baby's head into sight, then releasing it back into the folds of the yoni. This 'breathing' massages the tissue around the opening of the yoni connected to the clitoris, and allows it to open gently. Breathe directly into the clitoris here, and ask for the love of your partner to be felt and for him to touch you here. This can happen by you telling him what is happening *and* by him being aware of this moment and moving with it. This can keep the intensity directed toward love and pleasure.

In this phase it is possible to reach down and feel the head of your baby emerging. This, compounded with the stimulation of the third gate clitoris, can bring a sense of orgasmic innocence, purity and joy. A woman can ride this wave through the climax of intensity, physically and emotionally, through to birth.

In these final moments, sometimes the urge arises to push. Pushing before this point can cause damage to tissues, not allowing the yoni to fully open and bloom of its own timing aligned with baby and hormones. Sometimes we push to avoid feeling a deeper discomfort of intensity. In the choice to surrender rather than push, a woman allows the experience of birth to happen *through* her, not *from* her.

There is something profound that happens when she softens and allows organic movement to move baby. This trust in herself, in her body in birth, in the journey, releases any trace of resistance or force, to relax into the magnitude of momentum moving through her. This is how, in birth, she ultimately lets go and lets God.
This is what truly enables us to inhabit our increasing capacities. In this simple distinction between action and surrendered action, we take our seat at the center of our world. The gravity of our being in alignment with that which is beyond us allows everything to move in accordance around us.

In the next few surges, yoni blooms baby into the outer world for the first time. The next few moments are a surreal time, when the child has not yet taken his first human breath, but has left incubation deep within its mother.

In these moments, parents can Call their children in, through sounding their soul song, through sound and toning, through touch, through eye gazing, through your love and tears. Anchoring them by sounding their name vibration at this point invites them to arrive into their first breath and become human.

THE GOLDEN HOURS

The Golden Hours are the first hours after a child has arrived on earth, and is a time of deep emotional and spiritual bonding. From a biological perspective, bonding is the process by which a secure attachment is formed which ensures the continued care necessary for the survival and growth of the new baby. It is the time when the hormone of oxytocin is peaking in mother and child. This facilitates bonding on deep physiological and somatic levels. The child is present and awake, and all three souls can commune through touch, hugs, holding, eye contact and sound.

From a soul's perspective, this first 'in-bodied 'welcoming, this first meeting with your child face-to-face, skin-to-skin, touch-to-touch, eye-to-eye, is a profound moment for feeling and imprinting love, welcome, safety, care and trust. The more welcomed and received a child feels in this first hour, the more directly their energetic field will anchor in the earth's magnetic field, literally anchoring their soul and emotional body to the planet. The awe and wonder is almost surreal. Everyone is a bit besides themselves, incredulous, happy, relieved, exhausted, inspired and in a cocoon of love. Everyone has been through a major journey of an enormous amount of primordial energy, deep connection, love and bliss.

In music, the space between notes are just as important as the notes themselves in creating a song. In breathing, the space between the breaths allows you to deepen into stillness. In meditation, the spaces between your thoughts allow you to rest in the silence. In many spiritual practices, when you have generated a lot of energy, it is as important to rest and deepen after it as in actually doing the practice itself. It is in this rest, this space between, where you reap the benefit of what you have sowed before. All your labours bloom and bear fruit.

In the Golden Hours you harvest the fruits of your labours. Yes, you have birthed baby. BUT, this is now a reaping time for mother and father too. Your initiations, your Rite of Passages, become more embodied in you in the Golden Hours. With mother, father, child and guides present in these hours of new life and a new pathway in life for you, you assimilate what has just happened on a cellular, emotional and spiritual level. All three of you Rest in an extraordinary bubble of light and love, enjoying everything that has just happened. You can now finally let go.

In this letting go, something happens with all three of you. Your electromagnetic fields morph and change, resetting itself to a new harmonic that includes all three of you in a mutual bond. This creates a third electromagnetic field, made up of aspects of all three of you. A new frequency grounds on earth and into all three of you. More Bonding occurs.
In love-making, magnetic fields are released from the woman who has been loved, who has opened, who has orgasmed deeply, who is deeply satisfied. These magnetic fields are important for man and woman to rest in after making love, as it is here that deeper emotional intimacy and bonding occur through our magnetics, our feeling bodies. It is here we become closer.

In birthing we go into similar states with our magnetic fields amplified. This is a potent field of creation that is very alive, juicy and coursing in the flows of creation itself. Everything is sensitized and this maybe the time when you have felt the most alive ever. Here you are connected to yourself in a new way, and connected to the pulse of life that courses throughout all beings in the web of life.

In the Golden Hours after birth, honor your baby's senses. Keep the lights dim, the room quiet and warm, and engage in skin-to-skin contact with both parents. Allow baby to smell you both. All of this will allow your child to gently shift into this new perspective outside the womb. The more gentle, caring and gradual this transition is, the more trust, confidence, and adaptability your child can potentially carry in the rest of their life.

The Golden Hours come after The Golden Spiral has revealed the magic of the very movements of creation through a woman's body. The new field or Golden Sphere created by the birthing is the manifesting of the Golden Spiral into a cohesive Sphere around all three of you. Love creates the most coherent and harmonious forms, geometries and feelings.

It is this harmony made manifest, infinity brought into form in harmonious order, that Birth reveals. This Golden Ratio Sphere activates when all three souls rest together. This Sphere is made of activated life force, hormonal cascades, love, bliss and peace. It is the culmination of your entire nine-month journey. All the energies that have been unleashed in labour coagulate and settle down into a new form. You three are that new form, and you are now changing and integrating this on biological, emotional and electromagnetic levels.

The Golden Hours are a time for the peace of love in the cocooned presence of mother, father and child. Let yourselves rest completely and totally in this. Be alone as a family together and enjoy!

THE PLACENTA and UMBILICAL CORD

'At the moment a baby is born, a third of its blood is still outside of its body in the cord and placenta. If you delay cord clamping by 90 seconds, they receive 50% more blood cells. They get enough iron to last a whole year. They get stem cells to repair their bodies.'
Dr. Alan Greene

The lotus interim period is the time between the birth of your child and the dropping away of the umbilical cord. The birth process is only complete after the dropping away of the umbilical cord and the subsequent Placenta Ceremony, for this closure seals the physical, emotional, energetic and spiritual experiences of labour.

The Placenta Ceremony allows integration for mother, father and child as the umbilical cord and placenta of your child, which was his/her second mother for the previous nine months, connects to them both. Without an integration of the birthing process and loving reconnection of the energetic umbilical cord to both parents, allied with reflection upon the birth-story and the profound experiences that have just happened, an aspect of mother, father and baby can remain stuck in the birth experience.

This can fragment aspects of the nervous system and soul of all three people involved. When all three souls have received all the pieces from birth and integrated them into themselves, all three can embody more, and move forward to share the gifts gleaned.

The placenta holds a tone of energy for father, mother and child to integrate the first few days after birth before the cord is cut. The placenta is the child's 'first mother', an aspect of the mother's innate energy. By sitting with this deep mothering feminine energy after birth she grows into a part of herself that is necessary for nurturing and loving the child.

The placenta is the first magnetic foundation for a fetus. It holds an aspect of the integral intelligence for a soul's embodiment into form. It is important not to separate the placenta from the child until both the physical and emotional transference has completely taken place.

One can energetically feel when the energy has left the umbilical cord; it will first be felt as a dense presence in the cord and placenta, and then become less dense, its energy beginning to rise up to a few centimeters above the physical mass.

When the wisdom of the placenta has been received by the mother (both as a cognition of qualities and an energetic transference) the cord can be cut. This is most natural approximately two-three days after birth, when the mother's milk replaces the colostrom (bringing deeper nourishment on a physical level) and the umbilical cord becomes brittle and lifeless. Often this is accompanied with what has been labeled as post partum syndrome, but this is a natural grief and clearing arising from the release of placenta and child.

The umbilical cord and placenta have both been intimate parts of your body for the last nine months. They have been part of you! In releasing this grief, the mother begins a natural process of re-inhabiting her womb, which is now carrying more light and a higher frequency. This is a natural time to record the birth story, which helps father and mother to integrate the experience of the birth. Once this integration has happened, and the ceremony is done, the birth process is completed. After this time the placenta and cord can be buried in the earth.

OUR FIRST CONNECTION, OUR FIRST SEPARATION

The placenta sustains and nurtures you within the womb until you are ready to step out into this world. Placenta and baby both arise from the very same cell, the fertilized ovum, and in one sense that makes the baby and the placenta one, sharing the same etheric field.

The placenta is the first mother to baby. It is our first connection, our first relationship to this world, our first nourisher, supporter, and companion. It feeds us and offers us all we need to grow. Our sustainer and protector, the placenta provides us with our first experience of unconditional love: it is our first love. When we are cut off from this first source of loving nourishment and care prematurely, it leads us to seek and need love from a place of desperation, loneliness and insecurity outside of our own selves.

Needing love is different to desiring it. As an adult, when we need love, it often leads us into making unhealthy relationship choices, life styles and ways of beings. To desire love is natural as an adult, as it does not come from a grasping, an insecurity, a loneliness, and a sense of something missing within us that forces us to look outside to fill the gap within.

Sadly, this is what happens to almost all of us when the umbilical cord is cut, because we are separated too soon from the life force and etheric-emotional connections that still pulse through the cord. This cutting usually happens straight after birth, before the placenta has transferred its immune-boosting physical nurturance which is upto one third of our blood supply, and before the emotional nurturing qualities of the placenta transfers to us.

Before the moment of cutting the cord, placenta, womb, baby, and mother are one. When the cord is cut, we experience separation maybe for the first time in our tiny body-minds. The loss and abandonment that we can experience as we enter this world, brutally and prematurely cut off from the nurturing, unconditionally loving envelope of the placenta, can also create shock and fear.

As an adult, you can heal this separation within yourself through a placenta healing, the power of which thousands of men and women who have experienced it can testify to. Indeed, this chapter is based on the experiences that many of these men and women have had with the placenta healing method, which connects the umbilical cord to the soul of the parents, *and* back to Source.

The effects of this healing can be both "wonderful and frightening," as D.K. reports. For him, it felt *"at first as if I was in the womb, surrounded by peace and love . . . a time before any thought. Then I experienced being born. The umbilical cord was cut and I experienced much fear and terror. I felt separate. I had a hard time catching my breath. Finally I was able to breathe through the fear and terror. Then again I felt the peace and love surrounding me, except this time it came from within, and not from without."*

The body-mind and soul feels how big this trauma is, for when we feel cut off from the umbilical cord, we feel cut off from the vital information of love. *"I feel my placenta is my own connection to the love of the universe, and a divine connection to other human beings. It's my first connection to universal, unconditional love."* SR.

When the placenta is cut off too early, we can experience a deep loneliness, sadness, emptiness and loss. When you are cut off from the feeling of love so early in life, many beliefs arise to fill this hole. For some people who have experienced the healing of their placenta, some of the beliefs they formed at the beginning of their lives included feelings of abandonment. One participant reported of her healing experience, *"I feel I could be abandoned every time I'm in relationship [so] I feel I have put on many subterfuges to not be abandoned. "*DM

As R.M. put it, *"The following day I literally fell in love with myself! It was a very new feeling to me. . . . I don't know how to explain it but I felt there wasn't a separation anymore between me and myself. I used to feel disconnected with who I am, not really accepting who I am. I felt I was back into myself. I wasn't harsh to myself anymore. . . . I was kind to myself."*

The healing of this separation can re-evoke in us the cellular memory of being connected, of being nurtured by Mother. This memory can re-gift us with a feeling of security about life, our own loving and nurturing capacities, and feeling ready to be vulnerable and enter more satisfying intimate relationships. Feelings of warmth, kindness, and gentleness return to this part of ourselves that has been forgotten and un-nurtured.

As M.C. put it, *"The energy that pulses through the cord from the placenta is the Mother nourishing us. It is neither wholly our biological mother's nor ours alone, but something that connects us to one another and to the Divine Mother. This divine energy is transferred to us, into our bodies by the mother through the placenta. Regardless of how our biological mothers feel or who they are, the Divine wants us to thrive more than anything.*

The energy we receive while in the womb is what brings Spirit into us. It is the part that can save us from destroying everything. It is possibly as close as we can get to Spirit before our souls are fully awakened. It is, in effect, a great mystery and miracle. The Divine Mother is in and around all of us—we all have the most wonderful mother, as loving as we can imagine and beyond."

EARTH'S CORD

In Cambodia, the placenta is known as "the globe of the origin of the soul" and for the Maori it is te whenua—the land which nourishes the people, just as the physical earth does. Mother, child, and land are all intimately interconnected from birth itself, each nourishing the other. 27 When one is looked after, the other benefits also. This living connection sustains the vital personal and soul link between the land and the child, and between human soul, physical body, and life force.

The Māori word for land, *whenua,* also means placenta. All life is seen as being born from the womb under the sea. The lands that appear above water are placentas from her womb. They float, forming islands. All life takes place within the womb of the world. In that womb, preparations are made for a new world. We are children within the womb of the world, soon to be born into another reality.

The place where one's umbilical cord is severed is a place of special importance for each person. It is their place of first emergence into the world, of first maturation and *foundation.* 28

When this connection is not honored, life itself is not respected, and mother, child, and land all suffer. A conscious way of honoring the connection between placenta and child includes not cutting the cord, letting it fall off naturally. It can later be buried underground, while the whole family connects to the land through ceremony. By these practices, the living threads of energy that interconnect and sustain us, our communities, and our planet are woven together in a web of life and love.

In healing umbilicus trauma, we can trigger our body's cellular memory and reconnect with the cord of love that roots us in Gaia. As S.M. shares, "My body was heavy . . . going into the earth. As I sat with this energy I was visited by three indigenous souls—the longer I sat quietly, the deeper the stillness, the deeper the peace, the more connected into body and earth I became . . . very nurturing and blessed."

In many sacred traditions, the placenta is seen as a twin soul, or double. The Baganda of Uganda believe that the placenta is actually the child's double, which has its own soul that resides in the umbilical cord. Ancient Egyptian Pharaohs believed one soul inhabited the body, while another inhabited the placenta. It was the job of this placental soul to act as the child's guardian from birth; the placenta was thus a valued part of each child, not separate or useless. In Egyptian ceremonies, the placenta was paraded in front of the Pharaoh on its own separate chariot, leading the way in front of the Pharaoh.

In the Old Testament the placenta was thought to be the external soul. The placenta gives us our first experience on Earth of a 'twin' soul. When the trauma of separation from it is

---

[27] The Golden Hours are the first part of truly cementing this connection of inter dependence, into the Web of Life.

[28] http://www.teara.govt.nz/en/papatuanuku-the-land/page-4

healed, we can find this connection within ourselves, rather than feeling compelled to find it outside. We find a source of nourishment and inner peace within ourself.

RECONNECTING THE CORD

Deep emotion and tears are common during and after an umbilicus healing, as are physical discharges from the womb, fatigue, fever, headaches, womb cramping, and physical pains and stiffness. These are all symptoms of release, because the severing of the cord has created a false body attitude in us. Our body learns to compensate for this loss from this early age, adapting strategies and postures to compensate, just as our emotional bodies adapt to this rip in our tender structures.

In prematurely cutting the umbilical cord, we feel loss, and we all adjust, cope and compensate to this loss in some way. All compensation masks unsafety, insecurity and neediness; we then try and compensate and cover this loss through adopting various masks and facades. It is this sense of loss that motivates us to seek, need and demand love from outside and create these masks covering our vulnerability.

These symptoms arise because of this split between body-mind and soul, and is healed by the reintroduction of the soft, enveloping feeling of the placenta's nurturing energy being felt and remembered on the physical level, which creates shifts in conjunction with the body's innate wisdom. As H.T. put it, *"I feel I'm making peace with my physical body."*

When the energetic cause of this false attitude is removed, the body-mind and soul can return to its natural state. After a placenta healing, many people feel a new sense of wellness in their bodies. Expanded states of peace arise, bringing a feeling that something has finally come to rest deep within: the cord that was cut has now been reconnected back to its source.

L.P. described the experience as *"very soft, flowing very sweet, gentle but powerful, and cleared out a lot of samskaras."*

As C.O. recounts, *"It felt as my womb felt after giving birth, as an emptying without the intense contractions, a warmth of the flow of something, similar to the bleeding in menses. In my emotional body there was the sense of letting go of something that has been with me my entire physical life."*

"Remembering this essence on a cellular level is like a "deep basking in the inner light—very sweet. I am becoming significantly less engaged with external drama ... getting triggered by the world around me far less. I am experiencing lovely feelings of contentment and a sense of being supported by my own Source—the inner light feels near and accessible. I also seem to have had a breakthrough in terms of my tendencies to judge those around me." (D.W.)

"Recurrent feelings of shame, self-judgment and worthlessness are simply gone. I do not react to triggers with an automatic response anymore." (U.C.)

The placenta healing can aid the psychosomatic healing of family and ancestral issues that linger on into our adult lives. For U.C., who had done a lot of healing around her mother issues but was unable to break through some of her inherited family dysfunctions, *"healing the placenta also means healing the information that was passed from mother to child in utero. The relief I now feel from this healing is indescribable. I feel that I can now move on and get out into the world in action . . . so that feels like being born, quite simply."*

In many births, the balance between the energetic and the physical is disrupted by the removal of the placenta and umbilical cord while the energetic cords continue to hold connection to the child's spirit and soul. In order to complete this unfinished part of the process of whole birth, we have to heal the energetic placenta, reconnect the cord, and then let go of it consciously. Bringing resolution to the spirit-placenta disconnection means that both the child's soul and the mother's soul are free to rest, restore, and regenerate Shakti.

You can remedy the placenta disconnection through gentle natural birth practices for your own children. When allowance is given for the umbilical cord to drop away naturally after birth, all the life force of the placenta gets transferred along the cord to the baby, and the etheric field around baby and placenta is sealed off properly. This complete field results in a stronger immune system and a baby who feels safe, loved, nurtured, respected, and balanced.

Such a child is ready to make the step into this world in a safe, secure way that suits its own rhythms. By honoring the placenta, you can help your children avoid a life programmed by the fears of scarcity, loss, insecurity and a grasping for love that so many of us have experienced. According to midwives who participate in Lotus Births, such as the births shared in the book Sacred Birthing by Sunni Karil, children who have not had their umbilical cord cut prematurely are more peaceful, less disruptive, more centred and better behaved.

The feeling of softness, nurture, comfort, and being held gently yet powerfully in an Umbilical healing reintroduces this frequency and feeling back to our body-mind and soul, uniting them. If this is done properly, the child, who is within the mother's auric field for the first seven years of life, can release this deep attachment in a healthy way.

As this happens, the mutual field that baby and mother share diminishes until the child is within itself, with its own free will fully developed by age twentyone. The child can remain unhealthily corded with separation anxiety with the mother for longer than this, for many of the reasons shared above.

WOMB, PLACENTA AND GALACTIC CENTER

"I feel my placenta is my own, prototypal connection to the love of the universe, and to a divine connection to other human beings. It's my first connection to universal and unconditional love." M.P.

Cords connect us all, from the first cord between mother and baby to the cords between the chakras, the cords of relationship that connect us to other people, and the cords that connect us to earth. Earths leylines or dragon lines keep the routes of communication alive between us and Gaia, an acupuncture network crisscrossing the planet in intricate geometric grids and patterns.

In the last centuries on Earth, many of these cords and connective pathways have been damaged because of our abuse of the earth, much of it borne from our own traumatic and premature separation from the placenta and womb, which acts as our first instinctual, primordial and love based connection to Earth.

This is one reason why the Hawaiian, Maori, African and many other tribes worldwide have let the cord fall away naturally and buried the placenta and cord in a special spot to the tribe and family in the earth. They have kept their living connection to the earth alive.

The traumatic severing of the umbilical cord has wide ranging and profound effects on the development of the human psyche, and how that plays out on the planet. These events are recorded in the collective human consciousness and the earth herself, and have damaged our natural and innate connection to the leylines connecting us to Earth.

If we are birthed naturally and connected to Earth from the beginning of our lives, this connection will always be with us. This connection also feeds the earth as much as earth supports us. It is a two-way communication.

These cords or leylines connect us to ourselves, our parents and ancestors, the Earth, and through the web of life to the planets and the Milky Way Galaxy. At the center of our Milky Way Galaxy lies a massive black hole. The size of our galaxy—and of other galaxies—is inextricably intertwined with the size of the black hole in the galaxy; the bigger the black hole, the bigger the galaxy. Scientists and cosmologists are now saying that black holes birthed our galaxy, and possibly even our universe.

The Womb Centre of our Galaxy emanates out superstring cords of vibration and resonance, resembling the spiraling structure of DNA, which nourish and connect all within its system, just as umbilical cords from our mothers connect to us. These cords connect us all to the black hole at the center of our galaxy—the Galactic Womb. Astronomers discovered this black hole in 2002, yet its presence, importance, and connection to Source have been known to the Mayans, Indians and Egyptians for thousands of years.

The Mayans call this cord of connection *Kuxan Suum*, a lifeline of vibration and communication connecting us from our navels through a spiraling energetic umbilical cord to the Galactic Center, the womb of creation. In India, this umbilical cord or Tortoise Tube connects the God *Vishnu* through his lotus-shaped navel into the *Padmanabhi*, the Galactic Center, where he dreams creation into being. In Egypt, the God *Khonsu* acts as the umbilical cord to the Galactic Center, where the all-powerful "hidden" Creator God *Amun* resides.

All these traditions tapped into the Galactic Center through the womb in ways that were known to their shamanic seers, high priestesses and kings, all of whom were initiated into these mysteries so they could ride the *Kuxan Suum* to Galactic Center. Through the Galactic Center they could enter other dimensions, and access knowledge about the mysteries of life and death.

This was also done for the benefit of their societies, to keep them in alignment with the flow of life force and the web of life that connects all life everywhere, to maintain this flow of love, and to evolve and develop their own connection to the center and source of creation.

All cords start at this place, our first connection to the womb. Cords connect us all, human to human, human to earth, human to galaxy, human to source. When we heal and reconnect these cords, following them all the way to Galactic Center, we become fully connected and whole in the web of life.

The Galactic Center is not accessed through the mind, but through your primordial creative center of womb and hara. Once the connection is established, it is always there. The womb and hara are our direct connection points to the Galactic Center and beyond. Each individual womb or hara is the gateway into this space. The Galactic Center is not only outside of us: it is within the dreaming space of our hearts and wombs united. Each person has this connection within, and each person can activate it.

The Galactic Center is the source of this galaxy, the place from which this galaxy was birthed. Where the galactic Equator crosses the ecliptic (the apparent line of the Sun's annual motion relative to the stars), Sagittarius points directly towards the Galactic Center. To observers on Earth, this appears as a dark road that begins near the ecliptic and stretches along the Milky Way.

Mayan creation myths describe creation taking place at this celestial crossroads, called *The Road to Xibalba*, the underworld, or the "Black Road." Through this entrance to the underworld road, one can travel upto the heart of the sky, the Galactic Center. In the ancient Mayan village of *Santiago Atitlan*, the villagers call their sacred site *umuxux kaj, u muxux ulep* (navel of the sky, navel of the earth), the place where all creation began at the center of the galaxy. To this day, women there, wear headdresses called the rainbow serpent, a representation of the serpentine umbilical cord connecting each person with this Source in the heavens.

The serpent has great importance to the Mayans and Aboriginals as a symbol of Shakti, DNA, and the waves of resonance connecting one thing to another. The serpent is also a symbol of the umbilical cord, the connection between placenta and mother.

The Galactic womb is where all humans have come from, and the place to which we shall all return. It is the source of a river of Shakti which unifies all parts of yourself. The wisdom and loving power of Galactic Center streaming towards earth accelerates our evolutionary process, as it reconnects us to our first breath, our first cellular division that occurs when one becomes two. The Galactic Center is where male and female are in union in an infinite space of fertile possibility, rich in every potential. It is the highest Tantra.

The Galactic Center is a vast yet intimate space, peaceful but incredibly creative and brimming with fertile vibration in a state of dynamic stillness. It is a ground of being, still yet teeming with the potential of all life within it, containing an almost infinite potential of bliss and the power of creativity within itself.

Most people who experience a reunion with the Galactic Center describe it as unconditionally loving, accepting and supporting of every part of themselves. In this sense it is our mother, the Galactic Womb that nourishes us. The return of this energy to human awareness and consciousness is also the return of the Mother in all her glory. It is the homecoming.

Your heart and your womb/hara are the gateway to the Galactic Center. It is here that all grids and reconnections to the web of life are grounded, and it is here that our ultimate reconnection lies. In this process, we have to learn to live in the present, bringing every part of ourselves back together again, weaving ourselves back into the web of life. In doing so, we become conscious co-creators and live our soul's purpose fully, giving freely of our gifts.

CEREMONY: RECONNECTING UMBILICAL CORD

Part 1: MEDITATION

Mother is deeply open and sensitized at this point in time, 3-4 days after giving birth. She does not need much to enter an expanded state of consciousness. Mother sits comfortably in a meditative space with baby and placenta in her lap. Father holds her from behind-he has her back. She can lean on him for support. He holds her gently yet is seated in his power and pillar.

Both of you: breathe deeply into your womb/hara, root chakra at the base of your spine., and feet chakras on the middle of the soles of your feet for a few minutes.

Drop down through this connected breathing to connect to the center of the earth. Keep breathing and connecting. Ask to be led into the gateway here into the galactic center.

Once you feel your womb/hara connect to this in a felt shift, keep doing the connected breathing from Galactic Centre, Earths Womb, your feet, womb/hara *into your crown*. On each inhale extend from your crown upwards to galactic centre, and on each exhale draw the energy from both directions to your heart and down to galactic centre.

Once you feel an alignment, move to the seed of your heart, just below your ribcage in the center. From the seed of your heart, connect to your baby's heart seed, as you have been doing throughout the pregnancy. When you feel this connection, say:

My Beloved Divine Mother, Divine Father, please send us your Divine Love.
(repeat x3)
Now: holding your child and the placenta, scan through the experience of the birth. Are there any memories or aspects that still hold an emotional charge? Breathe through and release them as you do this.

Say: *My Beloved Divine Mother, Divine Father, please help us feel and release any pain, grief, fear, or anger from our birth experience. My Beloved Guides, Please hold us in this transition from First Mother (placenta) to Human Mother. Please help me embody the purity and frequency of my placental wisdom. My Beloved Divine Mother, Divine Father, Thank you, for your Divine Love, and for all the gifts in our life. Thank you. Amen.*

Sit as long as needed, until Mother feels integrated.

Then move onto part 2, to be done with both mother and father.

Part 2: CEREMONY

Prepare the bathtub with warm water. You will need a pair of sterilized scissors nearby to cut the umbilical cord. Burn sage and smudge all participants.

Mother holds the child in the water, making sure the cord and navel are completely immersed; after a few minutes it will soften. Pour some water over your child's crown, third eye, throat, and heart. When he/she has relaxed, father can recite the following prayers inserting the child's name where indicated.

My Beloved Divine Mother, Divine Father. Please send us your Divine Love. My Beloved Birthing Guides, Mother God, please guide (name) in his/her graceful and full arrival onto earth now. Please help him/her release all spiritual, emotional, energetic, and physical bonds with this placenta. Please help (name) now bond more deeply with us.

Beloved Divine Mother, Divine Father, Holy Opener of the Infinite Way! Please open all the Ways for (name) to Be in Source on Mother Earth now!

Beloved Mother Earth, please ground (name) soul with his/her physical body and Earth. Help us finish what we have started.

Beloved Mother Earth, Please manifest more of Your Divine Love and Divine Will into us and our Physical World. Please help (name) win the first initiation of Ascension. Please guide us to shape our world into more love and more truth. Thank You Beloved for our Body-world! Amen.

Now it is time to cut the cord. Bring the scissors about an inch from the child's navel. Keep your fingers between the scissors and your baby, and squeeze the cord tightly. Cut the cord, and keep the fingers squeezed to keep any energy from leaking out.

Take the baby out of the tub, and allow him to nurse. You can sprinkle goldenseal herb onto the cord and navel to keep it free of bacteria. In a few days the remaining cord will drop off, keep the area dry and clean in the meantime.

To further help spirit ground in the child, first hold the base of their occiput bone (where the skull meets the neck), then with one foot at a time, hold the little toe and the center sole of the foot. These points help the child to renegotiate boundaries and space (after leaving the gentle confinement of the womb), and also address many common symptoms related to this, such as colic.

Mother, father and child can remain in a quiet space together afterwards for the rest of the day, to allow integration and bonding. Try not to see anyone else at this time, go out, or do anything too active out of the sanctity and nest of your own home. It is recommended to do the practice of *Running the Light* later in the day.

PART 4:
THE FOURTH TRIMESTER

40 DAYS OF BEING

We are at our most tender, open and sensitive after birth. We have been opened biologically, sexually, emotionally and spiritually beyond our believed capacities, and it warrants gentleness, nurturing, connection and slowness to call all the parts of our being back into our new reconfiguration.

Just as we hold and care for the new born baby in our arms, so we must care for the parts of us that are newly born, vulnerable and seeing the world through fresh eyes. After-birth care is vital for the new mother to regain her psychological and soulful sense of who she is, to become physically healthy again, and to embody more of her soul, all of which has changed throughout pregnancy and the birthing process.

The initiation and Rite of Passage you have just undertaken needs integration upon your Return. Just as you have Pre-Conception and pregnancy preparation to clear the way and ready yourself to become a conscious and loving parent, so there is a process after birth to integrate aspects of your new self-emerging.

REINHABITING THE WOMB

The following meditations can be gentle hand rails for a mother to gently integrate, gather, and emerge into herself.

This meditation can be done after the birth for as long as needed. It helps the mother reconnect with her sense of her own womb after the transition of birth, and integrate the higher embodied frequency that follows conscious birth into the rest of her being. [29]*It is important to re-establish tone and presence in the womb and yoni following birth.*

Lie down. Make yourself comfortable. Relax. Do some deep belly breathing, and connect each inhale with each exhale, with no gap in between. Deep, connected, continuous belly breathing. Let go of everything with each deep belly breath. Breathe like this for a few minutes until you feel more relaxed and a shift has happened in your consciousness.

Starting with your fingertips at the base of your pubic bone, slowly draw the womb up with your fingers toward your navel 10 times, stretching the cervical ligaments at its base.

Now, cross the hands, fingers pointing down at a 45-degree angle, and draw the hands toward each other, gently wrapping the womb and holding her supportively. Hold her gently and firmly with your hands whilst breathing gently but deeply from your womb in a deep, connected, continuous belly breathing.

---

[29] *The Liquid Crystal Chrysocolla can be used while invoking the Master Deva Chrysoel. This can aid in accessing and connecting to the deep quiet space of the womb, and helps to tone the tissue after birth.*

Connect your heart to your womb through *a golden infinity loop* whilst breathing. Feel your wombs texture, feel her frequency, now, without child, without placenta, without the big belly you have had for nine months! Feel her essence.

Hold yourself in your two pulses, your two feminine centers, of womb and heart. Feel them together. Allow yourself to hold, and be held. Feel the comfort of being yourself again, yourself but now different: more embodied, more womanly, more here, more in your body, more alive.

Now, whilst breathing, cast your mind back into the labour and birth process: feel into all the memories, all the sensations, all the events, the people there, how they were, the joys, the bliss, the pains, how you felt, how the baby felt in your womb, how your womb and yoni felt, how your seven gates felt, how your body felt, how your sexual energy felt, how your heart felt at different times.

Feel any thoughts, disharmonies, hardness, sharpness, shards of pain, or any remaining emotions from the birth.

Breathe into them all. Feel them, release them.
Keep breathing. Allow yourself to surrender down deep into her. Be held by her. Be enveloped by her love.

Now, extend your breath deep down into the core of the earth. Feel the silence and stillness here. Now extend it to the Galactic Center, the black hole of our universe. Feel the resonance here echoed in your own womb. Feel your innate connection to this place of the emanation of all creation.

As you sink in more deeply, tune into the womb within, and the womb 'outside'. *They are the same. You are simultaneously in the space of holding and being held.*

Now pray, from the seed of your heart and your womb:
"My Beloved Divine Mother, please send me your Divine Love."
(add anything else you feel to pray for specifically relative to your womb)

Bring your awareness back to the comforting infinity loop between your heart and womb. Sit in this space as long as you feel, allowing any thoughts and emotions to be felt, embraced and released.

As one mother shares: *Last night I felt such a deep weight in my chest I almost couldn't breathe. I could smell the placenta strong, it was like She filled up the entire space. When I breathed into this weight, I felt intense pain in my womb, where the placenta had been. It felt like we were mourning the loss of Her. It was very heavy.*

I just breathed into the space like during birth, expanding myself in every direction. I began the Reinhabiting the Womb exercise and fell asleep holding my womb. This morning I felt something had cleared, the energy and heaviness was gone. As i woke up and picked my baby up to give her milk, she pooped and kicked her cord at the same time. Felt like a big release for us all.'

WEAVING THE NEW MOTHER INTO UNITY THROUGH THE ELEMENTS

In labour all the elements of body and spirit are powerfully spun into different cycles because of the intense forces that mother had to surrender to. All the elements of earth, air, fire, water and space are flung into a new order, a new pattern, at a higher frequency if the birth is conscious and joyful.

If the birth is traumatic, induced, drug led and painful, the configuration of the elements within the biology and spirit still change, but down into a lower frequency, leading to potential depression, post partum emotions, fatigue, lethargy and a general loss of self.

The element of space or ether shifts too within you. The spaces between the cells, the spaces between thoughts, the spaces of consciousness, the space within the body itself, will become larger and more spacious. It is this space that the new mother can move into and inhabit, embodying more of her presence and soul. These spaces within the new mother shift during birth, as well as the magnetic foundation and womb space of the new mother. *Everything changes.*

The elements are the building blocks of nature, the universe, and our bodies. Without the dynamic interplay and dance of the elements, creation would be an amorphous sea of light with no form. You, me, your baby, your partner, would not be here!

Living with the elements in harmony and order is the basis of most healing systems like Chinese Medicine and Ayurveda from India, amongst others. In order for the new mother to integrate and adjust herself to this new octave of her body, mind and soul, she has to reconnect to all the elements, if possible within eleven days of birth.

In this process, you are integrating the 'new you'! You are getting to know the new you in a fundamental manner, pre-verbal, pre-thought, in your instinctive and intuitive self. This re-connection to the elements will become part of your new foundation for life and love, providing a basis upon which to raise your child and cement your new family unit into place.

To attune to the 'New You 'through the elements after birth we do:

Earth Embrace
Fire Ceremony
Air Immersion
Water Baptism
Space Cleansing

EARTH'S EMBRACE

A deeply healing action a new mother can do is to be buried in the earth or sand for three hours, ideally at dawn or at twilight. If not, any comfortable time is good. In these hours, she will receive the full support of Mother Earth and will be nourished, nurtured, woven and integrated into the next higher octave of her new connection to Gaia.

In this process, she can connect to the womb of Earth, gateway to the Galactic Centre. As she does, she will receive profound nourishment in a very tangible, physical, spiritual and soulful way. There may be some deep detoxing, catharsis, healing, bliss, and profound movements of energy, so it is loving and wise for mother to have father there the whole time.

There are sacred sites and Centers where this can be done, OR you can have someone dig the hole for you in your back garden or in a sacred site of your choosing, preferably where there are ley-lines. To do this is quite simple.

A vertical hole wide enough and deep enough to accommodate the new mother is dug into the earth. When she eases herself down into this hole, she will be standing up BUT totally supported by the earth with just her head free. She will not have to use a single physical muscle to be held upright, and it will be quite comfortable and relaxing. The new mother is in the earth itself, supported and cuddled on all sides.

When the new mother has become comfortable in her space and feeling with the earth, she can begin to go deeper.

Begin by: Centering in the Seed Center of your heart. Do some gentle Heart Seed Breathing.

Now, from the Center and seed of your heart, feel: the beauty of this sacred spot on earth. Feel your love for it, and expand it to all of nature, all of Mother Earth.
Say, '*I love you Mother Earth. Please send me your love,*' x3. When you feel this love fully, say '*Beloved Mother Earth, please send me your love.*' x3
Wait for this love to return. It always will.
Say these prayers whenever you feel to, throughout the time you are in Earth's Embrace.

Pray, "*Beloved Divine Mother, Blessed, Holy, Sacred Shekinah and all nature, I love You. Help me heal and re-whole myself from my birth. Help me integrate into the next higher octave of my Self, here on Earth, for the benefit of all beings!*"
Say this prayer whenever you feel to, throughout the time you are in Earth's Embrace.

Now: start the infinity loop breathing from your heart-womb down into the womb of the Earth, weaving yourself through breath and prayer into this primal unity.

Stay in this space, and now connect to Beloved Divine Father. Feel the beauty, vastness, the wonder, the shining purity of the sun, the stars, the thousands of galaxies. Feel your awe, wonder and love for Father's creation.

Say, "*Beloved Divine Father, I love You!*" x3
When you feel this love fully, send this love up to the Sun.
Now say, '*Beloved Divine Father, please send me your love.*' x3.
Wait for the love to return. It always will.

Pray, "*Beloved Divine Father, please send me Your Divine Love. Beloved, bring me into Source. Let my physical body receive the DNA Re-codings and support from my Beloved, Blessed, Holy Mother Shekinah! Help me be One with You, Beloved!*"

At this moment you are now connected in love with Mother Earth, and connected in love with all Creation. [30]

---

[30] *Thank you to Drunvalo Melchizedek and Sri Yuketeswar for this meditation.*

WATER CEREMONY: SACRED BATHING RITUAL

For thousands of years we have engaged in the sacred and sensual ritual of bathing in the earth's pure rivers, lakes and oceans. When we become naked in the waters of nature, we can consciously align ourselves with our own fluids of breast milk, tears and yoni juices.

For a new mother to stand ankle deep in the waters of the earth and gently sponge her body with pristine, living water helps weave her back into the liquid support and nourishment from her earthly mother. For her to fill a jug from a natural spring and drink it, allows her cells to receive a deep and intimate intelligence from Gaia's breast.

It is ideal to do this in a natural river, stream, lake or ocean. If this is not possible it can be done in a bathtub at home with added rose essence.

Stand naked in ankle or knee-deep water. Using a natural sponge, or having your partner do this, lean over and gently sponge the water up your legs to the inner edge of your thigh, using long and sensual strokes.

Allow yourself to really receive the water, feel it's temperature, texture, and energy.

If the water is clean, bring the sponge to your yoni lips, and gently invite the energy in. Follow your intuition as to what to do next. You may stroke the rest of your body with this water. *It is not medically advisable to fully immerse in water for a long period of time straight after birth.*

REPEAT the words, "I AM LOVE,' as you bathe yourself with the water. Keep caressing your body, all the way up to your face with the sponge and fresh water.

Next, using natural spring water sourced directly from earth, fill up a glass jug of water. Holding the water between your hands, repeat the mantra, "I AM LOVE," charging the water with this vibration. As you drink the water, feel it moving into your cells, nourishing, hydrating and blooming them into their fullness.

When we are birthed into our next frequency through giving birth, our inner fluids also shift. When we connect them to earth's waters post birth, we re-enact the infinity loop of nurturing with Earth Mother that helps sustain us in caring for a new child.

WATER MEDITATION 2

The following meditation can be done in the bath, in a pool, or the ocean.

Take a few deep breaths into your heart.
Touch into your appreciation of the water element, and offer the following prayer from your heart and your feeling body.

I feel and appreciate the water element within,
in my blood,
my lymph,
my yoni juices,
my sweat,
my tears,
my breast milk.

I feel and appreciate the water element,
As the conduit of connection for my emotional bonds,
With my child,
My partner,
My parents,
My friends.

I feel and appreciate the water element without,
The rain,
The ocean,
The rivers,
The lakes,
The snow,
The clouds.

I feel and appreciate the water element
As the giver of life,
The quencher of thirst,
That washes our wounds and
Sanctifies our bodies.

I feel and appreciate the water element as me.

Sit silently in the water and feel your inner waters connecting with the outer waters. Allow yourself to be softened, sensualized, cleansed, and purified.

FIRE CEREMONY

Fire creates, warms, nurtures, transforms and dissolves. It is the element that carries a woman through the throes and intensity of birth, and yet can be extinguished by the aftermath of birth's energy storm. When our fire is blown out, we can feel depressed, dampened and disconnected to our passion, desire and essential life force. These are quintessential symptoms of post-partum depression.

Losing our internal fire is akin to a pilot light being blown out by the wind. The pilot light needs to be relit in order for the stove, the fuel for our inner alchemy, to engage again.

First we must *rekindle* our fire after the cyclone of fire energy brought on by birth. Second, once the flame is fanned, we use that energy to cleanse and dissolve all remaining residue from birth so we can be more present to who we are now. This is where the cleansing aspect of fire comes in, dissolving all that stands in the way of the deeper embodiment of our soul here on earth.

FLAME MEDITATION

Fire, our flame of desire, is housed deep in our heart. To rekindle this inner fire, sit in front of a candle or a real log fire *in the dark*. Gaze into the heart of the flame and connect to it from the seed of your heart; feel the seed of your heart, and send it to the flame, and then have the flame return into the seed of your heart. From your heart, feel the warmth, listen to the whisper of flame licking the stillness around it. Sit with it. Be with it. Breathe it in.

Watch as the flame dances before you, rising and reaching to become greater that it was an instant ago. Smell the heat, the burning atmosphere around it. Draw this fire into your heart through all your senses, allowing it to seek out the places deep within you waiting to ignite.

Once you feel an aspect of your inner flame relight, fan it gently and delicately with soft prayer.
'I love you Mother Earth. Please send me your love,' x3.
When you feel this love, say *'Beloved Mother Earth, please send me your love.'* x3
Say, *"Beloved Divine Father, I love You!"* x3
When you feel this love fully, say, *'Beloved Divine Father, please send me your love.'* x3.

Allow the warmth from this to fortify the flame of desire in your heart. Feel your love for yourself, for your new child. Feel the unique mothering force and feminine power behind this love, that motivates you into action.

After this fire has been relit in some way, move onto the second part of this practice.

BUILDING YOUR FIRE MEDITATION

This meditation was so profound for me I decided to do it every day for a week. It burned through much of my mental chatter, surface emotions I was spinning in, and touched some misunderstandings and beliefs within me.

After each meditation I felt centered, still, more connected and confident in my soul. Once I committed myself to doing the meditation every day for a week, it was as if all day long the beliefs and thoughts would line up, waiting for their release that evening in front of the fire.

I knew I was complete when, after a week, *my heart and mind felt still*. I had released all that needed to be released to rise into my next octave of being.

Build a fire in your fireplace or a fire pit outside. Have wood nearby to be able to add during your hour-long meditation. Sit comfortably and stare into the heart of the fire. Gaze into the heart of the flame and connect to it from the seed of your heart; feel the seed of your heart, and send it to the flame, and then have the flame return into the seed of your heart

Feel the warmth on your skin, smell the scent of the burning wood, listen to the crackle, and look deeply at the myriad of colors in the flames. Breathe and draw the fire into you, into your soul.

Next, pray from the seed of your heart,
"My Beloved Divine Mother, Divine Father, please send me your Holy Cleansing Fire."

Repeat this a few times until you feel the intensity of this fire within you.

For this hour-long journey, be a loving witness to all that is arising in you to be felt and released through the flames as you rise into re-inhabiting your own inner fire.

When it is complete, close the meditation by giving thanks to Source, to yourself, and to the fire for its gift of illumination and cleansing.

Note: Fire Mantras can be used here too.

AIR CEREMONY

For a woman to reconnect afresh with Air Element, find a spot in nature, on a hillside, mountain top or ocean side, with good, fresh air, quiet and privacy.

Lie on your back, knees up, hands resting lightly on your womb, and do some deeply relaxing, continuous, belly connected *womb breathing* in nature's fresh air. On each inhale allow the belly to rise up and expand, and on each exhale allow the air to leave the belly as it comes down. Continue this breath for 20 minutes. This breathing can release birth and pregnancy residues and can clear out any remaining debris and energies that still need to move and release.

You can also do a gentle version of Womb Breathing as mentioned previously.

SPACE CEREMONY

Human beings vibrate at 570 trillion HZ per second. This means that we are moving incredibly fast every single second of our lives - we are just not aware of it. We are vibration, and in the constantly vibrating, ever shifting web of waves that we are in is an exquisite and delicate dance of vibration creating the patterns that we are. This dance is happening all the time.

The spaces in-between this dance lie within you. These spaces of silence, of peace, of stillness, the spaces between your thoughts, the spaces between your in-breath and out-breath, the spaces between your words, increase the more we evolve. As the new mothers physical body changes, the body opens up.

Let us journey through the body into the spaces between.
Begin by lying down.

Take a few deep breaths and center into your womb. Relax and breathe deeply. Feel the outline of your physical body, from the tips of your toes to the top of your head. Become aware of a gentle flow of energy caressing the outline of your physical form.

Now, tune into your left palm chakra; feel the sensation there. Feel the pulse, the warmth, the energy flow. Breathe and bring this energy up your arm, into your forearm, left elbow joint, upper arm, left shoulder joint, left collarbone, and down to end gracefully at the heart.

Now, tune into your right palm chakra; feel the sensation there. Feel the pulse, the warmth, the energy flow. Breathe and bring this energy up your arm, into your forearm, right elbow joint, upper arm, right shoulder joint, right collarbone, and down to end gracefully at the heart.

Now, focus on your left ankle and breathe three times into it.
Focus on your right ankle, and breathe three times into it.
Focus on your Right knee, and breathe three times into it.
Focus on your left knee and breathe three times into it.
Focus on your Left hip, and breathe three times into it.
Focus on your right hip and breathe three times into it.
Focus on your right Shoulder joint, and breathe three times into it.
Focus on your left shoulder joint and breathe three times into it.
Focus on your right elbow and breathe three times into it.
Focus on your left elbow and breathe three times into it.
Focus on your right wrist, and breathe three times into it.
Focus on your left wrist and breathe three times into it.

End at the back of the neck and breathe three times deeply into here.

Now, imagine you are journeying through your cellular self. See the apparently solid structure of the body as nothing but a mass of tiny atoms vibrating. Zoom into one of these atoms. There are bright, tiny pinpricks of light called electrons whirling in a precise orbit around each atom.

Now, journey into the heart of the atom nucleus, which is empty, spacious, clear and clean. This is a black hole, within a nucleus that is surrounded by an endlessly rotating wave composed of innumerable frequencies meeting, dissolving, re-creating itself, and resonating with each other.

Breathe into this space, focus, and rest here.

ENTERING SPACE 2

Stand on the earth in bare feet, hips width apart, on a clear and starry night. In a slow, rhythmic, and internal motion begin spiraling your pelvis in an ascending spiral motion toward the heavens. This will replicate the similar birth spiral, but will be much slower, spacious and diffused.

As you move this spiral through your pelvis, inhale the stars into your body, exhale your essence into the stars. Continue with this until you feel no separation between yourself and the cosmos. This is quite easy after giving birth as women are very open and sensitized.

YONI REJUVENATION EXERCISES

These exercises have been practiced by Tantric practitioners for thousands of years to strengthen and circulate energy throughout the lower chakras as well as strengthening the internal yoni muscles. They are helpful during pregnancy and after birth to support the tissue, integrity, circulation of energy and presence in yoni. You can also work with a Yoni Egg. Working with the First Gate of the Yoni Lips with your partner is also very helpful for emotional and soulful integration IF you feel upto it.

Flex your PC muscles (vaginal and anal muscles) as if you are sucking your vagina and anus up into your body. Hold the flex as described, and then release and relax your muscles.

1) **Quick Flex**
Flex your PC muscle, hold for 2 seconds, and then completely relax the muscle. That is one rep. Wait 1 second between reps.
Start with 20 reps. Add ten reps per week x 1 set. Add 1 set every 2 weeks. Work up to 4 sets daily.

2) **Slow Flex**
Slowly flex your PC muscle, hold for 15 seconds, and then release slowly, completely relaxing the muscle. That is one rep. Wait 5 seconds between reps.
Do 10-25 reps. Add 3 reps per week x 1 set. Add 1 set every 2 weeks. Work up to 4 sets daily.

3) **Super Flex**
Slowly flex your PC muscle, hold for as long as you can upto 60 seconds, and then release. That is one rep. Wait 30 seconds between reps.
Do 10 reps. Add 1 rep per week x 1 set. Add 1 set every 2 weeks. Work up to 4 sets daily.

4) **Push Out**
This exercise will help you develop the ability to ejaculate and to expel the ejaculate from your body. Push out slowly with your vaginal muscles as if you are trying to push an object out of your vagina, hold for 5-10 seconds, and then release slowly, completely relaxing the muscle. That is one rep. Wait 5 seconds between reps.
Do 10-25 reps. Add 3 reps per week x 1 set. Add 1 set every 2 weeks. Work up to 4 sets daily.

PART 5:
RAISING YOUR NEW CHILD

In moving through the healing journey of preconception to birth and beyond, you will have grown in many ways into becoming able to intuitively and effectively parent your baby. All the experiences and initiations you have taken will have equipped you physically, emotionally, mentally and soulfully to naturally know what your child needs, and what you need to stay balanced.

Your clear womb-heart and deepened connection with your soul are your best guides for what your child needs. The evolution that happens after birth from this solid foundation, where mother, father and child are bonded and have taken their Rites of Passage, means that much learning happens spontaneously, intuitively and in the moment. The true bonding between all of you means you are all tuned into each other.

In the emerging New Paradigm, parents need to be equipped with the tools their children need to help them adapt their expansive vibration to a harmonic resonance with earthly life. Part of the reason these souls have chosen you is for the active and dormant gifts within you waiting to be developed and used. Parenting will bring some of these dormant gifts forth.

A facet of your soul's design is a deep-seated desire, genetically and soulfully seated in your core: you want your child to be better than you, to go beyond you, to do greater things than you, and yes, to be more evolved, loving and wise than you.

We share with them valuable earthly lessons and soulful learning's that took us years of mistakes to learn, not to take this learning away from them, but to enable them to build their souls foundation on deeper roots than we ever did, or could.

In following this innate desire, we love selflessly and unconditionally. We extend our souls in ways we never did before. We develop a greater patient kindness AND a greater detachment, the detachment of true love that allows all things and embraces all things, accepting all things and the choices everyone makes.

The deeper the love you have for your child, based on your own solid foundation of sovereign Self-love, the freer you allow your child to Be. It is this freedom your children need in order to be themselves.

The love you share for your partner in front of your child, the vulnerabilities you display that make it ok for your child to be vulnerable and expressive, and the unspoken and unseen acts of love you do that permeates the family atmosphere, informs your child on profound levels. The more love you show, and the higher the mutual regard you hold for each other, will inform baby for their entire life.

BONDING

If loving, safe and consistent care is not given by both parents during an infant's life between 9-27 months, emotional problems occur which become part of that person for their whole life unless consciously healed. In other words, if love is not consistently shared with your child at this time, if you are not there for them emotionally and physically, the brain will not grow to its full potential and emotional capacity.

This results in many personality disorders, deep emotional issues with bonding and intimacy, (which will arise in later relationships,) and psychological problems. Co-dependence, attachment without healthy bonding or healthy emotional boundaries, over detachment, emotional coldness and sexual issues are common issues connected with this.

You can be unhealthily attached to someone which is the opposite of being healthily bonded. You can have very strict boundaries or very poor boundaries with others if you have experienced this lack of being loved at such an early formative age. You can veer to mentally dominated views of spirituality which negate the emotions in favour of a transcended 'witnessed' reality. You can become emotionally detached believing this is right and true. You may never bond with another person truly unless this is healed in you.

Science has traced these issues back to the growth of the amygdala and hippocampus during 9-27 months. These brain centers are forming at this time, and literally become fixed after 3 years old and do not grow much further. These brain centers prune neurons for proper emotional bonding and attachment. 31 Thus, if loving, safe and consistent care is not given by both parents physically and emotionally during an infant's life between 9-27 months, the amygdala and hippocampus parts of the brain do not grow to their proper size.

What I noticed with my child is that by 26 months he had a fully formed and loving bond with both of his parents. He felt happy and secure in himself alone and with both of us. He was expressive in his love towards us, freely giving and delighting in it. He had bonded healthily and his brain has received and registered this safety.

This shift at 26 months was a culmination of all of our love and care towards him, and we could visibly notice the difference in him now that he was secure in our love for him as individuals and as a family unit. Interestingly enough, we only found out this information about the brain and bonding after it had happened in him, and we had both observed the shift in him. We had already done it, observed it, and then science confirmed it.

The love and harmony between both parents is also crucial for this. It is one of the most important imprints a child will ever get. If he/she can feel and see the harmony and love between you, that will make that childs day! He/she wants that love and thrives on it. It feeds and sustains them. It imprints them. It gives them safety in your solidarity. It is a safe home.

---

[31] Schore "Affect Dysregulation and Disorders of the Self"

They delight in it and the field created by this harmonious love of solidarity allows them to be more of who they are: it is a field of permission for their own sovereign self to come out more and express itself. It allows their inner security to blossom, and from this their soul will shine forth.

It is important for both parents to also have their own bonding time alone with their child. Consistent attention, holding, wearing the child, engagement, play, fun and love in a safe, secure environment where the child is allowed to do and be how he/she wants to be is vital.

THE AMYGDALA

Located deep in the oldest part of our reptilian brain, the amygdala is an almond-shaped structure. The rest of the brain grew up over the amygdala in layers, with cognitive reasoning taking place in the topmost layers.

The amygdala detects danger or emotion associated with past experiences from childhood that were stamped within the brain as being dangerous or emotionally significant. If the amygdala detects incoming stimuli that match these stamps, then it will alert us to potential danger by pumping increased levels of stress hormones and neurotransmitters through the brain.

As this happens, you will typically experience fragments of the experience ("flashbacks"), but with the force of the original emotion. The trigger of these flashbacks can be practically anything connected with the original event: an accent, a sound, a picture, a person, a dream.

The amygdala does not give you a chance to think. It just acts instinctually. When the amygdala is not working at its optimum, there is a gap of what we feel ourselves to be, and who we think ourselves to be. In this gap lies the inability to express what we are feeling. It is in this gap where much disempowerment and frustration can occur. When you connect what you are feeling to what you are thinking, your sense of identification also shifts.

The courage to step out of a limiting and false emotional safety net and ways of relating that have served you, but not fulfilled you is the key. One has to become aware of the emotional patterns that we call home. It is easy to become comfortable with what has served you emotionally SO FAR; it is a challenge to go beyond this point and strive for a higher emotional resonance grounded in the soul. This is deep subconscious work.

When the amygdala is triggered in conjunction with the hippocampus, sexual polarities and phenomenon including out-of-body states, hallucinogenic and dream-like recollections involving the experience of god, demons and angels, rapture, the ecstasy of orgasm, intense sexual arousal, dread, terror, euphoria and the "nirvana" of a heroin "high."

This is because the hypothalamus and amygdala are major pleasure centers, and contain opiate-producing neurons and opiate (enkephalin) receptive neurons, thus generating feelings of numbness and a narcotic high. They also help to generate serotonin production, serotonin being the hormone of ecstasy. The amygdala makes it possible to experience spiritual awe and the dread of the unknown. And yet, it is also the amygdala that has the capacity to transcend the known.

The amygdala opens up through combining polarities – the extremes of light and dark, angelic and demonic, sexual and spiritual. The amygdala is the uniter of primal polarities and extremes – the breaker of taboos and judgments about the sexual force, about the nature of love, about the judgments of the mind on what love is.

The fear, anxiety, terror, excitement, visions of demons, fear of going into the unknown, all contrast with its opposites in the amygdala: ecstasy, peace, transcendence, visions of angels and God. It affects our opening fully to joy and happiness through avoidance and fear, leading us to becoming polarized. The experiencing of emotions of darkness and light in order to reach enlightenment is something we all have to do in order to reach the middle way.

The amygdala is a primal impulse that is biologically based. The amygdala governs our capacity to deeply feel love or affection, and to recognize family or friends. The amygdala becomes excited when it detects that someone is gazing directly at them, or when making threatening gestures with the hands. Hence, many divine beings with multiple faces or arms appear in the East.

Past traumas and deeply felt emotional memories and shocks are stored in the amygdala. We know when the amygdala is out of balance when we have fear, panic and stress attacks; our mouths and yoni's go dry; we need drugs like Prozac or valerian to be calm; we have an inability and fear of orgasming; a fear and judgment of darkness; lack of joy; fear of death, fear of life, feelings of depression, sadness, helplessness and disempowerment.

It affects the feminine part of our brain that holds memories and feelings of having separated from the masculine qualities of strength, courage, power, wisdom and will. It affects the masculine part of your brain that holds memories and feelings of having separated from the feminine qualities of nurturing, caring, compassion, empathy and kindness.

The healing of the Amygdala increases your levels of emotional openness, for the amygdala is the heart chakra of the brain. When it opens, the whole brain starts to heal. It governs the love brain and emotional intelligence, hence the term 'think with the heart, respond with the brain'.

The amygdala is part of the portal to the feminine lunar entrance to the third eye, found at the back of the brain. When it heals, the third eye channel starts to open from the back, not just the front or masculine solar entrance. Making love with the open and healed amygdala is an experience that takes love making to a new octave. One literally makes love inside the brain, resulting in explosions of light, bliss and full brain orgasms in a new context.

To open the amygdala to its full potential requires that we travel into our deep subconscious emotions from childhood and the womb. We have to enter and release our deepest fears, anxieties and judgments about ourselves, and bring this into recognition, acceptance and resolution. When it is healed, it brings your souls expression into the present moment in a responsive rather than reactive way, being with what is occurring right now. We end up feeling more love with a healed amygdala, as there is freedom from past trauma, shocks, emotional impacts and emotional illusions.

For you as an adult, healing your amygdala and its emotional imprints within you will impact and benefit your child. They will receive an aspect of this healing if you do it before they are seven years old. As the amygdala has a strong sexual orientation, it will also help in your lovemaking and bonding NOW with your partner, which will also affect your child now and in the future.

In raising a child, this awareness about the amygdala, and care taken by both parents to ensure that loving bonding occurs in the first 27 months of your child's life, can greatly assist your child now and in later life with all that has been shared above, and their intimate relationships.

THE SOULS DESIGN FOR PARENTING

In the Souls Design, our soul blueprints as a family are in harmony. This means that living our soul's purpose AND raising our children are not only in alignment with each other, but are integrally related and feed each other.

When our souls are partially fulfilled in this way, we find pleasure in all that unfolds from our playing, growing, and sharing together. In order to keep this flowing, we must be humble and responsible to all that is being asked of us, and all that arises.

As humans, the attachment and bonds we feel with our children are not just emotional, but also genetic. In some ways, these old genetic impulses are not in alignment with our evolving soul's blueprint.

In truly loving our children and ourselves unconditionally, we are asked to embrace and therefore transcend some aspects of our physiological and genetic make-up. This means feeling and releasing genetic wounds that keep us in contraction. The biological and cultural imperative prevalent in the old paradigm holds a limiting expression of family, and of love.

Not all pregnancies arise out of a loving or conscious male/female partnership. Many 'partnerships' end. In these circumstances, it is still possible to honour the Souls Design for birth. The needs of the child will be strong enough, if you are open enough, to draw the right people in to play these roles.

This raises an interesting point. Our children are not our own, they simply come through us. Our roles with each of them are as individual as the children themselves. For many mothers who find themselves in the potential role of a single mother, if they heal the aspects in themselves that mistrust the masculine, they can draw the appropriate masculine presence to them to bring wholeness to herself and her child.

I have found in myself, and many other mothers, a deep confusion around a true mother's love and the impulse to over coddle and over protect our children. This can stem from an abandonment wound. It is often mistaken for 'compassion,' when in fact it is a compromise of love based on the fear of abandonment.

When this wound is truly felt, released and finally transcended, we can love our children unconditionally, make decisions truthfully on their behalf and for their sovereign growth as an individual soul, encouraging their own exploration and soul's growth from a place that is not protecting our own needs and wounds first.

Raising a Child means opening up to many possibilities and opportunities that are being presented. These Children draw to them the exact scenarios and people they need to be stimulated and supported in their upbringing.

This may bring unconventional arrangements for living and family outside of the old paradigm nuclear family unit. Opening up to these new expressions of living in truth and love allows the greatest opportunity for all involved to honor their soul covenants with each other, and their own soul's purpose.

Raising a Child also means stepping out of the old paradigm of what we know about raising children. These children need help adapting into a physical body far more than we ever did, and their wisdom and intelligence potentially exceeds most of ours. It is a process of guiding them gently into this 3D reality, while allowing space for them to grow and express who, and what, they are.

Many new children will not fit into normal systems of growth, healing and development. Often the perspective of professionals (even alternative health professionals) will be coming from a limited system for understanding that does not take into account the upgraded blueprint for the human design that many children are coming in with NOW.

There are some systems just emerging that are oriented around this evolved human blueprint. Do your research and you will be drawn to the best support for you and your child. Rely strongly on your intuition, and information received from your soul guides relative to your child. Of course, the best avenue for advice comes from your child itself, and reading your child intuitively.

FATHERS ROLE IN RAISING A CHILD

Father is responsible for creating an ever-expanding field of awareness 'in front of' mother and baby to pave the way for them, allowing them to keep on growing, spiritually, soulfully and emotionally. Father is a guide, walking ahead of mother and child with his consciousness, his care, his vision, his actions. He helps create a larger field and clear pathway in front of mother and child they can then step into gracefully.

His clear seeing, his foresight and insight sees things before they happen, before taking action. A good shaman always assesses his choices before he takes action on them, seeing what choices lead to what possible future outcomes. Father sees each potential timeline for his family and in consultation with mother will put this into manifest action:

Spiritually: what is the best course of action for his family's spiritual growth?
Soul-purpose: what are all 3 souls soul-purpose, how are they interconnected on deeper levels, what is each person's soul-purpose with the other, what is each person's passion and how to fuel that, and how can this all continue to unfold, bloom and be fulfilled?
Location: which place on earth is best for the new family to grow into, and what does the child want and need to grow?
Which people are best suited to be around his family, and who does not need to be around his child?

Father guards and actions this for the whole family, guiding them all into the timeline that is the best for all three souls.

What further priorities do you have? Write them down and discuss them.

Father opens up internal spaces of consciousness for mother and child as an opener of the way, a navigator paving the way for mother and child to move gracefully forward.

Father's responsibility in raising his child is also having a responsibility for himself, to feel and follow his own heart's passions and soul's desires. In so doing, he becomes truly himself. Being yourself is the greatest gift you can give to your baby, your partner, yourself, all others and the world.

In being this, father helps creates a foundational awareness and a subconscious energy pillar that baby feels, aligns to and is imprinted by. This pillar of soul purpose, why we are here, and being yourself, being a sovereign being, is a priceless attribute of freedom that can be imprinted at an early age to his child.

If father is being himself, and has assumed responsibility for his soul and what his own purpose is, baby will receive this in baby's root chakra, in the very tap roots of baby's preverbal sub-conscious, primordial mind. He or she will therefore always have this awareness. This is important because purpose is seeded at an early age, and even though it may not be fully manifested until the child has grown up, the preverbal subconscious awareness or guiding spark is established.

One reason few people are living their true soul purpose and hearts desires on earth is because their parents are not, and have not modeled this for their children in a caring and clear way. Most parents have been primarily dedicated solely to the material upbringing of their children. This is important, yet the father in the old paradigm was just earning money and rarely doing what he really wanted to do, his soul purpose, the reason he is on earth. This factor is subtle, but deep and prevalent.

The energy for soul-purpose, for fulfilling the reason for your existence, for fulfilling the age-old question, ''Why am I here?" is primarily received by the baby from father. Baby receives it from mother to a lesser degree, for baby is more concerned with the nurturing aspects that comes from mother, not direction, strength and purpose which are more masculine attributes. Baby is looking to father for the alignment to soul-purpose, and to Source.

In raising a child, father allows the child to unfold. Following the child's deepr soul choices and inclinations, many of which may not be known to the child at an early age, he encourages and allows his childs soul to take root, flower, and bear fruit in the child's own way. This is his loving guidance in love and non-attachment. For the father, it is a dance between structure and fluidity, emotion and direction. In raising a child, father needs to take care of all three of them, mother, himself and child in many dimensions.

This may mean father has to make some 'unpopular' decisions, such as discipline and timing, creating healthy boundaries a child may rebel against in wanting its own way, and setting a child on educational pathways that the child itself has said, whilst in the womb, that it needs in order to fulfil its soul-purpose, but which it may have forgotten in the throes of early childhood and its distractions of video games and other old paradigm distractions. It is important not to impose your ideas on the child, but read and follow the child. The previous method of communicating with the child in the womb and asking them questions is invaluable for this.

Father provides a spark of life, a spark of power, a spark of excitement, a spark of adventure, a spark of Shakti. This solar power, the power of Ra, is initially transmitted from father to baby, igniting neuronal patterns within the baby's brain, stirring the soul and spirit body of baby. Baby is looking to father for this, which literally sparks the neurons of the child into joy, growth and expansion. He can also receive this partially through mother but again, baby is looking for other primary qualities from the more lunar mother.

For a father to show vulnerability and tears before his child is important, for it allows the child to recognize and feel comfortable with their own emotions. To have this permission and safe reference point inculcated from an early age for a child is important, for in fathers displayed, open vulnerability, the child can feel safe in its own emotions, knowing they are ok and not needing to repress them or hide them. This will spark a further remembering in the child of the soul, as soul is feeling in nature, and soul purpose arises from deep feelings and knowings within oneself.

Feelings bring forth compassion. The sooner they remember, integrate and incorporate this, not being drawn into it, but just aware of it, the sooner they will be able to enter into their soul and soul purpose, and become who they are.

In raising a child, many of the things father did during pregnancy will also be applicable on a soul, emotional, and spirit level. Father is still looking after mother and child, still helping mother engage more deeply with her own soul purpose.

As each child unfolds, as each relationship unfolds, father needs to be fluid with the dynamic of the three. Just allow it to flow where it needs to go, whether that is moving to a new home, leaving things behind, making new friends, doing things that are unexpected or unknown. Father just needs to flow with it. And father will, if he has emotionally traveled throughout the pregnancy and has embodied himself as a result of the birthing process.

SOUL EMBODIMENT FOR CHILDREN

RHYTHM, WARMTH and CONTAINMENT

For their first nine months, children know the warm, cozy enclosure of their mother's womb, enclosed in gently swaying waters, resonating in the softly swelling sound of the placenta's comforting, rhythmic pulse, echoed by mother's heartbeat. This creates a safe hammock to guide them gradually and gently into form. The elements of rhythm, warmth and containment are key factors in their safe and loving gestation, and need to be continued after birth to sustain a nurturing, loving environment for your child.

Rhythm helps a child to organize itself in time and space. It gives reference, regulated and comforting movement and a felt, grounded relationship to the experience of inhabiting a physical body here on earth. It brings simplicity, order and reassurance to the movements of life. We discover rhythm in our innate biology, movements, and instincts as well as the natural world around us.

Rhythm is first felt and heard in the steady, constant and foundational beat of our hearts, reassuringly felt by our children for nine months in the womb. Its familiar resonance is accessible after they are born through our cuddling of them, or being carried on our chest. Rhythm resides in the steady suckling of a newborn at its mother's breast, nursing for nourishment in nodding, rhythmic pulses.

This instinct often accompanies them into sleep and can be heard and seen long after they have unlatched from nursing. Rhythm enables a gentle transition from the 3D plane to the astral plane of the dream state, and dream state travel into other dimensions and planes of reality beyond the third dimension. It also facilitates a safe return from the childs explorations. We enable this transition through rocking to comfort and lull our children to sleep.

Rhythm is the steady pat of your hand on your child's back to remove wind after feeding, and to comfort them. Rhythm is embedded in the cadence of our voice as we speak softly, repetitively, and simply to our children. It is woven into the melody of simple spontaneous song we as parents sing, inspired by the accomplishments and unique traits of our child's emerging character and soulful expression. It is the beat of every child's unique soul song.

There is a rhythm in routine on the 3D plane that builds a framework of organization and structure, familiarity and discipline, bringing sense to the new experiences, swirling emotions and growth pains all children have.

Bathing, feeding, changing, walks, play and bonding time become familiar activities that give shape, safety and security to our children's expansive experience of sensory perception. This rhythm and repetition is how a child begins to organize an understanding of life.

Time in nature, immersed in the elements of air, sun, water and the green grasses and fertile soils of the ground allows children to connect to the rhythms of the earth and cosmos, grounding them within their bodies and the larger cycles of life. Children hold an innate sense of the harmony of life, and spending time connecting to the earth and sun reinforces this internal harmony.

Waking up with the Sun at dawn and going to sleep with the Moon after twilight weaves our children into the greater rhythm of the solar system, aligning their internal biorhythms with the outer rhythms of our universe. Rituals and routines around seasons, Solstices and Equinoxes brings rhythm and harmonic order to the year, that begins to mark a reference for their earthly experience.

Rhythm is relationship. It is the clock that the web of life finds its pulse and how we tune our own unique pulse within the pulse of all life. Rhythm is the organic return to order from chaos. Rhythm helps us find our way through duality and polarity. When rhythm is innate in our understanding and in our bodies, we are free to express and dance the melody of our soul and express who we really are, feeling comfortable, fluid and available to all that life has to offer, and all that we have to give.

WARMTH

Warmth is a conductor of relationship, a nurturing closeness that invites us to drop down from mind and stresses, expand, open and relax. Warmth is the gravity that begins bonding, the all-attractive universal language of affection that compels us to be vulnerable and engage with another. Warmth is loves invitation, and without it we stop growing, stop connecting, and eventually stop living. Life is warmth-death is cold.

Warmth radiates from the Sun, penetrating and softening us, bringing health and vibrancy to our complexion and our spirits. Without the sun, there is no life on earth. It is the central reference point for us and our children to orient their senses, subconsciously map their position in the universe, and on a deep level feel the sustaining of life on this planet.

Warmth emanates from our hearts, our smiles, our outstretched arms. The daily expressions of love and warmth we share with our children imprint them in the limbic part of the brain, increasing their capacity to give and receive love. Warmth is exchanged through cuddles, frequent hugs at least 10 times a day according to modern science, and skin on skin contact, carrying with it the intelligence of healthy biological function.

It is through direct contact with the mother's skin that a newborn baby learns to regulate its temperature, heartbeat, and respiratory rate. Warmth is maintained in soft clothing of natural fibers, and intentional protection from harsher climactic elements. As love is the fuel to sustain and evolve our souls, warmth is the key ingredient to sustaining our bodies and spirits here on earth.

CONTAINMENT

In good boundaries, we find great freedom. Healthy boundaries allow us to become who we are. For nine months, a child knows the snug comfort of the womb before emerging into a world of intense stimulus, of bewildering colors, shapes, noises and many more people than just its mother.

Being held or contained, physically, emotionally and soulfully enables a slow and gentle transition into this earthly world. Stimulus can be received as impetus for growth and expansion or it can be a shock that causes shut down if a child is not properly contained and held.

Physical containment is felt in a partially enclosed sleeping space, or in mother or father's arms. When a newborn's arms and legs are gently physically contained for periods of time to allow a break from uncontrolled movement and reflexes, he can feel a settled peace. Containment is also felt in the safe confines of a clean and uncluttered home.

Baby wearing is common in many indigenous cultures. Studies have shown that babies who are worn in a sling around the chest or in a carrying pack for the first nine months of life become emotionally independent earlier in life.

The heart-arc line, (see the chapter on breasts) which extends from nipple to nipple, is a natural energetic field of loving resonance. This heart-arc line field holds a comforting resonance to a child, (and adult men!) especially when it is the child's parents, and a person in a loving state of consciousness. It is comforting for a child to rest here, for he/she feels safe, snug, secure and protected in this energy field (when it has been cleared by the individual holding the child). It is a good place for them to be when you are traveling, or in public places.

Emotional containment is also experienced in our boundaries with our children. This becomes increasingly important as children grow older. Knowing what is expected of them and what is appropriate, gives them a sense of safety and security and the freedom to more confidently know and express themselves.

Spiritual containment is felt in the strength and integrity of the field around the parents, the child and the home. This field is maintained by the emotional health of each of the individuals, as well as the relationships of those living with the child. When there is harmony and love with good boundaries between mother and father, a child will thrive.

This love is determined by the authentic, honest expression of truth and love in the parents relating. Another factor is how deeply is each parent living from their true souls desires? Are you doing what you really want to do? Are you living what you are here on earth to live or doing something else? Children living in such a field of passion, soulful alignment, love and truth flourish.

When we are engaged and humble on our own spiritual path, our children do not get burdened with playing out our unhealed emotions. When we are in our own process of feeling and releasing our personal wounds, our children feel the fruit of release. They too will feel the joy, the lightness, the greater love and expansion of our own consciousness in them that comes when healing is accomplished. They greatly benefit from our soulful and emotional evolution, for they are partially healed by our own healing.

Because the child is part of the mother's aura for the first seven years of life, who ever the mother intimately interacts with is experienced by the child. For example, I received a massage from woman who was in a deep grieving process, and I decided I could handle this. However, during the massage my son, who was six miles away from me at the time, cried for almost two hours and was very upset. Upon seeing him on my return, I was shocked as I had never, in his entire life, seen him so disturbed. This was a big lesson for me in having a higher degree of discernment in my interactions.

Soulful containment allows our children the space and feeling of safety to fully open up, engage with you and others, and express more of who they really are. Traditionally, it was seen as the father's role to be a protector, yet mother too has to learn this vital skill, for there will be times when she will be alone and will need to learn how to be a protector.

People are attracted to the light and innocence of a child, and there have been many times when we have experienced physically invasive and totally inappropriate advances on our son made by complete strangers, who see his light and want this for themselves on their own healing journey back into innocence. Both mother and father need to be aware of this and be able to be a protector.

Protecting your child from others, with grace yet firmness, is a part of parenting, as your child is defenseless and relying on you for support and guidance in almost every area of life.

Another way of soul containment is when we make time every day to commune with our children's souls. In this sacred time, an inviting window is created for their souls to express, expand and incarnate more fully. Singing, deep eye contact, calling them by their soul's name, singing their soul song, sharing affection, playing and music, repeated over time, will help create a soulful container for your child to engage with life and express who they really are.

Wouldn't you like that?

CLEARING AND INTEGRATING FOR CHILDREN

In today's world, there is an overload of electrical equipment dependency that interferes with our natural harmonic resonance with our own biology, our own electromagnetic fields, and the earth. This is one reason why it is so important for our children and ourselves to spend time in nature. Here, our body can be reminded of its resonant frequency by aligning to earth.

With this connection intact, life feels smoother, more fluid and expansive. We are grounded and reminded that we are part of a continuum moving through the entire living web of life beyond our skin and our bodies.

The circuitry of children is sensitive and refined. The unnatural frequencies generated from televisions, computers, video game addiction to artificial dopamine creation, wireless and telephone networks, as well as the collective field of negativity and density in cities, interfere with them. When children show signs of being agitated, unsettled, holding excessive tension in their small bodies, and excessive neediness, it can be a sign that they are overloaded.

The density of the third dimensional reality is quite different to the frequency of these souls. Their bodies cannot physically handle the frequency of their soul incarnating here all at once. It happens in stages throughout the first seven years. As the soul moves through its stages of embodiment, the physical body will adapt, and sometimes this adaptation will bring symptoms of stomach discomfort, tense muscles, hyper-activity and general fussiness.

The following massage regime is a quick way to help your child balance their energetic system and integrate with their nervous system and physical body. Skin on skin contact, baths, and nappy free time with loving tender touch are also helpful.

PRACTICE: CLEARING AND INTEGRATION MASSAGE

The following exercise is a quick and simple way to bring Children back into alignment when their spirit body has been impacted by excessive electromagnetic, toxic, or human pollution.

1. Lay your child on their back on your lap or the ground. If they are fussy or fidgeting, begin patting their belly and torso to help them to rhythmically settle.

2. Next, beginning at the hands and wrists, wrap your hands around their arms and legs and squeeze. Do quick squeezes all the way up their arms to their shoulders five or six times.

3. Now return to a belly pat. At this point they may be laughing with you as they delight in the movement, sound and sensation.

4. Now move your hands to their feet and do the same motion up their legs to their pelvis five or six times.

5. Next grab their thighs at the base of their pelvis and do some bicycle motions with their legs. This will help the energy to move through-out their pelvis.

6. You can return to belly pats at any time if they begin to get restless again. Bringing song or sound into the exercise makes it more fun and engaging for both of you. Use firm touch with the intention to penetrate and release any tightness in their meridians due to an overload of energy in their circuits.

WHY BABIES CRY

Babies cry. Sometimes they cry a lot. Why? Because they cannot communicate any other way for the first years of their lives, or so we have been led to believe. Bouts of inconsolable crying are seen to be 'normal' for a baby and there is even a term for it: "purple crying."

This is not normal in the Souls perspective on children and how we have been designed to grow up. When babies cry inconsolably, and resist all conventional soothing techniques, something else is happening. It is not normal or natural.

It is abnormal and unnatural, but because we have become so used to the abnormal and unnatural in our lives and society, and therefore the lives of our children, we accept it as part of the zeitgeist of how babies are 'supposed' to be.

Babies cry and are inconsolable many times because of emotional reasons. Maybe they are not receiving the love they need from a soulful place from within the parent. Maybe they are reflecting the repressed, suppressed emotions within the parents that the parents are not addressing. Maybe they are a mirror to assist the parent to see their own self and resolve the pain and sadness hidden deep within them from their past.

Maybe the baby's birth journey, through their parent's pregnancy, traumatic and painful labour and birth, brutal umbilical cord severing, epidural drugs and cold, hospital births surrounded by strangers who do not really know or care about YOU or baby creates this inconsolable crying.

Maybe baby is suffering from all of these birth trauma pains, with parts of their delicate little bodies still in shock from the experience. Maybe baby is simply not wanted by its parents, or the parents have an unhealthy relationship, which of course impacts the child greatly. Maybe baby is voicing the pain and hurt already imprinted on them, and is complaining about it, hoping for a resolution somewhere, somehow.

Maybe their primordial trust in existence, in life and love, in their parents, has already been tainted and shaken by these experiences. Maybe their crying comes from the depth of their souls, having been shaken into this world with no other way to express and be taken seriously.

Maybe baby is reaching out for soul to soul communication. Maybe the parents do not know their soul agreement with their baby and this is being voiced by the baby, who has a primordial sense of knowing about why he/she came here and in particular why he/she came to their parents, and is confused as to why this agreement is not being honoured and love is not being shared between them in the ways they agreed to before they incarnated.

Pain may arise when we feel the places where love has not yet been felt and embraced within us, but it is not love. So many of us believe that we need to continually feel pain in order to love, and stay in this cycle believing that it is necessary, not knowing that embracing and grieving our wounds can lead to them being erased completely.

Inconsolable crying is not normal. It is a sign that there is a felt absence of love occurring for a baby. If we take this as our basis for the birthing experience, and indeed our own lives, then we can start to see something is distorted in babies inconsolable crying. It is seen as 'healthy' and 'normal' in today's world for a baby to cry for hours at a time, and that this does not affect their physical health. Even a cursory glance at this sentence does not make sense.

What is sick and what is not? What is normal and what is not? The Sufi's say that anyone who is not living in love is sick and needs healing and love to reach the status of being normal. Normal for them is being whole, healed and loving.

So, what is normal? The redefinition of these terms has to come to pass in order for humanity to reclaim its birth rights, and live in the same way as we have been created: in love.

A self-aware and conscious parent will know most of the time why their baby is crying because they have developed a relationship and an intuitive bonding based on their conscious pregnancy and birth experience and the initiation they have taken. Therefor they can read and understand what baby is expressing because they take the time to do so, and are connecting from their own soul to the baby's soul.

The soul communicates to another soul through feeling and emotion, and this form of communication is not just between you and your baby: this is how you communicate most deeply to other souls and to the universe as well. For a parent to communicate like this with a baby requires they have a good awareness of their own soul, and can communicate with the many parts of their own self.

Parents have to, in some degree, have healed their primordial woundings to live in primordial trust, feeling supported by life and safe within their own self. They know they deserve love and do not have to earn it. This then creates the container for baby that both parents provide, by having these qualities recognized and active within themselves.

In the felt container of trust and safety, we open and receive. Many impulses such as inconsolable crying arise from fear and its contractions in mind and body. We place our trust in what we choose to value. The mind shapes all experience according to what it values. If what we learn in the womb shapes our future values, what do we trust in? What do we learn to value? Innately, babies trust deeply, yet this can be tainted by our own selves, and the pregnancy and birth experiences.

In the choice of trust, you withdraw the value you have given to a certain perception of reality, a certain veil surrounding the real. To trust means we feel safe and secure in our essence, in our inner reality. We can only do this by exploring and coming to know our inner reality from our more feminine side.

Here, we know we are loved, that we value love, and we trust this flow in our lives. This flow is always there; it is ever present as our support, our ground, constant and reliable, even when we forget it for a moment. When we have integrated this, then we experience true strength. We become naturally strong, confident and fearless, as we feel held, supported, and nurtured within self and by Life.

This strength does not waver, as it is based in the eternal, whereas our trust in another person, parent, teacher, or teaching will change over time, for our perceptions change as the soul's growth deepens. Evolving becomes easier and quicker once we have true strength, and we can then pass this onto our children, and indeed even learn from their demonstration of trust.

In this, we experience life as wondrous and spontaneous, like a child does, for we can allow what is unfolding. Children do not suppress their emotions, at least initially. If they are hurt, they cry, they release the emotion, and then it is done! They don't hold onto the experience like many adults do, and "suck it up" or have a "stiff upper lip." This is something we learn, usually from our parents and others, who themselves are repressed and pass this behaviour onto us, and thus we onto our children.

If we knew everything that was going to happen there would be no real fun, no real discovery, and little play. Life would be boring! Trust allows existence to continually weave its magic, bringing more into our lives and taking us into previously unimagined possibilities.

As we travel the path, trust sustains, supports, and gives you solid ground. As you evolve, trust deepens and changes its nature, until the soul gives itself to, and fully surrenders to, existence, which then becomes the support, and the ground, for the soul. The ground that gives rise to you, also gives ground and support to all life. When one experiences the trust that is our support is the support of all beings, we open a doorway to Self-Realization.

Safety and trust are keys to our babies living in harmony. For them to be this, we have to live in trust and inner safety within ourselves first! This then becomes the 'normal' way for our children to relate to themselves and to us, their parents.

Parents who have developed this within themselves will find their baby does not cry much, and when the baby does, the parents will know what to do because they have developed a soul-to-soul relationship with baby that is not dependent on normal language.

How does one do this? *Through feeling*, for the soul communicates primarily through feeling. In this sharing and communication, there will be little if any inconsolable crying, and any distress the child feels will be minimal and easily resolved. Harmony and love reign. *This is normal. The rest is not.*

It is normal for a baby to cry to communicate its needs. It is helpful to understand the many reasons behind a cry, so it can be addressed in the moment.

HUNGER
PHYSICAL DISCOMFORT
OVERTIRED
PHYSICAL PAIN/ILLNESS
SENSORY STIMULATION
WANTS TO BE HELD
FRUSTRATION
FEELING UNSAFE: NEGATIVE SPIRIT INFLUENCE
PARENTAL SUPPRESSED EMOTION
NIGHTMARES
ANGER, FEAR AND PAIN
BABY FEELING THEIR OWN EMOTIONAL WOUNDS
MOTHER'S POST NATAL DEPRESSION

A parent or caregiver who is tuned in can often hear a distinct difference in the sound of a cry, between hunger or needing to be held, an over tired cry or that of their child feeling unsafe or emotionally stressed. When we know the reasons behind the cry, we can more effectively and lovingly address the situation.

1.HUNGER

A hunger call often has a sense of urgency behind it. It is a call that stems from a base need for survival, and this can be felt in the underlying tone. Just before my son would start to cry out of hunger, my milk would rush in through my breasts as my body was attuned to his needs. A newborn baby needs to eat around every 2-3 hours. The stimulus of engaging with a new world, and the rapid rate of growth burns a tremendous amount of calories.

2. PHYSICAL DISCOMFORT

Gas/colic, inability to regulate temperature, uncomfortable positioning and soiled, full nappies are primary reasons why babies feel physical discomfort. Another primary reason are growing pains, such as teething, and the fact that their brains, organs, bones and bodies are all growing very rapidly, some of which can be discomforting and unnerving.

One of the most common reasons is distress in their digestive system, which can be remedied with regular and rhythmic burping sessions after feeding. Babies have a difficult time regulating their own temperature, and are extremely susceptible to extremes in heat or cold. Always keeping a hat on baby whilst venturing outside or into public places will keep them warm and protected, as the bones in their cranium have not yet fused and their crown is open and vulnerable.

Babies have different positions of comfort, and these positions are constantly changing. I remember the first few weeks after my son's birth he slept on his side. When I transitioned him to stomach sleeping he began to sleep almost entirely through the night. He never liked lying on his back, and would often cry after a few minutes of lying that way. Being attuned to what is comfortable and what is not can help avoid crying spells of discomfort.

I have noticed when my son has a soiled nappy and is upset with it, he almost tries crawling away from his lower half, as if to escape the discomfort. Changing nappies often, and giving babies time without their nappy each day can help avoid diaper rash and uncomfortable sores from too much time in a wet diaper. Alternating between disposable and cloth nappies can also help alleviate this.

3. OVER TIRED

Sometimes, when babies get over-tired they have trouble transitioning into a sleep state. To let you know this, they will cry. Simply rocking or singing to them can be enough to help lull them into a gentle dream state. However, at this point we can also explore why we did not listen to the child's needs, and ask: why did I push them? Why did I not listen to my intuition when I knew it was time for a rest but my child convinced me otherwise ...and now we are both paying for it!

4. PHYSICAL PAIN or ILLNESS

A child's baby teeth are formed in the womb, and can begin to emerge through their gums anytime during the first six months. This is a painful process for a child, and will often bring on fevers and long crying spells. You can help alleviate this discomfort by putting a piece of ice in a wet cloth and helping them suck on it, or massaging the gums with your finger (you may even feel the tooth emerging).

Amber teething necklaces can be helpful in that the amber releases its calming oil into the skin which soothes the baby. A good remedy in all instances of physical pain is to help your child connect to itself beyond the physical experience, and remind him or her that it is not just a body.

Taking a walk in nature, toning, 'running the light' (see meditation), humming, singing their soul song, immersing them in a warm bath or shower, or rhythmic movement are all ways to connect to the soul of your child and remind them they are more than just their physical body.

It is common for babies to run a fever, and it is not abnormal for their temperature to run as high as 103-104 degrees F. (Never try to cool down a fever, the body is heating up to ward off an unfriendly inhabitant.) Any kind of sickness is actually exercising the immune system and with a steady supply of breast milk and nurturing, they will move through this quickly.

Often after an illness a child will make a developmental leap, either physically or cognitively. Remember during these times that your child is ultra-sensitive, so be especially gentle to their senses through being aware of loud noise, extreme temperatures/elements, and rough fabrics or touch.

5. SENSORY STIMULUS

On one level babies are a mass of sensory organs with no filters. They are unable to tune out or control the intensity of input coming into their experience through their senses. During and after birth, a mother's senses are extremely heightened as well. This enables her to be more aware of the immediate environment of her child, and to protect their senses.

Even the sound of dishes being stacked can be overbearing to a newborn's sensitive ears. Strong smells such as perfumes or smoke can upset a baby, just as stubbly beards or rough fabric can be painful to their extremely sensitive skin. While we cannot control the environment perfectly for our newborn, we can be aware of possible irritants that might upset them and make them cry.

On the flip side, sometimes gentle stimulus is necessary. As a baby is so open to an unfiltered experience, giving them a focused stimulus is helpful to soothe them, or draw them out of over stimulation. Rocking, ambient music, singing, or allowing them to push into their legs helps them focus their energy and embody, bringing order to chaos. And it is healthy to allow children to have some sun early mornings and later evenings without sunscreen!

6. WANTS TO BE HELD

After spending nine months in the womb, with the warmth and familiar sound of mother's heartbeat and placenta, babies are most comfortable when they are held close to the familiar sounds, smells, and warmth of those that love him/her. We all have a need for love, and this stems from emotional *and* biological reasons.

The more babies are touched, the more their nerves and brain are stimulated into growth and development. Studies have shown that babies left to cry all day in cribs compared to babies that are held periodically throughout the day, are much more likely to develop disabilities in brain function.

Many indigenous cultures wear their babies close to their chests and heart chakras all day long, while they work, cook, and engage in their daily activities. These cultures do not experience many of the same deep wounds of emotional insecurity and separation that we do in more 'developed' countries.

In wearing a child, or holding a child often throughout the day, they feel emotionally safe and secure, and *often become more independent at a younger age*, since this sense of security becomes innate within them. Sometimes babies cry to communicate this basic need for love.

The more they are carried and anchored to our bodies, the more easily they can learn to adjust their expanded consciousness to the physical. When we wear our children, we act as a grounding rod. They can stay open to the vast amounts of life force available to them and not be overwhelmed by it.

Eventually, through entrainment, they learn how to anchor this Shakti themselves, and are ready for more independence. This gentle transition process ensures that these children will maintain their gift of sensitivity whilst being able to integrate it into healthy functioning here on earth.

7. FRUSTRATION

Do you remember what it was like to emerge onto the earth plane, in a body that is foreign and with limited means of communication? I have witnessed my son on numerous occasions put all of his effort and might into crawling or speaking and while at moments he would taste success, he would end up crying in utter frustration.

The truth is, our neuro biology body takes time to coordinate and adapt to life on this planet. Whilst it is good for our children to test their limits and push possibility, there is also a time when the frustration overwhelms them. As parents, we can break them out of this conundrum and reassure/distract them.

8. SAFETY

As most babies brought into the world in a natural way are quite open, they are sensitive to threatening or 'unsafe' energies. Sometimes people or energies that don't feel bothersome to us, *can* have an impact on our child.

In most cases babies and children can feel the underlying intentions in people, but because they do not have filters or the means to move themselves out of an experience, they are dependent on us to protect them and maintain their feeling of safety.

If your baby cries in public, or when someone approaches, pay attention. So often we are distracted by our own thoughts, our external activities, that we may miss the fact that our baby feels unsafe. Even if you cannot understand the reasoning behind why, even if it is a family member, it is important to honor your child's call for a boundary.

When babies grow up with parents setting clear boundaries for their emotional and physical safety, they come to develop a deeper trust in themselves and the capacity to set their own boundaries and become who they are.

The sense of threat and not feeling safe can also happen with the invisible world of negative/ wounded spirits. Negative spirits are attracted by your and your baby's wounds, which they can hook into and influence. Your deep seated emotional wounds create holes in your auric field and weaknesses in the integrity of your soul, which can allow these spirits to influence you. Babies are especially vulnerable and sensitive to these spirits.

These spirits resonate and share similar wounds to you and hence gravitate towards you, just like your share similar interests with your human friends. For example, if there is an alcoholic spirit he will want to come to you if you have a tendency towards drinking, and then will encourage you to drink so he can vicariously live out his own addiction. The same with the sex addict, the drug taker, the sex abuser, the spirit angry with men/ women and so on.

If you have the same wound as these spirits, they will come to you so they can continue to play it out. It is a blessing in a way, because then you can see where your holes lie that allow them to hook into you, as they tend to exaggerate the symptoms of your wound. This may accelerate you to really look at your stuff and heal it fast, for your sake and the sake of your child.

Of course, there are ancestral and parental wounds you will have that will also play out here, and a baby will also have its own wounds and will attract spirits. It is good to be aware of this, and help protect your baby. Babies can often cry in deep fear as they are approached by these dark spirits, and it is time to reassure them love them, hold them and if you are capable, banish the negative spirit.

Yet, babies are intelligent. Do not underestimate them. They can release and heal emotions far quicker than most adults, if they are talked to about what is happening. Talk to your baby as an adult person, on a soul and telepathic level. They will receive it. The babies who are spoken to as real, whole people from early on in their life mature and become more independent, without constantly needing mommy and daddy to do everything for them later in life.

9. PARENT'S SUPPRESSED EMOTIONS

It is important to be aware of your own feelings when your child cries, and tune into what you are feeling to bring light to why your child is crying. Sometimes tending to your child is simple, as in answering a call for food or bringing him close to your heart.

But when you have run down the list of physical and emotional needs and your child is still crying, there may be something not so obvious happening. Your child could be reflecting an emotion or behavior that is suppressed in you, and as they grow up, this reflection can become more and more prevalent IF we are suppressing emotions and wounds within us. Conversely, they can reflect the joy within us too!

Our children will play out our own repressed emotions to us. This happens to all parents. Whatever you have not healed will come out in some way at some time, and our children are the best mirrors of this. Because of their sensitivity, a child will feel that which is suppressed or held back in us, and act it out.

To end this depends on the parent acting in a self-responsible way to see their wound, recognize it, feel it as their own, and then take whatever other steps are needed to heal it.

This takes humility and self-reflection. The more we reclaim and take responsibility for our own emotions, the less of a burden we place on our children.

STORY OF MAUREEN P (Real name changed)
by Gail T, Child Carer

When I met M, she was a bright, in-pink, seven month old. Her parents were nice people, and their only request was for her to be happy. They didn't want to see or hear her cry, and they admitted they felt like they were not being good parents if she was crying or upset.

As I spent time with M, I could feel her beauty, her soul shining through. She is a bright clear one, and as she looked straight into my eyes and smiled, I could feel a discomfort and unease building up within her.

As I connected in deep presence with her soul, I opened my heart to her, letting her know I could see her, and she was safe to express with me whatever she needed to. Words are not paramount in this exchange; it is mainly about emotional presence and telepathic communication, whilst gazing into each other's eyes.

She physically relaxed and surrendered into her body. She started to cry, and as her parents were around they became increasingly worried that something was wrong. I put M into a front strap on pack and took her on a long walk into the woods. I wasn't attempting to console her or distract her from crying. I reassured her that it was just us, her and I (and her Creator), she was safe, and whatever she required I would hold her.

We stopped and sat down by a stream in the woods. I held her close. I looked into her eyes and asked her to let it go. She looked at me and I could feel her soul saying "Thank you." She immediately welled up and broke down, tears streaming, full on wailing.

It was beautiful to witness her feeling like she was really letting it all go for the first time in her young life. Every time she started to wind down her sobbing, she would look into my eyes and I would ask her "Are you finished yet?" Then she would break down again and tap into her cry for another round. Time after time she let go, and let go even further.

Her release lasted for nearly 45 minutes. All I had to do was be present and listen to her soul, and hold space for what she was asking for. She told me that she wasn't allowed to cry, and her little body was having a hard time sleeping because she was being stuffed with a pacifier, coddled, overfed and distracted. She didn't feel comfortable because she wasn't being allowed to feel and express everything due to her parents "just trying to be good parents".

When we returned, I had a conversation with M's parents about the importance of allowing her to cry and feeling their own emotions in her reflection. I shared that they are harming her more than helping her by not letting her fully be in the moment with however she is feeling, and whatever she wants to express.

We talked about how, as first time parents, they were trying to do the 'right' thing, but didn't realize that THEIR emotional state of being, their repressed emotions, their own fears, were actually being reflected through their daughter.

The next few days, I witnessed the parents relaxing around M's emotional outbursts and tantrums, and not rushing to coddle her as they took more responsibility for their own states of being.

M actually became more temperamental as she started to push and test the boundaries she was not allowed to previously do or feel, but she then also felt lighter, freer within, laughing more with everyone, and at peace within to be able to discover herself.

Her parents became more accepting as they embraced the reality that they go through their own daily emotions, and it is perfectly acceptable for M to feel hers as well. This beautiful family shifted in the week I was with them.

M's mother emailed me later and said "I don't know what happened, but I feel completely different and something magical took place this past week. I may never know, but I think you changed our lives in a profound way that I'll never understand. Thank you."

10. NIGHTMARES or NIGHT TERRORS

Nightmares occur to a child for the same reason adults get scared. There is a wound that negative spirits can hook into and manipulate. This wound can also be reflected by the parent, i.e the parent can have a similar wound. As children are so open, these spirits can influence them easily and show them scary images and scenarios. Children are more easily frightened and more powerless to do something about these visions, and so have nightmares.

Negative spirits come to us to show us our wounds. This is a blessing even if we do not feel like it at the time! When negative spirits come to your child, pick your child up, and ask what is happening. Tune into what your child's real wound is. Speak to them about it.

Obviously, this is easier if you have done this process inside you before. BUT, you may be surprised what your baby shares with you. Your baby is having deep emotions arising within it, and nightmares/ excessive crying (even during the day) are showing *you* that your baby needs to release these emotions, *which you can help facilitate for baby.*

11. ANGER, FEAR and PAIN

To scientists at Brown University the subtle acoustic features of a cry, many of them imperceptible to the human ear, (but not to the emotional body) can hold important information about a baby's health. As Stephen Sheinkopf, professor of psychiatry and human behavior shares, " Crying can be a window into the brain, and differences in cry are linked to problems stemming from malnutrition, prenatal drug exposure, and other risks. Cry is an early warning sign that can be used in the context of looking at the whole baby."

It is not easy to know why a newborn cries, especially amongst first-time parents. "Crying is a baby's principal means of communicating its negative emotions and in the majority of cases the only way they have to express them," explains Mariano Chóliz, researcher at University of Valencia.

"When babies cry because of anger or fear, they keep their eyes open, *but keep them closed when crying in pain.* As for the dynamic of the cry, both the gestures and the intensity of the cry gradually increase if the baby is angry. On the contrary, the cry is as intense as can be in the case of pain and fear."

As Chóliz notices, when babies are angry they tend to keep their eyes half-closed, either looking in apparently no direction or in a fixed and prominent manner. Their mouth is either open or half-open and the intensity of their cry increases progressively. Many adults do not properly identify which emotion is causing the cry, especially in the case of anger and fear. When a baby cries, there is a lot of tension in the forehead, eyebrows or lips, opening of the mouth and raised cheeks.

When babies are scared, their eyes remain open almost all the time, and at times they have a penetrating look and move their head backwards. Their cry seems to be explosive after a gradual increase in tension. More physical touch and close cuddling with rocking helps them as they express.

When a baby is in pain it will have closed eyes and when the eyes do open it is only for a few moments and a distant look is held. There is also a lot of tension in the eye area and the forehead remains frowned. The cry begins at maximum intensity, starting suddenly and immediately after the stimulus. Babies often close their eyes whilst crying for basic needs, and this usually lasts a very short time.

12. CAUSAL WOUND RELEASE

Most children incarnate with wounds, and still need to release causal wounds carried in their genetics or acquired during their gestation period. Usually their causal wound manifests when they are resisting receiving love from a parent, or refuse to make eye contact. When a child is ready to release a deep emotional wound, they may be irritated, agitated, overly subdued, or unwilling to connect.

When children are taught from an early age the means to allow their emotions to flow and move through them, and when their parents also freely show their vulnerabilities and tears, children can remain more fluid in life, and have no need for fear or judgment around feeling and moving beyond difficulty or pain.

Sometimes babies cry to release their own deep-seated wounds and emotions that are arising to be felt, embraced and healed. One day, I noticed my four month old son would not look at his father. This was unusual, as often in bonding and play he would gaze deep into his father's eyes. This avoidance went on for a day and a half. It was literally like he couldn't see his father, for even if he was standing right in front of him, he would turn his head the other way.

One afternoon, the three of us lay down on the bed together, while I nursed my son. I looked deep into his eyes and told him his Papa loved him. He whimpered in pain. I told him again, and again he moaned and sniffled. I took him off my breast and handed him to his Papa.

My son instantly looked away from him and began crying a very loud, powerful, aching cry, a cry totally different to what I had ever heard from him before. It was not any of his usual repertoire – this was totally different, coming forth from the depths of his soul.

His deep belly crying and oh so sweet tears continued for over half an hour while his father held him on his chest, gently stroking him, speaking softly of all the ways he loved him, all the sweet things they would do together, reassuring him that as long as Papa was alive, he would be there for his son.

Each time his crying began to taper off, and his Papa again shared his love, it released a layer of abandonment our son had been carrying, since his time in the womb *and before.*

Finally, from his tear drenched eyes he began to look his Papa in the eyes, first momentarily, and then for longer. He melted onto his chest, soft, tired, and vulnerable. I stayed in the background so as not to distract my son, aware to not bring him into a comfort zone away from feeling what he needed to feel.

I held a loving and tender space in my heart for him. Within the sound container we held, he felt safe to truly enter his sadness, and release it from his heart and soul. I was touched by his sincerity of feeling, his earnest expression, and his vulnerability in opening to his father.

We kept him close for the rest of the day, and the next day he was joyful, full of laughter, deeply open and connected to his father again. I experientially understood the wisdom of feeling and releasing our pain, our wounds, our sadness, is innate. In children the process is quicker than it is for most adults, and is more efficient and thorough IF we recognize what is happening *and* hold a loving space for their release and healing.

Sunyam trusts his Papa so deeply on a soul level that he is instantly able to surrender to that place of release when his Papa brings him to his chest. There is no story attached to the pure raw emotion for a child, so the release is quick and thorough. It is nice to be gentle with them for the rest of the day as they may still feel a bit vulnerable.

As parents we are not perfect. We will do things that impact our children. We will make choices on behalf of our own desires and growth that will bring up emotions in our children.
If we are humble and open in acknowledging our mistakes, if we are firm in our actions to follow truth and love, we allow our children to grow as well, especially in experiencing their emotions, the gateway to their souls. They come to learn that feeling and releasing emotions as they arise is normal and healthy.

They learn to flow with all feelings in their entirety, and let go of it when it has completed. In this way they can surrender and trust the flow of expression. They become strong in their softness and firm in their souls. This is one of the greatest gifts we can offer our children; setting an example of healthy emotional expression, to feel and be with all the experiences life is bringing them in each moment.

13. POST NATAL DEPRESSION

Mothers who are depressed respond differently to their crying babies than do non-depressed mothers. Their reaction, according to University of Oregon, is much more muted than the robust brain activity in non-depressed moms. An infant crying is normal, but how mothers respond affects a child's development, says Jennifer Ablow, professor of psychology.

The brains of 22 women were scrutinized using functional magnetic resonance imaging (fMRI). "Non-depressed mothers were able to respond to crying as a positive cue," Laurent said. "Their response was consistent with wanting to approach their infants. Depressed mothers were really lacking in that response.'[32]

Depression can exert long-lasting effects on mother-infant relationships by blunting the mother's response to her infant's emotional cues. "A mother who is able to process and act upon this information will have more sensitive interactions with her infant, which, in turn, will allow the infant to develop its own regulation capacities," Ablow said.

"Some mothers are unable to respond optimally to their infant's emotional cues. Some of these prefrontal brain problems may be changed by addressing current symptoms, but there are deeper, longer-lasting deficits at the motivational levels of the brain that take more time to overcome."

These brain responses shape mother-baby relationships during this critical period of babies' emotional *and* brain development. Baby will cry more if mother is depressed as baby will feel this as an emotional "cut-off" that he/ she simply cannot understand. All baby will feel is lonely, isolated and separated.

This will become the 'norm' and baby will then develop coping mechanisms, emotional denial strategies, and shields to be "ok" with this. Baby is deeply affected by the lack of mothers emotional empathy, caring and response to her/him if mother is too depressed to lovingly move to her baby when baby is in distress.

The cocktail of hormones, adrenal, oxytocin and the sheer power of birth can spin anyone into a vortex of emotion. After the high comes a low. Yet this level of non-reaction top her baby comes from a mother who has not journeyed into the sad and painful cause of this depression *before birth*. This is also why healing before and during pregnancy is important.

---

[32] H. K. Laurent, J. C. Ablow. A cry in the dark: depressed mothers show reduced neural activation to their own infant's cry. *Social Cognitive and Affective Neuroscience*, 2011; DOI: 10.1093/scan/nsq091

PRACTICE: HEART MEDITATION FOR YOUR CHILD

Children are naturally connected to their feelings and emotions. Through this, they naturally connect to all beings, as we all do. Giving and receiving love interconnects us all, and love is the quality all beings recognize universally. It is the universal language.

When your heart is open, the flow of love in and out naturally occurs. You are transparent, a meeting space and vessel of the forces of heaven and earth, part of the unbroken flow of harmony and order that weaves all beings together.

Giving and receiving love allows us to open to all parts of our Self. It is our birth right, how children are, how we are designed to Be. When we expand our capacity to freely give and receive love, we are in harmony with ourselves, the flow of life, others and God.

Children have this innately, until they are conditioned out of it by their wounds, life's experiences, their parents and the world. For them to be reminded of this essential quality of giving and receiving love, and indeed to amplify it, is a crucial part of their souls upbringing in this world. They can always Know that this is the way they can connect to everyone, no matter what the world says or does.

All of us, and every single part of us, wants to taste love, to receive it, to feel it, and to give it to self, others and all. This is the Native American *Sacred Hoop*, living in the Egyptian *Ma'at*, in the Indian *Rtam*, in Hawaiian *Pono*: the truth of order, harmony, goodness and rightness.
We all want love. This lies at the heart of deep healing for all people. For your child to have this Remembrance and live it is priceless.

The following heart meditation can be done after 2 years of age by your child, every night before they sleep, or at any point in the day where you feel it. It can be done every day or a few times per week. You and your child will both benefit from it, and can enjoy it together.

Ask your child to lie down. Ask them to feel their bodies, feel their heart beat, close their eyes and relax.

I love myself. I really love me!
I love my mama. Please Send me your love mama!
I love my papa. Please Send me your love papa!
I love my brother (name) and my sister (name) Please Send me your love!
Beloved (best friend/person closest to child's name), I love you. Please send me your love.
I love my teacher (name). Please Send me your love!
Beloved Mother Earth, I love you. Please send me your love.
Beloved Father Sun, I love you. Please send me your love.
I love all people everywhere on earth. I love you. Please send me your love.

PART 6:
THE NEW CHILDREN

Savitri

I saw the Omnipotent's flaming pioneers ...
Come crowding down the amber stairs of birth;
Forerunners of a divine multitude

Out of the paths of the morning star they came
Into the little room of mortal life.
I saw them cross the twilight of an age,
The sun-eyed children of a marvelous dawn,
great creators with wide brows of calm,
The massive barrier-breakers of the world ....
The messengers of the incommunicable
The architects of immortality,
Into the fallen human sphere they came

Faces that wore the Immortal's glory still
Voices that communed still with the thoughts of God
Bodies made beautiful by the spirit's light,
Carrying the magic word, the mystic fire,
Carrying the Dionysian cup of joy
Approaching eyes of a diviner man
Lips chanting an unknown anthem of the soul
Feet echoing in the corridors of Time.
High priests and priestesses of sweetness, might and bliss,
Discovers of beauty's sunlit ways
And swimmers of Love's laughing fiery floods
dancers within raptures golden doors

Their tread one day shall change the suffering earth
And justify the light on natures face.

-Sri Aurobindo

THE NEW CHILDREN

Christ said, 'Become again as a child to enter the Kingdom of Heaven.'

As enough minds and souls become unplugged from the ancient collective mindset, a Way is becoming clear for the Birthing of a New Paradigm. This New Paradigm will become established and bear fruit through the New Children.

The pathway for the New Children was paved by souls who started to incarnate in the 1970's. A higher frequency wave of these Children incarnating here began at the end of the twentieth century. The Third Wave of The Children of Light began in 2013, heralded by the two previous Waves. [33]

All these children are humanity's future Leaders and Teachers and collectively they will revolutionize the planet, establishing a tangible basis for an awakened civilization in all facets of life, from the economic, artistic and scientific, to the technological, spiritual and environmental.

The Third Wave of Children are in connection with their pure soul essence, and are being born to conscious parents who have prepared themselves spiritually and sexually to receive them, thereby reducing the amount of amnesia and baggage the children have to carry. This Third Wave of children are more sensitive than the previous waves, and need a conscious foundation and container to be received into.

These Children activate those that come into contact with them. They are magnetic joy and pure innocence, touching the souls of all they meet. These Children resonate with the very underlying fabric and wave of creation, and create ONLY according to this. As Yeshua said, 'Blessed are the peacemakers; they shall be called the children of God.'' In the eyes of the soul and love, the ONLY creations that matter are those that make Love more visible in the world.

These Children are a source of creations that serve healing because they are conduits for new creations. They bring forth the unseen into the seen, and see the world with different eyes.

It may be hard at first to comprehend 'what' these children are. They are magical, refined, and exquisite. Their innocence, auric manifestation and soul gaze stands out in any crowd. They come to give the world what it needs, which is a return to the source of Creation.

These Children will be the creators of a new wave of technology that will harness the very Source of Creation, ranging from space travel to genetics, free energy and the elimination of pollution. They will create environments and atmospheres in tune with Source, creating viable infrastructures in alignment with this, allowing humans on Earth to follow natural laws in a practical, accessible way.

---

[33] These children are being born in small numbers all over the world

All of their creations are based on simple laws, and simple ways of seeing things that will appear obvious to them, and miraculous to most people. It is through these Children that the tangible and felt awakening of the collective consciousness from the grip of fear will happen. Through these Children, the collective genetic pool and lineages of humanity will change and mutate. These Children may be perceived as "special", but they simply reflect our natural divine essence and Divine birthright. They are the true potential of the Souls Design for Birthing.

THE COVENANT WITH THE NEW CHILDREN, EARTH AND HUMANITY

'Often He did not appear to his disciples as Himself, but was found amongst them as a child.'[34]

The New Children hold a key to the Template for the Fifth Dimensional Earth and the next evolution of the human species. Fifth Dimensional Earth can only fully manifest when enough of us are embodying the soul, and the majority of these souls will be the New Children.

Laying their bodies on the Earth's ley-lines helps them connect to the Five-Dimensional Earth Blueprint, and they need to feel this energetically AND physically so they can play more. Through their play, they manifest.

This connection into Earth's Grids helps stimulate their physical, psychic and soul's growth, along with the unfolding and manifestation of their DNA. [35] The four elements of earth, air, fire and water are all useful, AND the intelligence and consciousness of Earth Herself is key in their development.

These New Children receive from Earth, and give to Earth through the blueprints they hold. When the New Children interact with the earth's fields, they help the earth itself to move into the Fifth Dimension. They nurture the earth into her next octave, just as they are being nurtured. This is a giving and receiving exercise for the benefit of all beings. The more regularly it is done, the better.

The ideal home environment for the New Children is in Nature, and in regular contact with the Earths ley-lines. The New Children will also appreciate that their parents are living with and around the right people, with the right attitude, and in their soul-purpose. The child will feel this deeply.

This DNA blueprint is key, because DNA is the code of all life. All life everywhere is held within our DNA, and the soul is the key to activating it. When more of our disconnected DNA is activated, god like abilities and capacities will become the norm for humanity. As Christ said, "Ye are like Gods." He saw this potential within all of us, and he himself activated it, through Grace and his own efforts.

---

34 Gospel of Judas
[35] This is the Blueprint that Christ Yeshua fully anchored, activated, and brought forth onto earth in his body. Most humans only use 6-10% of their brain capacity, with 90% of DNA being classified as "junk" or unusable because it has been disconnected by genetic manipulations and errors from the past history of the human race.

The human being is a physical body (particle) AND a spirit (wave). As a wave, the individual is part of the collective consciousness, in touch with it in its entirety. From 2013, there has been a New Particle introduced into the human collective and this NEW particle, the Golden Children, who have not existed before in the collective, is the pre-cursor to the next step in the evolution of human consciousness and the birthing of a new species.

This wave/particle will continue and propagate, on and on as a wave, to reach all parts of the collective, building a bridge for all beings to cross to a new level of evolution for the species. This wave is cascading out like a spider's web to resonate and permeate the entire collective via its wave form or resonant frequency, building a bridge by "catalytic proximity" in the Zero Point Field.

Evolution can be triggered by a mutation of one member of a species, which is then passed onto other members of the species by DNA and vibrational resonance through the collective gene pool field. Many have speculated that the most efficient way for a species to mutate is through a virus, which can "infect" all cells rapidly and mutate their resonant information.

When a member of a species moves to a higher vibrational frequency and crosses from being identified as just a physical being to being part of the Wave of the Creator, (in Aramaic: Ha-Shem) this information is then seeded into the collective consciousness through a resonant wave form and a new pathway is opened that others can follow.

This wave obeys the law of resonance, and in the same way as a physical mutation is passed along to the rest of the species by DNA, it is passed into the collective consciousness via the law of resonance. This new frequency resonance permeates the field, to be matched by those beings who approximate the source frequency. If the evolutionary trigger is one member of the species, and the whole is the sum of its parts, it therefore follows that the parts influence the nature of the whole.

In this case, the New Children are having a catalytic effect on the whole of humanity. Their vibrational footprint has been at work in the collective consciousness already, and we are probably too close to observe it properly, but its effects will become more visible as time goes on.

These New Children come in with a Blueprint that blooms into manifestation from the solid foundation the child receives from the parents. This foundation of love, care, presence, solidity, soulful interaction, protection and nurturing that these children receive, especially in the first three years of life, sets a tone for their entire incarnation.

The parent has the responsibility to find the means to allow a natural unfolding of the inner light of the child. For although the innate potential is there in the child, [36]it is not manifested as yet, and needs nurturing and care from the parents *who have done this process already within themselves.*

---

[36] and through the wisdom and practices given in this book is made more accessible for parent and child

Our responsibility is to create a physical, psychological and spiritual climate that will allow for the shining of these Children's light. This climate has to be created within us first through our own growth, healing and evolution, and only then can this climate, container and environment be lovingly created for our child.

Every parent has a responsibility to Represent light to the Child: the mother represents Divine Mother, Earth Mother and the Womb, the father represents Divine Father, the Seed of Light, and the Pillar. This responsibility allows both parents to grow too. The sharing is mutual. *Once you are a parent, start to see yourself through your child's eyes.* Then you will change exponentially.

The primary responsibility of the parents is not to give the child a good school and a nice house; *the primary task of the parents is to represent spirit and soul to the child.* Children will soon feel whether their parent's emphasis is on the inner reality of soul, or the outer material reality of forms, and the child will then begin to mimic that through the mechanism of mirror neurons, learning and structuring their own reality and behaviors accordingly.

The only thing that matters to the Child is that they live surrounded by love. It does not matter if the child has little materially and lives in a palace or in a ghetto. If the parents are living in love, the child will be content, happy, and in a far better place then having a 'nice' home, 'good' school and all the material things we think are so important today.

By focusing much effort on settling down, finding a good home, a good school, a 'good this and a good that,' *externally*, we miss the mark. Yes, these things are important, *but only as secondary things.* Focusing more energy on our souls growth in an authentic way and becoming closer to our own Realization enables other things to fall into place naturally and gracefully, both for the parents and their children.

As Christ Yeshua shares, "Seek ye first the Kingdom of God and His Righteousness, and all other things shall be added unto you." The only way father and mother can represent, to any degree, Divine Father and Divine Mother to their Children, is by having a direct relationship with the Divine themselves.[37] They both make time for deep Communion in their prayers and meditations, putting this into action, caring for the Works and souls entrusted to them, fulfilling their own soul-purpose and roles in the divine plan alone *and* with the family.

When the father is soul centered and situated in Self, representing the Divine Laws of love, the Child will feel safe and able to trust in the goodness of existence. Children with such a father will know what true manhood is, because they have felt and seen the example. When mother embodies the womb of nurture, foundation, caring and feminine power, the Child will know what the true feminine is and will have successful, honouring and soulful relationships in their life.

This is the Childs solid foundation that will inform and guide the Child's other forms of education naturally, and through synchronicities. Once this foundation is established, all other earthly skills required for the Child can be added gracefully. If this foundation is not in place, then no matter how many skills the child may acquire, at his/ her core the child will be shaky, and can be swayed and misled. This foundation is set by three years of age, and if it is not, it will then take years of healing and spiritual growth much later in the child's life to re-create this Sovereign Inner Foundation.

These Children will not be living their lives by the rules by which we live, our parents lived, or our grandparents lived. They are making a transition from the old ways of doing things, which were largely ignorant of the patterns, rhythms and processes of how life and the universe operates. The upgrading of the earth and humanity is happening, and for the purposes of the renewal of the earth and humanity, a whole new order of these Children of Light are incarnating here.

The lessons these children need to learn are sometimes different to our own. The lessons they have come to teach must not be obstructed by old forms of 'education'. Supplementing their normal education is vital. Perhaps they will become their own teachers, designing curriculums beyond our ability to do, beyond the paradigm taught in the school systems of today. In Russia, China and America, this is already happening.

As the Golden Children share:

Play with me: learn with me in laughter. Sit with me in Silence: Gaze upon your own innocence. I Am what you are: Reminding you of your own child, nestled in the folds of the heart we share, in this moment.

Allow yourself to care for me: as I care for you. Allow me to open the cracks in your heart a little wider, so we can play together, free, and easeful.

We come to share through Being, what you have never dared:
the easiest flow, radical in approach, simple in design.

NEW CHILDREN, NEW SPECIES

Suffering on Earth will cease with the birth of a new species. The New Children are a bridge between the old *homo sapiens* and the new *homo luminus*, or light being. They are building this bridge one body, one soul at a time, and they are flocking in droves to earth to achieve this.

Some adults and the New Children are paving the Way for the new species *homo luminus* to incarnate, and to provide this new species with the best possible chance of growth here. *Homo luminus* purpose is to create a new civilization and an uncorrupted vessel for the latent energies within the DNA to fully bloom so humanity can become like gods (part of God) on earth.

To admit this is possible and do-able to yourself is the beginning of anything great.

The New Children carry within them the seeds for a new humanity. When watered with our love, and protected in the safe container of their parent's home and field, they will bear fruit and help realign humanity's path to the next higher expression of possibility. They carry a light that we can raise ourselves to in its purity, instead of trying to dumb them down to our experience and society. In this surrender to what they bring, we will arrive at our next evolutionary possibility.

The New Children and these new families create a tunnel through the old paradigm into a new birth for humankind. This will happen beyond our lifetime, yet our choice to birth in our true soul's design is laying the foundation for this greater evolution to occur.

The New Children have much to share with us if we are willing to listen and open ourselves beyond our normal means of communication. They will take us on journeys beyond the edge of our universe and show us a greater plan.

"One morning I was resting in bed nursing my son. He began to speak to me, as he often does, in images, and he took me on a journey beyond the earth to a distant star. From here I could see earth and the whole of humanity. Within the larger pattern of chaos, I could see subtle waves forming, waves of love and harmony.

I understood that there were a few souls who had incarnated on earth at this time whose purpose it was to help bring harmony back to humanity, and these soft waves were the momentum of their actions manifesting. My son indicated that these souls were laying the foundation for the work that the New Children would further, that of paving the way for the next species of human being to emerge.'

Sri Aurobindo, an enlightened sage, visionary and founder of Auroville Community in India, foresaw this new species in the 1950's, and this legacy is being followed today by millions worldwide. As he shares, *'The true process of evolution is to add a new principle, degree or stage to the already existing order. These gradations serve the purpose of the transition ...without leaving a gap so wide as to disturb the evolutionary order of the universe.*

"...A hope would be there and a promise available to all which now only the few can share in or realize ....This is a result of the new evolutionary order and it would mean a considerable extension of the evolutionary field itself. Spiritual powers have been illustrated in the lives of many, but as something exceptional and occasional, the casual or incomplete manifestation of an acquired capacity, rather than the organization of a new consciousness, a new life, and a new nature. "

This is what the new children and new species they are heralding are bringing and will be living naturally.

"For the manifestation of a divine body here on earth there must be an initial transformation, the appearance of a new, greater and more developed type, not just a continuance with little modifications of the present physical form and its limited possibilities."

What we can do is provide the conditions and environments, inner and outer, to facilitate this for these children. This new species can only bloom and anchor on earth by a spiritual change in our being, as they bring fundamental and radical change in our evolution akin to a revolution in our very nature.

To live into the opportunity gifted to us by these New Children, which is the opportunity to move into the next evolution of the human species, creating a new humanity, Version 2.0 in flesh and spirit, we have to enter the state of consciousness they are already in. They help us, we help them, and the soul covenant is complete for all three souls.

Evolution on earth has been a long and slow process, but this does not have to be so. It has only been long and slow because it has been an emergence from subconscious beginnings, struggling against inertia and resistance. With the New Children this is not the case, as they do not have the same burdens we have had.

Sri Aurobindo continues, '*Their evolution is not from ignorance and wounding to knowledge and consciousness; it is from knowledge to greater knowledge, consciousness to greater consciousness, from Being to even greater Being. In this, there is no longer any necessity for the slow pace of ordinary evolution; there can be rapid conversion, quick transformation after transformation, which would seem to us now a succession of miracles.* "

The New Children still have lessons and wounds left to work out and release, but this can be done before they mature if the parents are aware and help facilitate this. In the process, the parents receive the gift that the child is bringing them for their very own evolution.

Sri Aurobindo shares, "*In this (new species) there are no contradictions: whatever would seem to be opposites for the mind, here carry in themselves their own right relation and reconciling agreement, if indeed any reconciliation were needed, for the harmony of these apparent opposites is complete.*

The finite does not cut up or limit the infinite, does not feel itself contrary to the infinite; but rather it feels its own infinity: the relative and temporal is not a contradiction of eternity but a right relation of its aspects, a native working or an imperishable feature of the eternal. Time there is only the eternal in extension and the eternal can be felt in the momentary.

In (this) life ... all the Divine is possessed, and when it descends on earth, it must bring the Divine with it and make that full possession possible here ...He will become one with cosmic being and universal Nature: he will contain the world in himself, in his own cosmic consciousness and feel himself one with all beings.

He will see himself in all and all in himself, become united and identified with the self which has become all existences. He will enter in the end into the bliss of Brahman and live abidingly in it, and for all this he will not need to shun existence or plunge into annihilation in some self-extinguishing Nirvana.

All relations with the Divine will be his: the trinity of God-knowledge, divine works and devotion to God will open within him and move towards an utter self-giving and surrender of his whole being and nature. He will live in God and with God, possess God, even plunge in him forgetting all separate personality, but not losing it in self-extinction.

The love of God and all the sweetness of love will remain his, the bliss of contact as well as the bliss of oneness and the bliss of difference in oneness. All the infinite ranges of experience of the Infinite will be his and all the joy of the finite in the embrace of the Infinite.

A divine life on earth ...will take up human being and human life, transform what can be transformed, spiritualise whatever can be spiritualised, and cast its influence on the rest. It will effectuate either a radical or an uplifting change, bringing about deeper communion between the universal and the individual.

Mind it will uplift towards a diviner light of thought and will, life towards deeper and truer emotion and action, towards a larger power of itself, towards high aims and motives. Whatever cannot yet be raised into its own full truth of being, it will bring nearer to that fullness; whatever is not ready even for that change, will still see the possibility open to it whenever its still incomplete evolution has made it ready for self-fulfillment. Even the body ...will become more aware of its own truth.

This change might happen not only in the few, but extend and generalize itself in the race. This possibility, if fulfilled, would mean that the human dream of perfection ....of all its ways of action and living, would be no longer be a dream but a truth, that could be made real, and humanity lifted out of ignorance.''

STAR CHILDREN SOUL EMBODIMENT PROCESS

When my son was only a few months old, I was nursing him to sleep. He was staring at me intently, the way he does when he has something to share or communicate with me. I opened my heart and spirit to him, to listen and receive. Through images and feelings conveyed through our heart seed connection, he took me on a journey.

I could see the earth, and a golden wave of consciousness moving and spreading like golden light. I understood this to be the morphic template for the New Children on earth that carries the next frequency of evolution for earth and humanity. Sunyam reminded me that that this was part of why he had come into incarnation at this time, to help usher in and anchor this new consciousness.

We travelled up into space and through many geometric forms I understood as star gates. I began to see that what he was showing me was relative to his embodiment. Because of the density of 3 Dimensional life on earth, and the high frequency of their souls, these Children embody in stages. Conceiving, gestating, and birthing him in the ways we had, gave his soul a solid foundation for entry into the earth plane. Raising him in love, truth, and presence would enable him to complete the journey.

All children move through star gates when they incarnate on earth. The most common star gate geometries for incarnating souls on earth are found through the Pleiades, Sirius, Antares and Arcturus. New Children maintain an active relationship with their star gates in order to retain their remembrance and bring more parts of their spirit and soul here onto Gaia.

They also communicate with other beings through the star gates, and relay information to other New Children, Earth and other beings in their different 'home' star systems. This relay of information and experience is important because it enables incoming waves of New Children to benefit from the incarnated Children's experience. This creates a morphic template or collective consciousness field for the New Children on Earth, their Soul family in different star systems and planets, and the incoming New Children.

This collective consciousness is a newly evolving field-grid different from the old human collective consciousness grid, and this field grows each time one of these Children incarnate on earth. They are weaving the field of a new collective consciousness through their successive waves of incarnation into the particles of physical bodies anchoring now on earth.

The speed at which they incarnate is partly dependent on the conditions in their own body, parents and home, and is also dependent on the state of the earth's morphic field, which they themselves are changing. The more all variables are expanding to receive and hold a higher frequency, the more of themselves they can bring here.

Often, the degrees of any child's embodiment are marked by physical milestones of sitting, crawling, standing, walking and talking. Sometimes it takes an emotional release for these

Children to enter their next stage of growth. Sometimes it takes their physical bodies clearing through fevers, or what may appear as illness to enable a leap of understanding and cognition to occur.

All of these are effects of a deeper process happening. When we as parents bear this in mind, we can support them. It is important to remember that these children are profound, magnificent and wise souls, AND small children who need and want the love and connection with their parents. It is our care, presence and understanding that is the strongest anchor and draw for their continued embodying.

RAISING A CHILD of LIGHT

New Children:

- Know they belong here *as they are*, and expect you to realize it as well.
- Are more confident and have a higher sense of self-worth
- Authority with no input from them does not work so well. The old educational system is a good example. They do not fit so well into left brained thinking and control, although they can adapt to it. They are insightful and often have a better idea of method then what has been in place for years.
- The fulfillment of their personal needs is important to them, and they will let you know.
- They are highly intuitive. They know what feels right to them and anything else is disruptive to their system.
- Have food sensitivities and may be picky.
- May see spirits: "dead" people, guides, angels, and extraterrestrial beings. Have telepathic abilities and speak to spirits. Are fascinated with and easily communicate with plant intelligences, animals and crystals.
- Are empathic, are sensitive to the feelings of others and sometimes pick them up and carry these energies with them. They are feelers rather than thinkers most of the time.
- They have an innate "knowingness" and resist untruths.
- Carry a higher vibration and therefore may not feel entirely comfortable in the denseness of today's world.
- Do not think just in linear fashion.
- They bore easily and can be fidgety or over excitable.

This said, each child is unique, so each path is different for each of them. The environment that the child's DNA resonates with will primarily be with its parents and then the physical environment. Being in nature, with less electronic signals, pollution, and people is best. But still, a child can be living in a flat in the middle of the city and if he/ she has the primary qualities of love around it and the parents are soulfully embodied and taking the child into nature, he/she can still thrive and manifest who he/she is.

The New Children need your help to support them to translate their higher frequency energies to Earth. This support will be unique for each child's soul-purpose, and each child's dynamic with their parents and caregivers. The child will have specifically chosen exactly the right parents and people to help him or her in this transition.

The best place to get the most accurate information to help your child is from your child itself! For a woman, this will be through her open, receptive womb, and for a man through the emotionally sensitive intelligence of his soul. It is amazing the information children can guide you to when you are attentive and present with their souls. In the process of soul-to-soul connection, the communications become clearer and clearer every day. It is like exercising a muscle: the more it is done, the greater the muscle will grow.

The extent to which the New Child makes the transition into the denser frequencies on Earth depends partially on their parent's soul evolution AND how much they have expressed and anchored their soul qualities into physical manifestation. The more the parents have done this, the more they will be able to share the appropriate action, frequency and support to their child.

Honestly, how much have you embodied your own soul presence, your own gifts and your love? The more you have embodied it, the more you will be manifesting it, and the more it will be easily accessible for the child *and the whole family unit.*

Some of the New Children have never been here on earth before. This is why they can hold the pure human blueprint intact. Some have never even been human before. Some of them are masters of time and have already been on earth, and decided at a previous time to return to earth in this period of time. These beings can move between time lines as easily as most people change their clothes.

Each of these children will ask for what it wants, and it is up to the parents to listen to their demands. And demand they will at certain times, for what they want in their unique path!

They will have chosen *you* for that, for your gifts and purpose to support, align or even be the same as their soul-purpose. How this plays out in your lives may be something quite different to what you think, but it will be the perfect foil and compliment to support the child into its own soul-purpose, its own gifts and its own flowering.

You being something totally different to what your child is may help fully align it to what it needs to be and do. Some of these qualities may be surprising but it will make sense if you look at it spatially, not linearly. If you look at it from the eyes of the soul, it will all become clear. You will align and support the child; and then the child may help reveal to you the next octave of your own gifts!

WHAT DOES A NEW CHILD NEED TO THRIVE?

There are a few things to take into account in raising your New Child that will be quite different to how you were raised, and how other children are being raised around you, even by your family and friends.

Firstly, your child will be different to other children, and will stand out, in a beautiful way. Get used to it! Take your Child to the right conscious nanny and a conscious kindergarten. Your intuition and your child's feelings are your best guide for finding the right fit. Totally include them in this process, almost like an adult. Remember, it is not just about finding someone to look after your child. It is about bringing in supporting energies that will continue to stimulate and care for your child in different ways than you do.

Our son's nanny was one of our students, so I knew her relatively well. The first few weeks she spent time with Sunyam, I stayed in the room, doing my work in the background. This enabled Sunyam to gradually trust her. He liked her immediately, and each morning when she came to greet him, she always asked, "Sunyam, do you want to spend some time together?" When he responded by leaning toward her and smiling, we knew he was agreeing to being with her.

Our nanny noticed early on Sunyam's natural gift with rhythm and sound. She played with him in ways to strengthen this. They quickly set up a routine in their few hours together of walks, singing and playtime, quiet time and meal time. Each morning she came, I would let him know his friend was coming to spend time with him. As long as he understood what was happening there were no problems, and the situation was enjoyable for everyone.

One reason our nanny was such a success was that she tuned into Sunyam's interests and what he was drawn to, and then built their time together around those interests. This is an important point, because these children are intelligent and have a lot of energy to pour into their unique purposes.

Symptoms such as ADD or ADHD arise when their free will, creativity and allowance for their uniqueness is not allowed to express. When they are free to explore, create, discover and learn of their own accord, they will be drawn to the necessary experiences to strengthen their gifts. Frustration, anger or acting out is a sign that they are not being given the outlets they need.

Recognizing the patterns they demonstrate grows an understanding of how to create a nurturing environment that helps them grow. It is their job to help transcend the values of the world age that is passing, and replace them with the values of the new paradigm.

1. Above all, New Children need love. Giving and receiving love is part of the human experience they have come to earth to partake in, as have we all! Unconditional love, especially from their parents, is the fuel to activate their potential. Without consistent love, their gifts will remain more inactive.

2. They need space to explore and create. They need an environment with ingredients that stimulate expression and exploration. They need the space to feel unhindered by our limited understanding or projections. Creating a safe contained play space that has a few toys they are drawn to is a good setting for them to begin to explore.

    Containers that they can open and close, rattles they can sound, and low furniture they can climb on are a few examples. They will feel most free to explore when they know their parents are nearby. Find the balance between allowing their independence, and engaging with them in a present and focused way. This will allow them to flow easily in their exploration and growth.

3. When you're communicating with them, make eye contact and show them that it's safe. Listen to what they are "really" saying. Soul communication happens through feeling the hidden message behind their sounds and words, through the feeling tone of their voice and cries, through pictures they transmit, and through intuition and telepathy.

4. Introduce them to other New Children or people who are soulful, energizing, loving and inspiring vibrations. People who can help them grow. If this is not possible, find a way to make it possible.

5. Create an environment in your home which allows for a flow of creativity in any regard, such as painting, music, dancing, inventing with building blocks or geometric play sets. Help them have free play.

6. Talk about God, angels, masters, love, creation etc. Make it fun, playful and engaging. Share your personal experiences with these beings and your own stories and experiences. They will enjoy this and it will make it more real for them, as well as having the pleasant side effect of them admiring and respecting you more.

7. Support a healthy lifestyle without drugs and medication.

8. Make yourself available to connect with them, and find out what's going on in their world. Have set times for soul to soul sharings, like bed time when perhaps they may be more open to share. Share that you are present, and give them the space they require to open up. Understand that you might be what is required to help them open up, and also it might not be you. You can support them in connecting with that person or energy to open up, if that is the case. Conscious group gatherings may also be useful for them to thrive and express another side to themselves.

9. With television, limit the time. Help them experience entertainment that stimulates the mind, movies that open the heart, that promote growth and have good vibes. Limit all screen time and video games, or stop them totally.

10. Be there for them. Be there when things get emotional. For a father and mother to show their emotions openly, be it sadness or bliss, tells them it is OK to be emotional and openly express. This creates stronger bonding between you both, and brings them into their soul.

11. Include them in spiritual activities you do, such as prayer, meditation, group sacred gatherings, sacred sound, yoga. They will resonate to the one they like most.

12. Put their bodies on the earth, especially on ley lines. This will ground them, stimulate their growth, and help the earth. Bring them into the elements: fresh air, a variety of places in nature, oceans, beach, forests, lakes. Ensure they have a regular, single earth spot or power spot to align to that they like.

13. Make sure they get regular exercise that they enjoy.

14. Wear them regularly (in a baby sling or carrier).

15. Treat them with respect and consult them on decisions that affect them.

16. Above all enjoy them! Have fun and play with them!

RESOURCES

The Music

The Souls Guide to Birthing is a Book to educate, inspire, heal and prepare women AND men on how to birth their child's body and soul blissfully and harmoniously. The music for The Souls Guide to Birthing, called The Souls Birth, has 7 individual soundscapes based on the 7 steps of conscious birth. This is designed to help mother, father and baby through pregnancy and labour, and is based on psycho acoustic frequencies and the sonic wisdom of many sacred traditions.

Psycho acoustic frequencies are frequencies scientists have recorded that different objects vibrate at. For example, water molecules have a certain frequency, as does the earth and the organs in the human body. Many of these frequencies have been recorded, and are used in the Music to provide mother, father and child with a depth of relaxation, harmony and vibrational guidance into the highest potential and peace for their birth.

The vibrational handrails and guide posts this music provides for mother, child and father helps entrain the family to supportive, peaceful and moving states of consciousness that can be used at any time during the pregnancy and after birth.

Visit the website for music samples and to purchase the music:

www.techoflove.com

THE AUTHORS

Katherine Zorensky

The Souls Guide to Birthing is written by leader in the field of Womb Consciousness Embodiment, Katherine Zorensky. She is a doula, womb shaman, healer, and mother. For a decade she has guided hundreds of women internationally into their intrinsic feminine embodiment and awakening. The extraordinary births of her children empowered her into remembering that birthing consciousness is a gateway into the soul.

The Soul's Guide to Birthing is a way of birth, a way of life, a way of living in alignment and harmony with the Divine Plan, the Will of Love, the forces of Creation. The distinct lineage of this wisdom emanates from Isis and expresses through the Soul Doulas of Gaia. The Soul Doulas midwife spirit into womb, spirit into world. Mother Mary, Mary Magdalene, and Mary Salome were a part of this lineage and in their time on earth taught the mysteries of birth to their students. Each of the three Mary's have their unique perspective on birthing through their individual lenses of Mother, Lover and Midwife.

This book is a culmination of practices and perspectives from this Lineage, allied with our own understanding and practical embodiment gleaned from our immersion into Womb Consciousness in love making, relating, parenting and our own birthing experiences. In teaching this Work and seeing the transformations that occur, and my initiation into this lineage of Doula's working with families in this way of Birthing, this lineage's wisdom on the feminine is anchoring once again.

This book, the teachings, practices and music are part of a larger movement landing on earth at this time offering a possibility for humanity to evolve into the next phase of evolution.

May it be received as a pillar of light. We offer this book and these teachings at this most crucial time of possibility. We are at a poignant crossroads between destruction and evolution.

www.techoflove.com

Padma Aon Prakasha

The Soul's Guide to Birthing presents information that is both new and ancient. New for these times we live in and the new children who are coming to earth now, and ancient in the sense that we have brought together a resurfacing of wisdom about the feminine, masculine and birthing that has been forgotten.

The Souls Guide to Birthing arises from my initiations into different sacred traditions such as the Indian, Tibetan, Gnostic, and Hebrew over the past seventeen years, which helped to bring many of the pieces in this book together again. My journey has taken me to more than fifty countries, to hundreds of sacred sites and teachers, known and unknown. All these lineage teachings gave rise to my direct experience and teaching, shared in retreats and workshops around the world for thousands of women and men.

The Souls Guide to Birthing also arises from my embodying a sacred father, which was rooted in me through taking the initiations of pregnancy, birthing and raising my son in a conscious and soulful way. As a father, I have viscerally experienced both sides of the birthing journey, as my first child came from an unconscious hospital birth and my second child came from a conscious birth. I have gone from one extreme of the birthing process to the other, so I now understand both polarities of the birthing journey, and what it takes to integrate the sacred masculine in all steps of the journey.

I wish the same for you!

www.padmaaon.com

ACKNOWLEDGEMENTS

I offer my profound gratitude to...

The lineage that has held me, guided me, and been the essential bridge between my earthly experience and my cosmic roots. You are an inextricable light woven into the fabric of my being, sustaining my soul and reminding me of my mission.

Thank you Isis, for the Black Light that nourished, sustained, and opened me to receive so much of what wanted to be shared.

Thank you Mary Magdalene, Mary Salome, Mother Mary for your continual guidance in birthing and guiding. For initiating me into this lineage of Doulas. For the handrail to return to this innate way of birthing.

Thank you to Padma. Thank you for your clarity and vision through this incredible journey that kept us moving toward a goal so much greater than ourselves. Without your essential contribution, guidance, love, support, this book would never have been born. Thank you for your unconditional love and commitment to truth.

Our journey of surrender brought us into The Souls' Guide to Birthing as it happened to us, and through us. Your wisdom, your brilliance put so much of it into tangible perspective, creating this handrail for others. I am the voice to bring it to the world. You continue unconditionally to be a pillar, a pioneer, protector, and spiritual and soulful provider for our family.

Thank you my son, Sunyam. Thank you for choosing me to birth and raise you. Thank you for bringing the seeds of this work through your gestation and birth. Thank you for your setting the course of possibility for the new paradigm, for our family, for humanity.

Thank you my daughter Bella, for initiating me into motherhood, for asking me to show up for a spectacular birth, and for choosing me to be your mother.

Thank you my parents, for seeding and birthing me, for raising and loving me in a grounded and wholesome way, and setting me free to fulfill my desires and purpose.

Thank you Aina, for your selfless service, your care and willingness to continue forward, with each of us.

Thank you families, who have entrusted me to be their guide on this pathway. Your 'becoming and blooming' makes my world richer. Your courage to follow your own knowing to birth in a way that is outside our cultural norms sends waves of potential into the field for humanity.

Thank you to all the self-less financial contributors that enabled the emergence of this book into the world for the benefit of all beings.

www.ingramcontent.com/pod-product-compliance
Lightning Source LLC
Chambersburg PA
CBHW081944230426
43669CB00019B/2915